AA

TRAVELERS' COLOR
GUIDE TO
BRITAIN

AA
TRAVELERS' COLOR
GUIDE TO
BRITAIN

BRITISH HERITAGE PRESS
NEW YORK

First published in 1982 under the title *Touring in Britain*, under licence from the Automobile Association of Fanum House, Basingstoke, Hampshire.

Maps in this book are based upon the Ordinance Survey Maps with the permission of the Controller of HM Stationery Office. Crown Copyright reserved. The Ordinance Survey is not responsible for the accuracy of the National Grid in this production.

The contents of this publication are believed correct at the time of printing but the current position may be checked through the AA. Nevertheless the publishers and the AA can accept no responsibility for errors or omissions or for changes in the details given.

Copyright © 1982 The Automobile Association.

Printed in Portugal by Edições ASA.

This 1985 edition published by British Heritage Press, distributed by Crown Publishers, Inc.

AA Travellers' Color Guide to Britain.
First published in Britain under the title: Touring in Britain, 1982.
Includes index.
1. Great Britain – Description and travel – 1971 – Guide books.
I. Automobile Association, (Great Britain).
II. Title. III. Title: Travelers' color guide to Britain.
DA650.A66 1982   914.1'04858   85-15159
ISBN O-517-492989

h g f e d c b a

Contents

Introduction

Britain is a varied and beautiful country that can be explored with the help of this book. *Travelers' Color Guide to Britain* uses maps, color photographs and descriptive text to make an attractive guide to this historic land.

The book is divided into six main sections: The West Country, Southern England, Central England, Wales, Northern England and Scotland. These regions are colour-coded on the key maps on pages 8–9. London is featured in a separate section describing many of the most interesting places to visit in the capital.

Each of the six main regional sections of the book opens with a road atlas of the region. This atlas is at a scale of 1:500,000, or about eight miles to one inch, and shows every major road and many minor ones as well.

Following the road atlas for each region are eight planned motor tours in various parts of that region. These have been selected and researched by AA experts, and each one can comfortably be completed in a day. A special map has been prepared for each tour, and this is accompanied by explicit route directions

and descriptions of the places of interest along the way. (In the route directions, the abbreviation 'SP' is used for 'signposted'.)

The tours are followed by an alphabetical gazetteer of the region, giving brief descriptions of the chief towns and villages. Each place described can be found on the road atlas by means of the reference number that accompanies the place name. This consists of the page number of this book where the place may be found on the atlas, followed by a National Grid reference number which both makes the place easy to locate on that page and also makes it possible to find the place on any other map.

Most of the castles, stately homes, gardens and other places of interest described in the book are open to the public at certain times, but the mention of such a property here does not necessarily imply that it is open. Opening details may be checked in the AA's annual publication *Stately Homes, Museums, Castles and Gardens in Britain*. Churches may generally be visited at all times; some are kept locked, but the key is usually available.

The National Grid

Modern maps of Britain use a standard system of reference for indexing places, and that system, known as the National Grid, is used in the regional gazetteers in this book. For example, on page 31 it will be seen that the National Grid reference for Plymouth is SX45. The two letters, SX, refer to the National Grid square; Britain is divided into 50 of these 100-kilometre squares, and each one is identified by two letters of the alphabet. These letters are marked on the pages of the road atlas. The 100-kilometre squares are shown by heavy blue lines on the atlas, and are subdivided by light blue lines into 10-kilometre squares which are identified by two numbers, in the above case 45. The first number, 4, refers to the vertical grid line numbered 4 at the foot of the atlas page, while the second number, 5, refers to the horizontal grid line numbered 5 at the side of the page. These two lines form the western and southern boundaries of the grid square in which Plymouth will be found.

Key to Tours

LEGEND TO TOURS

Main tour route
Detour/diversion from main tour route
Motorway with access
Motorway service area
Motorway & access under construction
A-class road
B-class road
Unclassified road
Dual carriageway
Road under construction
Battlefield
Castle
Church as route landmark
Ferry
Folly/tower
Place described on tour
Place not described on tour
Industrial site (old & new)
Level crossing
Lighthouse
Marshland
Memorial/monument
National boundary
National Trust land
National Trust for Scotland land
Notable religious site
Picnic site
Prehistoric site
Radio/TV mast
Railway (BR) with station
Railway (special) with station
River & lake
Scenic area
Seaside resort
Stately home
Summit/Spot height
Viewpoint

A466
B423
unclass
A48

River Leven / Chelford
Deddington

LC

NT
NTS

River Arun

CLEEVE CLOUD 1049

This map is colour-coded to show the six regions in the book. The areas numbered and outlined in red show the location of the 48 motor tours; see the Contents page for details and page numbers. The starting point of each tour is shown on the map in italic type.

LEGEND TO ATLAS

Motorways with junction numbers and service areas — M1 — 9 — S

Motorways under construction

Dual carriageway   Primary routes — A28

A roads — A12 — under construction

B roads   Unclassified roads — B2103

Toll roads — TOLL

Spot heights — 1335 THE WREKIN

Boundaries of counties (England & Wales), regions and island areas (Scotland)

Rivers, lakes and lochs — River Hull

Overlaps and numbers of continuing pages — 21

AA Service Centres 24–hour Breakdown / Information Service — AA 24 hour

AA Service Centres Breakdown / Information Service normal hours — AA

AA Road Service Centres Breakdown & Road Service Information. Normally 0900 – 1730 hrs — AA 19

AA Port Service Centres — AA

AA Motorway Information Service Centres. Normally 0900 – 1730 hrs Callers only — AA info

AA and RAC telephones

PO telephone boxes in isolated areas

The road atlas is divided into six sections, which correspond to the six regions in the book. Each atlas section appears at the beginning of the appropriate region, and the numbers on this map indicate the pages on which the atlas sections occur. Some atlas pages (e.g. 14 or 38; 104 or 126) occur in more than one region and are therefore repeated for easy reference.

Map labels

166

166   167

Thurso

Inverness

162   163   164   165

Kyle of Lochalsh

Fort William   Aberdeen

Oban   Dundee

Perth

Stirling

158   159   160   161   Edinburgh

Glasgow

Ayr   Berwick

Dumfries   132   Newcastle   133

Stranraer   Carlisle

156   157

Workington   Middlesbrough

130   131   Kendal

Douglas   Scarborough

Lancaster

Blackpool   York

Preston   Leeds   Hull

126   127   128   Bradford   129

Liverpool   Manchester   Doncaster   Grimsby

Holyhead   Llandudno   Sheffield

Chester   Lincoln

104   105   Stoke

Shrewsbury   Nottingham

Leicester   King's Lynn   Norwich

Aberystwyth   Wolverhampton   Great Yarmouth

Birmingham   78   79

76   Coventry   77   Peterborough

Worcester   Northampton   Cambridge   Ipswich

102   103   Hereford   Colchester   Felixstowe

Fishguard   Gloucester   Chelmsford

Carmarthen   Oxford

Pembroke   Swansea   Newport   Swindon   Southend

Cardiff   Reading   LONDON   Maidstone

Bristol   Guildford

14   Guildford   40   41

Barnstaple   38   39   Dover

Taunton   Winchester   Folkestone

12   13   Southampton   Brighton

Exeter   Bournemouth   Portsmouth

Truro   Weymouth

Plymouth

Penzance

The West Country

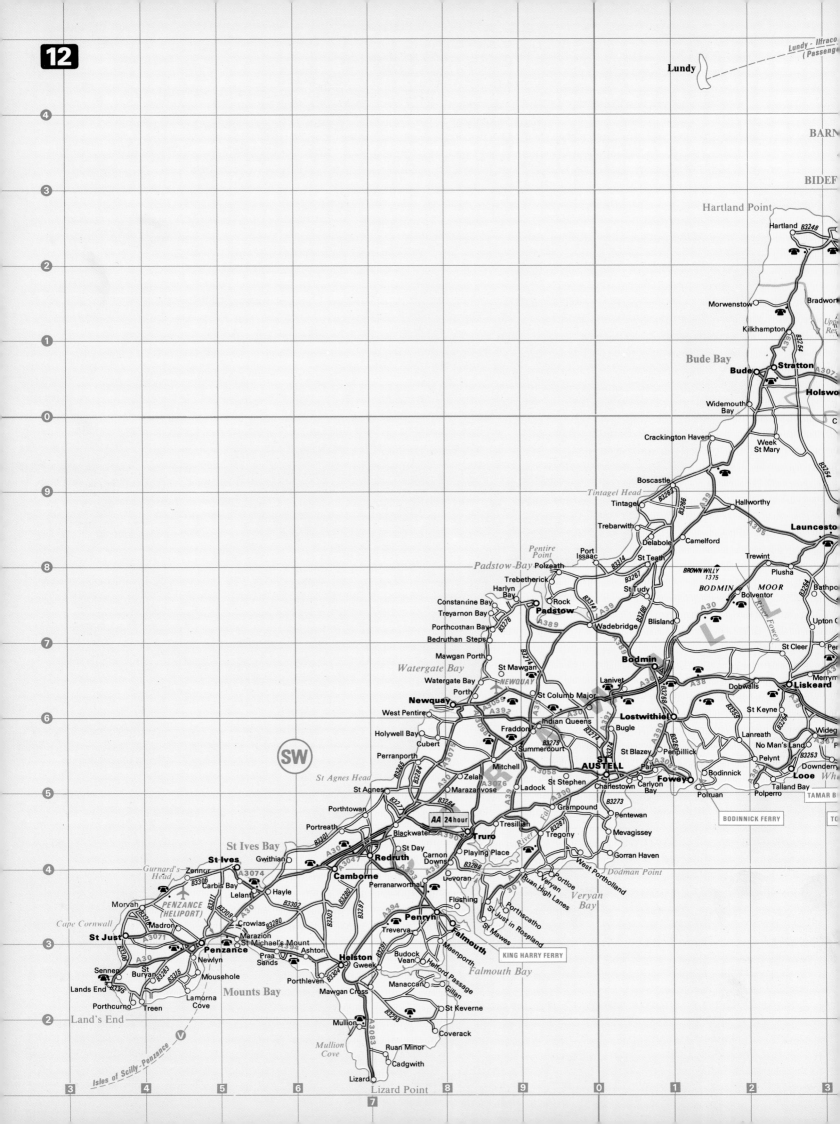

Cornish Coasts and Lanes
40 miles

NEWQUAY
One of Cornwall's busiest and most famous resorts, Newquay offers excellent beaches and a host of amenities for the holidaymaker. Towan Beach, somewhat sheltered from the Atlantic breakers, is especially suitable for children, since it offers a paddling pool as well as rock pools and caves to explore. An amusement park, a miniature railway and Cornwall's only zoo are among the attractions of Trenance Gardens.

Before the advent of the railway brought tourism to Newquay, the town was a prosperous pilchard-fishing centre. A man known as the 'Huer' was employed to keep watch for pilchard shoals, and the Huer's Hut, still to be seen on Towan Head, is a reminder of this unusual office.

TRERICE MANOR
Fourteen acres of grounds surround this fine Elizabethan mansion built by Sir John Arundell in 1573. Fine plasterwork and fireplaces are notable features of the house, which is owned by the National Trust.

LAPPA VALLEY RAILWAY
This narrow-gauge line once formed part of a Great Western route between Newquay and Chacewater. Today the steam locomotives that run on its 15-inch track haul tourist trains round a 2-mile circuit through lovely countryside.

ST NEWLYN EAST
The Church of St Newlina here is the burial place of several members of the Arundell family of nearby Trerice. The church dates mainly from the 14th and 15th centuries with some Norman work, including the font.

TRURO
Set on the Truro River, which flows into the beautiful Fal estuary, Truro is Cornwall's administrative capital and cathedral city. The latter is a comparatively recent role, for the graceful cathedral, built in the Early English style, was completed only in 1910, some years after Cornwall became a diocese in its own right. But Truro has been a place of importance since the 13th century. For five centuries, until 1752, it was one of the four Cornish stannary towns, where the quality of locally mined tin was controlled. The late 18th century saw an upsurge in Truro's maritime prosperity. Wealthy sea merchants of this period are responsible for the city's many fine Georgian streets, such as Lemon Street and Walsingham Place.

The history of Truro and of Cornwall is traced in the County Museum and Art Gallery. The mineral gallery is of particular interest, reflecting the story of the Cornish mining industries.

ST AGNES
This large village is set back from the dramatic cliffs of the north Cornish coast, here strewn with the remains of old mine-workings. Copper and tin ore were once shipped from nearby Trevaunance Cove – the nearest thing to a sheltered harbour that this inhospitable coast affords.

A fine, dune-backed bay stretches for three miles north of Perranporth

St Agnes itself is a pleasant village whose quaint old streets are lined by slate and granite cottages that were once the homes of local tin-miners. The church, rebuilt in 1848, is worth a visit to see its unusual poor box supported by a wooden figure of a hungry man, and its 15th-century font, made from stone quarried in the village.

ST AGNES BEACON
It is said that 32 church towers and 23 miles of coast can be seen from 628ft St Agnes Beacon, perhaps the most prominent landmark in the area. Bolster's Dyke, a two-mile earthwork on the Beacon, is named after a legendary giant who is supposed to have lived here in ancient times.

WHEAL COATES ENGINE HOUSE
A Wheal Coates engine house stands precariously on a forbidding cliff to the west of St Agnes Beacon. Once it contained an engine which provided the essential services of winding, pumping and ventilation for the mine below; now it is being restored as an important relic of Cornwall's past.

PERRANPORTH
Three-mile-long Perran Beach has made Perranporth one of Cornwall's most popular small resorts. The beach is backed by extensive sand dunes, and at its northern end is Penhale Point, a spectacular rocky promontory with magnificent views.

ST PIRAN'S CHURCH
Perranporth is in the parish of Perranzabuloe, which means 'St Piran in the Sand'. St Piran is thought to have come to Cornwall from Ireland in the 6th century. He is said to have taught the Cornish the art of smelting and was adopted as the patron saint of tinners. He built his church north of Perranporth on the Penhale Sands, but

by the 11th century shifting dunes had closed in and completely enveloped the little building. It was not excavated until the 19th century and is now housed in a concrete shell to protect it from further damage. The mile-long walk to see the church is well worth the effort.

HOLYWELL
Separated from Perran Beach by Penhale Point, Holywell Bay is a smaller and quieter beach, and offers good bathing except at low tide. At the north end is a freshwater spring – one of the holy wells of Cornwall – that gave the place its name. It can be reached at low tide by steps cut into the cliff.

CRANTOCK
This peaceful village near the Gannel Estuary is named after St Carantoc, who founded an oratory here in the 5th century. The medieval parish church is still dedicated to him, and his life is illustrated in its modern stained-glass windows. The old village stocks may still be seen in the churchyard. They were often used to punish smugglers; it is said that a secret chamber in the village inn was used to store contraband. Near the village is Crantock Beach, a popular bathing spot at the mouth of the Gannel.

TOUR 1 ROUTE DIRECTIONS
From Newquay drive along the A392 (SP Truro, St Austell) to Quintrel Downs. Drive over a level crossing, then at the crossroads go forward on to the A3058. In ¾ mile turn right on to a narrow unclassified road (SP Newlyn East), and drive for 1 mile to Trerice Manor. Continue for 1 mile, then turn left at the crossroads. (After ½ mile a detour can be made to the Lappa Valley Railway by turning left on to an unclassified road for ½ mile.) The main route continues to St Newlyn East. Leave the village by the road for Truro and Redruth and continue for 1 mile to Fiddler's Green. Turn left here, then after 1¼ miles go forward at the crossroads and turn right on to the A30 for Zelah. In ½ mile turn left at the crossroads on to an unclassified road (SP Shortlanesend). Continue for 2 miles to the Shortlanesend Inn and here join the B3284 for Truro. Leave Truro by the A390 (SP Redruth). In 4 miles at the roundabout take the second exit. After 2¼ miles, at the roundabout, take the third exit, the B3277 (SP St Agnes) and drive to St Agnes. Leave by the B3285 Perranporth road and drive on, passing through Trevellas, to Perranporth.

Take the B3285 (SP Newquay) from Perranporth and drive for 2 miles to Goonhavern. Turn left on to the A3075 and in 2½ miles turn left on to an unclassified road for Cubert. (From Cubert a detour can be made to Holywell, about 1¼ miles away.) Leave Cubert on an unclassified road for Crantock, 1½ miles away. Take an unclassified road (SP Newquay) from Crantock. In ¾ mile turn left on to another unclassified road and continue for 1 mile to the A3075. Turn left and return to Newquay.

South-east Dartmoor
48 miles

ASHBURTON
Tin-mining was Ashburton's first source of wealth; as early as the 12th century it was one of Devon's four stannary towns. Later centuries saw it prosper as a wool town and a coaching stop. The slate-hung houses, cobbled streets and old warehouses that lend the little town much of its charm are reminders of these earlier days of importance. The church, dating from the 15th century, has a magnificent tower and a fine medieval roof.

BUCKLAND-IN-THE-MOOR
Thatched cottages, lovely woodland and a little 15th-century church help to make this village one of Dartmoor's showpieces. St Peter's Church, built of stone quarried on the moor, has a fine Norman font and a 15th-century painted screen.

WIDECOMBE-IN-THE-MOOR
This song-famed and much visited village still holds its famous fair on the green every September, and the tale of Uncle Tom Cobbley is commemorated on the village sign. The Church of St Pancras is set on a rise behind the village.

BECKA FALLS
Best seen after heavy rain, these falls are made by the picturesque Becka Brook as it leaps and plunges 70ft down a series of great boulders.

MANATON
Old stone cottages surround the shady green at the heart of this scattered village high up on Dartmoor. Also at the village centre is the granite church, which has an attractive 15th-century screen and some stained glass dating from the same period.

NORTH BOVEY
Another of Dartmoor's 'show' villages North Bovey has all the characteristics of a picturesque English village. Thatched cottages and the pretty Ring of Bells Inn surround a green planted

The Church of St Pancras at Widecombe is often called the Cathedral of the Moor

with oaks, while nearby a war memorial lych-gate leads to the 15th-century church.

GRIMSPOUND
This fine example of a Bronze Age shepherd settlement consists of 24 small hut circles in a walled enclosure with a paved entrance.

WARREN HOUSE INN
A traditional welcome in the form of a peat fire that has been burning continuously for over 100 years awaits travellers who stop here. The inn takes its name from one of Dartmoor's many rabbit warrens.

POSTBRIDGE
The East Dart River is spanned here by two bridges. One carries the road, whilst the other is an ancient clapper bridge, one of several on Dartmoor. Despite its primitive appearance, it is thought to date from the early days of tin-mining on the moor.

TWO BRIDGES
A pub and little else stands at this junction of the only two major routes across central Dartmoor. To the north-east is Crockern Tor, where the so-called Tinners' Parliament met at intervals to enact special laws governing the stannary towns.

DARTMEET BRIDGE
Here, where the East and West Dart Rivers join forces to descend through a deep valley to Dartmouth, is one of the most popular beauty spots in the Dartmoor National Park.

RIVER DART COUNTRY PARK
Oak coppice, marshland, and valley bogs make up the varied landscape of this country park, which adjoins Holne Woods and occupies both banks of the River Dart.

HOLNE
This small village high above the River Dart was the birthplace of Charles Kingsley, author of *Westward Ho!* and *The Water Babies*. Son of the parson, he was born in the vicarage in 1819. The village church dates from around 1300, and features a fine screen and a pulpit incorporating an hour glass.

BUCKFAST ABBEY
Buckfast Abbey was founded in the 10th century and rebuilt on the old foundations by the Benedictine monks themselves between 1907 and 1938. A magnificent mosaic pavement has been laid inside the church. Nearby is the House of Shells museum, which demonstrates the use of shells in arts and crafts.

BUCKFASTLEIGH
Old mills and workshops characterize much of this market town, once an important centre for the wool trade. High above the town is Holy Trinity Church, reached by a flight of almost 200 steps. The treasures inside include a fine Norman font of red sandstone.

DART VALLEY RAILWAY
The northern terminus of this revived steam line, originally built in 1872 to serve the mining and farming industries, is in Buckfastleigh. Great Western rolling stock and a number of locomotives are stored here. The 14-mile round trip to Totnes Riverside takes 63 minutes.

TOUR 2 ROUTE DIRECTIONS

From Ashburton take an unclassified road (SP Buckland). Drive to Buckland-in-the-Moor, then follow the East Webburn valley to Widecombe-in-the-Moor. Leave Widecombe by the Bovey Tracey road and climb on to open moorland. Descend to the Bovey valley and after 3 miles, by the Edgemoor Hotel, turn left. After ½ mile turn left again on to the B3344 (SP Manaton). Later go through the woods that surround Becka Falls, following the B3344 to Manaton. Turn right ¾ mile beyond Manaton church on to an unclassified road (SP North Bovey), then descend steeply to cross the River Bovey and climb again to North Bovey.

Turn left to leave the village, and in ¼ mile descend and bear right (SP Princetown). Recross the river, climb steeply and bear right. In 1¼ miles, at a T-junction, turn left on to the B3212 (SP Princetown). (After 2 miles a detour can be made by turning left on to an unclassified road for Grimspound.) Continue on the B3212 past the Warren House Inn and through Postbridge to the edge of

Two Bridges. Turn left here on to the B3357 (SP Ashburton) and after 4¼ miles descend to Dartmeet Bridge. Climb steeply again and continue to Poundsgate, then descend to cross the river at New Bridge. Enter the woodland of Holne Chase and in ½ mile turn right on to an unclassified road. (A detour to the River Dart Country Park can be made here by keeping forward on the B3357 for 1¾ miles.)

The main route continues to Holne. From here follow signs for Buckfastleigh along a narrow road and in ½ mile bear right. After another ½ mile descend (1 in 5), and at the bottom keep left. In 1½ miles, at the crossroads, turn left (SP Buckfast, Totnes). In ¼ mile bear right then immediately left, and after ¾ mile enter Buckfast village, passing the abbey. Continue for ½ mile to a T-junction. (A short detour can be made into Buckfastleigh by turning right here.) The main route turns left, crosses the River Dart and turns left again. In 1¾ miles, at a T-junction, turn left on to the B3357, then shortly right on to an unclassified road to return to Ashburton.

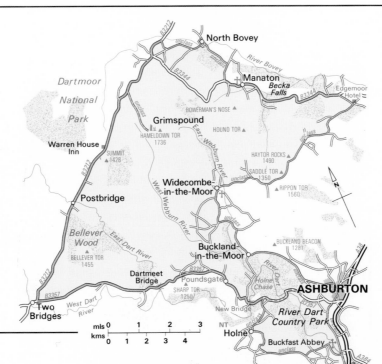

Resorts of East Devon

73 miles

EXMOUTH
This large and popular seaside town on the Exe estuary offers plenty of amenities for the holidaymaker. The resort's architectural pride is The Beacon – a row of fine Georgian houses overlooking the bay.

To the north of the Exeter road stands A la Ronde, an unusual circular house built in 1798 by sisters Jane and Mary Parminter. Its rooms are arranged around an octagonal hall.

BUDLEIGH SALTERTON
This town gained its name in the 13th century, when it was a salt-panning village. Today, Budleigh has plenty to offer the visitor. The beach is of pebbles, but Budleigh boasts an excellent golf course and is surrounded by attractive woodland that makes ideal walking country.

In Fore Street is the Fairlynch Arts Centre and Museum, whose exhibits include a costume display, a local history exhibition and a 'smugglers' cellar'.

EAST BUDLEIGH
This pretty, thatched village was the birthplace of Sir Walter Raleigh. He was born in 1552 at Hayes Barton, a thatched 16th-century house in a wooded dale about 1 mile west of the village.

BICTON GARDENS
These splendid formal gardens feature a lake, terraced lawns, a pinetum – one of the finest conifer collections in England – and an attractive 19th-century summer house. In addition to these attractions, modern visitors to Bicton can tour the gardens by narrow-gauge railway or visit the fascinating countryside museum.

SIDMOUTH
This popular resort is as well known for its Regency architecture as for its dramatic 500ft-high cliffs of red sandstone. Many of the sparkling white villas, often embellished with wrought-iron balconies, were built in the 1820s and the resort soon became one of the most fashionable in England. Queen Victoria spent her first seaside holiday here – aged seven months – in what is now the Royal Glen Hotel.

BRANSCOMBE
A lovely wooded valley leading down to the sea at Branscombe Mouth is the setting for this tucked-away village. The church, which is mainly Norman, has a three-tier Georgian pulpit and a 16th-century gallery. Thatched cottages and an old forge stand nearby.

HONITON
The intricate craft of lace-making, for which this old town was once so famous, has now almost died out here. However, displays of Honiton lace, and sometimes lace-making demonstrations, can be seen in Allhallows Museum. Much of the town is Georgian, having been largely rebuilt after a fire in 1765. Honiton was an important coaching stop, and a 19th-century castellated toll-house called the Copper Castle can still be seen on the Axminster road.

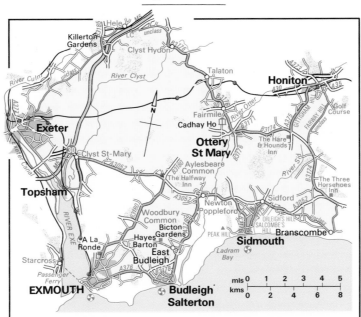

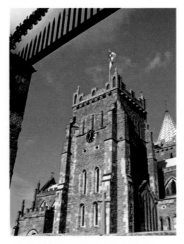

Much of Ottery St Mary's church dates from the 14th century, when it became a collegiate foundation

TOUR 3 ROUTE DIRECTIONS

Leave Exmouth on the A376, and drive through Budleigh Salterton. Two miles beyond it, turn left for East Budleigh. Turn right by East Budleigh church and shortly rejoin the A376. Pass Bicton Gardens and in 1½ miles turn right on to the A3052 into Newton Poppleford. Later turn right on to the B3176 for Sidmouth.

Leave Sidmouth by the B3175 (SP Honiton) and drive to Sidford. Turn right on to the A3052, climb Orleigh Hill and, ½ mile beyond the top, turn right for Branscombe. From Branscombe follow signs for Beer as far as the top of a hill, then turn left (SP Honiton). In 1 mile turn left on to the A3052. After ¾ mile pass the Three Horseshoes Inn and turn right on to the B3174. After 2½ miles bear right on to an unclassified road and cross Farway Hill. In ¾ mile keep forward for Honiton, and turn left by a golf course to descend into Honiton. Turn left into the High St (the Exeter road), and in ¾ mile turn left on to the

A375 (SP Sidmouth). Climb Gittisham Hill and continue to the Hare and Hounds Inn. Turn right on to the B3174 into Ottery St Mary. Leave along Hind St (the B3176) and cross the river to Cadhay House, then cross the A30 at Fairmile and follow signs for Cullompton. Continue to Clyst Hydon and, at the end of the village, turn right. In ¾ mile turn left, then in 2 miles, at the B3185 junction, turn left and right for Hele.

Pass under the M5, cross the River Culm and turn left. After 1½ miles keep forward on the B3185, recross the Culm and in ¾ mile turn right for Killerton Gardens. Follow signs for Poltimore, then Exeter. Leave Exeter by Topsham Road (SP Exmouth, B3182). In 2 miles keep forward at a roundabout for Topsham. Continue from Topsham to a T-junction in Clyst St George. Turn left here and, at the roundabout at Clyst St Mary, take the third exit (SP Lyme Regis, A3052). In 4¾ miles, at the Halfway Inn, turn right on to the B3180 and return to Exmouth.

Opened in 1566, the Exeter Ship Canal is the oldest canal of its kind in Britain

OTTERY ST MARY
This little town has a majestic church said to have been modelled on Exeter Cathedral. Its interior is a treasure-trove of craftsmanship ranging from an elaborate Victorian font to a medieval wooden eagle lectern. Ottery St Mary was the birthplace of poet Samuel Taylor Coleridge, and was also the setting for W. M. Thackeray's novel *Pendennis*.

CADHAY HOUSE
Considered one of the finest examples of Tudor building in Devon, this superb house was built in 1550.

KILLERTON GARDENS
The lovely grounds that surround 18th-century Killerton House include an arboretum, a folly called the Hermitage and an Iron Age hill fort. The house now contains a museum of costume.

EXETER
This busy modern city has kept much of its rich historic heritage, despite heavy bomb damage in the Second World War. The oldest feature is the city walls, built by the Romans. The medieval city began to grow after the bishopric was moved here in 1050. The magnificent cathedral's twin Norman towers are survivals of the first cathedral here, though the rest of the building dates from the 13th and 14th centuries. Rougemont Castle, now a ruin standing in pleasant gardens, was built soon after the Norman Conquest, when the city was already a thriving port. Exeter's long associations with the sea are reflected in the Maritime Museum, where over 100 craft from all over the world can be seen.

TOPSHAM
A port since Roman times, Topsham's importance grew as Exeter's maritime trade declined with the silting up of the Exe in the 14th century. Wealthy merchants who traded with the Low Countries in the 17th century are responsible for the Dutch-influenced houses here. Narrow streets, attractive old pubs and a distinctly nautical atmosphere ensure that Topsham keeps its charm today.

Cliffs of Two Counties
72 miles

BUDE
Originally the only safe harbour among the inhospitable rocks of this exposed stretch of coast, Bude is now a popular holiday resort and one of the best surfing centres in Britain. The long rollers that sweep in from the Atlantic over Bude's two fine beaches provide ideal conditions for this exhilarating sport. The rugged coastal scenery around Bude is ideal walking country, and the town itself offers all the usual leisure amenities for the holidaymaker.

KILKHAMPTON
In the 12th- to 15th-century church are 157 carved bench-ends dating from the 16th century. The Norman doorway is elaborately carved, and there is a splendid barrel roof.

MORWENSTOW
Standing above the highest cliffs in Cornwall, this village is noted for its church, which features beautiful Norman carvings. The churchyard contains the graves of victims of the many shipwrecks that occurred in the days of sail on this notorious stretch of coast.

STOKE
Hartland's 14th-century church stands here, its magnificent 128ft tower forming a local landmark. Inside are a carved Norman font and a fine, unrestored rood screen.

HARTLAND QUAY
The quay that stood here has long since been washed away by storms, but the fine beach is a constant attraction. Some of the most exciting shorescapes in the West Country are formed by the strangely twisted and fractured strata of the local cliffs. A clifftop path leads to the spectacular Speke's Mill Mouth waterfall, which lies 1 mile to the south.

Contorted cliffs and jagged rocks tumble into the Atlantic near Hartland Quay

HARTLAND POINT
Dramatic red cliffs plunge 350ft to the sea here. This spectacular coast has an ugly history and has been the death of many a storm-battered ship. Because of this the point carries a small white lighthouse which emits the strongest light of any on Britain's coast. Much of the hinterland is part of a designated area of outstanding natural beauty.

HARTLAND
To the west of this pleasant little town is an 18th-century house called Hartland Abbey. The abbey itself was founded as a college in the 12th century and later became an Augustinian abbey, but very little of the original building remains today.

CLOVELLY
One of the most famous villages in the West Country, Clovelly is unique in being completely closed to traffic. Its stepped, cobbled street means that visitors must leave their cars at the top of the hill.
Below, charming cottages, piled almost one on top of the other, spill down to the little fishing harbour – the only shelter for ships for many miles. The village is justly popular with artists.

BUCK'S MILLS
This unspoilt fishing village of thatched cottages nestles at the bottom of a wooded valley, on a section of coast noted for its picturesque cliff scenery.

ABBOTSHAM
Abbotsham Church features a good 15th-century barrel roof bearing trade emblems and coats of arms, and also preserves carved bench-ends and a Norman font.

WESTWARD HO!
Specially developed as a resort after the publication of Charles Kingsley's novel from which it takes its name, Westward Ho! has grown to meet the needs of 19th- and 20th-century holidaymakers.

A three-mile-long sandy beach and a famous golf course are among its attractions. To the west of the town the sands merge into rocks scattered with pools.

NORTHAM
This village on the Torridge estuary has a long maritime history. The tall west tower of St Margaret's Church has for centuries been a landmark for shipping, and the churchyard below contains many sailors' graves.

APPLEDORE
This sleepy village, its cobbled streets lined with fishermen's cottages, is the unlikely site of Europe's largest covered shipbuilding dock.

BIDEFORD
The 24-arched medieval bridge that spans the River Torridge still contains some of the original 13th-century timbers within its stonework. Old Ford House, at the south end of the town, marks the site of an even earlier river crossing. Trade with the American colonies brought great wealth to Bideford in the 17th and 18th centuries, and some of the town's attractive streets and elegant buildings date from this period.

GREAT TORRINGTON
This unspoilt country town high above the River Torridge retains two old market buildings – the Victorian Pannier Market and an older market building with a row of booths. Today Torrington is famous as the home of Dartington glass.

HOLSWORTHY
A thriving local centre with a large cattle market, Holsworthy is Saxon in origin, and still holds its annual fair, a tradition dating from the 13th century, every July.

STRATTON
A warren of quaint, narrow streets leads up to the 15th-century church here, creating a peaceful atmosphere that belies Stratton's turbulent past. In 1643 a Civil War battle was fought here when Sir Bevil Grenville led his Cavaliers to victory at Stamford Hill, just outside the village.

TOUR 4 ROUTE DIRECTIONS

Leave Bude by the A3072 (SP Bideford). After 1¼ miles turn left on to the A39, pass the edge of Stratton and drive through Kilkhampton. (Three miles beyond it a detour can be made to Morwenstow by turning left on to an unclassified road.) Continue on the A39 for 3 miles, pass the West Country Inn and branch left on to an unclassified road (SP Stoke). Cross a short stretch of moorland to reach Tosberry Cross, and bear left then right to reach Stoke. Continue for ½ mile and descend steeply to Hartland Quay.
Return to Stoke and follow signs for Hartland and Bideford. (After ½ mile a road on the left leads to Hartland Point.) The main route continues to Hartland. Take the B3248 (SP Bideford, Clovelly) for 3 miles and turn left on to an unclassified road. In ½ mile turn left on to the B3237 and

drive to the car park for Clovelly.
Return along the B3237, then in 1¼ miles turn left on to the A39 Bideford road to reach Buck's Cross. (From here a detour can be made to Buck's Mills by turning left on to an unclassified road.) Drive 5 miles further on the A39, then turn left on to the B3236 to reach Abbotsham. Continue on the B3236 to Westward Ho! and Northam. (At Northam a detour to Appledore can be made by turning left on to the A386.)
Follow the A386 from Northam to Bideford, then follow signs for Torrington and follow the River Torridge to Great Torrington. Leave by the B3227 (SP Holsworthy, Bude). After 6 miles, at Stibb Cross, keep forward on to the A388 for Holsworthy. Leave Holsworthy by the A3072 (SP Bude). Later cross the River Tamar to reach Stratton, from where the A3072 (SP Bude) leads back to the starting point.

Between Exmoor and the Sea
34 miles

LYNTON
Perched high on a cliff above Lynmouth, its sister village, Lynton was reached by the railway in 1898, so was transformed, in the early 20th century, into a popular resort, whilst more inaccessible Lynmouth remained a relatively uncommercialized fishing village. Lynton still has much of the air of a Victorian resort, with churches and public buildings dating from the turn of the century. It is within reach of magnificent moor and coastal scenery and has plenty to offer the visitor, including the Lyn and Exmoor Museum, which is housed in a 17th-century cottage. A mile to the west is the Valley of the Rocks, a spectacular place of jagged tors and rocky outcrops.

WATERSMEET
As its name suggests, this National Trust beauty spot is the place where the tumbling waters of the East Lyn River converge with the Hoaroak Water, which cascades down a rocky bed in a series of waterfalls. It is best to leave the car and explore the cool beauty of this wooded gorge on foot.

BRENDON
This picturesque village is situated on the banks of the East Lyn, which is spanned here by an attractive medieval packhorse bridge. The Church of St Brendon has two Norman fonts.

MALMSMEAD
Ponies can be hired here for a 2½-mile trek along the deep valley of Badgworthy Water, leading to the legendary Doone Country. The journey can just as easily be undertaken on foot.

DOONE VALLEY
The valley of Badgworthy Water, together with adjacent Hoccombe Combe and Lank Combe, is now immortalized, even on Ordnance Survey maps, as the 'Doone Country' of R. D. Blackmore's famous romantic novel *Lorna Doone*. No roads run along the valley, but it can be reached on foot or horseback. The path, never far from the sound of tumbling water, runs through magnificent scenery with wild moorland, magical rocky chasms and a lovely dell that in early summer is full of rhododendrons.

EXMOOR NATIONAL PARK
In its northern reaches this vast national park meets the sea with magnificent results. Rugged hog's-back cliffs stretch continuously from Lynton to Porlock, falling steeply to the sea and affording views across to the coast of South Wales. Lush combes wind deep into remote and heather-clad moorland, scattered with tiny hamlets and picturesque villages.

OARE
Set in a beautiful Exmoor valley, this tiny village consists of little more than a few farms, a manor house and a church. However, many people visit the village for its connections with *Lorna Doone*. The marriage of the heroine is set in the little church here, and there is a memorial to its author R. D. Blackmore, whose father was Rector of Oare from 1809 to 1842.

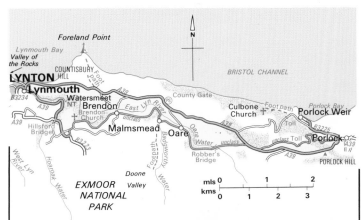

TOUR 5 ROUTE DIRECTIONS
From Lynton descend Lynmouth Hill (1 in 4) to Lynmouth and turn right on to the A39 (SP Barnstaple) for Watersmeet. Continue alongside Hoaroak Water for ½ mile then turn left on to the B3223 (SP Simonsbath). Cross Hillsford Bridge and in ¾ mile go round a hairpin bend and keep forward on to an unclassified road (SP Brendon Valley).
   Pass Brendon church and descend to Brendon, then continue alongside the East Lyn River to Malmsmead. cross the river bridge here and continue to Oare, then follow the road for Oareford and Robber's Bridge for 1½ miles. Cross the bridge and continue climbing to join the A39. Go down Porlock Hill into Porlock, and leave on the B3225 for Porlock Weir.
   Return to Porlock and take the Lynmouth Road, then branch right on to an unclassified road (SP 'Alternative Route via Toll Road'). Turn right on to the A39 and after 2½ miles pass the footpath leading to Foreland Point. Continue to Countisbury Hill, go down it (1 in 4) into Lynmouth, then climb Lynmouth Hill to return to Lynton.

Culbone church can be reached from Porlock Weir by an attractive footpath

Deep, bracken-clad combes and tumbling streams are an essential part of the landscape of north Exmoor

PORLOCK HILL
The notorious incline of this hill to the west of Porlock is one of the steepest in Britain, and there is a breathtaking view from its summit. A prehistoric stone circle survives close by.

PORLOCK
Now more than a mile inland, this large village once stood on the coast. Gradually the sea has receded, leaving an expanse of farmland between Porlock and the sea. Samuel Taylor Coleridge is said to have been staying near here, at Ash Farm, in 1797 when he wrote his famous poem 'Kubla Khan', a description of a drug-induced dream. It was the interruption of 'a person from Porlock' that jolted him out of his fantasy, forcing him to leave the poem uncompleted.
   Notable buildings in Porlock include 15th-century Doverhay Manor House and a mainly 13th-century red stone church containing the tomb of John Harrington, said to have fought at Agincourt. The remarkable monument is topped by almost life-size effigies of Harrington and his wife.

PORLOCK WEIR
This quaint little harbour, surrounded by old pubs and thatched, colour-washed houses, is the only survival of Porlock's days as a busy port. Pleasure craft now set out from here to sail or cruise in Porlock Bay. Woodland cloaks the steep coastal strip to the west, and a pleasant walk leads from Porlock Weir to Culbone.

CULBONE CHURCH
Measuring only 33ft long by 13½ft wide, this is the smallest complete parish church in England. Enchantingly situated by a stream, the building is basically Norman, and probably replaced a Saxon church. The tiny slated spire was added in the 19th century. Inside are old benches and a 14th-century screen.

FORELAND POINT AND LIGHTHOUSE
The footpath to this lighthouse runs through magnificent coastal scenery owned by the National Trust, and affords extensive views across the Bristol Channel.

COUNTISBURY HILL
Stagecoach drivers had to change horses at the ancient inn on top of this exceptionally steep hill. Prehistoric earthworks overlook the inn and sea to the west, and superb cliff walks can be made beyond the small local church.

LYNMOUTH
Tucked beneath 500ft cliffs, this attractive former fishing village is where the East and West Lyn rivers funnel into the sea. This had disastrous consequences for Lynmouth in 1952, when a severe rainstorm caused the swollen river to burst its banks. Thirty-one people were drowned, and many houses were swept away in the deluge. One of these was a cottage where, in 1812, the poet Shelley stayed with his first wife, Harriet. He praised the little resort for its mild climate and magnificent scenery.

Wessex and the Isle of Portland

60 miles

WEYMOUTH
A popular resort for the past two centuries, Weymouth is said to be the place where the bathing machine was first used, in 1763. Later in the 18th century King George III spent several holidays here, and Weymouth soon became a fashionable place to stay. Many of the elegant terraces along the seafront date from this period. The old harbour, which long before this had sent ships to resist the Armada, is now busy with yachts and cargo ships. The history of Weymouth and Portland is vividly depicted in the Museum of Local History in Westham Road.

CHESIL BANK
This pebble ridge is 200yds wide and extends approximately 12 miles from Portland to Abbotsbury. It is separated from the mainland by a tidal lagoon called the East and West Fleet.

FORTUNESWELL
North of the village high cliffs drop to the waters of Portland Harbour. Close by is the highest point in the peninsula, a 490ft eminence bristling with the 19th-century forts and batteries of Verne Citadel.
   Also nearby is Portland Castle, built by Henry VIII in 1520. This massive fortress was part of a defensive chain that stretched from Kent in the east to Cornwall in the west. Its 14ft-thick walls were built to absorb cannon fire.

EASTON
Avice's Cottage, a 17th-century Portland Island dwelling now containing a museum, was featured as the heroine's home in Thomas Hardy's novel *The Well Beloved*. Nearby is the pentagonal tower of Bow and Arrow Castle, said to have been built by William Rufus in the 11th century. Pennsylvania Castle was built during the 19th century for the Governor of Portland, grandson of the founder of America's Pennsylvania state.

PORTLAND BILL
This barren mass of limestone rises to only 20ft above the sea at the southern tip of the isle. Nearby Pulpit Rock is a pinnacle rising from the sea in a series of crags and caves. For years its labyrinthine tunnels were used by smugglers.

WESTON
Portland stone, made famous by architect Sir Christopher Wren while he was rebuilding London after the Great Fire, is quarried near this village.

PORTESHAM
This village has an attractive green and stands at the foot of hills dotted with ancient monuments. The nearest ones include burial mounds and standing stones.

ABBOTSBURY
This long village of golden stone cottages is most famous for its swannery, which lies ½ mile to the south. Little survives of the monastery in Abbotsbury village, apart from the tithe barn, which is one of the largest in England. In the porch of the church is an effigy of a 13th-century abbot.

Fortuneswell stands on high ground overlooking Chesil Bank, which stretches for 12 miles north-westwards to Abbotsbury

The statue of Thomas Hardy in Dorchester was raised in 1931, three years after his death

TOUR 6 ROUTE DIRECTIONS
Leave Weymouth by the A354 (SP Portland) and cross Small Mouth, with Chesil Bank on the right. Continue on the A354 on to the Isle of Portland to reach Fortuneswell and Portland Castle. Climb steeply from Fortuneswell (SP Portland Bill) and continue to Easton, then drive on to Southwell. At the Eight Kings pub, turn left for Portland Bill.
   Return to the Eight Kings and turn left to drive through Weston, then climb to the top of Portland Hill and turn left. Descend into Fortuneswell and return to the mainland. In 1 mile join the B3157 (SP Bridport) and drive through Chickerell to reach Portesham. Continue on the B3157 to Abbotsbury. Leave on the Bridport road and follow the B3157 through Swyre and Burton Bradstock. (Two miles beyond Burton Bradstock a detour can be made to West Bay.) Continue to Bridport.
   Leave Bridport on the A35 (SP Dorchester), pass the Nine Stones and at the end of Winterbourne Abbas village bear right on to the B3159 (SP Weymouth), then immediately right again on to an unclassified road (SP Hardy Monument). Climb on to heathland and turn left to reach the monument, then continue for 2 miles and turn right at a T-junction on to the B3159 to enter Martinstown. At the end of the village branch left on to an unclassified road. Drive for 1¼ miles to a T-junction and turn right on to the A35 for Dorchester. Leave on the A354 (SP Weymouth). (A detour can be made to Maiden Castle by taking an unclassified road on the right.) Continue on the A354 through Broadwey and back to Weymouth.

ABBOTSBURY SWANNERY
Swans have been bred here since the 14th century, when they were reared as food for the monastery at Abbotsbury. They still breed here today, and the swannery is also a haven for many species of wild birds.

BURTON BRADSTOCK
Thatched cottages line the charming old streets of this peaceful Dorset village, which has an interesting Perpendicular church.

WEST BAY
Formerly the harbour for nearby Bridport, West Bay is now better known as a resort, with a promenade and a shingle beach. A commercial fishing fleet still operates from the little port.

BRIDPORT
The spacious Georgian main streets here were once used for the twisting and drying of nets and ropes, which have been manufactured here since the Middle Ages. The history of this unusual industry is the subject of a permanent display in the Museum and Art Gallery in South Street.

NINE STONES
This ancient stone circle stands ½ mile west of Winterbourne Abbas and is the most notable of many tumuli and configurations of stones in the Dorchester area.

HARDY MONUMENT
Admiral Hardy, who was beside Lord Nelson at his death during the Battle of Trafalgar, is commemorated here by an obelisk on top of Black Down.

DORCHESTER
Unofficial capital of Hardy country, Dorchester is only two miles from the novelist's birthplace at Higher Bockhampton, and is the 'Casterbridge' of his novels. Hardy spent the last few years of his life at Max Gate, on the edge of the town.
   Dorchester has witnessed several events of historic importance, including the trial of the Tolpuddle Martyrs, six farm-workers who were sentenced to transportation after banding together to campaign for higher pay for agricultural labourers. The famous trial took place in 1834 in the courtroom of the Old Shire Hall. Some 150 years earlier the ruthless Judge Jeffreys made his mark on the town when he held one of his notorious 'Bloody Assizes' here. A house in the High Street where he stayed is now a restaurant named after him.
   Dorchester has two museums: The excellent Dorset County Museum, in an elegant Victorian building in High West Street, and the Dorset Military Museum, in the Keep.

MAIDEN CASTLE
This vast prehistoric hillfort occupies 120 acres and is the finest of its kind in Britain. It probably developed from a simple bank-and-ditch defence against neighbouring tribes. After successfully storming it, the Romans used the castle as a base and built a temple within its ramparts.

WELLS

The Cathedral Church of St Andrew is undoubtedly the showpiece of this delightful little city. Of particular interest are the exquisite carvings on the west front, the chapter house with its fine fan-vaulted ceiling and the 14th-century clock. The ecclesiastical precinct in which the cathedral stands has been the heart of Wells for more than ten centuries. The buildings that stand there today are mainly medieval.

Wells is compact enough to be easily explored on foot, and its ancient streets are full of interest. The museum is also worth a visit to see its displays on the history and natural history of the Mendip Caves.

GLASTONBURY

Steeped in ancient myths and legends, Glastonbury is said to be the place where Joseph of Arimathea founded Europe's first Christian church, later the burial place of King Arthur and Lady Guinevere. Rising abruptly nearby is 520ft Glastonbury Tor, sometimes claimed to be the place where the Holy Grail is buried.

The abbey ruins in Glastonbury today date from the 12th and 13th centuries. They include the Abbot's Kitchen and the tithe barn, now home to the Somerset Rural Life Museum.

BRIDGWATER

The pleasant streets of this market town on the River Parrett tell little of its former importance. It is no longer the major port it once was, and the 13th-century castle was completely destroyed by the Roundheads after the Civil War. However, Bridgwater is remembered for its role in the Duke of Monmouth's rebellion in 1685. Here Monmouth was proclaimed King by his followers, and here he spent the night before his defeat at the Battle of Sedgemoor.

The gaunt tower of a vanished 14th-century church crowns Glastonbury Tor

BURROW BRIDGE AND BURROW MUMP

The curious conical hill known as the Mump is topped by a ruined chapel, from where there are excellent views over the Somerset Levels. Nearby, Victorian steam pumping engines are on display at the Burrow Bridge Pumping Station Museum.

MUCHELNEY

The first abbey was founded here in the 7th century, but the ruins that can be seen today belong to later buildings. The 16th-century abbot's lodgings survive almost intact, with a beautifully carved original fireplace in one of the upstairs rooms.

HUISH EPISCOPI

Glass by Burne-Jones and a fine Norman doorway whose stonework was burnished to a rich reddish-brown colour in a fire are features of the local church. Its crowning glory is a 15th-century tower considered to be the finest in the county.

SOMERTON

This attractive little town was the ancient capital of Wessex. Many of the buildings, including the 17th-century market cross, are built of local blue lias stone. The church has an unusual tower with an octagonal top and is noted for one of the finest tie-beam roofs in Somerset.

YEOVILTON

Concorde 002 is among the exhibits at the Fleet Air Arm Museum here. The collection includes historic aircraft and other memorabilia of the Royal Naval Air Service.

CADBURY CASTLE

Once it was thought that the myths linking this hilltop fort with King Arthur's Camelot had been disproved by excavations revealing evidence of Stone and Bronze Age occupation. However, digging in 1966 suggested that the site had been re-defended during Arthur's period.

CASTLE CARY

The Victorian market hall in this handsome little town is now the home of a small museum. In the square behind is a tiny, round lock-up – one of only four in the country.

PILTON

This tranquil village has a church with a splendid angel roof, a manor house that was the summer residence of the abbots of Glastonbury, and a magnificent stone tithe barn.

SHEPTON MALLET

This busy market town, permanent home of the Bath and West Show, is famous for its church, whose wagon-roof is among the finest in the country. It has 300 intricately carved bosses, each one different from all the others. In the market place is the Shambles, a curious timber stall or shed thought to date from the 15th century.

CROSCOMBE

This former wool village is known for the furnishings in its church. The rood screen, pulpit, readers' desks and box pews are all superb examples of Jacobean woodcarving, donated by the Fortescues, lords of the manor, in 1616.

TOUR 7 ROUTE DIRECTIONS

From Wells drive along the A39 to Glastonbury, then take the B3151 (SP Meare). Drive through Meare and in 1¼ miles turn left (SP Shapwick). Turn right by Shapwick church. Cross a main road after ¾ mile, then in ½ mile turn right on to the A39. After 5 miles bear sharp left over a dyke, then cross the M5 and enter Bridgwater. Follow signs for Langport on the A372, and 1 mile beyond Middlezoy turn right to follow the A361 to Burrow Bridge. Cross the River Parrett and immediately turn left (no SP). Follow signs to Stathe, then signs for Curry Rivel. After ¾ mile branch right, and bear right at the top of Red Hill. After ¾ mile turn left on to the A378 to enter Curry Rivel, and in ¼ mile turn right (SP Drayton, Muchelney) for Muchelney.

From here follow Langport signs for 1 mile and at the T-junction turn right to enter Huish Episcopi. Turn right on to the A372 (SP Wincanton, Yeovil), pass the edge of Long Sutton and turn left on to the B3165 (SP Somerton). Enter Somerton, turn right by the church into New Street (SP Ilchester), and in ½ mile turn right on to the B3151. In ¾ mile cross the A372 and in 1½ miles turn

right, then take the first exit at the mini-roundabout (SP Yeovilton). Continue for 1½ miles and pass the Fleet Air Arm Museum at Yeovilton, then in ¼ mile turn right (SP Queen Camel). In 2½ miles keep forward on to the A359 (SP Sparkford, Frome) to enter Queen Camel. In ¾ mile turn right on to the A303 for Sparkford (where a detour can be made on the A303 and an unclassified road to Cadbury Castle).

From Sparkford bear right across a railway bridge, then turn left on to the A359 (SP Frome). In 3¼ miles branch left on to the B3152 for Castle Cary. Leave Castle Cary following signs for Bath and Bristol (A371). After 1 mile turn left on to the A371 (SP Shepton Mallet).

In ½ mile, by the Brook House Inn, turn left (SP Alhampton, Ditcheat). At Alhampton bear right (SP Ditcheat, Glastonbury). At Ditcheat, turn left at a T-junction (no SP). Turn right by the Manor House Inn then bear left (SP East Pennard). Turn right at the crossroads in Wraxall on to the A37 (SP Shepton Mallet), then at the crossroads past Wraxall Hill turn left on to an unclassified road (SP East Pennard). In ½ mile turn right for Pilton.

At the crossroads in Pilton turn left, then by the church turn left (SP Shepton Mallet). At a T-junction turn right on to the A361 and in 1 mile turn left on to the B3136 for Shepton Mallet. Follow signs from Shepton Mallet for Wells, A371, to reach Croscombe and drive along the A371 back to Wells.

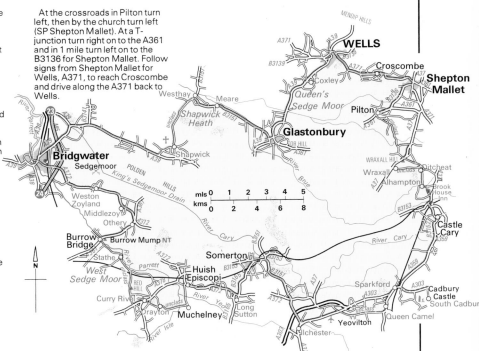

Bristol and the Mendips

81 miles

WESTON-SUPER-MARE
Plenty of traditional seaside amusements have made Weston Somerset's largest and most popular resort. Wide streets, lawns and the famous Winter Gardens overlook the large, sandy beach. Weston's facilities include swimming pools, two piers, dance-halls, theatres and the fascinating Woodspring Museum, which includes a display on the Victorian seaside holiday, an old chemist's shop, a dairy and a gallery of local wildlife.

CLEVEDON
This Bristol Channel resort has been popular for almost two centuries. This part of the Channel is known for its high tides, which caused Clevedon's pier to collapse in 1970. An early visitor to the resort was the poet Coleridge, who spent his honeymoon here in 1795.

Clevedon Court is a superb 14th-century house that is one of the oldest of its type in Britain. One of its towers is even older, dating from the 13th century. The house is considered typical of its period, with a screen passage dividing the buttery and kitchen from the great hall and the lord of the manor's living quarters. Its grounds feature fine terraced gardens and the Clevedon Craft Centre and Countryside Museum, where visitors can watch craft displays at weekends.

PORTISHEAD
Portishead is a small resort and dock situated on the lower slopes of a wooded hillside overlooking the Bristol Channel.

ABBOTS LEIGH
Set deep in the shelter of Leigh Woods, this village was once the property of the Abbey of St Augustine in Bristol. Good views of the Clifton Suspension Bridge can be enjoyed from the wooded ravine of Nightingale Valley, off the A369.

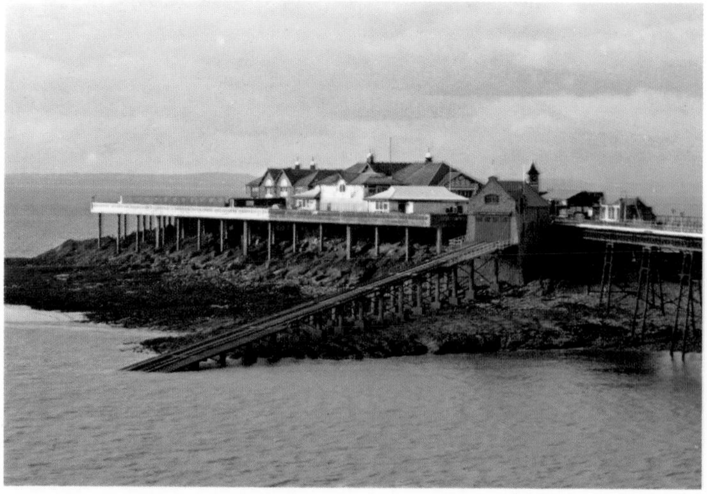

Birnbeck Pier at Weston-super-Mare is built on a rocky outcrop

CLIFTON SUSPENSION BRIDGE AND AVON GORGE
Here, where the sheer limestone cliffs of the Avon Gorge constrict the river to a silver ribbon some 245ft below, is the spectacular suspension bridge by the brilliant 19th-century engineer Isambard Kingdom Brunel. This was the last of his many great and innovatory works.

BRISTOL
This important and historic city on the River Avon has been a harbour since Anglo-Saxon times. The Normans built a castle here, and during the 15th and 16th centuries ships from Bristol travelled the world in search of new commodities such as tobacco, wine and chocolate – still staple raw materials of the city's manufacturing industries.

The Victorian era saw the launching here of Brunel's great ships; today the restored *Great Britain* – the largest iron ship of its time – can be seen in Bristol again, having been brought back from the Falkland Islands, where she was wrecked almost a century ago.

Many of the city's old buildings suffered heavy bomb damage in the Second World War, but among those that survived is the imposing cathedral, originally the church of a 12th-century abbey but much altered and extended in later centuries. Equally well known is the Church of St Mary Redcliffe, noted especially for its rib-vaulting and its unusual north doorway. Among Bristol's nonconformist churches is Wesley's Chapel, the oldest Methodist chapel in the world, built by John Wesley in 1739.

BURRINGTON COMBE
High above this secluded valley is 1,065ft Beacon Batch, the summit of Black Down and the highest point of the bleak Mendip range. There are several caves in the area.

CHEDDAR
This popular place is as famous for its gorge and caves as for its cheese. The gorge, hemmed in by cliffs reaching 450ft, stretches for almost a mile to the north of Cheddar village, now the home of many gift shops where, among other things, Cheddar cheese is on sale. It has been made locally since the 12th century.

AXBRIDGE
This quaint little town was a royal hunting centre as long ago as Saxon times, though the building known as King John's Hunting Lodge dates from the 16th century. The Perpendicular church that overlooks the little square has unusual plasterwork and an outstanding 15th-century font.

LOWER WEARE
Collections of waterfowl and a variety of small pets can be seen here at the Ambleside Water Gardens and Aviaries.

BURNHAM-ON-SEA
Extensive sands overlooking Bridgwater Bay account for Burnham's great popularity as a resort. Sand foundations are also responsible for the leaning tower of its 15th-century church. Inside is a famous marble altarpiece designed by Inigo Jones and made by master craftsman Grinling Gibbons.

BRENT KNOLL
This isolated village takes its name from a nearby 457ft hill surmounted by an ancient camp. Inside the 15th-century church are some interesting carved bench-ends.

TOUR 8 ROUTE DIRECTIONS

Drive from Weston-super-Mare on the A370 (SP Bristol) to Congresbury. Turn left, cross the River Yeo, then turn left again on to the B3133 (SP Clevedon). Pass through Yatton and Kenn, cross the M5 and continue to the clock tower in Clevedon.

From Clevedon clock tower follow signs 'seafront, B3130'. After ½ mile bear right to join the seafront, then in ½ mile bear left, pass the pier and keep forward for 1½ miles. At a T-junction turn left on to the B3124 (SP Portishead), then in ½ mile at Walton-in-Gordano crossroads turn left (no SP). After 2 miles turn left into Nore Road and continue to Portishead.

Leave by the A369 (SP Bristol) and in 2¾ miles, at the M5 roundabout, take the fourth exit (SP Clifton, toll) and go through Abbots Leigh. In 1¼ miles turn left on to the B3129 (SP Clifton), and cross the Clifton Suspension Bridge. In 200yds turn left (SP Motorway M5), and shortly left again into Clifton Down Road. In ¼ mile turn left on to the B4468 (SP Weston). Descend Bridge Valley Road and at the bottom turn left on to the A4. Pass under the suspension bridge and in ¼ mile keep left (SP City Centre).

From Bristol centre follow signs for Weston, A370, to cross the Cumberland Basin and Avon bridges, then keep forward on to the A370. At a crossroads 1½ miles beyond Backwell (West Town), turn left (SP Bristol Airport), and at a T-junction turn right on to the A38 (SP Taunton). Descend Red Hill, cross the River Yeo and in ½ mile branch left on to an unclassified road (SP Burrington, Blagdon). In 1 mile turn right on to the A368 (SP Burrington Combe). After ¼ mile turn left on to the B3134 and ascend to Burrington Combe.

Continue to a crossroads and turn right on to the B3371 (SP Cheddar). Later turn right on to the B3135 through Cheddar Gorge. From Cheddar follow signs for Bristol and in 1 mile turn right on to the A371 (SP Axbridge, Weston). Branch left, go through Axbridge and follow signs for Taunton, Exeter (A38). Take the first exit at a roundabout and in ½ mile turn left on to the A38. Cross the M5 and in ½ mile keep left at a roundabout. In 1½ miles at another roundabout take the third exit, the B3140. In 1½ miles, at another roundabout, keep forward into Burnham-on-Sea. Turn right (SP Berrow, Brean) and in 1½ miles, at Berrow, turn right (SP Weston). Turn left in Brent Knoll, then at East Brent turn left on to the A370, and follow this road back to Weston-super-Mare.

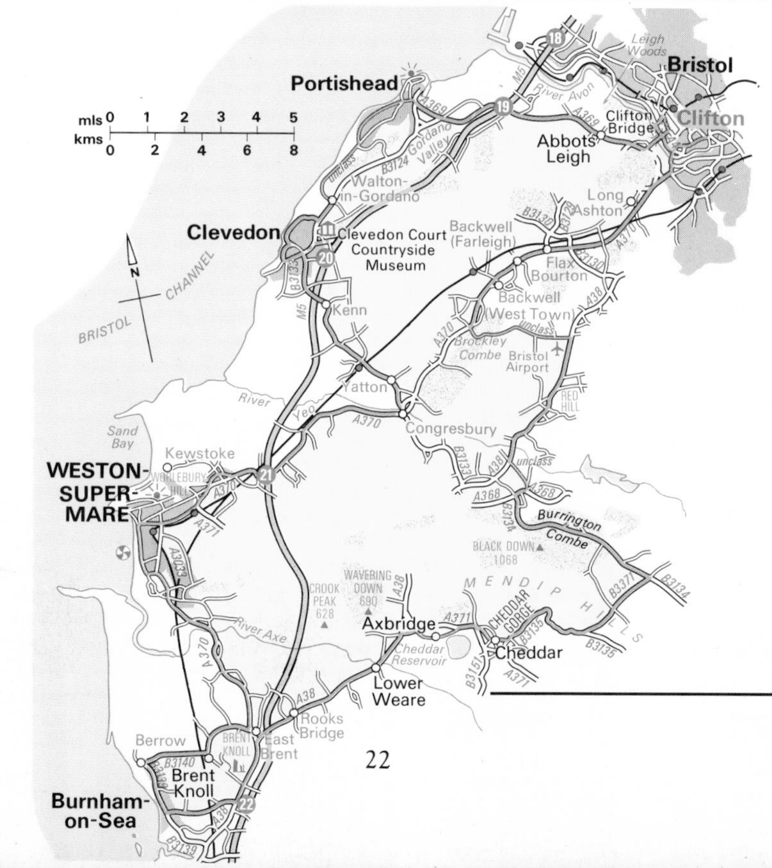

West Country Gazetteer

ASHBURTON, Devon *13 SX76*

Once an important tin and cloth centre on a popular coaching route, Ashburton is attractively sited on the River Yeo and makes an ideal base from which to tour this side of the Dartmoor National Park. Cobbled streets and old tile-hung houses impart great charm to the town, and the fine church features a characteristic Devon stair turret.

AXMINSTER, Devon *14 SY29*

This little town on the River Axe gave its name to a kind of carpet invented by Thomas Whitty in 1775 that resembled Turkish carpets. Caster Hill House, where these carpets were originally made, can still be seen. In the town centre is a church with a Norman door and a Jacobean pulpit. The original church, founded before AD755, was endowed by Athelstan after his victory over the Danes in 937, in a great battle during which five kings and seven earls are said to have been killed.

BADMINTON, Avon *14 ST88*

Badminton House has given its name to the familiar game played with net, rackets, and a shuttlecock. The seat of the dukes of Beaufort for centuries, it is a 17th- and 18th-century Palladian mansion with fine paintings and furniture. The three-day Badminton Horse Trials are held in the great park every April.

BAMPTON, Devon *13 SS92*

This small market town is situated by the River Batherm near its junction with the Exe. Ponies culled from the wild herds that roam the moor are sold at the October Pony Fair. The limestone quarried to the south of the town is highly prized, although the quarries are of geological rather than commercial interest. St Michael's Church, built around 1300, was rebuilt with a north aisle in the 15th century. Inside are notable carved rood and tower screens and a pulpit dating from the 16th century.

BARNSTAPLE, Devon *13 SS53*

Barnstaple has been the administrative and commercial centre of North Devon since Saxon times. It may even be the oldest borough in England. The River Taw is still spanned by a 13th-century bridge, built by a London merchant who saw a woman drowned here while atempting to cross the river.

Queen Anne's Walk, an 18th-century colonnade on the river side of the Strand, was once the town's merchant exchange. The Tome Stone that can be seen here was used as a money table. Castle House stands in the grounds of the former castle, and was partly built with stones from the previous structure – of which only the mound now remains. The 16th-century Church of St Peter is easily identified by its twisted lead spire.

BATH, Avon *14 ST76*

Justly spoken of as England's most elegant city, Bath is a spa resort of Georgian terraces, crescents and squares arranged round spacious landscaped parks in the Avon valley. Warm local stone is set off by trim lawns and mature trees, and the mineral waters that were the source of the city's prosperity still bubble into cisterns and baths built by the Romans some 2,000 years ago. Many centuries after the invaders left *Aquae Sulis*, the dandified high society of Georgian England came here to gossip with royalty and 'take the waters', and the legions of the wealthy occupied magnificent houses built for them by John Wood and his son. Bath today mainly reflects the cultured tastes of the 17th and 18th centuries, but it also contains relics from more distant periods. The ancient baths themselves receive half a million

gallons of water each day at a constant 49°C, and their history is interestingly related in an associated museum. Overlooking the baths is the city's splendid 15th-century Abbey Church, while nearby is the Pump Room where people came to drink the waters. Rebuilt in 1795, this popular meeting place still offers a choice of coffee or spa water in a genteel atmosphere. The work of the Wood family is everywhere, and some of the best examples can be seen in the Circus, the superb Royal Crescent (No. 1 is open), and the Assembly Rooms. Several museums can be visited in the city, including the Holburne of Menstrie Museum, the Burrows Toy Museum and the Bath Carriage Museum.

BEAMINSTER, Dorset *14 ST40*

This small town is situated in a beautiful natural amphitheatre formed by the surrounding hills. The church's richly ornamented Tudor tower is perhaps the finest in Dorset. Beaminster features in Hardy's *Tess of the D'Urbervilles* under the name Emminster.

BEER, Devon *14 .SY28*

This small resort and fishing village, with its interesting buildings and quaint narrow streets, was once the stronghold of smugglers. Beer Head is a magnificent chalk promontory which can be reached by public footpath, and the shingle beach is easily accessible for bathing.

BERKELEY, Glos *14 ST69*

In 1327 King Edward II was murdered in this magnificent 12th-century castle, the home of the Berkeley family for some 800 years. Many Berkeley monuments can be seen in the Early English church, which has a detached tower of 1783 and a Norman doorway beneath a fine rose window. Buried in the church is Edward Jenner, a local man who discovered smallpox vaccine. He died in 1823. A small Jenner museum may be visited in the village.

Overlooked by the soaring tower of 15th-century Bath Abbey, the Roman Great Bath was rediscovered in 1880 and still has its original lead lining and pipes

This five-arched medieval stone bridge crosses the River Exe near the fascinating old village of Bickleigh, where there is a Norman castle and a restored mill

BICKLEIGH, Devon　　　　*13 SS90*
Bickleigh Castle dates from Norman times. Its great sandstone gatehouse and chapel, with a fine font, are part of the original castle while the other buildings are mainly late Tudor.

Near Bickleigh Bridge, on the River Exe, is Bickleigh Mill Farm. An old farmstead has been preserved as a living museum of agriculture. Nearby is Bickleigh Mill, where the old mill machinery has been restored and a working craft centre established.

BIDEFORD, Devon　　　　*13 SS42*
Between 1550 and 1750 this town was the principal port of north Devon and the home of a renowned shipbuilding industry. Sir Richard Grenville, who obtained a charter for the town from Queen Elizabeth I, crewed his ship *Revenge* entirely with Bideford men. That brave little vessel will always be famous for its stand against 15 Spanish ships in the Azores.

Bideford's mile-long, tree-lined quay remains lively, and the estuary is popular with yachtsmen and small-boat sailors. Bridgeland Road preserves evidence of a prosperous past in the shape of 17th-century merchants' houses. Predating these is the bridge over the River Torridge, a 15th-century structure unusual in that all 24 of its arches are of different widths. It has been considerably renovated and widened to take the burden of 20th-century traffic.

BLANDFORD FORUM, Dorset　*14 ST80*
All but 50 or so of the town's houses were destroyed by a terrible fire in 1731, which explains why handsome brick and stone architecture of the late 18th century is so much in evidence. Earlier survivals include the Ryves Almshouses of 1682, Dale House of 1689, and the early 17th-century Old House. Much of the countryside round Blandford is rich arable and dairy-farming land, watered by the beautiful River Stour to the south and fringed by the lovely countryside of Cranborne Chase to the north and west.

BODMIN, Cornwall　　　　*12 SX06*
This is the county town of Cornwall and is set on the steep edge of Bodmin Moor. St Petroc's Church was rebuilt in 1469 and houses a fine Norman font. The waters of St Guron's well, near the churchyard, were once recommended as a cure for eye complaints. The town has an interesting county regimental museum, and the district is rich in prehistoric remains.

BOSCASTLE, Cornwall　　　*12 SX09*
The combined Valency and Jordan rivers meet incoming tides with dramatic effect at Boscastle. A local blowhole amply demonstrates the force of the water. Boscastle itself is an attractive village arranged round a long, broad street that climbs steeply through woodland. Close to the harbour is a museum of interesting relics associated with magic and witchcraft.

The great fire of 1731 which destroyed old Blandford Forum is commemorated by this classical portico

BOVEY TRACEY, Devon　　*13 SX87*
The church here, dedicated to St Thomas à Becket, is traditionally held to have been built by Sir William de Tracey to expiate his part in Becket's murder in 1170. The original building was burned down around 1320, and the present church is Perpendicular with a Decorated tower. The carved pulpit and screen are outstanding examples of characteristic Devon style. In January 1646, Cromwell took Royalist troops at Bovey by surprise and captured many prisoners. The name Cromwell's Arch was given to an old gateway which once formed part of an early priory.

BRADFORD-ON-AVON, Wilts *14 ST86*
The River Avon here is spanned by a 17th-century bridge incorporating a small lock-up. A tiny Saxon church rescued from obscurity in the 19th century has turned out to be one of the most important buildings of its age in Britain. Old weavers' cottages stand in Dutch Barton Street, and Barton Farm Country Park contains a superbly preserved 14th-century tithe barn. The park itself is an unspoilt area of country between the canal and the river.

BRAUNTON, Devon　　　　*13 SS43*
The sand dunes of Braunton Burrows are noted for their flora and fauna. St Brannock's Church has a Norman tower with a later broach spire, and houses 16th-century benchends and a Jacobean pulpit, reading desk, and gallery.

BRIDPORT, Dorset　　　　*14 SY49*
For over 750 years Bridport has been associated with rope- and net-making, and it is still Europe's principal centre for the production of fishing nets, lines, and cordage. These fascinating local trades are featured in a permanent exhibition at Bridport Museum and Art Gallery. Also here are exhibits showing the archaeology, geology, and natural history of the area.

BRISTOL, Avon   14 ST57

During the 16th century ships out of Bristol sailed to every part of the known world in search of new markets and exotic produce, opening up international trading routes in a way never before imagined. In 1843 Brunel launched his SS *Great Britain*, the largest iron ship of the time, and in 1970 its rusting hull was rescued from the Falkland Islands and returned to the Bristol dry dock where it was originally built. Extensive renovation has restored it as a proud memorial to its great designer and the city of its birth. Nowadays the city's dock area is at Avonmouth, which is more fitted to coping with the vast ships of 20th-century world traffic. Bristol's many lovely old buildings include a cathedral that was founded as an Augustinian monastery and contains examples of Norman, Early English, Gothic and Victorian architecture. St Mary Redcliffe, one of the city's finest churches, was built and extended between the 13th and 15th centuries and carries a massive tower with a 285ft spire. The 16th-century Red Lodge houses interesting oak carvings and furnishings of contemporary and later date, and the Georgian House features furniture from the 18th century. Various displays and exhibitions can be seen in St Nicholas' Church and the City Museum and Art Gallery.

BRIXHAM, Devon   13 SX95

This fishing town and resort, with its picturesque harbour, is popular with holidaymakers and artists alike. Sands giving access for bathing are found at Mudstone Bay. St Mary's Church, a little way inland, has a buttressed tower. William of Orange landed here in 1688—a turning point of English history commemorated by a statue on the quay.

BRUTON, Somerset   14 ST63

Bruton is a fine old town where an old packhorse bridge called Bruton Bow spans the River Brue. The church has two towers – the larger of which is a splendid example of the Perpendicular style – and an 18th-century chancel with attractive rococo plasterwork. Part of the 12th-century abbey walls can be seen in the street named Plox, and a dovecot survives on a hill above the town.

BUCKLAND-IN-THE-MOOR, Devon   13 SX77

Although visited by many people as one of the county's show villages, Buckland-in-the-Moor remains unspoilt. Its 15th- and 16th-century church contains a notable rood-screen, and the church clock has an unusual dial on which the hours are marked by the letters 'My Dear Mother' instead of numbers.

BUDE, Cornwall   12 SS20

One of Bude's main attractions is its huge surfing beach, where strong winds that have caused hundreds of wrecks over the centuries provide a constant supply of rollers ideal for the sport. The town itself is sheltered from the full force of the weather by ridges of downland between it and the sea. Visitors interested in sun- and sea-bathing are catered for by Summerleaze beach, a sheltered area of sand at the mouth of the River Neet. Here there is a large swimming pool that is naturally refilled every high tide.

BUDLEIGH SALTERTON, Devon   13 SY08

During the 13th century this village was a salt-panning community supplying the local priory. At the mouth of the River Otter is a shingle beach backed by red sandstone cliffs, and less than a mile away are the challenging fairways of the best golf course in south Devon. Several Georgian houses can be seen in the town, and a small but interesting museum called the Fairlynch Arts Centre is in an 18th-century thatched house.

BURNHAM-ON-SEA, Somerset 14 ST34

This little red-brick town has grown to cope with holidaymakers who come in large numbers every year to enjoy its miles of sandy beach. Bridgwater Bay Nature Reserve lies a little to the south-west.

CADGWITH, Cornwall   12 SW71

Cadgwith's attractive thatched cottages overlook a stone strand dotted with beached boats and the paraphernalia of a working fishing community. All along the coast are sandy coves, and to the south is the great tidal chasm of the Devil's Frying Pan. This was formed when a vast sea cave collapsed, and is at its scenic best in stormy weather.

CAMBORNE, Cornwall   12 SW64

Although most of the deep copper and tin mines in the area are no longer worked, Camborne still has a School of Metalliferous Mining. The local museum displays items of archaeological, historical, mineralogical and mining interest. Richard Trevithick, a pioneer of steam locomotion, was born here in 1771.

CASTLE CARY, Somerset   14 ST63

Several fine old houses, a Victorian market hall and a pretty duckpond are grouped together at the heart of this pleasant small town. The old lock-up, an unusual circular structure once used for the restriction of petty mischiefmakers, dates from the 18th century. It measures only 7ft across, and has no windows.

CASTLE COMBE, Wilts   14 ST87

Built of Cotswold stone and set deep in a stream-threaded valley, this old weaving centre is acknowledged as one of England's most picturesque villages. Numerous old buildings are grouped round the canopied 13th-century market cross and the 17th-century manor house, now a hotel. A stream called By Brook runs alongside the main street.

Left: The charming thatched cottages of Buckland-in-the-Moor nestle in a wooded valley surrounded by bleak moorland

Right: Sunset lends a haunting beauty to the extensive sands around the busy little resort of Burnham-on-Sea

CERNE ABBAS, Dorset   14 ST60

The village of Cerne Abbas derives its name from a Benedictine abbey founded here in 987. Remains of this include a beautiful 15th-century guesthouse, and the contemporary tithe barn has been converted into a house. Early examples of heraldic stained glass can be seen in the windows of the church. Outside the village is the 180ft-long hill figure known as the Cerne Abbas Giant. It is believed to be associated with fertility rites, and may date from before the Roman occupation.

CHARD, Somerset   14 ST30

Judge Jeffreys' notorious Bloody Assize was held in the former manor house at Chard after the 1685 Monmouth rebellion. The building, opposite the handsome Guildhall, dates from Elizabethan times. The old court room on the first floor can be visited. The Choughs Inn has an Elizabethan interior, and the mainly Perpendicular church displays a number of interesting monuments.

CHARMOUTH, Dorset   14 SY39

The Regency houses in this small resort line the lower slopes of a steep hill, which dips down to the sea and a sand-and-shingle beach. The cliffs are of great geological interest and contain numerous fossil ammonites. A fossilized ichthyosaurus found nearby in 1811 is now in London's Natural History Museum. Charmouth is described in Jane Austen's *Persuasion*.

CHEDDAR, Somerset   14 ST45

Every year many thousands of people come here to see the spectacular limestone scenery of Cheddar Gorge. Underground the region is honeycombed by caves and potholes, many of which feature weird crystalline formations created by water action. Particularly good examples can be seen in Cox's and Gough's caverns. Various archaeological finds are displayed in the Cheddar Caves Museum, and Cheddar village has a museum of motor transport.

Members of the Pole family are commemorated in Colyton church by several elaborate tombs

CHIPPENHAM, Wilts   14 ST97

Situated on the River Avon near the edge of the Cotswold Hills, this pleasant industrial town has been a market centre since Saxon times. Several attractive half-timbered houses, a 15th-century town hall and an old lock-up are preserved here.

CHIPPING SODBURY, Avon   14 ST78

This old market town has a Perpendicular church displaying a lofty pinnacled tower. The 15th-century pulpit is canopied, and a 16th-century cross stands near the church.

Dodington Park is 2 miles south-east. Designed by James Wyatt in 1813, this Palladian mansion stands in 700 acres of parkland laid out by Capability Brown. Features of the park include two lakes, a carriage museum and a children's farm.

Dodington Park, near Chipping Sodbury, is the home of a fine carriage museum containing over 30 vehicles

CLOVELLY, Devon   12 SS32

Clovelly is one of the West Country's most picturesque fishing villages. No cars are allowed here because the steep cobbled street, lined with lovely old houses, descends 400ft to the sea in a series of steps. Donkeys are used to transport visitors' luggage, and zig-zag steps allow pedestrian access down the wooded cliffs to the tiny quay and a pebble beach. The village, discovered by holidaymakers in the 19th century, is popular with artists and has a climate as mild as that of south Devon.

COLYTON, Devon   14 SY29

Picturesque winding streets and a 600-year-old bridge over the river add an almost medieval charm to this market town in the Coly valley. The cruciform church houses some particularly interesting monuments, and there is also a well-preserved Saxon cross. The Great House in South Street is the old home of the Yonge family, and was probably built by John Yonge, a merchant adventurer who died in 1612.

CORFE CASTLE, Dorset   14 SY98

Dominated by the picturesque ruined stronghold from which it takes its name, this Purbeck-stone village owes its existence to the curiously symmetrical hill on which the castle stands. The mound rises exactly in the centre of a gap in the Purbeck Hills and was probably first fortified by King Alfred against the Danes. When the Normans came they occupied the site and began the magnificent 12th- to 15th-century castle whose remains can be seen today. After the Civil War Cromwell made sure that it could never again be used against him by blowing it up. On the village side of the hill is a deep moat spanned by a bridge, and in a garden off the main street is a perfect replica of the village and castle in miniature. Various relics from the village can be seen in the local museum.

COVERACK, Cornwall   12 SW71

Smugglers once frequented this small fishing village, and wreckers lured unsuspecting vessels on to the nearby Manacle Rocks to plunder their cargoes. Nowadays Coverack has a lifeboat station that was established after a particularly bad series of disasters. The harbour is overlooked by thatched cottages.

CREDITON, Devon   13 SS80

Crediton was a Saxon bishopric before the Christian centre was transferred to Exeter. Tradition says that St Boniface was born here in 680. He later became Bishop of Mainz, in Germany, and converted large areas of Europe to the Christian faith. Crediton's splendid red sandstone church is almost a miniature cathedral.

CREWKERNE, Somerset   14 ST40

Crewkerne has long been a centre of the flax-weaving and sail-making industries. Interesting buildings include an ancient grammar school, and almshouses of 1604 and 1707. The church is an exceptionally beautiful, mainly 15th-century structure, displaying a notable west front.

Exhibits in Dorchester's elegant Victorian museum include memorabilia of Thomas Hardy

CULLOMPTON, Devon   *13 ST00*
This market town on the River Culm is noted for its apple orchards, which supply the local cider industry. Much of the town was burnt down in 1839, and Victorian additions stand alongside Georgian houses that escaped the blaze. The fine church has a spendid tower, screen, waggon-roof and fan vaulting.

Five miles south-west lie Killerton House and Gardens, given to the National Trust in 1944 by Sir Richard Acland, whose ancestors have lived here since 1778. The gardens feature a beautiful hillside arboretum.

DARTINGTON, Devon   *13 SX76*
Dartington Hall is a restored 14th-century manor house with ancient buildings grouped round a quadrangle. These are now owned by a trust which has made the manor a centre for rural education and a cultural centre for the district. It comprises a school, a college of arts and an adult education centre. Activities include farming, horticulture, forestry, weaving and building. The 14th-century banqueting hall is open to the public at certain times, and the entire complex is set amid gardens, courtyards and terraces.

DARTMOUTH, Devon   *13 SX85*
A market town and fishing port of great historical interest, Dartmouth is sited on the west bank of the River Dart. Many naval expeditions, including the fleet sent by Edward III to assist at the Siege of Calais, sailed from here. A ruined stronghold built by the townspeople in 1537, with an inscribed stone recording the sailing of the *Mayflower* in 1520, can be seen in Bayard's Cove. Also here are 17th-century houses. The remains of an old Butterwalk— a colonnaded arcade with carved overhangs —have been restored to house a nautical museum. The town church of St Saviour dates

from the 14th century and contains a fine carved screen and matching pulpit. Dartmouth Castle, a Tudor building on the site of an earlier castle, lies about 1 mile south.

DAWLISH, Devon   *13 SX97*
This is a quiet seaside resort near the mouth of the River Exe, with a sandy beach and red cliffs. On the banks of Dawlish Water, in the town centre, is the Lawn, a miniature garden, complete with waterfalls and black swans. It was laid out in the 19th century. Local architecture is partly Regency and partly Victorian; The Strand was built in the early 1800s, and still retains its elegant Regency character. Luscombe Castle was built by John Nash in 1800. A large national wildfowl refuge is sited at Dawlish Warren.

DEVONPORT, Devon   *13 SX45*
Although Devonport started life with an identity of its own, the establishment of the important naval dockyard on the Hamoaze in 1691 resulted in its rapid development into the navy quarter of neighbouring Plymouth. Its fine 19th-century town hall was by the architect John Foulston. Older foundations include the Gun Wharf of 1718 and the Royal Naval Hospital, also of the 18th century.

DORCHESTER, Dorset   *14 SY69*
Thomas Hardy was born 2 miles north-east of Dorchester in a cottage at Higher Bockhampton. The town itself is featured in several of his novels as 'Casterbridge', and the original manuscript of *The Mayor of Casterbridge* can be seen among other relics, in the County Museum. Excellent finds from periods before and after the Romans founded their major walled town of *Durnovaria* here around AD43 are also displayed, and foundations of a Roman villa complete with tessellated pavement can be seen at Colliton Park.

In 1834, the infant trades union movement was dealt a public blow at the trial of six agricultural workers later to become known as the Tolpuddle Martyrs. They were tried in the courtroom of Dorchester's Old Shire Hall, now a Tolpuddle memorial, and were sentenced to transportation for joining forces to request a wage increase for local farmworkers.

DULVERTON, Somerset   *13 SS92*
The River Barle is spanned here by an attractive three-arched bridge and is known for its excellent trout and salmon fishing. Dulverton itself is a shopping centre and administrative centre for south-east Exmoor. Local painters exhibit their works each summer in Exmoor House, by the bridge.

DUNSTER, Somerset   *13 SS94*
Dunster is a beautiful medieval village that has often been described as a 'perfect relic of feudal times'. Its unspoilt condition is largely due to its ownership by one family, the Luttrells, for some 600 years until 1950. The castle was the family seat, and is well worth visiting. Its oak-panelled halls display magnificent ceilings and fascinating relics. In the centre of the village is the octagonal Yarn Market, which

was built in 1609, when Dunster was an important cloth centre. No far away is the lovely Luttrell Arms, which is said to have stood for three centuries and was originally the house of the Abbot of Cleeve. Among its many features are an interesting 15th-century porch and a fine chamber displaying a wealth of carved oak. The parish church is by far the finest in this part of the country.

This Portuguese fishing boat is one of the vessels in the Exeter Maritime Museum

EXETER, Devon   *13 SX99*
In recent years the centre of this long-established city and county town has been developed into a massive shopping complex. The old city, farther down the hill towards the River Exe, contains many interesting old buildings. The most imposing structure is undoubtedly the cathedral, which is noted for its fine proportions and the beauty of its two Norman transeptal towers. The present building stands on the site of an 11th-century church, and the towers date from the 12th century. Among its most famous features is the elegant gothic fan-vaulting inside, claimed to be the finest and most extensive in the world. Town Quay features the Maritime Museum, which preserves over 100 vessels. Nearby is the fine Custom House, built in 1681. Other features not to be missed are St Nicholas Priory, Rougemont Museum and the castle remains, and the Albert Memorial Museum in Queen Street.

EXFORD, Somerset   *13 SS83*
The kennels of the Devon and Somerset Stag Hounds are here, and horses are very much in evidence at all times. Exford's annual Horse Show is generally held on the second Wednesday in August. The nucleus of the village is an attractive grouping of cottages, shops, and hotels around the local cricket and football field. The little church contains an interesting 15th-century screen.

Left: Best known for its fossils and its oil-wells, Kimmeridge Bay also offers magnificent coastal scenery and pleasant walks. The bay is overlooked by a ruined tower that was built in the early 19th century

Right: The Dorset coast around Kimmeridge is particularly rich in fossil ammonites, ancient sea creatures with tightly coiled shells

FALMOUTH, Cornwall　　　12 SW83

Falmouth is a leading holiday resort with a mild climate. The bay forms an excellent base for yachting, and the beaches offer safe bathing.

Shipping from all over the world uses the harbour, which is the largest in the county and includes a dry dock capable of handling tankers of up to 90,000 tons. There is a safe anchorage on the estuary of the Fal. Falmouth began to develop as a port after Sir Walter Raleigh recommended its natural strategic advantages. It became a station for the Mail Packet Service in 1688, and by 1827 had 39 overseas-mail vessels.

Henry VIII's Pendennis Castle, built in 1543, overlooks the harbour entrance and provides a good viewpoint. An east window in the 17th-century church of King Charles the Martyr, dedicated to Charles I, depicts the king holding the execution axe. Attractive 18th- and 19th-century buildings can be seen in the older part of the town; the Customs House and Grove Hill House are two good examples.

FOWEY, Cornwall　　　12 SX15

Fowey, pronounced 'Foy', stands at the estuary of a river of the same name. Once one of the West Country's busiest ports, it still has a harbour and some quaint, narrow old streets. The town hall of 1792 retains several 14th-century windows. St Catherine's Fort was built by order of King Henry VIII. The sign of the King of Prussia Inn commemorates a famous Cornish smuggler, John Carter, who operated some two centuries ago.

FROME, Somerset　　　14 ST74

The name of this busy market town is pronounced 'Froom', and its main industries are the manufacture of cloth and carpets. It is criss-crossed by steep, narrow streets and its well-restored, richly decorated church contains numerous chapels. Cheap Street has a central watercourse running down the middle of the road. The Blue House almshouses, dating from 1726, stand by a bridge spanning the River Frome. Most of the old houses here also date from the 18th century.

Three miles south-east is Longleat House. This great Elizabethan mansion, the seat of the Marquess of Bath, stands on the site of a 13th-century priory and is a treasure house of old furniture, paintings, books, and interior decoration. It was one of England's first unified designs, and the grounds were landscaped by the brilliant 18th-century designer Capability Brown. The estate includes a large safari park, the first of its kind in Europe.

GLASTONBURY, Somerset　　　14 ST53

High above the skyline of this ancient town is the 520ft pinnacle of Glastonbury Tor, a mystical place associated in myth with fabulous Avalon and the Celtic Otherworld. Glastonbury was probably founded in Celtic times, but according to legend it was created by Joseph of Arimathea. Other traditions connect St Patrick and King Arthur with the abbey, and it is said that Arthur is actually buried here. The well-preserved remains that exist today date from the 12th and 13th centuries, and include St Mary's Church, the abbey church, and a number of monastic buildings. By far the best preserved is the superb Abbot's Kitchen. Features of the town itself include two medieval churches, the George and Pilgrim Inn, and a 15th-century abbey courthouse known as the Tribunal, which now houses late prehistoric finds from lake dwellings at nearby Meare and Godney.

HELFORD, Cornwall　　　12 SW72

This lovely little village on the wooded banks of the Helford River is a favourite haunt of anglers and yachtsmen. The river is dotted with small villages and creeks, and a passenger ferry sails from here to Helford Passage, where there is an attractive inn.

HELSTON, Cornwall　　　12 SW62

Until the Loe Bar formed across the mouth of the River Cober in the 13th century, Helston was a busy port. Well-preserved Regency houses can be seen along Cross Street, and behind the early Victorian Guildhall is an interesting museum with many old implements including a cider press.

Some would say that 8 May is the best day to visit the town, for that is the time of the Furry or Floral Dance. From early in the morning the inhabitants dance through the winding streets and in and out of houses – supposedly to celebrate the time a dragon dropped a rock on the town without causing any damage.

HOLT, Wilts　　　14 ST86

Local weavers once brought their disputes to The Courts to be settled, but this 17th-century building now enjoys a peaceful retirement amid fine gardens that include topiary work, a lily pond and an arboretum.

HONITON, Devon　　　13 ST10

This town gave its name to Honiton lace, a material which is still produced in neighbouring villages and can still be bought in some local shops. Examples can be seen in a small museum housed in the old chapel beside the parish church. A 17th-century black marble tomb to Thomas Marwood, physician to Queen Elizabeth I, can be seen in the church. Marwood House, Honiton's oldest building, dates from 1619 and contains one of many antique shops that thrive in this acknowledged centre of the trade.

ILFRACOMBE, Devon　　　13 SS54

This one-time fishing port is now a popular holiday resort. Summer steamers cruise along the coast and connect Ilfracombe with Swansea, Cardiff, Bristol, and Lundy Island. A 14th-century chapel near the harbour is now a lighthouse. There are plenty of public parks and gardens, and a zoo is sited on the old Barnstaple road.

ILMINSTER, Somerset　　　14 ST31

Ilminster church carries a very fine Perpendicular tower. Inside is the family tomb of the Wadhams, founders of Wadham College in Oxford. The grammar school, dated 1586, is now a school for girls. Barrington Court (not open) is a splendid Tudor mansion built of Ham Hill stone, four miles north-east. A former stable block dates from 1670, and a remarkable ten-faced sundial stands in the grounds.

KIMMERIDGE, Dorset　　　14 SY97

Thatched and slate-roofed cottages make up this tiny village, which is situated near the shallow bay from which it takes its name. A toll road leads to the coast.

Very low cliffs of black shale ring wide, sandless Kimmeridge Bay, and the beach is littered with great chunks of rock packed with fossil ammonites. A condition of entry to the beach nowadays is that hammers and chisels should be left behind. A well sunk here in 1959 produces 10,000 tons of crude oil each year.

LACOCK, Wilts   *14 ST96*

A wide architectural range from medieval times to the 19th century has been preserved in the stone, half-timbered, and thatched buildings of this delightful village, which is owned by the National Trust. Its abbey was the last religious house to be suppressed at the Dissolution in 1539, and was later converted into a private dwelling incorporating many of its medieval buildings. Over the centuries its ancient structure has acquired an octagonal Tudor tower and a 17th-century gothic hall. The abbey gatehouse contains a museum of work by W. H. Fox-Talbot, a 19th-century pioneer of photography who once owned the abbey. Elsewhere in the village is a great tithe barn with eight massive bays, and a small medieval lock-up known as the Cruck House.

Almost every style of English cottage architecture is represented at Lacock

LANGPORT, Somerset   *14 ST42*

The River Parrett – once famous for its eels – flows below the main street of this old market town, which was an important port with its own fleet of ships until the last century. Traces of the old quays can still be seen. The Perpendicular church houses some medieval glass, and a curious hanging chapel over an arch, built in the 15th century for a craft guild, can be seen above the road near the church. The guildhall dates from 1733.

LAUNCESTON, Cornwall   *12 SX38*

The ruined Norman castle in this ancient town has an imposing keep, and a gateway survives from the former town walls. St Mary Magdalene's Church shows remarkable 16th-century granite carving on the exterior, and fine woodwork inside. St Thomas's Church houses the largest Norman font in Cornwall.

A Norman doorway which came from the old priory is incorporated in the White Hart, and Georgian houses are to be found in Castle Street. St Stephen-by-Launceston lies 1½ miles north and was the mother church of the town.

LISKEARD, Cornwall   *12 SX26*

Local miners once brought their metal to this stannary town for weighing, assaying, and taxation. The large, mainly 15th-century church has a 17th-century carved pulpit, and a tower of 1902. A bull ring can be seen in the castle park. The town is now the scene of one of Cornwall's busiest livestock markets.

LIZARD, Cornwall   *12 SW61*

A mile from Lizard is the headland of Lizard Point, the southernmost tip of a peninsula that has become famous for its beauty. Some of the area is leased to the Cornwall Naturalists' Trust. Splendid walks extend along the clifftops of the point. To the east the countryside is sheltered from the full force of Atlantic gales and is lush and green, but round the point to the west it becomes wilder and more desolate. Much of the land on this side is pitted with holes left by people digging for the mineral serpentine, a lovely stone prized for the rich shades of greens, reds and purple released by cutting and polishing. Souvenirs made from it are much in evidence in the gift shops of Lizard Town. Magnificent views from Lizard Point extend many miles – in very clear conditions, as far as Bolt Head in Devon. This superb vantage point is the site of the Lizard Lighthouse, built in 1752.

LOOE, Cornwall   *12 SX25*

The twin fishing towns and holiday resorts of East and West Looe are joined by a modern bridge spanning the Looe River. West Looe church has a detached bell-tower. East Looe features quaint streets and a pillory is preserved outside the 16th-century guildhall. An interesting monkey sanctuary is sited to the east at Murrayton. Looe Island lies offshore, and the area is well-known for its shark-fishing.

LOSTWITHIEL, Cornwall   *12 SX15*

Once the capital of Cornwall and a centre of the tin trade, Lostwithiel is set on the River Fowey. A medieval bridge spans the river, and the church retains its 13th-century tower surmounted by an octagonal lantern.

Duchy House includes remains of the Stannary court, and is of 14th-century date. An old building which formerly served as the Malt House bears an inscription recording its 3,000-year lease, commencing in 1652. Restormel Castle is a well-known 12th- to 13th-century ruin, 1 mile to the north, which has retained its circular keep.

LYME REGIS, Dorset   *14 SY39*

A steep main street runs down to the harbour in this charming little resort on Lyme Bay. The restored mainly Perpendicular church contains a 17th-century canopied pulpit, a double lectern and a gallery of 1611. The Duke of Monmouth landed on The Cobb to begin his revolution against James II in 1685. The Cobb and the town are featured in Jane Austen's novel *Persuasion* and in John Fowles' novel *The French Lieutenant's Woman*, which has been filmed here.

LYNMOUTH, Devon   *13 SS74*

Disastrous floods that made national headlines in 1952 caused serious damage and loss of life here. Afterwards the East and West Lyn rivers, which pour into the sea here, were widened, and strong walls built to prevent a recurrence of the tragedy. The clearing-up included the rebuilding of the Rhenish Tower, which was originally constructed to store salt water for indoor bathing.

LYNTON, Devon   *13 SS74*

This pleasant and very popular resort is sited high on a cliff some 500ft above its sister village of Lynmouth. Tree-covered Summerhouse Hill shields it from the blustery sea gales, and a solid ring of hills protects it from the worst of Exmoor's rain. Victorian architecture predominates in the town, and there is an unusual water-powered cliff lift.

Exmoor meets the coast at Lynmouth Bay, where cliffs plunge almost 1,000ft to the sea

MALMESBURY, Wilts   *14 ST98*

This pleasant hill-top town above the River Avon has a splendid partly ruined abbey church which shows Norman and Decorated workmanship. The richly carved south porch is particularly outstanding, and a rare watching loft or musicians' gallery is situated above the nave arcade. A window recalls the monk Elmer, who attempted to fly from here with artificial wings.

The Green Dragon Inn preserves a 14th-century window, and the fine 16th-century octagonal market cross is of interest. Old houses in the town include St John's Almshouses and the fine Bell Inn. John Aubrey, the county antiquary, was educated at the local grammar school during the 17th century. The philosopher Thomas Hobbes was born here in 1588, and Joseph Addison represented the town as MP from 1710 to 1719.

MEVAGISSEY, Cornwall   *12 SX04*

Two harbours are a feature of this picturesque resort and fishing port. It was once famous for smuggling, and for the building of fast sailing boats that could outrun the Excise cutters. An old boatbuilder's workshop now houses a folk museum. Interesting monuments of 1617 and 1632 are in the church, as well as a carved Norman font. Fine coastal scenery may be enjoyed to the south, towards the headland of Dodman Point.

MILTON ABBAS, Dorset   *14 ST80*

Set in unspoilt rural surroundings, this peaceful village of thatched and whitewashed cottages was designed and built from scratch during the 18th century. It was probably the first integrally planned village in Britain. The Brewery Farm Museum is housed in the old brewery and contains antique agricultural implements, old photographs and other interesting bygones.

MINEHEAD, Somerset   *13 SS94*

The natural beauty of its surroundings combined with its delightful situation and mild climate have made this a popular seaside resort. The Esplanade commands sweeping views over the bay, where the sands are good and bathing is safe. A prominent feature of the high ground behind the town is North Hill, which overlooks the quaint little harbour some hundreds of feet below and affords fine views across the Bristol Channel. On the landward slope is the parish church, where years ago a light burned constantly to guide travellers on the moor and lead ships to the harbour. During these times Minehead harbour was a busy port, but now it is just a pleasant holiday town. Among its attractions are the beautifully kept Blenheim Gardens, where there is a model town which is floodlit in the evening.

MONTACUTE, Somerset   *14 ST41*

This beautiful stone-built village preserves the Perpendicular gatehouse of its small priory, and a fine church tower. Montacute House is a splendid Elizabethan building of 1580 which was built in golden Ham Hill stone by the Phelips family. Lovely gardens and Jacobean pavilions grace the surrounding grounds, and the 189ft-long gallery is the longest in England.

MORETONHAMPSTEAD, Devon   *13 SX78*

The eastern edge of Dartmoor National Park sweeps down to the borders of this quiet market town, which forms a good centre for touring the moor. Picturesque colonnaded almshouses of 1637 can be seen in the town, together with a stout granite church that is a prominent landmark. Memorials in the church porch recall two French soldiers, taken prisoner during the Napoleonic Wars, who died here while on parole from Dartmoor Prison.

The moorland around Morvah is rich in prehistoric remains. Lanyon Quoit is one of the finest examples

MORVAH, Cornwall   *12 SW43*

This little mining and farming village is attractively set on the edge of the Penwith moorland. About 1 mile south of the village are Chun Castle and Chun Quoit, respectively a circular Iron Age fort built of stone and the remains of a large neolithic dolmen, or tomb chamber. Two miles south-east is Lanyon Quoit. Perhaps the best known and most visited of Cornwall's megaliths, this neolithic tomb resembles a huge three-legged stone table.

MOUSEHOLE, Cornwall   *12 SW42*

Pronounced 'Mous'l', this delightful small port and harbour is situated on Mount's Bay and shelters a pilchard-fishing fleet. The Spaniards landed here in the 16th century and burnt down the entire village except the Keigwin Arms, a former inn.

MULLION, Cornwall   *12 SW61*

This large village boasts a fine 15th-century church which contains some fine 16th-century carved bench ends. Dramatic Mullion Cove is fringed by steep, cave-pocked cliffs that form a splendid counterpoint to rocky Mullion Island, just offshore. The small harbour is used by local fishermen and visiting skin-divers.

NAILSWORTH, Glos   *14 ST89*

Old houses and woollen mills here include several Georgian buildings. Nailsworth Ladder is a hill with a 1-in-3 gradient, used for motor trials. The Friends' Meeting House dates from 1680. W. H. Davies – the tramp poet – died at Nailsworth in 1940.

NEWLYN, Cornwall   *12 SW42*

This busy fishing port used to be famous for its artist colony. Many of the painters moved north to St Ives, but a few still live and work among the quaint old cottages and fish-cellars. The Passmore Edwards picture gallery shows some of their work.

The tiny, picturesque harbour at Mullion Cove is now owned by the National Trust

NEWQUAY, Cornwall   12 SW86

Magnificent beaches, fine scenery and a wide range of amenities for the holidaymaker have made Newquay one of the most popular seaside resorts in Cornwall. The original Iron Age settlement was to the north-east at Porth Island, where today's tourists admire the grand cliffs and splendid caves. Since the first train arrived here in 1875 tourism has been the main factor in Newquay's growth. The railway originally came to bring china clay and tin to the port, but the harbour proved too small and shallow for large cargo ships. Because of this the harbour has retained some of its original character.

Two miles inland is Trerice Manor, a lovely 16th-century house with distinctive Dutch-style curved gables and a richly decorated interior with outstanding plasterwork and fireplaces.

NUNNEY, Somerset   14 ST74

Modelled on the French Bastille, the fine 14th-century castle in this delightful village is surrounded by a moat which may well be the deepest in England. The church carries a good Perpendicular tower, and houses effigies of the Delamares, who built the castle.

OKEHAMPTON, Devon   13 SX59

Okehampton is the market town for a large farming area and is situated north of the highest point in the Dartmoor National Park. The town hall dates from 1685. A little to the west are the ruined chapel, keep and hall of a 13th- and 14th-century castle – once one of the largest in Devon.

PADSTOW, Cornwall   12 SW97

Padstow stands on the Camel estuary and has an ancient harbour reached by quaint old streets. A curious Hobby-Horse dance is held here annually on May Day. The interesting Tropical Bird and Butterfly Garden is situated in Fentonluna Lane. Birds, plants and butterflies from all over the world may be seen here.

PAIGNTON, Devon   13 SX86

This popular Torbay resort offers a harbour, good sands, golf and bathing among its many amenities. St John the Baptist Church is notable for its richly carved 15th-century Kirkham chantry. A tower from a former episcopal palace still stands near the church. Oldway, a 19th-century house, displays rooms modelled on the Palace of Versailles. The zoo and botanical gardens are also of interest.

PENZANCE, Cornwall   12 SW43

The most westerly town in England, Penzance enjoys a mild climate all year round. The town grew to prosperity through tin-mining, and possibly smuggling, and was immortalized by Gilbert and Sullivan in *The Pirates of Penzance*. Evidence of its popularity in Regency times can be seen in the fine period buildings still standing in Chapel Street. Also here is a museum whose exhibits include finds from the ship *Association*, wrecked off the Scillies in 1707. There is a museum in Penlee Park, and many exotic plants grow in Morab Gardens.

Right: Trerice Manor, near Newquay, is an attractive Elizabethan mansion built in 1573 by Sir John Arundell

Below: Nunney's small but redoubtable castle succumbed to Cromwell in the Civil War, but only after a long siege

PLYMOUTH, Devon   13 SX45

Sandwiched between the estuaries of the Plym and the Tamar, this popular yachting resort and important maritime city is the venue for national sailing championships and a stop-off point for round-the-world yachtsmen. In the 17th century the Pilgrim Fathers stopped here on their way to the New World in the *Mayflower*. Their last glimpses of England would have included much of the present-day Barbican – Plymouth's Elizabethan quarter. Today the craft and antique shops of the Barbican make it an exciting district of modern Plymouth as well as a historic memorial.

A prominent statue of Sir Francis Drake shares the Hoe with Smeaton's Tower, which is the re-erected base of the old Eddystone Lighthouse. It was removed from the rocks in 1881 because of serious erosion. Nearby is the 17th-century Royal Citadel. Rising from the waters of the Sound, almost in front of the Hoe, is the rocky, tree-scattered hump of Drake's Island.

The Church of St Andrew is the largest in Devon and dates from the 15th century. Close by is Prysten House, the city's oldest building, thought to have been built in 1490 by monks from nearby Plympton.

Most of the city centre was rebuilt after appalling war damage, and Plymouth now has one of the finest shopping complexes in Europe. The 200ft-high Civic Centre affords excellent cross-town views from its roof deck.

Spanning the Tamar north-west of the city centre are two famous bridges. The oldest is the Royal Albert, a railway bridge designed by the brilliant engineer Brunel and completed in 1859. Close by is a graceful modern, single-span suspension road bridge.

POLPERRO, Cornwall   12 SX25

Narrow streets and quaint old houses give this picturesque fishing village its famous character. The old home of Dr Jonathan Couch, grandfather of Sir Arthur Quiller-Couch, houses a smugglers' museum. The curious House on Props is of interest. Rugged coast scenery can be enjoyed in this district, which is a very popular part of Cornwall. A natural pool west of the harbour is used for swimming.

The coastline near St Agnes is scattered with the ruined engine-houses of disused tin and copper-mines

PORTHCURNO, Cornwall *12 SW32*
The first transatlantic cable was brought ashore in this modern village, which has a very good beach of almost white sand. Just to the west is the unique Minack Theatre – built out of living stone on the cliff.

PRINCETOWN, Devon *13 SX57*
Sir Thomas Tyrwhitt founded the great prison here in 1806 and named the town in honour of his friend, the Prince Regent. Prison labour built many of the roads that allow modern motorists to tour comfortably through remote parts of the moor, and the town church was built by prisoners in 1883.

PUDDLETOWN, Dorset *14 SY79*
Thomas Hardy's Weatherbury in *Far from the Madding Crowd*, this village is one of the most attractive in Dorset and features a beautiful 15th-century church with an unusual panelled roof. Between the village and Wareham are stretches of moorland that were part of Hardy's Egdon Heath.

REDRUTH, Cornwall *12 SW64*
William Murdock, the inventor, lived in this important mining town and had the first gas-lit house in the country, which has been restored as a memorial. The area has associations with John Wesley and with George Fox – the founder of the Society of Friends. A local museum of mineral specimens is of interest.

ST AGNES, Cornwall *12 SW75*
St Agnes has retained its charm and character despite two centuries of mining and one century of tourism. Decaying engine houses and wildflower-covered burrows nearby bear silent witness to the mineral booms of years gone by. Among the pleasant streets and by-ways of the village is the quaint Stippy-Stappy, a steep row of slate-roofed cottages on Town Hill.

ST AUSTELL, Cornwall *12 SX05*
China clay is extracted and worked in this area, which is famous for its landscapes of spoil heaps and vast clay pits. Interesting features of the town include the Market House of 1791, the Menagew Stone in Fore Street, and the Menacuddle Holy Well.

ST IVES, Cornwall *12 SW54*
Until her recent death the sculptress Barbara Hepworth was the leading light in a famous artists' community that lived and worked in this attractive and very popular fishing village. Quaint old houses and winding alleys cluster beneath the 120ft rough-hewn granite spire of the church, a fine building dating from the 15th century.

ST JUST, Cornwall *12 SW33*
Also known as St Just-in-Penwith, this enchanting village is especially noted for the contents of its old church. Among these is a wall painting, an interesting inscribed stone of 5th-century date, and the shaft of a 9th-century Saxon cross.

ST MAWES, Cornwall *12 SW83*
Beautifully situated on the Roseland peninsula, St Mawes faces Falmouth across the Carrick Roads. The Percuil River winds inland to the east, and the resort offers good sands and yachting. King Henry VIII built the castle as a coastal blockhouse in 1542.

**ST MICHAEL'S MOUNT
Cornwall** *12 SW53*
This little granite island rises to a 250ft summit from the waters of Mount's Bay and is accessible on foot via a causeway at low tide, or by boat from Marazion. Its splendid castle and priory, both founded by Edward the Confessor in the 11th century, stand high above a small harbour and hamlet.

SALCOMBE, Devon *13 SX73*
Salcombe is beautifully situated at the mouth of delightful Kingsbridge estuary, in the South Hams district. As well as being a sheltered harbour, it offers sea bathing from its sandy beaches. A round tower from a ruined Tudor castle is still standing.

SENNEN, Cornwall *12 SW32*
According to legend Sennen was the battleground for the last Cornish fight against invading Danes. The 15th-century church contains a medieval statue of the Virgin Mary and is the most westerly church in England. Sennen Cove offers good sand and excellent bathing.

SHAFTESBURY, Dorset *14 ST82*
Situated on the edge of a 700ft plateau, Shaftesbury is an ancient town full of quaint corners and attractive little streets. Its most famous street, cobbled Gold Hill, slopes steeply down towards Blackmoor Vale. Shaftesbury's history began with the abbey established here around 880, a foundation that became the burial place of Edward the Martyr and grew to be one of the richest in the area until it was destroyed at the Dissolution in the 16th century. One of the houses in Gold Hill is now an interesting museum of local history.

Exhibits in Shaftesbury's museum include these pretty embroidered motifs (top). The museum stands in Gold Hill (bottom)

SHERBORNE, Dorset 14 ST61

Winding streets of mellow stone houses dating from the 15th century onwards weave a fascinating web across this beautiful and historic town. From AD705 to 1075 Sherborne was a cathedral city, but the great church was adopted by a slightly later monastery that flourished until the Dissolution in the 16th century. Many of the foundation's buildings were adopted by other bodies and survive in a good state of preservation. Some were occupied by the famous Sherborne School, and the Abbey Gatehouse now accommodates the Sherborne Museum. Over all stands the Norman to 15th-century Abbey Church, a magnificent building best known for its superb fanvaulting. The older of the town's two castles stands ½ mile east and dates from the 12th and 13th centuries. It was reduced to ruins in the Civil War. Sherborne's 16th-century castle was built for Sir Walter Raleigh.

SIDMOUTH, Devon 13 SY18

Sidmouth boasts a shingle beach backed by spectacular red cliffs, and is a popular holiday town. Rows of architecturally outstanding Regency terraces are reminders of the resort's prosperous early days, while elsewhere are the more ancient Old Chancel and Manor House. The former incorporates parts of the old parish church, and the latter is now a museum.

SIMONSBATH, Somerset 13 SS73

At 1,100ft above sea level, Simonsbath is the highest village in the Exmoor National Park and stands at the centre of what used to be the Royal Exmoor Forest. Deer were once commonplace here, but today these timid creatures are rarely seen. The 100-year-old church administers the largest parish in the park.

SOUTH MOLTON, Devon 13 SS72

Known to have existed as a Saxon colony around AD700, this lovely little town lies just south of Exmoor and is an agricultural centre for the region. Between the Middle Ages and the mid 19th century it became a thriving wool town; it was also a coach stop on the route to Barnstaple and Bideford, and the nearest town to the iron and copper mines of North Molton. A square of elegant Georgian houses is complemented by the town's grand 18th-century Guildhall and 19th-century Assembly Rooms, all built with the profits from wool and minerals. Since 1961 the town has been the centre for busy livestock market. Opposite the square an avenue of pollarded lime trees leads to the church, which houses a beautifully carved pulpit and carries a 15th-century tower. A small museum behind the Guildhall displays examples of pewterware, a cider press, and an intriguing old fire engine dating from 1736.

STOKE-SUB-HAMDON, Somerset 14 ST41

Hamdon Hill rises 426ft above this village, and is where the lovely golden Ham Hill stone is quarried. An extensive British camp on the summit has yielded many Iron Age and Roman finds, which can be seen in the Castle Museum at Taunton.

South Molton's market place is overlooked by the elegant ironwork verandah of the 19th-century Medical Hall

The village itself, together with its fine Norman church (¾ mile east, at East Stoke), is built of Ham stone. The 15th-century priory was formerly a chantry house, and now belongs to the National Trust. Behind the Fleur-de-Lis Inn is an 18th-century fives court.

STOURTON, Wilts 14 ST73

Good paintings and Chippendale furniture can be seen inside Stourhead House, but this famous Palladian mansion is best known for its superb grounds. These were laid out by Henry Hoare, who owned the estate, and show one of Europe's finest 18th-century layouts, with classical garden temples and a delightful lake.

STREET, Somerset 14 ST43

Footwear has become the staple product of this small manufacturing town. Street is also known as the home of Millfield School, which lies in the area. A tall monument to Admiral Lord Hood stands on nearby Windmill Hill.

STURMINSTER NEWTON, Dorset 14 ST71

The most important livestock market in the southern part of the Blackmoor Vale is held here. A fine six-arched medieval bridge spans the River Stour.

TAUNTON, Somerset 14 ST22

Cider is the best-known product of this town in the Vale of Taunton Deane. The partly 12th-century castle contains a museum, and was one of the places where Judge Jeffreys' Bloody Assize was held after the Battle of Sedgemoor in 1685. St Mary's Church and St James's Church both display lofty Perpendicular towers which have been rebuilt. Gray's Almshouses date from 1635. An ancient priory barn is also of interest. Three public schools include one of 13th-century foundation, and the former thatched leper hospital has been restored as council offices.

TAVISTOCK, Devon 13 SX47

Light engineering and timber-working firms in this pleasant little market town continue an industrial tradition that started at least as far back as the 14th century. At that time tin-mining was the big money-maker, but cloth came into its own in the 15th century and the discovery of copper brought a new mineral boom in the 19th. Despite this activity the town remains unspoilt, and is an ideal touring base on the western fringe of the extensive Dartmoor National Park. Tavistock is linked to the River Tamar at Morwellham by an unusual underground canal.

Taunton Castle (below left) has been rebuilt several times since it was founded in Saxon times. It now houses the County Museum, whose exhibits include a Roman mosaic illustrating Virgil's 'Aeneid' (below right)

Ruined Tintagel Castle, set on a wild clifftop, is said to have been the birthplace of King Arthur

TEIGNMOUTH, Devon   *13 SX97*
Pronounced 'Tinmouth', this popular resort offers a beach of sand and fine shingle; sea bathing; and golf. In 1821 the Dartmoor granite used to build London Bridge was shipped from the harbour, and today clay is shipped from here. A bridge crosses the Teign estuary to the yachting centre of Shaldon, below the wooded headland of The Ness.

TETBURY, Glos   *14 ST89*
This pleasant Cotswold town stands on the River Avon. The pillared Elizabethan market hall is thought to have been the place where local merchants brought their wool to be weighed. The church was rebuilt in 1787, but the tower and spire date from the 19th century. It is thought to be one of the country's finest examples of the gothic revival style. The interior has a gallery, box pews and slender wooden pillars.

To the south-west of the town is Highgrove (not open), the country home of the Prince and Princess of Wales.

TINTAGEL, Cornwall   *12 SX08*
The name Tintagel is highly evocative of the Arthurian legends, but the only King Arthur's Hall here nowadays is the modern home of the Fellowship of the Round Table. The local post office, owned by the National Trust, is a superb slate-built structure that dates from the 14th century and was originally a small manor house. Norman workmanship is very evident in the local church, but its origins probably lie farther back in Saxon times. A Norman font and a Roman milestone can be seen inside.

High on the jagged, broken cliffs near Tintagel is a romantically ruined castle that, according to legend, was the birthplace of King Arthur. Its remains postdate that giant of Western folklore by some seven centuries, but traces of a Celtic monastery founded early enough to have accommodated him can be seen close by. The castle itself was built on its wave-lashed promontory by Reginald, Earl of Cornwall and illegitimate son of Henry I, in the 12th century.

TIVERTON, Devon   *13 SS91*
After the conquest of the south-west in the 7th century, Tiverton became one of the first Saxon settlements, and later during the 17th- and 18th-century heyday of the clothing industry the town became the principal industrial area in the county. Architecturally, the town has benefited greatly from the prosperity of its inhabitants. Rich wool merchants have bequeathed such fine buildings as St Peter's Church, Blundell's School, and three sets of almshouses. The church, particularly noted for its richly carved Greenway Chapel, stands in front of a 12th-century castle which preserves its towers and gateway although they are now part of a private house. Also of interest is the local folk museum, which is housed in a 19th-century school building and displays a particularly good selection of farm implements.

TORQUAY, Devon   *13 SX96*
Mild weather is a feature of this well-known resort, yachting harbour and spa. Its situation on Tor Bay offers an excellent beach of sand, pebbles and shingle, and the climate allows subtropical plants to grow in the public gardens. Torre Abbey includes a notable Spanish barn, a 14th-century gateway, and two crypts. An art gallery is housed in the 18th-century mansion. Important prehistoric finds have been made in nearby Kent's Cavern.

TOTNES, Devon   *13 SX86*
Situated on the River Dart, this delightful town is one of England's oldest boroughs and is noted for the shell keep of its ruined Norman castle. Other features include many Elizabethan and Georgian houses, and a picturesque butterwalk. A restored Elizabethan house in Fore Street is now a museum. The fine Perpendicular church carries a 120ft tower, and the beautiful stone screen dates from 1450. A fine 18th-century house contains the grammar school, founded in 1554, and the town museum is in the Guildhall. Ancient walls once surrounded the town, and their line can still be traced. The historic Brutus Stone is set in a pavement near the East Gate.

TROWBRIDGE, Wilts   *14 ST85*
The Suffolk-born poet George Crabbe was rector here and was buried in the chancel of the Perpendicular church in 1832. There are good 18th-century houses in the town, and the former clothiers' group in the Parade is of particular note. A large collection of early documents, including the 14th-century Savernake Collection, is housed in the County Hall. Broadcloth has been manufactured here since the 14th century. Trowbridge was the birthplace of shorthand inventor Isaac Pitman – a fact recorded by a tablet in the town hall.

TRURO, Cornwall   *12 SW84*
Cathedral city of Cornwall and the county's unofficial capital, Truro was a stannary town and an important centre for the export of mineral ores, and in the 18th century became a focus of social life to rival even Bath, then the country's most fashionable town. Among the fine Georgian work here is the outstanding Lemon Street, which was laid out around 1795. It is complemented by Walsingham Place, a beautiful early 19th-century crescent. The former Assembly Rooms date from about 1770, and were the main gathering place for 18th-century society. Various types of Cornish granite were used in the building of the fine cathedral, which was begun in 1880 and stands on the site of the 16th-century Church of St Mary. Part of the older building is retained in the east end. The County Museum, in River Street, is considered to be the finest in Cornwall and has a famous collection depicting the history of the local mineral industries.

WADEBRIDGE, Cornwall   *12 SW97*
One of the finest medieval bridges in England can be seen here. Built about 1485 and widened in 1849, it spans the River Camel with 17 arches and is 320ft long. It is thought that packs of wool may have been sunk into the river bed to make firm bases for the piers. Also of interest is the Cornish Motor Museum, which has vintage cars and traction engines amongst its many displays.

WAREHAM, Dorset   *14 SY98*
This quiet port has an ancient quay which now serves anglers and pleasure craft. In Saxon times the settlement was defended by earthworks, and their grass-covered remains still almost encircle the town. Much of Wareham was rebuilt after a great fire in 1762, which explains why so many attractive Georgian houses can be seen here. The parish church preserves original Saxon work and contains an effigy of Lawrence of Arabia. To the north of the town are the sandy heathlands and coniferous plantations of 3,500-acre Wareham Forest, which covers much of the isolated area described by Thomas Hardy as Egdon Heath.

WARMINSTER, Wilts   *14 ST84*
Warminster was once an important market for wheat. The church has been greatly rebuilt, but retains a 14th-century nave. The beautiful old grammar school was founded in 1707, and numbers both Dr Arnold of Rugby and Dean Stanley among former pupils.

The great Mendip cave system of Wookey Hole (left) was inhabited some 2,000 years ago. Archaeological finds from this period are displayed in a museum on the site, and an old mill near the cave entrance is a store-room for Madame Tussaud's waxworks, with shelves full of astonishingly lifelike waxwork heads (right)

WELLINGTON, Somerset   *13 ST12*
The Duke of Wellington took his title from this town and a tall stone column was erected on a nearby spur of the Blackdown Hills in 1817 to commemorate the great duke. A midside stair turret reminiscent of those seen in Devon is a feature of the local Perpendicular church. Inside is the fine tomb of Sir John Popham, a former Lord Chief Justice who died in 1607.

WELLS, Somerset   *14 ST54*
Wells is a delightful cathedral city situated at the foot of the Mendip Hills. The west front of its fine 13th- to 15th-century cathedral is adorned with statues, and inside are a graceful branching staircase, leading to the chapter house, and a 14th-century clock. With its associated buildings the cathedral forms part of England's largest medieval ecclesiastical precinct. Vicar's Close preserves picturesque 14th-century houses, and across the cathedral green is the moated Bishop's Palace, where Wells' famous swans ring a bell near the drawbridge for food. Other interesting old buildings include a medieval tithe barn and the 15th-century parish church. Wells Museum includes a display on the Mendip Caves.

WESTBURY, Wilts   *14 ST85*
Features of the Perpendicular church here include the fine tomb of the First Earl of Marlborough and a chained New Testament. The oldest of the well-known Wiltshire White Horses was cut into the downland turf 1½ miles away in 1778.

WESTON-SUPER-MARE, Avon   *14 ST36*
Good beaches and lavish entertainment facilities are features of this large Bristol Channel resort. Among many places of interest are a small zoo, a marine lake with boating, an aquarium and a model village.

WEYMOUTH, Dorset   *14 SY67*
Weymouth's early claim to fame was as the only safe port for miles around, but the town became fashionable for seaside holidays after King George III began coming here in 1789. Georgian terraces still line the wide Esplanade, and quaint little back streets wind round the old harbour. Local waters are busy with the comings and goings of cross-Channel ferries, cargo boats and pleasure craft. Among Weymouth's places of interest are the Museum of Local History and No. 3 Trinity Street.

WOOKEY HOLE, Somerset   *14 ST54*
Inhabited for some 650 years from 250BC, this gigantic cave system was hollowed out of the Mendip limestone by the River Axe. Finds relating to the period when it was inhabited can be seen in the associated museum. The old mill at the cave entrance demonstrates the art of paper-making, and is a store for Madame Tussaud's waxwork museum.

WOOLACOMBE, Devon   *13 SS44*
Firm sands stretching for about three miles are a feature of this resort, and Barricane Beach is noted for its shells. Bathing and surfing can be enjoyed here. The prominent nearby headlands of Baggy Point and Morte Point are both owned by the National Trust.

WOTTON-UNDER-EDGE, Glos   *14 ST79*
The restored 14th- to 15th-century church here retains a fine old organ case and several good brasses. In the Rev. Rowland Hill's Tabernacle can be seen the Wotton Mosaic, a faithful copy of a Romano-British pavement found in a Roman villa at nearby Woodchester. The mosaic covers 2,000 sq. ft and depicts. Orpheus charming the beasts with the music of his lyre.

YEOVIL, Somerset   *14 ST51*
The 15th-century church preserves its 13th-century crypt and a notable brass lectern. Hendford Manor Hall houses the museum, which includes collections of costumes and firearms.

ZENNOR, Cornwall   *12 SW43*
At one time this village was a prosperous tin-mining community. The famous authoress Virginia Woolf lived in a local house called the Eagle's Nest, and writer D. H. Lawrence lived nearby in a cottage near the cliff top. A folk museum in the village illustrates Cornish life and archaeology. One of the benches in the 15th-century church carries an unusual mermaid carving.

The present Westbury White Horse dates from 1778, but a white horse is believed to have been here since 878

Southern England

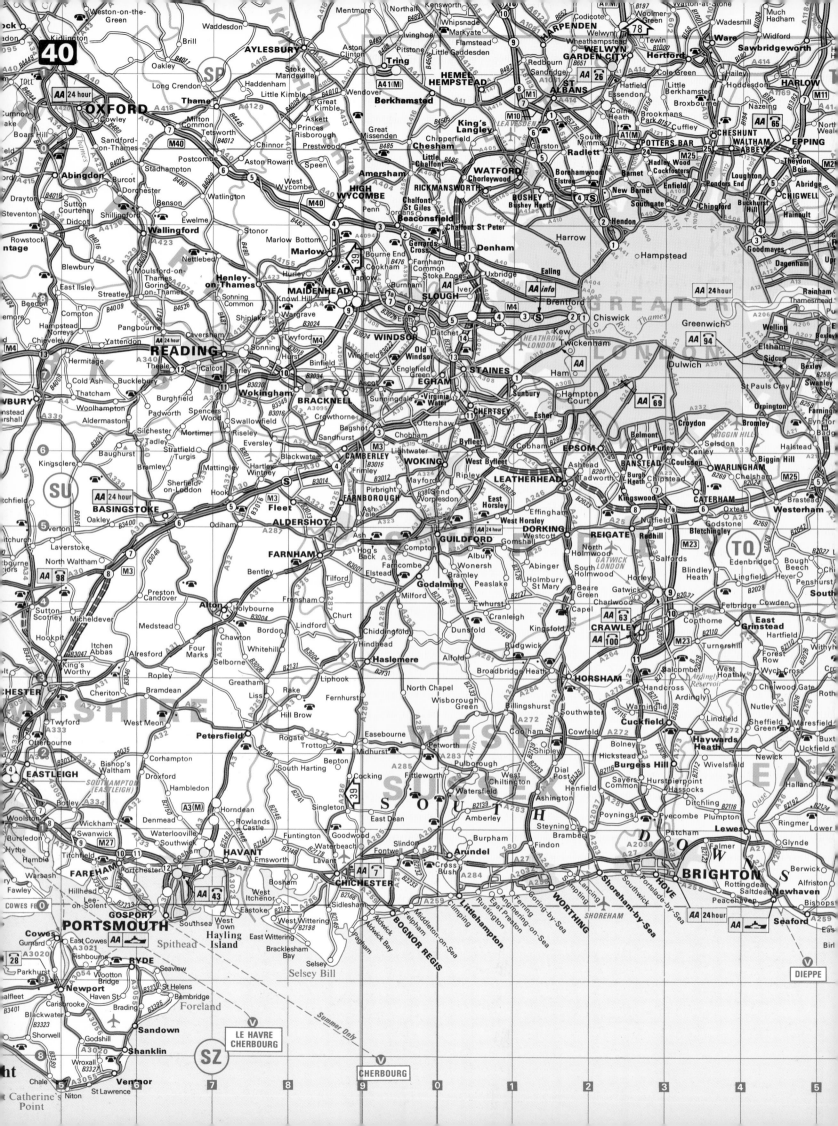

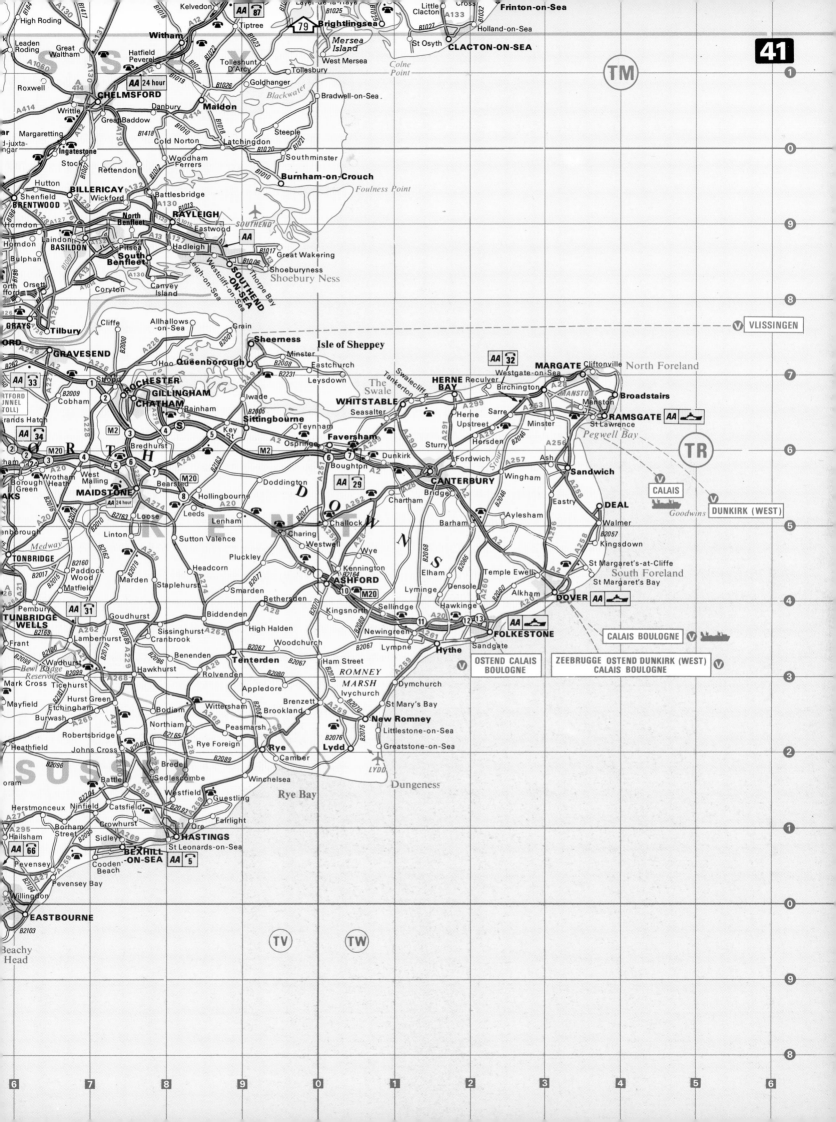

Around the Ridgeway
73 miles

The cathedral-like tithe barn at Great Coxwell is more than 150ft long

SWINDON
Now a sprawling new town, Swindon began to expand from a small market town when the Great Western Railway from London to Bristol was built in the mid 19th century. The company's engineering works were here, and Swindon's railway associations continue in the Great Western Railway Museum, in Faringdon Road, where a collection of locomotives is on view. Another interesting museum, concerning local wildlife, is at nearby Coate Farm, the birthplace of naturalist and writer Richard Jefferies.

LECHLADE
The elegant spire of a 15th-century church – one of the great Gloucestershire 'wool' churches – overlooks this pleasant little town on the upper Thames. The river is spanned here by Halfpenny Bridge, so called because of the toll once charged to cross it. A little 19th-century toll-house stands nearby.

BUSCOT
This charming village and the woodland around it are protected by the National Trust, as is Buscot Park. Built in 1780, this fine mansion is known for its collection of paintings, including works by Rembrandt, Gainsborough, Reynolds and the pre-Raphaelite artist Sir Edward Burne-Jones.

RADCOT
The earliest of the bridges that span the Thames's three channels here may well be the oldest on the river. In 1387 its central arch was broken during a battle between supporters of Richard II and his rebellious barons.

FARINGDON
Built in the 17th century, Faringdon's eye-catching little town hall, set on Tuscan columns, now houses the local library. The imposing cruciform church lost its steeple in the Civil War when it was hit by a cannon-ball.

GREAT COXWELL
The showpiece of this beautiful little village is its stone tithe barn, built around 1250 by Cistercian monks.

UFFINGTON WHITE HORSE
Probably cut in the late Iron Age, this 374ft-long white horse is among the oldest chalk-cut figures in England.

UFFINGTON CASTLE, THE RIDGEWAY AND WAYLAND'S SMITHY
The Iron Age hill-fort of Uffington Castle stands on the Ridgeway, a pre-Roman track along the crest of the downs. The chambered long barrow of Wayland's Smithy stands just off the track. It was constructed between 3700 and 3400 BC.

LAMBOURN
Racehorses are trained near this lovely village on the River Lambourn. The cruciform church, which dates from Norman times, houses several old brasses and the village stocks.

MARLBOROUGH
This little town on the River Kennet is well known for its public school, founded in 1843. Marlborough has a very broad and attractive High Street, where a market is held twice a week. Most of the buildings that line the street date from the mid 17th century or later, since the town lost many of its earlier buildings through Civil War damage and several serious fires. One of these, in 1653, took its toll on St Mary's Church. The Norman west doorway survived, but much of the rest of the church had to be rebuilt.

SILBURY HILL AND THE WEST KENNET LONG BARROW
Situated close to the A4 near Avebury, these superb prehistoric monuments are among the best known in Europe. Silbury Hill, an enormous artificial mound that covers almost six acres, is still as enigmatic as when 18th-century Cornish miners employed to explore it emerged baffled and empty-handed. A footpath from the A4 leads ¾ mile to the West Kennet Long Barrow.

AVEBURY
This enchanting little village lies within one of Europe's foremost prehistoric monuments – a huge stone circle with a bank and ditch enclosing about 28 acres of land. Two smaller rings stand inside the main one. Some of the stones have now gone, though concrete plinths show their positions.
A museum in the village traces the history of the stones and houses finds from excavations on the site. Nearby is Avebury Manor, a fine Tudor house whose attractive gardens contain a magnificent old dovecot.

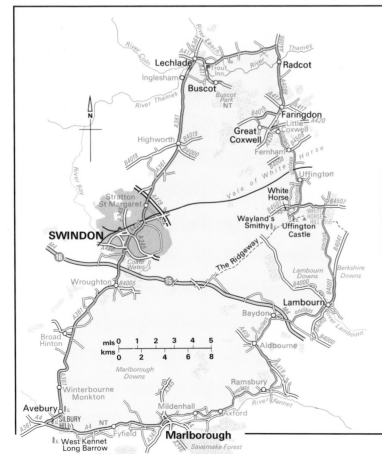

Part of Avebury stone circle

TOUR 9 ROUTE DIRECTIONS

From Swindon first follow signs for Oxford, then take the A361 (SP Stow) through Highworth and past Inglesham to Lechlade. Turn right and right again on the A417 Faringdon road, then in ¾ mile, by the Trout Inn, turn left on to an unclassified road (SP Bampton). (Here a detour can be made along the A417 to Buscot.)
Follow the B4449 to a T-junction and turn right on to the A4095 (SP Faringdon). Cross Radcot Bridge and drive to Faringdon, then follow signs for Swindon (A420) and in ½ mile turn right into Highworth Road (B4019). In 1¼ miles turn left on to an unclassified road for Great Coxwell. Turn left (no SP) and in ½ mile turn right at a roundabout, then at a T-junction turn left on to the A420. In ¼ mile turn right on to an unclassified road for Little Coxwell, then at the far end of the village turn right and drive to Fernham. Turn left on to the B4508, then in ¼ mile branch right for Uffington. On the near side of the village turn right, then take the second turning right (SP White Horse Hill). In 1 mile cross the main road and climb White Horse Hill to Uffington Castle. Following the exit signs, descend to the B4507 and turn right. In 2 miles, at a crossroads, turn right on to an unclassified road (SP Lambourn). Turn right on reaching the B4001 for Lambourn.
Turn right at the crossroads in Lambourn on to the B4000, then turn left (SP Baydon). In 2¼ miles, at a T-junction, turn right for Baydon. Turn left in Baydon and drive to Aldbourne, then turn left on to the A419 (SP Hungerford). In 1¾ miles turn right for Ramsbury. Turn right in Ramsbury and keep forward through Axford and Mildenhall to Marlborough.
Leave Marlborough on the A4 (SP Chippenham) and continue through Fyfield and past Silbury Hill to the Beckhampton roundabout. Take the third exit, the A361 (SP Swindon) and in 1 mile keep left for Avebury. Continue from Avebury on the A361 Swindon road through Winterbourne Monkton and Wroughton, turning left at the end of Wroughton village to return to Swindon.

The New Forest and the Solent
74 miles

LYMINGTON
This pleasant little town is a popular yachting harbour and the ferry terminal for Yarmouth on the Isle of Wight. A weekly market is held in the broad High Street, overlooked by the cupola of the church, and from here a quaint, cobbled street lined with attractive cottages leads down to the marina, at the mouth of the Lymington River.

BUCKLER'S HARD
Great oaks from the New Forest once supplied a thriving shipbuilding industry at this little port on the Beaulieu River. Several ships that fought at Trafalgar were built here, including Nelson's *Agamemnon*. The history of the industry is traced in a fascinating maritime museum.

BEAULIEU
Well known as the home of Lord Montagu and of his National Motor Museum, Beaulieu Abbey is a beautiful ruin. The Palace House was originally the abbey gateway, whilst the former refectory now serves as the parish church of Beaulieu village. The Domus Building contains an exhibition of monastic life at Beaulieu.

EXBURY
Exbury Gardens are famous for their magnificent rhododendron and azalea displays in late spring. The village itself stands near the Solent shore, in a designated area of outstanding natural beauty.

CALSHOT
The great chimney of a modern power station towers above the low, round tower of Calshot Castle, a coastal fort built by Henry VIII. It occupies a commanding position on a promontory at the end of a long shingle beach. Calshot foreshore is part of a country park.

HYTHE
Excellent views of Southampton docks and the shore can be enjoyed from the Hythe ferry. Ship-spotting enthusiasts will find the village pier a handy vantage point.

ELING
Situated on a creek off the head of Southampton Water, this ancient port is protected from through traffic by a toll-bridge reputed to be the smallest of its kind in Britain.

New Forest ponies are frequent visitors to the commonland at Buckler's Hard

LYNDHURST
The ancient capital of the New Forest, this pleasant and popular little town preserves its role as seat of the Verderers' Court. This was set up in Norman times to protect the forest, and still meets every two months at the 17th-century building known as Queen's House. The court room still contains the roughly hewn old dock, where those who broke the forest laws were sentenced, and a stirrup that, according to legend, belonged to William Rufus.

KNIGHTWOOD OAK AND ORNAMENTAL DRIVE
With a girth of over 21ft, this great tree is thought to be more than 600 years old. It stands beside Ornamental Drive, a 5-mile stretch of road that is bordered by some of the finest trees in the forest. Both native and imported species are represented. Several specially planned nature trails may be followed from points along the drive.

BROCKENHURST
Set between woodland and heath, Brockenhurst is an ideal touring base for the New Forest. The cricket pitch by the Balmer Lawn Hotel is a popular venue on Sunday afternoons in Summer. The church dates from Norman times, though the brick tower was added in 1761.

BURLEY
Nearby Castle Hill rises to 300ft and gives good views over this pretty village. An intriguing collection of souvenirs, trophies and weapons can be seen in the Queen's Head Inn.

BARTON ON SEA
This modern resort's low clay cliffs form part of the Barton Beds, a geological series noted for its fossil shell, bone, and shark remains. Good views from the grassy clifftop extend to the chalk stacks of the Needles, and the Isle of Wight.

MILFORD ON SEA
A popular resort since Victorian times, Milford on Sea offers good bathing from its sand and shingle beach and excellent views across the Solent to the Isle of Wight. On a promontory about 2½ miles south-east is Hurst Castle, built by Henry VIII in 1544 and later occupied by Cromwell's forces. Charles I was held prisoner here in 1648. The castle can be reached either on foot or by boat from Keyhaven.

Leave Lymington by the B3054 Beaulieu road. Cross Beaulieu Heath and turn right by Hatchet Pond. After 1 mile turn right again to visit Buckler's Hard then return to the B3054 and continue to Beaulieu. Drive along the Hythe road for 1 mile, then turn right and immediately right again (SP Lepe). Drive to Exbury, turning left into the village, then in 2 miles bear left, continue through Lepe and turn inland. In ¾ mile turn right on to the Calshot road. In 2½ miles, at a T-junction, turn right on to the B3053 to enter Calshot. Return along the B3053 to the roundabout beyond the edge of Fawley, and here take the unclassified Hythe road. In 1 mile turn right into Frost Lane and continue to Hythe.
  Follow signs for Totton from Hythe Pier and in ½ mile turn right at a T-junction. Continue for 2 miles, then on the near side of the next roundabout turn sharp right (SP Marchwood). Two miles beyond Marchwood, turn right at a crossroads for Eling. Cross the toll bridge in Eling, then join the A35 and drive to Lyndhurst.
  Follow the Bournemouth road to the Swan Inn and turn right on to an unclassified road (SP Emery Down). In ½ mile, by the New Forest Inn, turn left (SP Ringwood). In 3 miles pass the Island viewpoint and a common on the left, then turn sharp left along the Bolderwood Ornamental Drive. Pass the Knightwood Oak after 2 miles, then continue and cross a main road to drive along Rhinefield Ornamental Drive to Brockenhurst, turning left across a ford to reach the village centre.
  Recross the ford and follow signs to Burley. Leave Burley by the Bransgore road, and by the Crown Inn in Bransgore turn left (SP Lymington). In 2 miles turn left and right across a main road near the Cat and Fiddle Inn. Beyond Walkford, turn left on to the A337, then in ¾ mile turn right for Barton on Sea. In ½ mile turn left then at a T-junction turn right to enter Barton. Drive to the end of the Promenade and turn left, then follow signs for Milford on Sea. Turn right on to the B3058 and continue through Milford, then turn right on to the A337 to re-enter Lymington.

Lymington Harbour is a popular mooring-place for pleasure craft

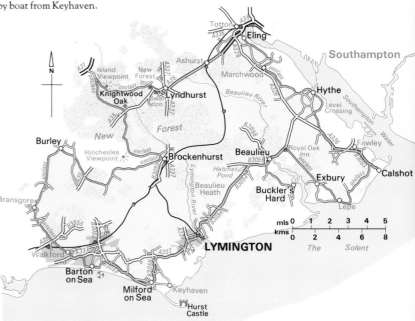

43

Surrey Heaths and Woodlands

55 miles

Clandon Park is a fine example of the Palladian style of architecture

The Guildhall clock is one of Guildford's most famous landmarks

TOUR 11 ROUTE DIRECTIONS

Join the A3 Guildford by-pass from the town centre, and follow signs for Petersfield. Drive under a road bridge and in 1 mile pass the turning for Compton and Loseley House (where a detour can be made). The main route continues for ½ mile on the A3, then turns right on to the B3000 (SP Farnham). Drive to Puttenham and turn left on to an unclassified road that leads along the southern slopes of the Hog's Back to Seale. Turn left beyond Seale church and in ½ mile, at a crossroads, turn left for The Sands. Cross a main road (SP Tilford), then at a crossroads turn left (SP Elstead). Soon turn left on to the B3001 and take the next right turn for Tilford.

Cross the River Wey twice (SP Frensham) and in ¼ mile turn left. After 1½ miles turn left on to the A287 (SP Hindhead). Go through Frensham and past the Great Pond, then in ¾ mile turn left (SP Thursley). In 1½ miles, cross a main road by the Pride of the Valley Hotel and after 1¾ miles turn right for Thursley. Continue for ½ mile and turn right on to the A3.

Pass the Devil's Punch Bowl and Gibbet Hill, then in Hindhead take the A287 for Haslemere, descend to Shottermill and keep forward on the B2131 for Haslemere. Leave Haslemere on the B2131 (SP Petworth) and in 2½ miles bear left (SP Chiddingfold). In ¾ mile, turn left at a T-junction on to the A283 for Chiddingfold. Turn right by the Crown Inn (SP Dunsfold), bear right on the far side of the green then in 1 mile turn left and go through Dunsfold. After 1 mile turn right on to the B2130 (SP Cranleigh). In 1 mile bear left, and ¼ mile later turn right. Drive over a staggered crossroads and in 1¼ miles turn right on to the B2128 for Cranleigh. Turn left at the end of the village on to the B2127 and in 2¼ miles turn left again into Ewhurst. Keep forward on to the Shere road. In ¾ mile bear left and drive to Shere. At a T-junction turn left (SP Guildford), and at the next T-junction turn left again on to the A25. Pass the Silent Pool, and at the crossroads 1 mile beyond Newlands Corner turn left on to the A246. (By keeping forward here a detour can be made to Clandon Park.) Continue along the A246 to Guildford.

GUILDFORD

This university and cathedral city lies at the eastern end of the great chalk ridge known as the Hog's Back. The red-brick cathedral, completed only in the 1960s, stands on Stag Hill, north-east of the city centre.

Plenty of old buildings remain, including the early 12th-century keep of the castle. The moat is now a colourful flower garden. Over the attractive cobbled High Street hangs the ornate clock of the 17th-century Guildhall. Nearby is the Guildford House Gallery, also a 17th-century building. Parallel with the High Street is North Street, where an open-air market is held on Fridays and Saturdays.

COMPTON

The Victorian painter and sculptor G. F. Watts is buried here, and a gallery in the village is devoted to his works. He is also commemorated by a mortuary chapel.

Nearby is Loseley House, a lovely Elizabethan mansion built by a relative of Sir Thomas More and still lived in by the family's descendants. The sumptuous interior has fine carvings, panelling and plasterwork, and an extraordinary chimneypiece made from a single block of chalk.

THE HOG'S BACK

At its highest point this great whaleback ridge of chalk, an outlier of the North Downs, rises to 505ft above sea level. It stretches from Guildford to Farnham, with parking and picnic areas along its length.

TILFORD

Features of this pleasant village include two partly medieval bridges over the River Wey, the graceful lines of 18th-century Tilford House, and a huge tree known as King John's Oak, said to be many centuries old. The village is noted for its Bach music festivals.

FRENSHAM

Much of Frensham Common, an area protected by the National Trust, is now a country park. Its two ponds are the largest in Surrey, and many species of British bird can be seen here. The Great Pond is popular for rowing and sailing. Beneath the tower of Frensham Church is a great copper cauldron said to have belonged to a local witch.

THURSLEY

Old houses and charming cottages straggle along a winding lane to the village church, which has a sundial on its shingled spire.

DEVIL'S PUNCH BOWL AND GIBBET HILL

The great wooded combe of the Devil's Punch Bowl was the scene of the gruesome murder of an unknown sailor in 1786. His murderers were hanged nearby on Gibbet Hill, now better known as a viewpoint and picnic site.

HASLEMERE

This attractive little town was once a centre of the Wealden iron-working industry, and is known for its literary associations. George Eliot and Sir Arthur Conan Doyle both lived here, and nearby Aldworth House (not open), on the slopes of Black Down, was the home of Alfred, Lord Tennyson, from 1869 to 1892. He is commemorated in the parish church by a stained-glass window designed by the eminent Victorian artist Burne-Jones.

CHIDDINGFOLD

In medieval times this lovely Wealden village was famous for its fine-quality glass. At the heart of the village is a pretty green with a thorn tree said to be 500 years old, a pond complete with ducks and water lilies, and the delightful 14th-century Crown Inn.

DUNSFOLD

A modern lychgate and a tunnel of clipped yews lead to Dunsfold church, which dates from the 13th century and has an attractive Tudor porch. Its pews may well be the oldest still used in England.

CRANLEIGH

Near the 14th-century church in this large village is a 16th-century building that houses one of the first cottage hospitals ever founded. The well-known public school at Cranleigh was founded for farmers' sons in 1865. The maples that line the main street were planted by Canadian soldiers in the First World War.

SHERE

This charming village is full of timber-framed buildings, some constructed from old ships' timbers. The 12th-century church retains traces of an anchoress's cell on the outside wall of the chancel. A tiny 13th-century bronze statue of the Madonna and Child is on display in the church.

SILENT POOL

The legend attached to this popular beauty spot is that a local girl drowned herself here after King John had seen her bathing naked. Fed by an icy-cold spring, the pool is crystal-clear and very deep.

NEWLANDS CORNER

Magnificent views across the Weald to the South Downs can be enjoyed from this well-known spot on the crest of the North Downs.

CLANDON PARK

Built in the early 1730s, this classical mansion features noteworthy plaster decoration, and stands in gardens refashioned by Capability Brown. A famous collection of china, furniture and needlework is displayed in these elegant surroundings.

The North Downs
71 miles

EPSOM
This well-heeled town on London's outskirts was known for its race meetings long before the most famous one – the Derby – was first held here, in 1780. Epsom's other claim to fame was its medicinal springs, which gave their name to Epsom Salts and made the town a popular spa.

CHESSINGTON ZOO
In 1931 Reginald Stuart Goddard founded this famous zoo in the grounds of Burnt Stub Manor. Now its 65 acres of lovely grounds are home to a large and varied collection of animals and birds.

STOKE D'ABERNON
Preserved in the local church are several fine brasses, including one of 1277 to Sir John d'Abernon. It is thought to be the earliest of its kind in the country.

COBHAM
The two settlements of Church Cobham and Street Cobham have merged, in the present century, to form this popular commuter town. St Andrew's Church retains some Norman work and two interesting brasses. An inscription on the bridge here tells of an earlier structure raised by Queen Matilda, wife of Henry I, because one of her ladies drowned while crossing the pool.

OCKHAM
Hidden among the trees of Ockham Park is the village church, which is well known for its lovely 13th-century east window of seven lancets, sometimes known as the Seven Sisters.

EAST CLANDON
This village was once the farming estate of Hatchlands, an 18th-century mansion built for his retirement by Admiral Boscawen, who died before he was able to enjoy it. Now owned by the National Trust, the house has a plaster drawing-room ceiling and library by Robert Adam.

EAST HORSLEY
A striking landmark on the main road here is the red-and-black brick neo-Romanesque lodge of Horsley Towers, a flamboyant 19th-century mansion – once the home of Lord Byron's son-in-law – that now houses Electricity Board offices.

FRIDAY STREET
Old cottages and a single street leading to a lake fringed with pine and oak are the main features of this village. The Stephen Langton Inn recalls a prelate of that name who played a leading role in the signing of Magna Carta.

The folly on Leith Hill dates from 1766 and is a replica of a 13th-century Wealden tower. The battlements and stair-turret were added in 1864

LEITH HILL
Much of the wooded countryside south of Friday Street is protected by the National Trust, including Leith Hill, Duke's Warren and the estate of Leith Hill Place. The hill itself carries a picturesque tower whose top is 1,029ft above sea level – the highest point in Surrey.

OCKLEY
The village green here is sited on the course of the Roman Stane Street. The church is in a delightful setting, and the King's Arms Inn has an unusual sign showing Nell Gwynne in the embrace of King Charles II.

NEWDIGATE
The church in this typical Wealden village has a 14th-century timber tower supported by four huge oak pillars. It is the most impressive of many timber-framed structures in the area – a reminder of the dense forest that once cloaked the countryside around here.

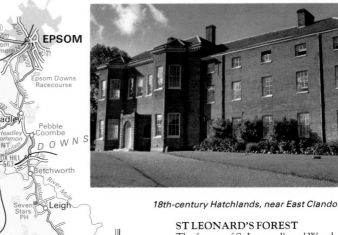

18th-century Hatchlands, near East Clandon

ST LEONARD'S FOREST
The forests of St Leonard's and Worth, along with various scattered woodlands, are among the only sizeable remnants left of the vast prehistoric forest of Anderida.

CHARLWOOD
An 11th-century tower is a feature of the church here, which also has some late 13th-century wall-paintings and a screen that displays some of the finest medieval woodcarving in the county.

LEIGH
Charming old houses in this village (whose name is pronounced 'lie') are complemented by a green and a 15th-century church famous for its memorial brasses. Particularly good examples of these are the ones to members of the Arderne family.

BOX HILL
Named after the box trees that grow on its flanks, 563ft Box Hill is a noted viewpoint and designated area of outstanding beauty, including both woodland and downland scenery.

HEADLEY
Yews mark the spot where Headley's 14th-century church was pulled down in the last century, and the spire of its 19th-century successor is a distinctive landmark. The church bell is at least 500 years old.

TOUR 12 ROUTE DIRECTIONS

From the roundabout at the southern end of Epsom High Street take the B280 across Epsom Common. (In 1½ miles, at the traffic lights, a detour can be made to Chessington Zoo by turning right.) The main route keeps forward at the traffic lights. In 2 miles turn left on to the A244 for Oxshott, then turn right on to an unclassified road for Stoke d'Abernon. Turn right here on to the A245 for Cobham, and turn left in Cobham on to an unclassified road (SP Downside, Ockham). Cross the river, then turn right and follow signs to Ockham. Turn right by the war memorial on to the B2039, take the next turning left, then go forward at the crossroads and drive for 3 miles to East Clandon. Turn left here on to the A246, and ½ mile beyond East Horsley turn right (SP Shere). In ½ mile bear left (SP Dorking), and in 1½ miles turn right (SP Abinger). Turn left on to the A25 and in ½ mile turn right and climb for 1¼ miles. (Here a detour can be made by turning sharp left for Friday Street.)
  The main route continues past Leith Hill. In 2½ miles join the B2126, then keep left for Ockley. Turn left on to

the A29, and beyond the King's Arms Inn turn right on to the B2126. In 1½ miles turn left on to the A24 and by the Crown Inn in Capel turn right (SP Newdigate). From Newdigate drive to Rusper, bear left (SP Crawley) and in ½ mile turn right for Faygate, then turn left (SP Crawley). Turn left on to the A264, pass St Leonard's Forest and in 2¾ miles turn left on to the A23 and follow London signs through Crawley's suburbs and past Gatwick Airport. At the roundabout 1 mile beyond the airport take the first exit and go through Charlwood and Leigh. At the Seven Stars pub, ¼ mile beyond Leigh, turn right for Betchworth, then turn left at a T-junction and right (SP Walton-on-the-Hill). At a roundabout take the second exit, the B2032. At the top of the hill turn left on to the B2033 (SP Box Hill) and bear left for Box Hill. After descending the hill, turn right at a T-junction (SP Mickleham) and in ¼ mile right (SP Headley). At a T-junction turn right on to the B2033, then turn left (SP Epsom) and drive to Headley. In 1¾ miles turn right at a crossroads, pass Epsom Downs race-course, then turn left on to the B290 and return to Epsom.

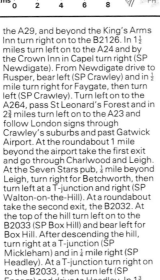

Ockley's pub sign depicts Charles II and his famous mistress Nell Gwynne

South Downs and Sussex Coast

53 miles

WORTHING
This popular south coast town offers holidaymakers all the usual resort facilities including a sand and shingle beach, a pier and excellent sea fishing. To the north is a golf course, on the edge of which is Cissbury Ring, a fine example of an Iron Age hill-fort which incorporates more than 200 neolithic flint mines. Flint tools and other finds from the site are among the exhibits in Worthing Museum and Art Gallery, which also has a large costume collection.

SHOREHAM-BY-SEA
This popular seaside town and busy harbour dates back to the 5th century, when the south Saxons settled in the area now called Old Shoreham. The Church of St Nicholas incorporates Saxon work, and the house known as Marlipins, now occupied by a local history and maritime museum, dates from the 12th century.

BRIGHTON
Until the mid 18th century this most famous of south coast resorts was a fishing village called Brighthelmstone. The young Prince of Wales – later George IV – was among the trendsetters who contributed to its growing popularity in fashionable circles. The lavish Oriental-style Pavilion, Brighton's best-known building, was built for the Prince in 1787.

Brighton's days as a fishing community are recalled by a stroll through the Lanes, a maze of narrow streets lined with quaint fishermen's cottages that are now antique shops, pubs and cafes. Elegant Regency terraces and the Victorian pier are among many features that enable Brighton to retain much of the atmosphere of its fashionable heyday, and its story is brought up to date by the brand-new Marina, the largest of its kind in Europe.

Architect John Nash was chiefly responsible for the Oriental appearance of Brighton Pavilion

Brighton offers numerous attractions for wet or chilly days. Apart from the usual theatres, cinemas and sports facilities there is a large aquarium, a museum and art gallery, and the Booth Museum of Natural History, which is particularly noted for its butterfly gallery.

BRAMBER
This attractive village on the River Adur was a busy port before the river silted up. Its long history is demonstrated by the ruined Norman castle on the ridge of the downs and by St Mary's, a fine 15th-century timber-framed house where Charles II hid on his escape to France. It now houses the National Butterfly Museum. Another fascinating museum here is the House of Pipes, a collection of more than 35,000 smoking accessories set in a 19th-century shopping arcade.

STEYNING
This little town at the foot of the downs is well known for its Norman church, which has an especially fine nave and chancel arch. There are some attractive old buildings in the High Street, some of them dating back to the 15th century. The tile-hung old Market House is topped by an appealing little clock-turret, and nearby in Mouse Lane is the medieval poor-house, a quaint timber-framed cottage.

CHANCTONBURY RING
The prehistoric earthworks of Chactonbury Ring occupy a 783ft downland summit which affords views over some 30 miles of countryside. The hill-fort has been a well-known landmark since 1760, when a group of beech trees was planted within it.

STORRINGTON
Celtic field patterns are preserved on the slopes of Kithurst Hill, and close by is 28-acre Sullington Warren nature reserve. A large tithe barn of 1685 stands at Manor Farm.

PARHAM HOUSE
This delightful Elizabethan house has a 158ft-long gallery and contains fine furnishings and pictures. The grounds include glasshouses and a walled garden.

BIGNOR
One of the largest and most impressive Roman villas in the country was discovered near this small village in 1811. The villa complex consisted of about 70 buildings in a 4¼-acre enclosure. A museum here includes coins and household items.

ARUNDEL
This attractive hill-town is dominated by its great Norman stronghold, largely restored in Victorian times. The fine art collection inside includes works by Reynolds, Gainsborough and Van Dyck. An attraction of a different kind is the Museum of Curiosity, where the extraordinary work of the Victorian naturalist and taxidermist Walter Potter is on display. Stuffed animals are arranged in tableaux, representing such scenes as 'The Kittens' Wedding' and 'The Death of Cock Robin'. To the north of the town, by the River Arun, is the 55-acre reserve of the Wildfowl Trust, where ducks, geese and swans from all over the world can be seen.

TOUR 13 ROUTE DIRECTIONS

Leave Worthing by the A259 (SP Brighton) and drive eastwards through Shoreham-by-Sea to Brighton. Return towards Hove and at the traffic lights beyond the King Alfred Sports Centre turn right (SP London) into Hove Street. In 1¾ miles turn right on to the A2038. Go through West Blatchington, then turn left at a crossroads on to an unclassified road (SP Devil's Dyke). In ½ mile bear right, pass a golf club, then in ¾ mile turn left. After ½ mile turn sharp left into Poynings.

Turn left and follow an unclassified road through Fulking and Edburton, then turn left on to the A2037 for Upper Beeding. Leaving the village, turn right and cross the River Adur into Bramber. Continue to Steyning and leave by the road for Storrington and Petersfield. Skirt Wiston on the A283 and continue past the turning to Chanctonbury Ring. At the roundabout on the edge of Washington, take the second exit and go through Storrington, then in 1 mile pass a left turn to Parham House. Continue for 1 mile on the A283 and turn left (SP Greatham). In 2¼ miles at Coldwaltham, turn left on to the A29 and ½ mile beyond Watersfield turn right on to the B2138 Petworth road. Take the next left turn for West Burton, and pass a right turn leading to Bignor. The main tour turns left (SP Bury). In 1 mile turn right on to the A29 (SP Bognor). Climb Bury Hill and at the roundabout take the A284 (SP Littlehampton). Skirt Arundel Park and in 2¼ miles turn left on to an unclassified road into Arundel. Leave Arundel by the A27 (SP Worthing) and return to Worthing.

Some of the best Roman mosaics in Britain have been found at Bignor's Roman villa

46

Inland from Eastbourne
80 miles

EASTBOURNE
Popular since the early 19th century, this elegant resort's natural assets include high sunshine levels and the dramatic cliffs of Beachy Head nearby. Grand hotels, a bandstand, two 19th-century fortresses and several museums are among Eastbourne's many man-made attractions.

BEACHY HEAD
This chalk promontory, where the South Downs plunge abruptly to the sea, is the starting point of the South Downs Way, a long-distance footpath that runs all the way to the Hampshire border.

BIRLING GAP
Long favoured by smugglers as a landing place, the rocky shingle and sand beach here is now more popular with bathers. To the west are the great chalk cliffs known as the Seven Sisters.

FRISTON
This village lies in a hilly area now popular with glider pilots. At one time its small Church of St Mary served as a landmark for mariners and smugglers.

JEVINGTON
A sturdy Anglo-Saxon tower is a feature of Jevington's flint-built church, and in the churchyard is the copper model of a square-rigged schooner once sailed by a Chinaman buried here.

MICHELHAM PRIORY
Remains of this small Augustinian priory founded in 1229 include a Tudor mansion, a 14th-century gatehouse, and an attractive bridge over the moat.

CROSS-IN-HAND
A working windmill stands in this charming Wealden village. Holy Cross Priory is partly in use as an old people's home, but the house and grounds may still be visited.

ROTHERFIELD
Tile-hung and weatherboarded cottages surround an interesting church in this charming village at the edge of Ashdown Forest.

ERIDGE GREEN
Pretty estate cottages stand behind the Victorian church here. Nearby is the sandstone outcrop of Bowles Rocks where trainee mountaineers practise.

HIGH ROCKS
Huge, weathered sandstone blocks amid the abundant foliage of oaks and rhododendrons make this a popular beauty spot that is also frequented by climbers.

ROYAL TUNBRIDGE WELLS
Mineral springs were discovered here in 1606, and fashionable Londoners soon flocked to Tunbridge Wells to take the waters. They included Queen Henrietta Maria, who came here in 1630 to recuperate after the birth of her son, the future King Charles II. Development later in the 17th century included the building of the Pantiles, still a delightful pedestrian shopping area.

**TOUR 14
ROUTE DIRECTIONS**

Leave Eastbourne by the B2103 and turn left to Beachy Head. Continue to Birling Gap and Eastdean. Turn left on to the A259 and right on to the B2105 to Polegate. Turn left on to the A22 and in 2¾ miles turn left to Michelham Priory. Cross the B2108, turn left on to the A22 and right (SP Horam). Join the A267 to enter Horam and continue to Five Ashes. In ½ mile turn left, go through Rotherfield and continue to the A26. Turn right and 1 mile past Eridge Green turn left (SP Groombridge) and in ½ mile right (SP High Rocks). After ½ mile bear right, pass High Rocks and in 1½ miles turn right. Cross Tunbridge Wells Common and turn left into Tunbridge Wells.
  Take the A267 Eastbourne road to Frant and turn left to Bells Yew Green, then turn right on to the B2169 (SP Lamberhurst). Later pass a left turn to Bayham Abbey, then another left turn to the Owl House. In 1¼ miles turn left into Lamberhurst. (One south, off the A21, is Scotney Castle.)
  From Lamberhurst take the B2100 and in 3 miles turn left on to the B2099 into Wadhurst. In 1¼ miles turn right on to the B2181 (SP Burwash Common). In Stonegate turn left and in ¾ mile turn right to Burwash. Turn right on to the A265 and left (SP Woods Corner) by the war memorial. In ½ mile pass a right turn to Bateman's. By the Swan Inn at Woods Corner turn right and left (SP Pont's Green). Follow the sign for Ninfield, then turn right (SP Hailsham) on to the B2204. Later turn right on to the A271 and ½ mile beyond Boreham Street turn left and pass Herstmonceux Castle. Bear right at Wartling, then turn right on to the A27 and go through Pevensey to Westham. Turn left on to the B2191 and later join the A259 to return to Eastbourne.

Herstmonceux Castle was first built in the 15th century when brick was just becoming fashionable in this country

FRANT
This village surrounds a spacious green, at one corner of which stands the early 19th-century church. The pillars, gallery screen and window tracery are all of ironwork – a reminder of the days when the Sussex Weald was famed for its iron-working industry.

BAYHAM ABBEY
Claimed to be the most impressive group of monastic remains in Sussex, this picturesque ruin dates from the 13th century and comprises a church, monastery buildings and the former gatehouse.

THE OWL HOUSE
Once the haunt of wool-smugglers, this small half-timbered building dates from the 16th century and stands in beautiful grounds featuring woodland lakes and flowering shrubs.

LAMBERHURST
The railings and ornamental gates for St Paul's Cathedral were wrought in the 18th century at this former centre for the Sussex iron industry. Lamberhurst retains many old features including a 14th-century church.

SCOTNEY CASTLE
Ruins of this 14th-century tower and an attached 17th-century house stand in a landscaped and moated garden planted with trees and flowering shrubs.

WADHURST
The Norman tower and tall shingled spire of Wadhurst church are a distinctive landmark for miles around. The churchyard is rich in decorated sandstone tombs, whilst inside the church are many handsome cast-iron grave slabs dating from the 17th and 18th centuries.

BATEMAN'S
Standing near the pretty village of Burwash, this fine house was built in 1634 for a local iron-master and is now best known as the home of Rudyard Kipling, who lived here from 1902 until his death in 1936.

HERSTMONCEUX CASTLE
Home of the Royal Greenwich Observatory since 1948, this fortified 15th-century manor house fell into ruin in the 18th century but was faithfully restored in the 1930s. The Astronomical and Historical Exhibition and the castle's moated grounds can be visited at certain times.

WARTLING
The church in this pretty hillside village has box pews, an 18th-century pulpit and some interesting Georgian monuments.

PEVENSEY
Pevensey's 3rd-century Roman fort was incorporated into a castle built by the Normans after they landed here in 1066. Once one of the principal ports of Sussex, Pevensey declined when its harbour began to silt up. Sizeable boats could reach it until the 16th century, but subsequent reclamation of the coastal marshes has left the village more than a mile from the sea.

Historic Homes of Kent

51 miles

Westerham's statue of General Wolfe was erected in 1910

SEVENOAKS
This popular residential town, now much favoured by London's commuters, dates back at least to the 12th century. The original seven oaks from which it took its name have gone, but seven more were planted on the common in a ceremony in 1955.

SUNDRIDGE
Sundridge's pride is the 15th-century timbered hall-house in its main street. The great hall is several storeys high, and its original stone hearth can still be seen. Sundridge church contains a number of good brasses.

BRASTED
The village street here opens on to a small green fringed by half-timbered houses. Brasted Place, in a fine park adjoining the village, was built by Robert Adam in 1784 and subsequently became the home of Napoleon III. About 1½ miles south of the village is 600-acre Brasted Chart, which offers pleasant walks and drives.

QUEBEC HOUSE
On the eastern outskirts of Westerham is early 17th-century Quebec House, famous as the boyhood home of General Wolfe. Relics of this hero of the Battle of Quebec are preserved inside the house.

WESTERHAM
This pleasant town at the edge of the North Downs is noted for its connections with two great men, both commemorated by statues on the green. At the top is General Wolfe of Quebec, while lower down is a statue of Sir Winston Churchill, who spent the last 40 years of his life at nearby Chartwell. On the corner of the green is Westerham church, which has a rare 14th-century timber spiral staircase leading up the tower.

CHARTWELL
Chartwell will always be associated with Sir Winston Churchill. It was his country home from 1922 until his death, and many of the rooms are arranged much as they were in his lifetime. Items on display include his Nobel Prize and some of his paintings.

Oast-houses are a familiar feature of the landscape in this part of Kent. They were used for drying local hops

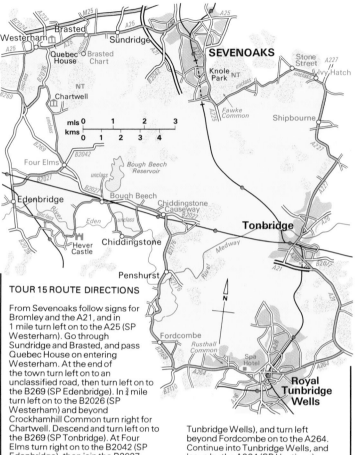

TOUR 15 ROUTE DIRECTIONS

From Sevenoaks follow signs for Bromley and the A21, and in 1 mile turn left on to the A25 (SP Westerham). Go through Sundridge and Brasted, and pass Quebec House on entering Westerham. At the end of the town turn left on to an unclassified road, then turn left on to the B269 (SP Edenbridge). In ¾ mile turn left on to the B2026 (SP Westerham) and beyond Crockhamhill Common turn right for Chartwell. Descend and turn left on to the B269 (SP Tonbridge). At Four Elms turn right on to the B2042 (SP Edenbridge), then join the B2027. After 1½ miles turn left on to the B2026 into Edenbridge, cross the River Eden, take the first turn left and drive to Hever Castle. Continue to Bough Beech, join the B2027 for 200 yards, then turn right for Chiddingstone. Turn left at the crossroads by Chiddingstone Castle, go through the village and in ½ mile branch left. In 1¾ miles turn right on to the B2027 for Chiddingstone Causeway, then turn right on to the B2176 for Penshurst.
  Leave Penshurst by the B2188 (SP Tunbridge Wells), and turn left beyond Fordcombe on to the A264. Continue into Tunbridge Wells, and leave by the A264 (SP Hastings). Later turn left on to the A21 (SP Sevenoaks), then branch left on to the A2014. Turn right into Tonbridge and follow signs for Gravesend, driving along the A227 through Shipbourne. Turn right on to an unclassified road (SP Ivy Hatch). From Ivy Hatch follow the Seal road, then turn left and continue through Stone Street. Bear left (SP Fawke Common), later crossing Fawke Common. Turn right on to the A225, pass the entrance to Knole Park and return to Sevenoaks.

EDENBRIDGE
Several old buildings survive in Edenbridge's main street, particularly between the 16th-century Crown Inn and the bridge over the River Eden. The mainly 13th-century church carries a massive tower crowned by a spire of later date.

HEVER CASTLE
In Tudor times 13th-century Hever Castle was the home of the Boleyns, whose daughter Anne married Henry VIII and bore him the future Queen Elizabeth I. The building began life as a fortified farmhouse, but was made into a crenellated mansion at the beginning of the 15th century. By the beginning of this century it had reverted to use as a farmhouse and a wealthy American, William Waldorf Astor, restored it to its present magnificence. The superb gardens feature Tudor-style flower beds and a 35-acre lake.

CHIDDINGSTONE
Owned by the National Trust, this picture-book village of Tudor timber-framed houses still looks much as it did in the 16th century. Nearby stands Chiddingstone Castle, a 19th-century mock-Gothic extravaganza that houses an interesting collection of Oriental art treasures.

PENSHURST
The showpiece of this pretty village is Penshurst Place, a lovely medieval manor house with later additions. In 1552 the house was given by Edward VI to Sir William Sydney, grandfather of the Elizabethan poet and statesman Sir Philip Sydney, and it remained the seat of the Sydneys for some 200 years. Penshurst church, reached through a cluster of half-timbered cottages called Leicester Square, has a fine modern stained-glass window commemorating the institution of its first parish priest by St Thomas à Becket.

ROYAL TUNBRIDGE WELLS
This well-known Regency spa town still has a chalybeate spring, which rises in the attractive promenade called the Pantiles. Nearby stands the 17th-century Church of King Charles the Martyr, noted for its plasterwork ceiling.

TONBRIDGE
This ancient town and thriving commercial centre on the River Medway is dominated by its ruined castle. The remains of the keep and the curtain walls are Norman, while the great gatehouse dates from the 14th century. There is a nature trail in the castle grounds.

KNOLE PARK
In 1456 Thomas Bourchier, then Archbishop of Canterbury, bought an ordinary manor house called Knole Park. He and his successors developed it into a great palace, but when Archbishop Warham died in 1532, Henry VIII seized the estate for himself. In 1566 Elizabeth I granted it to Sir Thomas Sackville who died while improvement work on the interior of the house was still in progress. Knole Park still looks much as it did then.

Cinque Ports and Romney Marsh

73 miles

ASHFORD
Local cattle and sheep reared on Romney Marsh have ensured Ashford's success as a market town. Livestock auctions are held here regularly, and Ashford's Cattle Show is one of the oldest in the country. The town grew rapidly after becoming an important railway junction in the mid 19th century, but many of Ashford's buildings are older than this, including the 15th-century church, the old grammar school and the market house. Templar Barracks houses the Intelligence Corps Museum, a collection spanning both world wars and continued through to the present day.

GREAT CHART
A 14th-century church with a 16th-century pest house in the south corner of its churchyard can be seen here. This long narrow structure is a timber-framed building once used to isolate victims of plagues. Court Lodge, a complete 13th-century stone house, stands to the west of the church.

BETHERSDEN
Marble from this village was used for the altar stairs at Canterbury Cathedral. The quarries are now worked out. Brass memorials to forbears of the 17th-century poet William Lovelace can be seen in the church.

TENTERDEN
Houses faced with typical Wealden weatherboarding are a feature of Tenterden's picture-book High Street. St Mildred's Church has one of the finest towers in Kent, dating from the 15th century. Set on a rise, it not only dominates the town but is visible for many miles both across the Weald and out to sea. Britain's first light railway, the Kent and East Sussex, was opened here in 1872 and has now been revived.

ROLVENDEN
The large 14th-century church here preserves two squire's pews, and there is a splendid restored postmill. Great Maytham Hall, now converted into flats, was designed by Sir Edwin Lutyens in 1910 and stands in gardens that were laid out by landscaper Gertrude Jekyll. In the High Street is the C. M. Booth Collection of Historic Vehicles, which includes several Morgan three-wheelers dating from 1913.

ROYAL MILITARY CANAL
Originally a defence against an expected Napoleonic invasion, this canal between Rye and Hythe now offers peaceful towpath walks and boat-hire facilities.

RYE
The hill on which this lovely old town stands was once almost surrounded by the sea. The harbour silted up during the 16th century, however, and today marshland stretches from Rye to the sea. As one of the Cinque Ports, Rye suffered many naval attacks and was burnt down by the French in 1377. Surviving features of the medieval town include parts of its wall (including 14th-century Landgate), the Norman

church and 13th-century Ypres Tower, later used as a prison and now a museum. Rye's narrow cobbled streets abound in beautiful old buildings, including the famous Mermaid Inn, a one-time smugglers' haunt. Novelist Henry James lived in 18th-century Lamb House from 1898 until his death in 1916.

LYDD
Like Rye, Lydd was once a coastal town, but it now lies a good 3 miles inland. Its 14th-century church has a 130ft tower and has been described as the 'Cathedral of Romney Marsh'.

DUNGENESS
This desolate shingle promontory is the site of a nuclear power station that can be seen for miles over featureless Denge Marsh. Much of the promontory is taken by a 12,000-acre nature reserve.

ROMNEY, HYTHE AND DYMCHURCH RAILWAY
Dungeness is the western terminus of a 13½-mile narrow-gauge line which is claimed to be the world's smallest public railway. Steam trains run from Hythe through New Romney and along the seaward fringe of Romney Marsh to Dungeness.

NEW ROMNEY
This former Cinque Port, the capital of Romney Marsh, is now about a mile from the sea. Its former importance is illustrated by the fact that it once had five churches. Only one of these, the Norman Church of St Nicholas, survives today.

DYMCHURCH
Now a popular resort on account of its sandy beach, this old port was the historic centre of government for Romney Marsh. New Hall dates from 1590 and preserves its old lock-up. A Martello Tower – one of a chain of defensive towers built in the early 19th century – is open to visitors.

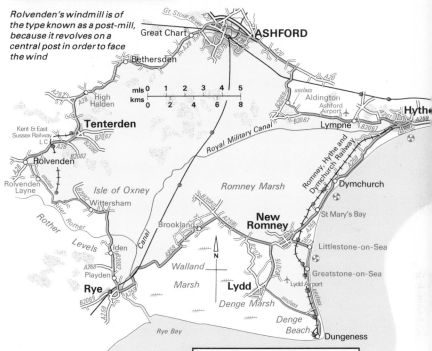

Rolvenden's windmill is of the type known as a post-mill, because it revolves on a central post in order to face the wind

HYTHE
This ancient Cinque Port was very prosperous in the 12th and 13th centuries; its wealth today is assured by its popularity as a resort. To the north is Saltwood Castle, the place from which Thomas à Becket's murderers are said to have set off for Canterbury. The castle dates from Norman times and was restored in the 19th century.

LYMPNE
As *Portus Lemanis*, this was already the site of a Roman fort in the 3rd century. Not far from the Roman remains is Lympne Castle, a 14th-century fortified manor house. Many species of animals including elephants, leopards and rhinos can be seen at Port Lympne Zoo Park and Gardens.

Weatherboarded buildings are a distinctive feature of Wealden towns and villages. These fine examples are at Tenterden

TOUR 16 ROUTE DIRECTIONS
Leave Ashford on the A28 (SP Tenterden). Go through Great Chart, Bethersden and Tenterden to Rolvenden, then turn left (SP Wittersham). Go through Rolvenden Layne and climb on to the Isle of Oxney. Turn right on to the B2082 and go through Wittersham and Iden, then follow the A268 to Rye.

Take the A259 (SP Folkestone) from Rye through Brookland, and in 1½ miles turn right at a crossroads. In 4 miles turn right again on to the B2075 for Lydd. Cross a railway bridge at the edge of Lydd, then branch left on to an unclassified road (SP Dungeness). Shortly turn left again and in 3 miles turn right to reach Dungeness, and the terminus of the Romney, Hythe and Dymchurch Railway. Return along the unclassified road for 1 mile, then turn right and follow signs through Greatstone and Littlestone-on-Sea, then turn left on to the B2071 for New Romney. Turn right on to the A259 (SP Folkestone) and go through St Mary's Bay and Dymchurch to Hythe. Leave by the A261 (SP Ashford) and in 1 mile turn left on to the B2067 for Lympne. Leave on the Tenterden road and in 2½ miles bear right (SP Aldington). Turn right in Aldington on to the B2069. Cross a railway and in ¾ mile turn left on to the A20 for the return to Ashford.

Southern England
Gazetteer

ALDERMASTON, Berks   39 SU56
This attractive brick-built village lies close to the Atomic Weapons Research Establishment. The Aldermaston Pottery is well known and sells its work all over the country. The River Kennet runs through Aldermaston Mill.

ALRESFORD, Hants   39 SU53
During the medieval period New Alresford grew to be one of the 10 greatest wool towns in the country. There is still a fulling-mill on the River Alre. Aptly-named Broad Street, perhaps the finest village street in Hampshire, leads downhill to Old Alresford, whose church is the burial place of Admiral Rodney.

The lovely countryside in the area can be seen by taking a 3-mile steam-hauled trip to Ropley on the Mid Hants Railway or 'Watercress Line', as it is known.

ALTON, Hants   39 SU73
In years gone by this historic market town grew prosperous on brewing and the manufacture of woollen cloth. Fine Georgian buildings grace the main street, and a Tudor cottage that was once the home of the poet Spenser is in Amery Street. Exhibits in the Curtis Museum include a collection of craft tools and other bygones.

AMERSHAM, Bucks   40 SU99
Amersham Old Town is a lovely collection of old houses, quaint cottages and ancient inns in the Misbourne valley. Sir William Drake built the Market Hall in 1682, some 15 years after the almshouses bearing his name.

AMESBURY, Wilts   38 SU14
At Amesbury the Avon is crossed by a five-arched Palladian bridge. Amesbury Abbey dates from the 19th century and stands in a park in which beech clumps have been planted to represent the positions of English and French ships at Trafalgar. The Church of SS Mary and Melor is a flint-built Norman structure containing a contemporary font fashioned from Purbeck marble.

North of the town is Woodhenge, an enigmatic prehistoric monument discovered by aerial photography in 1925. It is thought that a huge, roofed timber building once stood here. The post-holes are now marked by concrete plinths.

ARUNDEL, W Sussex   40 TQ00
Looming large over Arundel to guard a gap made in the downs by the River Arun is ancient and much-restored Arundel Castle, seat of the dukes of Norfolk. Behind its walls are rooms rich in furnishings and art treasures. A prominent town existed here before the Norman conquest, but comparatively few ancient houses remain. The only real rivals to the castle are the 14th-century Church of St Nicholas and the superb Church of Our Lady and St Philip Neri.

ASCOT, Berks   40 SU96
Ascot has strong Queen Anne connections. In 1711 she instituted the Royal Ascot race-meeting, a fashionable event still held every June and patronized by the Royal Family. The Ascot Gold Cup was first presented in 1807.

AVEBURY, Wilts   39 SU06
Many experts consider Avebury the most significant prehistoric monument in Europe. It is certainly one of the largest stone circles in the world, comprising 100 standing-stone positions enclosing some 28 acres of land. Inside the large outer circle, which has quite a few gaps due to superstitious destruction in the past, are two smaller rings about 300ft in diameter. The village itself is a collection of handsome old buildings, featuring a small museum of archaeology and Avebury Manor, a 16th-century house set in fine gardens.

BATTLE, E Sussex   41 TQ71
The town takes its name from the Battle of Hastings, fought here in 1066. William the Conqueror promised to erect an abbey if he won the battle, and the proof of his victory is St Martin's Abbey, built on the hilltop where Harold was killed. A fine 14th-century gatehouse, a roofless refectory, and a 13th-century Abbot's House can still be seen. Close to the abbey are the Norman Church of St Mary and a fine Deanery (1669).

BIDDENDEN, Kent   41 TQ83
This picturesque Wealden village has several weavers' cottages and a fine medieval Cloth Hall. Its church has a good 15th-century tower and contains a wealth of brasses. The 'Biddenden Maids' were Eliza and Mary Chulkhurst, a pair of Siamese twins who lived here in the 12th century and bequeathed 20 acres of land to provide an annual dole for the poor. Representations of the sisters are stamped on cakes distributed free every Easter Monday.

BISHOP'S WALTHAM, Hants   39 SU51
The great ruin of a 12th-century bishop's palace – part of the See of Winchester – is the most striking feature of this quaint little town. William of Wykeham, founder of Winchester College and of New College, Oxford, died here in 1404.

BOGNOR REGIS, W Sussex   40 SZ99
This popular resort began life as a Saxon village. The name 'Regis' commemorates a visit by George V, who stayed here during his convalescence in 1929. The Dome House (1793) is now part of the West Sussex Institute of Higher Education.

BOSHAM, W Sussex   39 SU80
This attractive fishing village and yachting centre is situated on a creek of Chichester Harbour. The partly-Saxon church has a fine Norman font, and appears on the Bayeux tapestry. Harold sailed to Normandy from here.

BOURNEMOUTH, Dorset   38 SZ09
In 1840 a marine-resort village was laid out here, and with its natural advantages grew quickly to become one of Britain's largest seaside resorts. Among its assets are a mild climate, six miles of sandy beach, attractive sandstone cliffs and deep ravines that provide pleasant wooded walks to the shore. Facilities for shopping and entertainment are excellent, and the cultural interest of the town is amply demonstrated by the world-famous Bournemouth Symphony Orchestra. Three major places of interest are the British Typewriter Museum, the Rothesay Museum, and the Russell-Cotes Art Gallery and Museum.

Left: Woodhenge, near Amesbury, is one of Wiltshire's many mysterious prehistoric monuments

Right: Lime trees and attractive Georgian houses line New Alresford's Broad Street

Left: Brighton's Palace Pier, built in the late 19th century, offers many traditional seaside amusements

Right: Jane Austen spent the last eight years of her life at Chawton Cottage

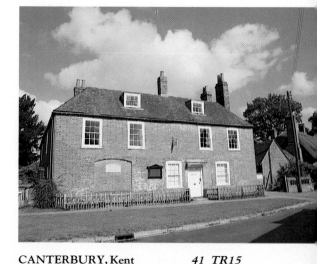

BREAMORE, Hants 39 SU11

Pronounced 'Bremmer', the village is known for its well-preserved Saxon church, which celebrated its millennium in 1980. Breamore House is of Elizabethan origin, and houses fine collections of paintings, china, and tapestry. There is also a carriage museum, housed in the stables, and a countryside museum. Reconstructions of a wheelwright's shop, a dairy and a brewery are among the many exhibits.

BRIGHTON, E Sussex 40 TQ30

This famous resort developed as a result of the 18th-century health fad for sea bathing. Its success was assured by the patronage of the Prince of Wales in 1784, and the many superb terraces preserved here today prove its continued prosperity. The most impressive building is the Royal Pavilion, a magnificent Oriental-style palace built for the Prince Regent by Henry Holland in 1787. There are various museums, galleries and theatres in the town, and visitors are offered all the usual distractions of the British seaside holiday. An excellent aquarium can be visited near Palace Pier, and the Volks Electric Railway – the first of its kind in the world – runs from here to the Black Rock area. Old Brighton is preserved in the winding streets of The Lanes, which contrast with the new conference centre and up-to-the-minute marina.

BROADSTAIRS, Kent 41 TR36

This popular resort is known for its associations with Charles Dickens. Bleak House – so called after his famous novel – was once his home. Part of it is now a museum. Across the bay is Dickens House, immortalized as the home of Betsy Trotwood in *David Copperfield*. Broadstairs holds a Dickens Festival every June, during which many of the local people dress in period costume.

BROCKENHURST, Hants 39 SU20

Many people find this handsome, lively village an ideal base from which to explore the New Forest. The local church is of Norman origin and claims to be the oldest foundation in the forest. *Domesday Book* records a church on this site, and the enormous yew in the churchyard may well have been planted more than 1,000 years ago.

BUCKLER'S HARD, Hants 39 SU40

This small Beaulieu River village thrived for several centuries as a shipbuilding yard. A fascinating little maritime museum recalls those times, and the deep estuary is put to peaceful use by yacht owners. The short village street of 18th-century houses was the creation of the Second Duke of Montagu, who planned a town and docks here to receive produce from his own extensive foreign estates.

BURWASH, E Sussex 41 TQ62

In Burwash churchyard is a cast-iron grave slab that is claimed to be the oldest in the country. Pleasant old buildings in the High Street include timber-framed cottages.

Nearby Bateman's, a 17th-century stone house built for a local ironmaster, is famous as the home of Rudyard Kipling. He lived here from 1902 to 1936, and wrote several of his books, including *Puck of Pook's Hill*, in the study, which remains much as it was in his lifetime.

A collection of mementoes of Milton is on display in his cottage at Chalfont St Giles

CANTERBURY, Kent 41 TR15

When the Romans came here they took over a Belgic Stourside community and developed it into the town of *Durovernum Cantiorum*. When the Romans left the area was swept by waves of invaders, and in AD597 St Augustine's mission arrived to convert King Ethelbert of Kent and restore the town's dilapidated churches. Shortly afterwards Canterbury became the Metropolitan City of the Church of England. Long stretches of the city wall survive on Roman foundations, and the present cathedral dates from 1070. This fine structure is best known as the place where Archbishop Thomas à Becket was murdered for his denial of the king's authority over the church.

Canterbury Castle has the third largest Norman keep in Britain, and King's School is thought to be the oldest in existence. Beside the River Stour stands the Weavers' House, built for a wealthy merchant in 1507 and used to accommodate refugee weavers from the Netherlands. Weaving demonstrations are held here in summer, and part of the building is a brass-rubbing centre.

CHALFONT ST GILES, Bucks 40 SU99

St Giles' Church dates from the 13th century but has a Victorian exterior. Bertram Mills, of circus fame, is buried in the churchyard. The village has a small green and ancient brick-and-timber cottages. One is Milton's Cottage, where the poet came to escape the plague in London. He completed *Paradise Lost* and began *Paradise Regained* here.

CHAWTON, Hants 39 SU73

In Chawton is the unassuming 18th-century cottage where novelist Jane Austen once lived. Now a Jane Austen museum, this was her home from 1809 till her death, and all her later books were written here.

CHELMSFORD, Essex 41 TL70

Chelmsford is an agricultural and industrial centre divided into three districts by the Rivers Chelmer and Can. Both rivers are crossed by several bridges, but the main one is the Stone Bridge of 1787. Although the Perpendicular Church of St Mary the Virgin became a cathedral in 1914, it is still a typical Essex parish church of the 15th century.

A detail from 'Christ Preaching at Cookham Regatta', which hangs in the Stanley Spencer Gallery at Cookham

CHERTSEY, Surrey   40 TQ06

The Thames is spanned here by a seven-arch 18th-century bridge. The pleasant riverside town was once famous for its wealthy Benedictine abbey, which was destroyed by the Danes but later rebuilt. Only a few ruins remain. Old buildings here include the partly 17th-century George Inn, and Curfew House of 1729. A curfew bell in the church commemorates Blanche Heriot, who saved her lover's life. Knowing that he was to be executed at curfew, she hung on the clapper of the bell to prevent it being sounded until he was reprieved.

CHICHESTER, W Sussex   39 SU80

This was the important Roman town of *Noviomagus*, and retains its original layout – a walled enclosure with four main streets. Substantial portions of the city walls remain; these defences were completed about AD200, bastions were added in AD350, and an inner rampart was built as a promenade in the 18th century. The remaining portions of wall are of medieval workmanship, but the foundations and core are Roman.

In 1075 the See which St Wilfred had founded at nearby Selsey in 681 was transferred to the city. The present cathedral was started in 1091 and completed in 1123, but has been considerably altered and extended since. It has a rare 15th-century detached bell-tower.

The remains of Greyfriars monastery in Priory Park now house a small museum. St Mary's Hospital is a group of almshouses dating from 1269, including a hall with a timber roof and a fine chapel screen. Many fine 18th-century houses survive in the city – particularly in St Martin's Square and the Pallant quarter.

The Chichester Festival Theatre, built in 1962, stages important dramatic productions during the summer festival season.

Chichester Harbour is a well-known yachting centre and has been designated an area of outstanding natural beauty. Fishbourne Roman Palace, the largest ever found in Britain, lies 1½ miles west of the city.

CHIDDINGSTONE, Kent   40 TQ54

Chiddingstone, a National Trust village, has a beautifully preserved street lined with half-timbered 16th- and 17th-century houses that were probably built with iron-industry money. At the top of the street is 19th-century Chiddingstone Castle. The Chiding Stone, from which the village takes its name, is a large sandstone rock behind the street. Nagging wives were once brought here to be chided by the assembled village population.

CHRISTCHURCH, Dorset   38 SZ19

Situated on the estuaries of the Avon and Stour, this town was originally called Twynham. The splendid Priory Church stands behind the quay and displays a mixture of styles from Norman to the Renaissance. Among its more notable features are the chantry chapels, a monument to the poet Shelley and the so-called 'miraculous beam'. Remains of a Norman castle and house stand nearby on the banks of the Avon. Red House is of Georgian origin and contains an interesting museum and art gallery.

COOKHAM, Berks   39 SU88

This delightful village faces the wooded Cliveden Reach of the Thames, a fine stretch of river that begins at Cookham Lock. The artist Stanley Spencer lived and worked here, and his painting *The Last Supper* is hung in the 12th-century church. Other examples of his work are displayed in the Memorial Gallery, on the corner of the High Street. Cookham is traditionally the home of Her Majesty's Swan Keeper, who presides over the annual 'swan-upping' ceremony on the Thames, when cygnets are marked to identify their owners. The ceremony is the subject of one of Spencer's best-known paintings.

COWES, Isle of Wight   39 SZ49

This busy island port has a good harbour on the River Medina and is connected to East Cowes by a floating bridge. The headquarters of the Royal Yacht Squadron is based at Cowes Castle, and the town is well known as England's premier yachting centre. 'Cowes week', held every August, is one of Britain's leading social and sporting events.

A number of oast-houses can still be seen around Chiddingstone, though they are seldom used nowadays for drying hops

CRANBROOK, Kent   *41 TQ73*

This former cloth-weaving town is now a busy commercial centre. Old buildings here include the Elizabethan Old Cloth Hall, once called Coursehorn Manor, which has associations with Queen Elizabeth I. The church is sometimes called the Cathedral of the Weald, and has an ancient porch of 1291 and a fine oak door. A windmill is preserved in the town.

DARTFORD, Kent   *40 TQ57*

This busy town preserves a gateway from its old palace, a Georgian galleried inn, and several timbered houses. The restored parish church has a Norman tower and contains old brasses. It also houses the tomb of Sir John Spielman (1626), said to have been the first English paper-maker. Paper mills still operate here. The Dartford Tunnel lies 2½ miles north-east.

DEAL, Kent   *41 TR35*

Henry VIII built a castle in the shape of a six-petalled flower at Deal, though considerable protection was already offered by the notorious Goodwin Sands. These vast, shifting beds lie just five miles offshore and have caused hundreds of wrecks. In its early history the town was a limb of the Cinque Ports, but most of its development dates from the end of the 17th century. Local exhibits as well as nautical items from all over the world are shown in the Maritime and Local History Museum.

DEVIZES, Wilts   *39 SU06*

Devizes once lay on the boundary between three manors; hence its name – a corruption of *ad divisas*, meaning 'at the boundary'.

A castle was constructed here, and although it was demolished after the Civil War, a little of the old building survives in the present 19th-century castle. St John's Church was built for the castle around 1150, and St Mary's for the town in about the same period. Both display fine Norman work, and the former has an impressive tower. The Bear Inn was visited by Fanny Burney in 1730, and the landlord was the father of painter Sir Thomas Lawrence. The museum has a rich and important collection of antiquities, including finds from local Neolithic, Bronze Age and Iron Age sites. Many good Georgian houses stand in the town, and timbered houses of 1500 can be seen in St John's Alley. An ornamental market cross carries an inscription telling the tale of Ruth Pierce, a woman who died suddenly in 1753 after cheating in the local market.

The Kennet and Avon Canal passes near the town, and rises with the aid of 29 locks built by Rennie. It is one of the longest flights of locks in the country, and is currently being restored.

DIDCOT, Oxon   *39 SU58*

The great towers of Didcot power station give the landscape a futuristic look, but lovers of the steam age are well compensated by the fine railway museum of the Great Western Society. Didcot was a sleepy Oxfordshire village until Brunel's Great Western Railway arrived in 1841, and the old locomotive depot makes a good setting for the collection of GWR relics including several engines.

DITCHLING, E Sussex   *40 TQ31*

Several Tudor houses here include one that Henry VIII gave to Anne of Cleves. The cruciform church is mainly of Early English style, and preserves a chest of the same period. Nearby Ditchling Beacon (813ft) is one of the highest points in the South Downs. A road climbs almost to the summit, from which an extensive view can be enjoyed.

DORCHESTER, Oxon   *39 SU59*

Dating back to the Bronze Age, this pleasant village is situated on the River Thame near its junction with the Thames. It was both a Roman station and subsequently a sizeable Saxon cathedral town. The large and exceptionally interesting Norman abbey contains some fine 13th- and 14th-century glass and preserves a superb Jesse window. Another of the windows has been restored as a memorial to Sir Winston Churchill.

DORKING, Surrey   *40 TQ14*

Bow-fronted shop windows facing on to narrow streets are a feature of this ancient market town, which is pleasantly set in the Surrey hills. The High Street follows the line of Roman Stane Street, and the Saxons had a village here. Charles Dickens stayed at the 15th-century White Horse Inn, and the hotel at nearby Burford Bridge is where Nelson finally parted from his wife in 1800.

DOVER, Kent   *41 TR34*

Formerly the Roman walled city of *Dubris*, Dover was chief of the Cinque Ports and has a magnificent castle, built on a site occupied since prehistoric times. It strategic position gives it total command of the harbour, and successive English kings spent vast sums on its development. It was last used for military purposes during the Second World War.

The Pharos, a surprisingly well-preserved Roman lighthouse, stands within the castle walls near the exceptionally fine Saxon Church of St Mary de Castro. Dover Town Hall incorporates the 13th-century Hall of Maison Dieu, and nearby Maison Dieu House dates from 1663. The oldest and best-preserved wall paintings north of the Alps can be seen in the Roman Painted House. A granite memorial in North Fall Meadow marks the landing of Louis Blériot in 1909, after his historic cross-Channel flight.

EASTBOURNE, E Sussex   *41 TV69*

Consistently top of the seaside sunshine league tables, the thriving resort of Eastbourne has been popular since the beginning of the 19th century. It lies in a sheltered position behind the chalk promontory of Beachy Head, which is accessible by an easy walk.

Several fine parks in the town include Devonshire Park and Hampden Park, and lawns and flower beds border the promenade. Also on the sea front is the Wish Tower, originally a Martello tower built in 1804, which now serves as a museum. Other places of interest include the picturesque old Lamb Inn, the Towner Art Gallery and 18th-century Compton Place. The 600ft pier dates from 1872 and 1888.

An exhibition of Epping Forest's wildlife is housed in Queen Elizabeth's Hunting Lodge

EGHAM, Surrey   *40 TQ07*

About ½ mile north-west of this town on the Thames are the 60-acre riverside meadows of Runnymede. It was here, in 1215, that King John was prevailed upon by his barons to seal the draft of Magna Carta. Overlooking the meadows is Cooper's Hill, which is crowned by the RAF Memorial and has the American Bar Association's Magna Carta Memorial at its foot. Halfway up its slopes is a memorial to the assassinated US president, John F. Kennedy.

Egham is also known for the extraordinary building of Royal Holloway College, a Victorian extravaganza that housed one of the first women's colleges in the country when it was completed in 1887. It is now part of London University.

EPPING, Essex   *40 TL40*

Standing on the northern edge of the forest that shares its name, Epping has managed to retain its own identity as a small market town of some charm, despite the proximity of London. Winchelsea House and Epping Place, in the High Road, are both of 18th-century date.

Epping Forest was created in Norman times and maintained as a royal hunting area through the reigns of various monarchs. In the reign of Charles I its bounds were fixed to embrace some 60,000 acres. On the forest's southwestern edge stands Queen Elizabeth's Hunting Lodge, a wood-and-plaster building thought to have been erected towards the end of the 15th century so that the sovereign of the day could enjoy a grandstand view of the chase. After having served as a keeper's lodge for a number of years it now houses the Epping Forest Museum.

EPSOM, Surrey   *40 TQ26*
In the 18th century this pleasant market town was famous for the medicinal springs that gave their name to Epsom Salts; even before that it was known for horse-racing. The popularity of the spa has waned, but that of the turf is still in good heart. The course has been the home of good racing since the reign of James I, and has been the venue for the Derby, perhaps Britain's most famous race, since 1780.

EVERSLEY, Hants   *39 SU76*
St Mary's Church at Eversley was built in the 18th century, and is distinguished in having had novelist Charles Kingsley as rector. He is buried in the churchyard, and the north aisle was built in his memory.

ETON, Berks   *40 SU97*
Eton College, across the bridge from Windsor, is a famous public school originally founded by Henry VI in 1440. The beautiful chapel houses paintings and brasses. Lupton's Tower is an impressive structure, and Upper School is attributed to Wren.

FAREHAM, Hants   *39 SU50*
This old market town and port is situated at the head of a small creek. Several good Georgian houses can be seen on the Wickham road. Other interesting buildings include the former 19th-century Corn Exchange, and Bishopwood – a thatched house of about 1800.

FARNHAM, Surrey   *39 SU84*
Farnham is one of the most outstanding examples of a small red-brick country town in England. The town's essentially Georgian character is best displayed in Castle Street and West Street. Wide Castle Street climbs to Farnham Castle, where a 12th-century shell keep adjoins the impressive 15th- to 17th-century former residence of the Bishops of Guildford. It is noted for its Great Hall and brick tower.

FAVERSHAM, Kent   *41 TR06*
Once a flourishing port, this quiet old market town has many interesting houses, particularly in Court Street and Abbey Street. Notable buildings include the arcaded town hall, the Freemason's Hall, a house in Court Street where James II was held in 1688, and the old Ship Inn. Also here is the house of Thomas Arden, whose murder by his wife became the subject of an Elizabethan play, *Arden of Faversham*. Manufacture of gunpowder was once an important local industry, and the last of the gunpowder mills has been preserved. The large church contains carved late 15th-century stalls, numerous brasses, and an Easter Sepulchre of 1535.

FOLKESTONE, Kent   *41 TR23*
A popular holiday resort and a harbour for cross-Channel steamers, this ancient port still has a fishing fleet and fish market. A wide grassy promenade known as The Leas extends along the cliff top, and attractively wooded walks slope down to the beach.

GODALMING, Surrey   *40 SU94*
This colourful town on the River Wey has a church displaying a lofty lead-covered spire. Houses of the Tudor and Stuart periods can be seen in the town. The 17th-century almshouses are of interest, and the attractive town hall of 1814, affectionately known as 'The Pepper Pot', now houses a museum.

GOODWOOD, W Sussex   *39 SU81*
The well-known race-course lies in a delightful downland setting. Goodwood House, built by James Wyatt between 1790 and 1800, contains a good collection of pictures. It shares a fine park with curious Shell House of 1739, and an early 18th-century Palladian temple known as Carne's Seat. Birdless Grove is a pleasant group of beeches, so named because it is said that no bird ever sings there.

The Star and Eagle at Goudhurst was once the haunt of smugglers

GORING-ON-THAMES, Oxon   *39 SU68*
This attractive Thames valley village is situated in a gap between the Chilterns and the Berkshire Downs. The mainly Norman church contains a bell dating from about 1290. The ancient Icknield Way crosses the river here to meet the Ridgeway; Goring was an important ford even in prehistoric times.

GOSPORT, Hants   *39 SZ69*
Trinity Church is of 17th-century date and contains an organ that once belonged to the Duke of Chandos. It comes from Canons in Edgware, and Handel is said to have composed some of his music on it. The naval hospital at Haslar, facing Spithead, was built largely in the 18th century. Fort Brockhurst dates from the mid 18th century, and is one of five similar structures in the area.

GOUDHURST, Kent   *41 TQ73*
This attractive Wealden village has fine old houses and a 15th-century church which is notable for its Culpeper monuments and brasses. The tower, which was rebuilt in the 17th century, provides a fine viewpoint. The Star and Eagle pub, which is connected to the church by a tunnel, was once a smugglers' base.

GRAVESEND, Kent   *41 TQ67*
This flourishing residential, industrial and commercial centre on the River Thames is connected to Tilbury by passenger ferry.

Three Dawes is an old inn near the town pier, built in such a way as to include several tunnels, and possibly used by smugglers. Weatherboarded houses can still be seen in the main street. Two windows in 18th-century St George's Church – now the Chapel of Unity – commemorate the Red Indian Princess Pocahontas who saved the life of John Smith in Virginia. She later married an Englishman, and died here during a visit to England. Her grave is in the church, and her statue stands in the former churchyard.

Pleasure craft converge on Goring Lock, set on a very popular stretch of the Thames

GREENSTED-JUXTA-ONGAR, Essex   *40 TL50*

The nave of St Andrew's Church is famous as the only surviving example of a Saxon log church. The brick choir was added around 1500. The body of King Edmund is known to have been rested here in 1013, but the building is probably much older than that.

GUILDFORD, Surrey   *40 TQ04*

Medieval kings built a great castle in this ancient town and merchants later developed it into an important centre of the wool industry. Nowadays the castle has vanished except for a three-storey keep set in flower gardens, but the prosperity of wool is reflected in many fine old buildings. Charles Dickens thought the steep High Street 'the most beautiful in the kingdom'. At its summit is the 16th-century Grammar School, the contemporary Hospital of the Blessed Trinity, and an 18th-century church. Farther down, the ornate clock of the 17th-century Guildhall hangs over the pavement near the Saxon tower of St Mary's Church, and the 19th-century Church of St Nicholas makes an interesting contrast at the bottom of the hill. The River Wey features an interesting 18th-century riverside crane powered by a 20ft treadmill. New buildings include Sir Edward Maufe's controversial cathedral on Stag Hill.

To the east of the city, near West Clandon, is Clandon Park, an 18th-century mansion built for the first Lord Onslow.

HADLEIGH, Essex   *41 TQ88*

Remains of Hadleigh's 13th-century castle, rebuilt in the 14th century as the residence of Edward III, were the subject of a painting by Constable. Hubert de Burgh was its original builder, and after Edward Henry VIII made it the home of Anne of Cleves. The church is mostly Norman and displays remains of a wall painting of Thomas à Becket.

HAMBLEDON, Hants   *39 SU61*

It is claimed that one of the very first games of cricket was played here on Broadhalfpenny Down in 1774. A stone commemorating this stands opposite the Bat and Ball Inn, and the pub itself contains interesting old relics of the game. Saxon workmanship forms much of the church's construction, although most of this is now hidden by later building.

HASTINGS and ST LEONARDS, E Sussex   *41 TQ80*

These popular twin resorts offer five miles of shingle beach and sand at low tide. The Old Town lies between the East and West Hills, and its picturesque old houses are dominated by the ruins of a Norman castle built by William the Conqueror in 1086. Hastings was one of the original Cinque Ports.

A miniature train runs along the front at Rock-a-Nore, passing a lifeboat station and several old net-houses – tall huts once used for drying fishing nets. The track ends near the Fishermen's Museum, which houses the last of the Hastings luggers to be built for sail. There are many fine houses in the town, particularly in the High Street and All Saints' Street.

The church at Greensted-juxta-Ongar has one of the oldest wooden naves in the world

HATFIELD, Herts   *40 TL20*

This ancient market town lies to the east of the A1000, adjacent to Hatfield New Town. Since the new town was built in 1946 the population of the area has doubled, but the old town is still full of charming old buildings. Fore Street has a row of Georgian houses stepped up the hillside, and several other interesting buildings can be seen in Park Street and Church Street.

Magnificent Hatfield House was built for Robert Cecil, Earl of Shaftesbury, and stands in a great park. Its superb great hall is richly appointed with panelling, carving and several unique paintings. The original Tudor palace, constructed entirely of brick (a startlingly new fashion for the period), stands in the grounds of Hatfield House. Elizabeth's Oak, said to be where Elizabeth I received news of her accession, is also in the park.

HENLEY-ON-THAMES, Oxon   *39 SU78*

This residential town is a popular Thames-valley resort. The famous regatta, founded in 1839, is held annually in the first week of July. Old Father Thames and the goddess Isis are represented by carvings on the keystones of the bridge, and St Mary's Church contains many interesting monuments. Numerous Georgian buildings can be seen in the town, including the Kenton Theatre, built in 1805 and the fourth oldest in England.

HEVER, Kent   *40 TQ44*

Hever's beautiful moated castle has associations with Henry VIII and Anne Boleyn, his ill-fated second wife, who lived here as a girl. A tomb and brass to her father can be seen in the local church, and the village inn displays a rare sign depicting Henry VIII.

Hever Castle was painstakingly restored earlier this century by the wealthy Astor family

HIGH WYCOMBE, Bucks   39 SU89

High Wycombe has been important since Roman times, and once earned a very good living from wool and lace. It is now well known for the manufacture of furniture, particularly chairs, and has a museum dealing solely with the craft in Castle Hill House. The Guildhall and octagonal Little Market House are scheduled as Ancient Monuments.

On the northern outskirts is Hughenden Manor, the home of Disraeli. Remodelled by him in 1862, the house is preserved as a museum, with mementoes of his personal and political life.

HUNGERFORD, Berks   39 SU36

This little town on the River Kennet is known for the picturesque Hock-tide ceremony which takes place on Tuesday of Easter week, featuring the Tutti-men. The town hall has a horn said to have been presented by John of Gaunt, who gave the town fishing rights on the Kennet. The area is still popular with anglers, and Hungerford is now a thriving centre for the antiques trade.

JORDANS, Bucks   40 SU99

The most famous of all Quaker Meeting Houses stands here. It was built in 1688 and overlooks a little graveyard where William Penn, the famous Quaker who founded Pennsylvania, is buried. The nearby Mayflower Barn has timbers said to have come from the ship that carried the Pilgrim Fathers to North America in 1620.

LEEDS, Kent   41 TQ85

Stone-built Battle Hall dates from the 14th century, and is just one of several old houses in this village, whose church has a massive Norman tower. Leeds Castle, 1½ miles north-east, is magnificently situated on two islands in the middle of a lake. The original stronghold was converted into a residence by Henry VIII. His first wife Catherine of Aragon lived at the castle, which was a royal palace for 300 years.

LEWES, E Sussex   40 TQ41

This county town of East Sussex lies in a downland setting on the River Ouse. The steep hill on which Lewes stands is topped by the keep of a Norman castle. The impressive barbican and gatehouse are below. The Barbican House is occupied by the Museum of Sussex Archaeology.

St Michael's Church carries a curious round tower. St Anne's Church and St John's Church (Southover) are both partly Norman; the former has a notable font of the same period, and the latter houses an engraved stone which covers the grave of one of William the Conqueror's daughters. Most of the old houses are of 18th-century date, and are best seen in Keere Street – where remains of the town wall also exist – and in the High Street. Anne of Cleves House, in Southover, is dated 1559 and contains a folk museum which includes a remarkable collection of ironwork.

John Evelyn, the diarist, attended Lewes grammar school from 1630 to 1637, and occasionally lived in Southover Grange. Bull House, once the home of Tom Paine, pamphleteer and author of *The Rights of Man*, is a half-timbered building noted for its carved satyrs.

The Battle of Lewes took place to the west of the town in 1264, when Henry III was defeated by Simon de Montfort and his baron army.

MAIDENHEAD, Berks   39 SU88

The Thames here is spanned by an 18th-century road bridge and a fine railway bridge built in 1838 by the brilliant engineer Isambard Kingdom Brunel. The river at Maidenhead is also known for Boulter's Lock, a popular boating rendezvous and beauty spot. To the west of the town is the Courage Shire Horse Centre, where the well-known brewery's 12 Shire horses can be seen, together with a display on the history of the horses. In the town itself are almshouses dating from 1659. The Harry Reitlinger Bequest is an interesting collection of paintings, sculpture, glassware and pottery.

MAIDSTONE, Kent   41 TQ75

Although this county town has some industry such as brewing and paper-making, it is still the agricultural centre of Kent. Maidstone has several interesting old buildings. The Archbishop's Palace is mainly Elizabethan, and was once a residence of the Archbishop of Canterbury. It stands facing the Medway, and its stables now house a museum of old carriages. Chillington Manor is an Elizabethan house now serving as a museum and art gallery. It includes a Japanese room.

MALDON, Essex   41 TL80

Oysters and fine-quality table salt are well-known products of this picturesque port and yachting harbour at the mouth of the Rivers Chelmer and Blackwater. All Saints' Church carries a unique triangular 13th-century tower, and the south aisle of 1340 is also notable.

In AD991 one of the decisive battles of England's early history was fought just outside the town. It is the subject of the Old English poem *The Battle of Maldon*.

MARGATE, Kent   41 TR37

Margate was once a port of some importance, and is now a popular resort with a harbour, fishing, golf, amusements and excellent sands. The restored flint-built parish church of St John houses many brasses, and a nearby 18th-century grotto displays shell-studded walls. The Theatre Royal dates from 1787, and is one of the oldest in the country.

MARLOW, Bucks   39 SU88

The fine Regency suspension bridge over the Thames at Marlow dates from 1829. It is overlooked by the graceful spire of All Saints' Church, and by the Compleat Angler Hotel, famed for its connections with Izaak Walton, after whose classic book it is named. Marlow also has associations with the poet Shelley, who lived in West Street. He composed *The Revolt of Islam* here, and his wife Mary wrote *Frankenstein* here in 1817-18.

The graves of William Penn, the Quaker founder of Pennsylvania, and members of his family are overlooked by the Friends' Meeting House at Jordans

MIDHURST, W Sussex   *39 SU82*

This small market town is full of lovely old buildings especially in the market place and the street that runs down from it to the delightful little duckpond. Midhurst stands at the centre of one of Sussex's most beautiful regions. To the south lie the downs, and to the east are the picturesque ruins of Cowdray House, set in a beautiful park that has a famous polo ground.

Nettlebed's bottle-shaped brick kiln was in use until 1927, and is the only survival of a trade carried on in the village for many centuries

NETTLEBED, Oxon   *39 SU78*

This village standing among Chiltern beechwoods is dominated by its tall, beautifully restored brick kiln. It was built about 300 years ago but the history of the industry here goes back much further. As long ago as the 14th century the kilns of Nettlebed made 35,000 tiles for the building of Wallingford Castle.

NEWBURY, Berks   *39 SU46*

Newbury's handsome parish church was rebuilt in the 16th century by Jack o' Newbury, a local clothier. The Jacobean Cloth Hall has been restored and is now a museum exhibiting relics of the Civil War. Donnington Castle, to the north of the town, was of great importance in the war, since it guarded the main route from London to the west. It was damaged when besieged by the Parliamentarians and gradually fell into ruin, but the mighty 14th-century gatehouse is still intact.

Today Newbury is well known for its racecourse, where major steeplechase and hurdling events are held. The course is unusual in having its own railway station.

NEWHAVEN, E Sussex   *40 TQ40*

Sited at the mouth of the River Ouse, Newhaven has an unusual, partly Norman church. Its chancel is at the foot of the tower, and it has an east apse. Bridge Hotel was the home of Louis Philippe and his Queen after the 1848 French Revolution.

The great gatehouse of Donnington Castle, near Newbury, commands panoramic downland views

NEWPORT, Isle of Wight   *39 SZ48*

Situated at the head of the Medina estuary, this town is the capital of the island and stands on a site that has been occupied at least since Roman times. Mighty Carisbrooke Castle stands on the foundations of a Roman fort 1 mile south-west. The remains of the castle include a Norman keep and a 16th-century treadmill that used to be worked by prisoners to raise water. Today it is one of many fascinating exhibits in the Isle of Wight Museum.

ODIHAM, Hants   *39 SU75*

Most of the houses in this town are Georgian, but the fine old George Inn was first licensed in 1540. The stocks and whipping-post have been preserved, and numerous old brasses, 15th-century screenwork, and a pulpit and galleries of the Jacobean period are features of the largely 14th-century church. The church tower is a 17th-century brick construction and a curious old pest-house which still stands in the churchyard dates back to the great plague of 1665. Remains of Odiham Castle, sometimes known as King John's Castle, lie 1 mile west near the Basingstoke Canal.

PETERSFIELD, Hants   *39 SU72*

In its early years Petersfield's prosperity was based on the wool trade, but as this began to decline it became an important coaching centre on the busy London to Portsmouth road. A once-gilded equestrian statue of William III guards the central square, where a market is held every Wednesday. The extensive waters of Heath Pond lie south-east of the town on the B2146.

PETWORTH, W Sussex   *40 SU92*

This old-world town has many 16th- and 17th-century houses, including Thompson's almshouses of 1618. The town hall is of early 19th-century date, and Somerset Lodge dates from 1653. Petworth House was presented to the National Trust by Lord Leconfield in 1947, and is a magnificent 17th-century mansion incorporating parts of an earlier house. Notable pictures, carvings by Grinling Gibbons, and a 13th- and 17th-century chapel are of great interest. The house stands in a huge, walled park landscaped in the 18th century by Capability Brown. The setting inspired some memorable landscape paintings by Turner.

Petworth Park, laid out by Capability Brown, is a fine example of 18th-century 'natural' landscaping

Left: Sunset over Poole Harbour transforms even modern industrial developments into a peaceful evening scene

Right: The old buildings of Rye look down over fishing boats at anchor on the River Rother

POOLE, Dorset   38 SZ09

Elizabeth I granted Poole county status which it kept until the late 19th century. Many fine old buildings in the town include the 18th-century Guildhall and a medieval merchant's house called Scaplen's. Both buildings contain local interest museums. Archaeological evidence suggests that Phoenician sailors were using Poole's vast harbour as early as 800 BC. It is the second largest natural harbour in the world, and its coastline measures over 100 miles. Brownsea Island, near the harbour mouth, was famous as the site of Lord Baden-Powell's first scout camp.

PORTSMOUTH AND SOUTHSEA, Hants   39 SZ69

The historic home of the Royal Navy, Portsmouth has docks that date back to the time of Richard the Lionheart and now cover more than 300 acres. Henry VIII built a castle at Southsea in 1539 to defend this vital harbour, and this now houses a naval museum. The Royal Navy Museum in Portsmouth itself contains a fascinating display of model ships and figureheads, together with a large panorama explaining the Battle of Trafalgar in 1805. That battle's most famous ship, HMS *Victory*, has been restored and is in dry dock here.

PULBOROUGH, W Sussex   40 TQ01

Attractive half-timbered and stone-built houses can be seen in this pleasant town, and several old bridges span the River Arun. The large Early English to Perpendicular church contains a massive 12th-century font, and is reached through a delightful 14th-century lych-gate.

PURTON, Wilts   39 SU08

The old village, off the main road here, has a fine cruciform church with both a central spire and a west tower. Nearby is a fine old manor house which includes a two-storeyed dovecote. A notable L-shaped tithe barn is also of interest, and Elizabethan Restrop House (not open) lies 1 mile west of the village.

RAMSGATE, Kent   41 TR36

Chalk cliffs fringe excellent sands at this popular resort and fishing port. Much of the town has a Victorian air, for the resort became fashionable in the 19th century after a visit by George IV in 1827. St Augustine's Roman Catholic abbey church of 1851 is considered Pugin's masterpiece and is where the great architect was buried. St George's Church has a tower topped by a lantern, and stained glass including a window commemorating the Dunkirk evacuation. Pegwell Bay and the cross-Channel hovercraft terminal at Ebbsfleet lie to the south.

READING, Berks   39 SU77

Many of Reading's historic buildings have been engulfed by modern development, but the town has a long and interesting past. It was occupied by the Danes as early as the 9th century, and in 1121 an abbey was founded by Henry I, who was buried here. The abbey ruins can still be seen, and the restored gateway was once a school whose pupils included Jane Austen. Other relics from the abbey can be seen in the Museum and Art Gallery, whose exhibits also include finds from the Roman town at Silchester. Whiteknights Park, now the campus of Reading University, is noted for the Museum of English Rural Life, a fascinating collection of agricultural and domestic items.

REIGATE, Surrey   40 TQ25

Reigate was important enough to have a castle in Norman times, though its remains are very sparse today. A network of medieval caves and tunnels has been discovered underneath, and these served as air-raid shelters in the Second World War.

The grave of Lord Howard of Effingham, who commanded the English fleet that defeated the Armada, can be seen in the parish church, which is one of the biggest in the county. Reigate Priory is a fine medieval house which now incorporates a small museum.

ROCHESTER, Kent   41 TQ76

Fortified by Romans, Saxons and Normans, this city on the Medway is still a major port and a thriving industrial centre. Slight traces of the old town walls remain, and Rochester's Norman legacy includes the 100ft-high castle keep and the magnificent cathedral. This great church has a large Early English crypt, many fine doorways and some 14th-century wall-paintings in the choir.

Later buildings include Eastgate House, an Elizabethan building described in *Edwin Drood* by Charles Dickens, who grew up in Rochester. The house is now a Charles Dickens Centre. A museum of local history occupies the nearby 17th-century Guildhall.

ROMSEY, Hants   39 SU32

The lovely Norman abbey church in this pleasant market town was saved from destruction at the hands of Henry VIII by the townspeople, who bought it for £100. The deed of sale can be seen inside the church, which includes among its treasures two rare pieces of Saxon sculpture and the exquisite 15th-century illuminated manuscript known as the Romsey Psalter. Visitors to the abbey come not only to see these ancient works of art, but also to pay their respects at the tomb of Earl Mountbatten of Burma, assassinated in 1979. His home was at Broadlands, an elegant Georgian house in lovely grounds by the River Test just outside the town. It was once the country home of Lord Palmerston. The Prince and Princess of Wales began their honeymoon here.

RYE, E Sussex   41 TQ92

Set on a small hill rising out of fenland by the River Rother, this collection of attractive old buildings and cobbled streets was one of the Cinque Ports. As such it was heavily fortified against the medieval French. This maritime importance seems odd today, but at that time Rye was almost encircled by sea. Its influence declined when the harbour silted up in the 16th century, and today the sea has receded. Many historic buildings have survived here, including the Norman and later church, which features a 16th-century clock with an 18ft free-swinging pendulum. Near by is the 13th-century Ypres Tower, which was built as a castle and used as a prison from the 16th to 19th centuries. Nowadays it holds a museum of local history.

ST ALBANS, Herts   40 TL10

Important remains of the Roman town *Verulamium* include a theatre, a hypocaust and good modern museum. The Roman settlement lay to the west of the present city centre, on the bank of the River Ver.

St Albans Cathedral dates originally from the Norman period. Considerable restorations in 1879 include the Victorian west façade. Roman bricks and tiles have been used in the building. Of particular interest are the remains of wall-paintings, the shrine of St Alban, the watching loft and the restored 15th-century screen. Other notable buildings in the town include an early 15th-century curfew tower and an octagonal timber-framed building called Ye Old Fighting Cocks, originally a monastic fishing lodge and later an inn.

SALISBURY, Wilts   38 SU12

The ancient city of Salisbury first came to importance following the abandonment of nearby Old Sarum in the 13th century. The bishop's See was transferred from the old to the new site, and in 1220 the new cathedral was begun. It is a wonderfully graceful building, with numerous slim columns of Purbeck stone and a magnificent 404ft spire that was added in the 14th century and is still the tallest in the country. The Cathedral Close preserves a beauty and atmosphere all of its own, and contains fine buildings dating from the 14th to the 18th centuries. Elsewhere in the town are 16th-century Joiner's Hall, the 14th-century Poultry Cross, and a great number of old inns. Interesting displays illustrating local history can be seen in the Salisbury and South Wiltshire Museum.

SANDWICH, Kent   41 TR35

The oldest of the Cinque Ports, Sandwich is now separated from the sea by two miles of sand-dunes. Among its many outstanding old buildings are the medieval Barbican, Fishgate, and a variety of houses and inns. St Bartholomew's Hospital guest-house dates from the 15th century, and both the Guildhall and Manwood Court were built in the 16th. The Old House is a fine example of Tudor design. Much of the old beach between the town and Sandwich Bay is occupied by Sandwich Golf Course, which is famous throughout the world.

Birds including a nightjar and a hoopoe are depicted in the Gilbert White window in Selborne church

SELBORNE, Hants   39 SU73

This lovely village gained fame through Gilbert White's classic field study *The Natural History of Selborne*. White, born in the Vicarage in 1720, made one of the first and best studies of wildlife within a defined area. He died in The Wakes, a fine house that now contains a Gilbert White museum.

SELSEY, W Sussex   39 SZ89

An important Roman settlement and later an Anglo-Saxon cathedral town stood here. Coins and other artefacts from these early days have been dug up, but Selsey's early architectural heritage has all been swept away by the sea. Today Selsey is a small resort, with excellent sands at low tide.

SHANKLIN, Isle of Wight   39 SZ58

A group of thatched buildings, the Crab Inn, and St Blasius's Church are all that remain of the fishing village that stood here before the seaside holiday fad took over. The excellent sea-bathing, sandy beach and good sunshine records attract many visitors every year.

SHIPLEY, W Sussex   40 TQ12

Fine Norman carving and the notable Caryll monument are features of Shipley church. Fragments of sarsen stones in the churchyard mark the grave of composer John Ireland. Shipley is also associated with novelist and poet Hilaire Belloc. He lived here until his death in 1953, and owned King's Mill – the last working smock-mill in Sussex.

SILCHESTER, Hants   39 SU66

Interesting remains of the Roman city *Calleva Atrebatum* exist here. The encircling town walls are in good condition, but the once-excavated city now lies beneath agricultural land. Parts of the old moat, early earthworks, and a small amphitheatre lie outside the wall. The fabric of the church includes a great deal of Roman material. Various finds are exhibited in the Calleva Museum and in the museum at Reading.

SINGLETON, W Sussex   40 SU81

This attractive downland village is the home of the Weald and Downland Open Air Museum, where historic buildings from the area have been re-erected and are preserved together with displays of rural industries and crafts.

SOUTHAMPTON, Hants   39 SU41

This important transatlantic port and busy commercial centre has a long maritime tradition, though it lost many of its old buildings as a result of heavy bomb damage in the Second World War. Parts of the medieval walls have survived, including the Bargate, an impressive gateway that was originally the northern entrance to the town. Its upper floor, once the Guildhall, contains a local history museum. Tudor House, a fine timber-framed building, is also a museum, and its garden has been restored to its original appearance. A partly ruined Norman house can also be seen here. The Civic Centre houses a good art gallery.

Southampton has no cathedral, but several fine churches escaped irreparable bomb damage. St Mary's, a late 19th-century building, is the mother church, and St Michael's, of Norman date, is the oldest. The 14th-century tower of Holy Rood Church has been preserved as a memorial to men of the Merchant Navy, while the Pilgrim Fathers are commemorated by the Mayflower Column.

SOUTHEND-ON-SEA, Essex   41 TQ88

This popular resort on the Thames estuary boasts a 1¾-mile pier that is the longest in the world. The Regency character of the town is preserved by the Royal Terrace, and Porters is a manor house of about 1600 which now serves as Mayor's Parlour. A museum of historic aircraft lies on the western outskirts.

Left: The graceful spire of Salisbury Cathedral is a 14th-century addition to an almost entirely Early English building

Right: Bayleaf House is one of several reconstructed buildings at the Weald and Downland Museum at Singleton

STOCKBRIDGE, Hants   39 SU33

People from all over the world come here to fish the Test, one of the most sought-after game rivers in the country. Stockbridge itself is a one-street town of mainly 19th-century buildings including the Town Hall, the Grosvenor Hotel, and the White Hart Inn.

STONEHENGE, Wilts   38 SU14

Originally Stonehenge comprised an encircling ditch and bank dating from the Stone Age, but this simple base was later developed into circles of sarsen stones around a horseshoe of trilithons enclosing the enigmatic Welsh bluestones. Several stones still stand where they were first erected thousands of years ago, and the largest measures almost 30ft high from its deeply buried base to its top. Very little is known about the original purpose of this most famous of monuments; theories of sun-worship and primitive astronomical computers remain mere speculation.

STRATFIELD SAYE PARK,
Hants   **39 SU66**

This stately home was built in the reign of Charles I and bought by the First Duke of Wellington with money voted to him by a grateful nation after Waterloo. The house stands in a superb park with a lake, and is still the home of the dukes of Wellington.

STUDLAND, Dorset   38 SZ08

Sandy beaches and sea bathing are offered by this Isle of Purbeck village. The unspoiled church preserves rich Norman work, particularly good examples of which are the tower and chancel. A curious 500-ton mass of ironstone situated on the heaths to the west is known as the Agglestone, and the chalk stacks of Old Harry Rocks lie offshore from Handfast Point.

Despite the efforts of countless scholars, Stonehenge remains a mysterious monument to a forgotten people

SWANAGE, Dorset   38 SZ07

This busy resort stands between towering downs that end as cliff-girded promontories on both sides of a sandy bay. Winding, switchback streets weave down to a shopping and amusement area concentrated on the only level piece of ground in the town – the sea front. An attractive group of old buildings clusters round the Mill Pond, off the Main Street.

TICHBORNE, Hants   39 SU53

Tichborne is a delightful collection of thatched 16th- and 17th-century houses with an unspoilt little church and a 19th-century manor house. Some 800 years ago the ailing lady of the manor, distressed by the poverty of the villagers, begged her husband to help them. Mockingly he agreed to set aside part of his estate to provide corn for the poor in

perpetuity, but that would be only so much land as she could crawl round while one torch burned. Tradition has it that she managed to encompass an amazing 23 acres. Every year the villagers still receive a dole of 30cwt of flour blessed by the local priest.

TILBURY, Essex   41 TQ67

Now an important container port, Tilbury has a fort that was built by Henry VIII in 1539 and later remodelled. This fort is noted for its ornate water-gate of 1682. An army raised to resist the Armada was reviewed here by Elizabeth I in 1582.

TUNBRIDGE WELLS, Kent   41 TQ53

In 1606 Lord North discovered chalybeate springs in the forest that stood here. Subsequently the town of Tunbridge Wells was founded, though building did not begin in earnest until the 1630s. By the end of that century it was a flourishing spa, and has remained so to the present day. Visitors to the raised parade known as the Pantiles may still 'take the waters'. Nearby stands the 17th-century Church of St Charles the Martyr.

WALLINGFORD, Oxon   39 SU68

The ancient earth ramparts of a former castle exist in this little River Thames town. The 17th-century town hall is mounted on stone pillars, and a fine old 14-arch bridge spans the river. Angiers Almshouses date from 1681. St Leonard's Church still displays some Norman work, and St Peter's Church was rebuilt in 1860 and carries a curious openwork spire.

WALMER, Kent   41 TR35

The Henrian castle here stands in attractive gardens and is the official residence of the Lord Warden of the Cinque Ports. The Duke of Wellington died here in 1852 and a number of his possessions are on display inside. Walmer Lifeboat is famous for the many rescues it has made from the Goodwin Sands.

The bronze busts in the gallery at Stratfield Saye House include one of Napoleon

In the market place at Wantage is a statue of King Alfred, a native of the town

WANTAGE, Oxon   *39 SU48*

King Alfred the Great is said to have been born here in AD 849, and a statue of him stands in the attractive market-place. Fine medieval craftsmanship is evident in the local church, including old woodwork, a 15th-century hammerbeam roof and five old brasses. The town has an interesting little local history museum.

WEST WYCOMBE, Bucks   *39 SU89*

This town has a beautifully preserved main street with architecture dating from the 15th to 19th centuries. The Church of St Lawrence stands isolated on a 600ft-high hill on the site of a village which has long gone. Artificial chalk caves in the area once housed the notorious Hell Fire Club founded by Sir Francis Dashwood, who owned the mansion in West Wycombe Park. The house contains many art treasures and is noted for its painted ceilings.

WHIPPINGHAM,
Isle of Wight   *39 SZ59*

Prince Albert built the ornate church here in 1860, and he and Queen Victoria built nearby Osborne House as a retreat from the pomp and ceremony of Windsor. Queen Victoria died here in 1901, and the State apartments remain as they were in her day.

WHITSTABLE, Kent   *41 TR16*

Fishing and bathing from a shingle beach can be enjoyed in this Thames estuary resort. The town is noted for its oysters. The railway from Whitstable to Canterbury was the first regular passenger service in the world.

WILTON, Wilts   *38 SU03*

Wilton is an interesting town best known as an important carpet-making centre. Good Georgian houses can be seen in Kinsbury Square, and a curious county cross stands near the market house of 1738. Wilton House was built on the site of Wilton Abbey in the 1540s, but was completely rebuilt by Inigo Jones after a serious fire. Subsequent work includes alterations by architect James Wyatt. Features of the grounds include fine cedars and a Palladian-style bridge over the Nadder.

WIMBORNE MINSTER, Dorset   *38 SZ09*

The fine Norman Minster Church carries two towers, one topped by a lantern. Other features of particular interest include the rare chained library, the 14th-century quarter-jack clock, and various monuments and tombs. Priest's House Museum displays Roman remains.

WINCHELSEA, E Sussex   *41 TQ91*

The old town of Winchelsea was completely submerged by the sea in the 13th century, and was rebuilt by Edward I on a rise above the marshes. The sea has long since receded, and it is no longer the prosperous port it once was. Three gates survive from the original walled settlement, and 14th-century Court Hall now houses a museum.

WINCHESTER, Hants   *39 SU42*

Venta Belgarum to the Romans, this one-time capital of Wessex boasts an 11th-century and later cathedral that is the second longest in Europe. Inside are richly carved chantry chapels, and coffins holding the bones of Saxon kings. Survivals from the 13th century include stretches of the city walls, the hall of Pilgrims' School, and the 13th-century and later Deanery. Winchester College, founded by William of Wykeham in 1382, retains much of its original structure and stands near the ruined Bishop's Palace of Wolvesey Castle. Castle Hall dates from the 13th century, and 16th-century Godbegot House stands on the site of a palace built by King Canute. Close to the centre of town the River Itchen rushes through a lovely old mill of 1744 before winding through attractive gardens alongside the medieval walls.

WINDSOR, Berks   *40 SU97*

Windsor is a largely Georgian and Victorian town that owes its existence to its magnificent castle. William the Conqueror first appreciated the site's strategic importance and built a palisaded fort within a moat. Practically every English monarch who has taken the throne in the 900 years since then has contributed to its development, and today it is the largest inhabited castle in the world.

Windsor Great Park encompasses an area of some 5,000 acres. It is noted for its fine gardens including the wooded 20-acre Savill Garden, where rare flowers grow in summer. At the park's south-eastern corner is Virginia Water, a beautiful 1½-mile-long artificial lake.

WORTHING, W Sussex   *40 TQ10*

Until the 1760s Worthing was little more than a fishing hamlet, but by the end of that century the patronage of George III's family had encouraged the smart set to take an interest in the new town. The 18th-century terraces preserve something of the old gentility. Today Worthing is a popular seaside resort with a pier and an extensive pebble beach.

One of the most attractive features of Windsor Great Park is the silvery expanse of Virginia Water. Near the shore is a totem pole brought from British Columbia in 1958 (detail, inset)

London

Inner London

London has something for everyone. Its museums and galleries are packed with a dazzling variety of man-made and natural objects that span the history of the earth from its creation to the present day. It has buildings of every type and age, interspersed by thousands of acres of beautiful parks. Its theatres, restaurants and shops are among the finest anywhere, and its great pageants and state occasions are unique.

Bank of England
Threadneedle Street, EC2

The 'Old Lady of Threadneedle Street' was founded in 1694 when City merchants decided that an independent national bank would be advantageous to all concerned. It operated from the Grocers' Hall until 1734 when the new building was opened in Threadneedle Street. The vaults traditionally house the nation's gold reserves, and the internal security system is therefore of the highest order. After the Bank was attacked by looters in 1780 the Bank Piquet was instituted, whereby a detachment of Guards marched to the building each afternoon and remained on watch all night. This ceremony continued until 1973 when an electronic security system was installed.

Banqueting House
Whitehall, SW1

Inigo Jones (1573–1652), the greatest architect of his day, designed this Palladian-style building, completed in 1622 as part of the old Palace of Whitehall, which James I wanted to modernize. A fire destroyed most of it in 1698, but the House was one of the few survivals. The sumptuous interior, with its ceiling painted by Rubens, is open to the public. From here Charles I passed on to the scaffold where he was beheaded in 1649.

Barbican
EC2

This impressive new development, built around the remaining portion of the old Roman wall, is an ambitious scheme to promote the City as a residential area rather than a place to be visited only for the purpose of daily work. It contains high-rise blocks of flats, shops, offices, pubs, the new City of London School for Girls, and the 16th-century church of St Giles Cripplegate. Other features include an ornamental lake, an arts centre, and the new Guildhall School of Music and Drama.

British Museum
Great Russell Street, WC1

Founded by Act of Parliament in 1753, the British Museum has grown to become the largest, and perhaps finest, museum in the world. A detailed study of the items on display would take several lifetimes, and these are only a selection of the vast number of objects that the museum holds, the rest being kept in its vaults and store-rooms. Exhibits not to be missed include the mummies and sculpture in the Egyptian Galleries, and the superb Elgin Marbles from Athens; British treasures include the beautiful 7th-century Sutton Hoo Treasure from a ship burial discovered in Suffolk, the exquisite 12th-century Lewis Chessmen, and two original copies of Magna Carta.

Buckingham Palace
The Mall, SW1

Formerly known as Buckingham House, this most famous of royal homes was built in 1703 by the Duke of Buckingham, and subsequently bought by George III in 1762. Nash altered and remodelled it for George IV in 1825, when its name was changed to Buckingham Palace. It was not much used until Queen Victoria came to the throne in 1837, when the court moved here. It has been the London home of the monarch ever since. The east wing, the side the public sees, was added in 1847 and the whole east façade was redesigned in 1913.

Many of the splendid art treasures belonging to the royal family can be seen in the Queen's Gallery, whose entrance is in Buckingham Gate. The Royal Mews, in Buckingham Palace Road, is also open to the public. It houses the state coaches and the horses which draw them.

Cenotaph
Whitehall, SW1

Designed by Sir Edwin Lutyens, the Cenotaph was unveiled in 1920 on the anniversary of Armistice Day. It was originally built to the memory of the men who lost their lives in the First World War. Now memorial services for the dead of both world wars are held here every year on the second Sunday in November.

Church of St Bartholomew the Great
West Smithfield, EC1

St Bartholomew's is one of the few surviving examples of Norman architecture in London. It dates from the 12th century and is the chancel of a great Norman monastery church which once stood here. After the Dissolution of the Monasteries it became private property, and for 300 years was put to a variety of uses, including a factory and stables. Its interior is dominated by huge Romanesque pillars, and contains the tomb of Rahere, the founder of the church and of St Bartholomew's Hospital. The church has a particularly interesting gateway, consisting of a half-timbered gatehouse above a battered 13th-century arch which was the original entrance to the nave.

Church of St Clement Danes
Strand, WC2

A church has stood on this site since the 9th century. Sir Christopher Wren rebuilt it in the 1680s, and it was rebuilt once more after it had been virtually destroyed during the Second World War. It is the memorial church of the Royal Air Force, and the crests of some 900 squadrons and Commonwealth air forces are let into the flooring. Many of the church's fixtures and furnishings have been donated by overseas air forces. The 115ft tower houses the bells that are immortalized in the famous lines of the nursery rhyme: 'Oranges and lemons say the bells of St Clement's'.

London as it was seen by the engraver J. C. Visscher in 1616. On the left is Old St Paul's, and on the far right is London Bridge

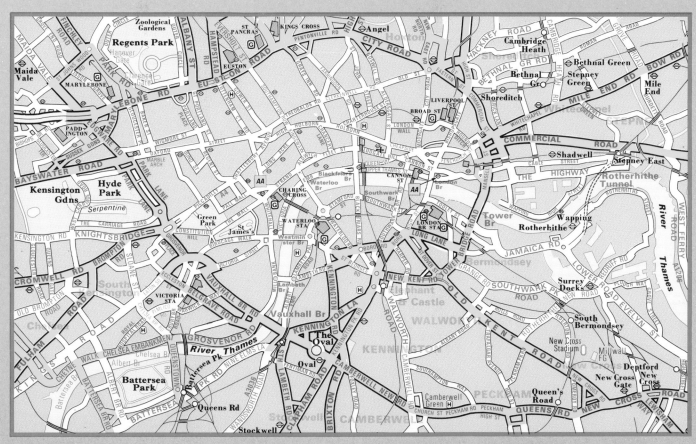

Church of St Martin-in-the-Fields
Trafalgar Square, WC2
The medieval church on this site, then surrounded, as its name suggests, by open fields, was extensively remodelled by James Gibbs in the early 18th century. It has an imposing temple-like portico, and a spacious galleried interior. Buckingham Palace is within the parish boundaries, and there are royal boxes at the east end of the church. The vaulted crypt contains a 16th-century chest and an 18th-century whipping post, but is better known for the fact that it is opened each night as a shelter for the homeless. This carries on the tradition of H. R. I. Sheppard, a First World War army chaplain, who, on his return from the Front, always kept the church open for servicemen or others who were stranded.

Courtauld Institute Galleries
Woburn Square, WC1
This superb collection of paintings was begun by Samuel Courtauld in the 1930s and presented to the University of London in memory of his wife. It is most famous for its Impressionist and Post-Impressionist pictures, but there is also a collection of Old Master drawings and Italian primitive paintings, as well as works by the Bloomsbury Group, which were presented to the university by the art critic Roger Fry.

Downing Street
Whitehall, SW1
This world-famous street was built by Sir George Downing, a secretary to the Treasury, in about 1680. At first it was an unimportant residential street with a pub – the Cat and Bagpipes – on the corner. In 1732 George II offered No. 10 to Sir Robert Walpole as a town house and since then it has been the official residence of the British Prime Minister.

Geological Museum
Exhibition Road, SW7
Most famous for its unsurpassed collection of gemstones, this fascinating museum illustrates the principles of geological science, together with the story of the earth's formation, and the world's economic geology and mineralogy.

Guildhall
Off Gresham Street, EC2

This building dates from 1411, when the livery companies raised money for its construction, but a good deal of restoration was carried out by Wren after the Great Fire, and a new façade was added by George Dance the Younger in 1788. The Great Hall, which was given a new roof in 1953, is now used for the Lord Mayor's Banquet and other civic functions. It has retained its original walls, and is decorated with the colourful shields of the livery companies, the banners of the 12 Great Companies, and several monuments to outstanding figures in the nation's history. At the west end of the Hall stand huge wooden figures of Gog and Magog, legendary British giants who are said to have fought against Trojan invaders around 1000BC. Beneath the hall is a magnificent 15th-century crypt, the largest of its kind in London.

HMS *Belfast*
Symons Wharf, Vine Lane, SE1

At 11,000 tons this is the largest cruiser ever built for the Royal Navy. She was built in 1939 and saved from a breaker's yard to be opened to the public in 1971.

Horseguards
Whitehall, SW1

Mounting the Guard, a ceremony in which detachments of the Household Cavalry participate, takes place here every morning (11 am weekdays, 10 am Sundays). The spectacular Trooping the Colour ceremony, which has origins stretching back to medieval times, is held on the Queen's official birthday (the second Saturday in June) on the parade ground behind Horseguards.

Houses of Parliament (New Palace of Westminster)
St Margaret Street, SW1

Officially known as the New Palace of Westminster, the Houses of Parliament buildings that exist today were designed by Sir Charles Barry and were started in 1840. The House of Lords was occupied by 1847, and the official opening by Queen Victoria took place in 1852.

The original Palace of Westminster was a royal residence from the reign of Edward the Confessor until Henry VIII, and comprised a walled and moated area of some 12½ acres. Henry VIII dispensed with the palace after it was damaged by fire in 1515, and in 1834 another fire destroyed all but Westminster Hall, the Crypt Chapel, and the cloisters. It is said that the fire was caused literally by red tape – the burning of exchequer tally sticks. The hour bell of the present clock-tower was named Big Ben after Sir Benjamin Hall, First Commissioner of Works, when the clock was installed in 1858. It weighs 13½ tons and the tower rises to 320ft. The entire building is in a rich Gothic style, and displays numerous fine carvings and statues both inside and out. Situated in the north end of the building, the House of Commons was restored in 1950.

Imperial War Museum
Lambeth Road, SE1

Founded in 1917 and established by Act of Parliament in 1920, this museum illustrates and records all aspects of the two world wars and other military operations involving Britain and the Commonwealth since 1914. An extremely varied collection of exhibits is on display, ranging from tanks and aeroplanes to paintings by official war artists.

Kensington Palace
Kensington Gardens, W8

William III bought what was a town mansion in 1689 and commissioned Wren to alter and improve it. The south wing is the best surviving part of his work. It was enlarged by William Kent for George I, and was the principal private royal residence until George II died here. Queen Victoria was born here and lived in the palace until she became Queen. It is now the residence of Princess Margaret. The State Apartments are open to the public.

Lambeth Palace
Lambeth Palace Road, SE1

Lambeth Palace has been the residence of the archbishops of Canterbury for 700 years. Its oldest part is the 13th-century crypt. The brick gatehouse dates from 1495, and the Great Hall, with its fine hammerbeam roof, from about 1660.

Lancaster House
The Mall, SW1

This massive palace was originally built in the 19th century for the 'grand old' Duke of York, and was acquired by the Duke of Sutherland. It is now a government hospitality centre and is usually open to the public.

London Zoo
Regent's Park, NW1

Set in the north-eastern corner of Regent's Park, this most famous of zoos was opened to the public in 1847 and has established a reputation for the care of its charges that is second to none. Over 6,000 species, ranging from the largest land animals to tiny sea creatures, are kept in environments as natural to them as

Far right: Giraffes and zebras, animals of the African plains, live happily together at London Zoo
Above right: The towers and pinnacles of the Palace of Westminster from the South Bank
Below right: Kensington Palace is the home of Princess Margaret, but the State Apartments are open to the public
Below: Life Guards riding down the Mall

possible, yet giving the public the best possible chance of seeing them. In the Snowdon Aviary birds nest, feed and breed as they would in the wild, while in the Charles Clore pavilion for small animals nocturnal creatures can be seen going about their secret business. At night Regent's Park is sometimes transformed into a wild forest by the howls of the inhabitants of Wolf Wood as they call to each other from the dark shadows of the trees.

Madame Tussaud's
Marylebone Road, NW1

This famous collection of waxworks was founded in Paris in 1770, moved to England in 1802, and found a permanent home in London in 1835. The exhibits, many of which are placed in appropriate settings, include historical figures, politicians, entertainers and, in the Chamber of Horrors, reconstructions of hideous crimes.

Mansion House
St Swithins Lane, EC2

In 1739 the Corporation decreed that the Lord Mayor should no longer be obliged to provide his own dwelling house, and the architect George Dance the Elder was commissioned to design an official residence. The imposing Palladian-style mansion that he built stands on the corner of Queen Victoria Street. Its principal rooms are the Egyptian Hall, or dining room, and the Salon, which contains 19th-century tapestries and an enormous Waterford glass chandelier.

Monument
Monument Street, EC3

Splendid views over the City can be obtained from the top of this famous landmark. Designed by Sir Christopher Wren and Robert Hooke, the Monument was erected in 1671–7

to commemorate the Great Fire of London which devastated the city in 1666. Its height (202ft) is said to equal the distance from its base to the place in Pudding Lane where the fire started on 2 September, destroying nearly 90 churches and around 13,000 houses.

Museum of London
London Wall, EC2

An integral part of the ultra-modern Barbican complex, the Museum of London is one of the most exciting establishments of its kind in the country. It is arranged chronologically and traces the capital's history from the very earliest times to the present day by means of brilliantly displayed exhibits, detailed models and audio-visual effects. Two of the most popular exhibits are the reconstruction of the Great Fire of 1666, complete with crackling flames, and the Lord Mayor's State Coach, a masterpiece built in 1757.

Museum of Mankind
6 Burlington Gardens, W1

This superb and endlessly fascinating collection embraces the art and material culture of tribal, village, and other pre-industrial societies from most areas of the world excluding Western Europe.

National Gallery
Trafalgar Square, WC2

The National Gallery houses one of the finest and most extensive collections of masterpieces in the world. All the great periods of European painting are represented, although only a choice selection of British work is on display as the national collection of this is housed in the Tate Gallery. One of the greatest, and most famous, paintings here is John Constable's breathtaking *Haywain*. Built on the site of a royal mews, the National Gallery is a classical-style building from whose majestic portico a panoramic view of Trafalgar Square may be enjoyed.

National Portrait Gallery
2 St Martin's Place, WC2

The collection of the National Portrait Gallery constitutes the world's most comprehensive survey of historical personalities. In addition to paintings the collection includes sculpture, miniatures, engravings and photographs. The portraits, arranged more or less in chronological order, are accompanied by furnishings, maps, weapons and other items to set them in their historical context.

Natural History Museum
Cromwell Road, SW7

Housed in a vast 19th-century Romanesque-style building decorated with terracotta reliefs of animals, birds and fishes, the Natural History Museum contains examples of nearly every animal species that has inhabited the earth. Life-size models of dinosaurs can be seen in the fossil galleries, while the Central Hall contains stuffed examples of the largest land animals on Earth today. In the west wing are galleries devoted to birds, insects and fish, and on the second floor is the Botanical Gallery, with dioramas of many different landscapes.

Above left: The fountains in Trafalgar Square, with the National Gallery in the background
Below left: Alfred Hitchcock and Agatha Christie, two of the waxworks in Madame Tussaud's
Below: The Monument, built to commemorate the Great Fire of London, and the view over the Pool of London from its top

Old Bailey
Old Bailey, EC4

The Central Criminal Court is popularly known as the Old Bailey from the name of the street on whose corner it stands. On this site, until 1902, stood the notorious Newgate Prison. On the first two days of each session the judges carry posies of flowers, and the courts are strewn with herbs, a custom dating from the time when it was necessary to do so to disguise the stench of the prison.

Planetarium
Marylebone Road, NW1

Spectacular representations of the heavens are projected on to the inside of the Planetarium's great copper dome and are accompanied by an instructive commentary.

Royal Albert Hall
Kensington, SW7

Queen Victoria laid the foundation stone of the building named after her beloved Prince Albert in 1867, and it was subsequently opened to the public in 1871. The huge circular wall is composed of red brick, adorned with terracotta and a mosaic frieze illustrating Triumphs of Art and Science, and is surmounted by a huge glass dome. The auditorium has a seating capacity of 5,600 and contains one of the world's largest organs, made by 'Father' Willis. Though the Albert Hall is particularly famous for the Sir Henry Wood Promenade Concerts, performed daily between mid July and mid September and entailing the services of some 15 orchestras, 30 conductors, and almost 200 soloists or singers, it is also the venue for concerts ranging from classical to pop throughout the year.

Royal Courts of Justice
Strand, WC2

Generally called the Law Courts, the Royal Courts of Justice were designed in the Gothic style by the distinguished Victorian architect G. E. Street and completed in 1882. The Courts are the central office of the Supreme Court of Jurisdiction for England and Wales, which was established in 1873.

Royal Hospital, Chelsea
Royal Hospital Road, Chelsea, SW3

The Royal Hospital, Chelsea, was founded in 1682 by Charles II for veteran and invalid soldiers. Sir Christopher Wren designed most of the buildings, and his work can be seen at its finest in the Figure Court and the chapel. Alterations and additions were subsequently made by Robert Adam and Sir John Soane. The Hospital now houses 500 army pensioners, who parade in their scarlet frock-coats on Oak Apple Day (29 May). The famous Chelsea Flower Show is held here every year.

Royal Parks

Of London's nine royal parks, five are set in the heart of the capital, and all of these have distinctive characters enhanced by their position in the centre of one of the world's busiest and most crowded cities.

With the towers and pinnacles of Westminster at its eastern end, and the dignified bulk of Buckingham Palace at the other, St James's is perhaps the best known and best loved of the central parks. Grassy areas dotted with clumps of trees and lovely flower beds surround a lake which is home to many kinds of water birds. Green Park, across the Mall from St James's, is principally a place of stately avenues of trees among grass that is enlivened by thousands of flowering bulbs in spring. Hyde Park is separated from Green Park only by the infamous road junction called Hyde Park Corner. Its most outstanding feature is the stretch of water called the Serpentine, but it gains its unique

character from its feeling of great space and freedom. Kensington Gardens are separated from Hyde Park by an even thinner strip of tarmac, but once more the change in character is marked. Kensington Park has a more enclosed and intimate feeling than Hyde Park, with which it shares the Serpentine, although here it is called the Long Water. Set away from the other four parks is Regent's, which, if Primrose Hill is included in its area, covers 870 acres. It was given its present appearance in the early 19th century by the great architect John Nash, who transformed it into a place whose elegant spaciousness echoes the Regency houses that surround it.

St James's Palace
St James's Street, SW1

The original palace was started by Henry VIII in 1531, and, after the destruction of Whitehall Palace, was the sovereign's official London residence. Foreign ambassadors are still appointed to the Court of St James's. The

Below left: Scene of many famous concerts, the Albert Hall was opened to the public in 1871
Below centre: Completed in 1882 on the site of some of London's worst slums, the Royal Courts of Justice stand at the point where the Strand merges with Fleet Street
Below right: Chelsea Pensioners on parade at the Royal Hospital, Chelsea. Their uniforms, dark blue in winter and scarlet in summer, have hardly changed in over 250 years. The three-cornered hats are worn only on special occasions
Right: St James's Park on a quiet autumn day. One of the best-loved of the royal parks, St James's was once the site of a colony for female lepers which Henry VIII dissolved to build St James's Palace

gatehouse facing St James's Street is the main remnant of the Tudor building, and has the initials of Henry VIII and Anne Boleyn carved over the doors. The Chapel Royal was originally built by Henry VIII but was much altered in 1837. However, the ceiling by Holbein is original. James II, Mary II, Queen Anne and George IV were all born here. George IV employed Nash to restore and redecorate the palace, but Queen Victoria moved the court to Buckingham Palace when she came to the throne. St James's Palace is now occupied by servants of the Crown, and is not open to the public. However, services may be attended in the Chapel Royal between October and Palm Sunday.

St Paul's Cathedral
St Paul's Churchyard, EC4
Other churches have unquestionably stood on the site which is now graced by this Wren masterpiece – although the actual number is uncertain. If it is assumed that it was King Ethelbert's foundation of AD604 that was burnt down in 1086, then a feasible number would be two with the present building as the third. The cathedral's predecessor is generally

known as Old St Paul's and was begun by Bishop Maurice in 1087. After a fire in 1561 the building fell into disrepair and its condition became something of a national scandal. Then, in 1666, the Great Fire of London dealt the last blow and caused irreparable damage to the building. Sir Christopher Wren had been instructed to examine the cathedral's state of decay, and the extent of damage sustained during the Civil War, just a few days before the fire. Instead he found himself demolishing the building with gunpowder and planning a new cathedral to form the heart of a devastated City. The foundation stone was laid in 1675 and the next 35 years were taken up with the

massive task of construction. Wren was buried in the cathedral's crypt in 1723.

The dome has a diameter of 112ft and the predominant material used in the construction of the cathedral is Portland stone. The overall height of the structure, from the ground to the top of the surmounting cross, is 365ft. Numerous monuments inside the building include a carving of the poet John Donne by Nicholas Stone – the only monument to have survived the Great Fire. There are tombs of famous soldiers, sailors, and artists in the crypt. A small charge is levied for entrance to the crypt, Whispering Gallery, Stone Gallery, and Golden Gallery; the last two afford superb views over London.

Science Museum
Exhibition Road, SW7
Housed in a handsome building that was completed in 1928 and added to in 1963, the collections which make up the Science Museum cover the applications of science to technology and the development of engineering and industry from their beginnings to the present day. It is also an Aladdin's cave of delights for children of all ages. There are working models of every description, a reconstruction of a coal mine, *Puffing Billy* – the world's first locomotive – and equipment which demonstrates the latest advances in physics. In the entrance hall is one of the most awe-inspiring exhibits, the Foucault Pendulum, whose gentle movement visibly demonstrates the rotation of the earth on its own axis.

Far left: After the Palace of Whitehall was destroyed by fire in 1698, St James's Palace became the official London residence of the monarch and remained so until Queen Victoria came to the throne
Left: Queen Mary's Garden, an enchanting glade within the huge expanse of Regent's Park
Below left: Designed in 1872, the Albert Memorial stands on the edge of Kensington Gardens, opposite the Albert Hall
Below centre: Exhibits in the Science Museum include the earliest steam locomotives and the Apollo 10 space capsule
Below: Sir James Thornhill painted the eight scenes from the life of St Paul which decorate the dome of St Paul's Cathedral

South Bank Complex
SE1

County Hall, at the south end of Westminster Bridge, was completed in 1932 and is the administrative headquarters of the Greater London Council. It was the first component of the projected South Bank scheme. When the scheme is completed there will be an uninterrupted riverside parade from Westminster Bridge to London Bridge. Also forming part of the complex, between Hungerford Railway Bridge and Waterloo Bridge, are the Festival Hall, the Queen Elizabeth Hall, the Purcell Room, the Hayward Gallery and the National Film Theatre. The National Theatre is east of Waterloo Bridge. Overlooking the whole South Bank area is the enormous Shell Centre, which has a 351ft tower and is one of the largest office blocks in Europe.

Southwark Cathedral
Borough High Street, SE1

A church has stood on this site since the 7th century, but it was not until 1905 that the basically 16th-century parish church of St Saviour was elevated to cathedral status. Despite rebuilding, particularly during the 19th century, its medieval Gothic style has remained largely intact, and parts of the church date back at least to the 13th century. Inside are many interesting memorials.

Street markets

London's street markets are a vital part of the capital's character. Many of them consist of little more than a few stalls on street corners, but some stretch for miles and are the haunts of some of London's most colourful characters. Vegetables, clothes and domestic goods are the

Far right: William the Conqueror built the White Tower, or keep, of the Tower of London. Sir Christopher Wren enlarged the windows and added the corner turrets
Right: A 15th-century boss in Southwark Cathedral.
Below right: Socks of every description on a stall in Petticoat Lane
Below centre: Tower Bridge
Below: Hundreds of antique stalls line the Portobello Road street market

items most often on sale, but there are some markets which specialize in furniture, antiques and the ubiquitous bric-à-brac. Portobello Road, in Notting Hill, is one of the most famous markets. It is at its most hectic on Saturdays, when over 2,000 stalls are open. Petticoat Lane, in the East End, operates on Sunday mornings and is as famous for its voluble stallholders as for the goods they sell. Camden Passage, in Islington, and the New Caledonian Market, in Bermondsey, are two of the specialist markets where high-quality antiques and *objets d'art* can be found.

Tate Gallery
Millbank, SW1

The Tate Gallery houses the national collection of British works from the 16th century to the beginning of the 20th. It also contains modern works by British artists born after 1850, together with foreign works from the Impressionists to the present day, and traces the development of art from Impressionism to post-war European and American art. The Tate is especially renowned for its modern works of art, some of which have aroused great controversy.

Temple
Crown Office Row, EC4

The Temple was originally the English headquarters of the Knights Templars. The order was dissolved in 1312, and the Temple eventually passed to the Knights Hospitallers of St John, who leased it to a number of lawyers. From this point on, the Inner and Middle Temples began to develop into Inns of Court. The oldest building in the complex is the Temple Church, which is one of only four round churches surviving in England.

Tower Bridge
EC3

This fairy-tale structure was built in 1894. All the original machinery for raising and lowering the bridge is still in place, though the steam engines were replaced by electric motors in 1975 as they had become uneconomic.

Tower of London
Tower Hill, EC3

Although universally known as the Tower, this famous complex of buildings is really a castle of the concentric type. Two fortified curtain walls mark the boundaries of the inner and

outer wards, and the entire structure is encircled by a deep moat.

White Tower is the central point of the castle and probably gave the structure its name. It was built in an angle of the old Roman wall by William the Conqueror, and the present curtain walls were erected between 1189 and 1306. It is thought that most of the work was by order of Henry III in the years after 1230.

Popular memory recognizes the Tower as a prison, but it has been much more in its long history. At various times it has served as a fortress, royal palace, arsenal, munitions factory, state prison, garrison, map-survey headquarters, mint, library, and treasury; but its tragic associations as a prison outweigh the past merit of its other functions.

Prisoners to be confined here ranged from upstarts eager to promote themselves from the lower echelons of the aristocracy, to heads of the Church and State. They usually entered the tower by the water-gate, and were conducted to their quarters to await ransom, execution, or interminable incarceration. Two traditional places of execution are Tower Hill and Tower Green, which is situated near the White Tower in the inner yard. Also in the inner yard is the Royal Chapel of St Peter ad Vincula, one of London's oldest churches.

Trafalgar Square
SW1

Pigeons outnumber people in this large and busy central square. They perch on heads and shoulders, and are fed, photographed, and fussed over. The square itself, dominated by Nelson's Column with its four lions designed by the Victorian painter Landseer, was laid out in memory of Nelson and completed in 1841, but the fountains were added in 1948. On the parapet nearest the National Gallery the Standard British Linear Measures are let into the stonework.

---

*Below: The Church of St Martin-in-the-Fields presides over Trafalgar Square with stately grace
Right: Banners in Westminster Abbey's Chapel of Henry VII*

Victoria and Albert Museum
Cromwell Road, SW7

This enormous museum, its galleries totalling nearly seven miles in length, houses the national collections of fine and applied arts. The exhibits range from outstanding masterpieces of painting, through superb examples of metalwork and textiles, to items whose function is simply to entertain and amuse. Specific exhibits include the enormous 16th-century Great Bed of Ware, a collection of furniture by Chippendale, and an unrivalled selection of works by John Constable.

Wallace Collection
Hertford House, Manchester Square, W1

This superb collection of works of art is housed in an elegant 18th-century town house. It is world-famous for its 18th-century paintings and furniture by French artists and craftsmen. Other paintings include *The Laughing Cavalier* by Frans Hals and works by Rubens, Holbein, and Titian.

Westminster Cathedral
Ashley Place, SW1

This imposing Byzantine-style Roman Catholic cathedral, built between 1895 and 1903, used to be completely hidden from view, but as the result of recent clearance it now stands at the back of a small piazza. Its nave is the widest in England and its bell-tower (at 284ft) is nearly 50ft higher than the west towers of Westminster Abbey. Cleaned of its grime, it is well worth a visit, not least for the view from the top of the bell-tower, which is reached by lift.

Westminster Abbey
Broad Sanctuary, SW1

The first church on this historic site was built by the last of the old English kings, Edward the Confessor. He died within ten days of consecrating the church, and the monks for whom he built it buried him within its walls.

Remains of the original building comprise the foundations and little else. Some 600 years of building, rebuilding, and alteration have completely altered the abbey's appearance. The general shape of the building is largely due to the first major rebuilding operation, which was initiated by Henry III in the 13th century. It was he who demolished the Confessor's original structure and gave the new abbey its Early English style. The king was unable to complete the work and building operations continued into the 14th century, conducted by Master of the King's Works Henry Yevele.

All but two English monarchs have been crowned here since the reign of Edward II, and the Coronation Chair of English oak has been used for this purpose since that time. One of the most magnificent chapels is that of Henry VII, the Chapel of the Order of Bath. It was built between 1503 and about 1512, has been used as a royal burial place, and displays some of the finest work to have survived from this period of English history. It is particularly noted for its fan-vaulting and its royal tombs include those of Elizabeth I and Mary Queen of Scots. Edward the Confessor's Chapel and the Sanctuary lie within the confines of the Ambulatory, which is surrounded by many fine chapels containing the remains of famous members of the nobility and church.

Outer London

BRENTFORD, Gt London　　*40 TQ17*

This ancient market town was once the capital of Middlesex, and is now part of Greater London. The Grand Union Canal joins the Thames here, and it is thought that Julius Caesar crossed the river by means of the ford that forms part of the town's name. Caesar's stone marks the place where the crossing was supposedly effected, and Roman remains have been found during recent excavations.

A fascinating piano museum is housed in a disused church in the High Street. Syon House, near the river and opposite Kew Gardens, was remodelled by Robert Adam in the 18th century. The interior displays what is perhaps the finest decorative scheme of his busy and highly successful career. The Gardening Centre was created in the grounds of the house in 1968. Also here is a comprehensive exhibition of London Transport buses and trams, which was transferred from a former museum in Clapham.

Boston Manor is an interesting three-storey house in a small park, built in 1622. To the west is Osterley Park, a fine mansion originally built in 1576, altered in 1711, and magnificently decorated by Robert Adam in 1763 and 1767. In Gunnersbury Park (between Acton and Brentford) is an early 19th-century house which now serves as a museum.

CHISWICK, Gt London　　*40 TQ27*

Situated by the Thames, this was a fashionable residential area in the 17th and 18th centuries. Chiswick Mall, opposite Chiswick Eyot, is a riverside street where numerous delightful houses include Kelmscott – the place where pre-Raphaelite artist and author William Morris lived and died.

DULWICH, Gt London　　*40 TQ37*

Dulwich Village contains many of the Georgian houses that dignify this residential suburb, and Dulwich College Art Gallery was the first public art gallery to be opened in London.

ELTHAM, Gt London　　*40 TQ47*

The Great Hall of Eltham Palace preserves a magnificent restored 15th-century oak roof, and a fine stone bridge spans the moat. The picturesque buildings of Well Hall, also moated, are the remnants of an Elizabethan manor house of 1568.

GREENWICH, Gt London　　*40 TQ47*

British sea-power and the historic town of Greenwich are inseparable. The *Cutty Sark*, a famous old clipper that shipped tea from China in the 19th century, is in dry dock near the pier, and *Gipsy Moth IV,* sailed round the world by Sir Francis Chichester, is nearby.

The Old Royal Observatory is part of the National Maritime Museum, and stands in Greenwich Park. The latter was laid out by Lenôtre, the famous French gardener. Current observatory work is now conducted at Herstmonceux Castle in Sussex, but interesting astronomical and navigational exhibits can still be seen in the Greenwich section.

The Royal Naval College has variously served as Greenwich Hospital and a palace for royalty. A Tudor building that once stood here was the birthplace of Henry VIII and his two daughters, Elizabeth and Mary. The existing complex was designed by Sir Christopher Wren, and added to by such famous architects as John Webb, Hawksmoor, Vanbrugh and Ripley. The chapel was rebuilt in the late 18th century, and the famous Painted Hall has a ceiling by Sir James Thornhill. The National Maritime Museum is in Queen's House, by Inigo Jones, and contains an exceptionally interesting collection of paintings and models concerning British seafaring. Buildings in Greenwich town include the forbidding pile of the Church of St Alfege, built by Nicholas Hawksmoor in the early 18th century and, in Crooms Hill, a delightful array of domestic architecture from many periods.

HAM HOUSE, Gt London　　*40 TQ17*

Sir James Vavasour, a courtier of James I, built this superb riverside mansion in 1610. In 1672 it came by marriage to the Duke of Lauderdale, who lavished such attentions on it that its name became a by-word for luxurious living and equally luxurious spending. He commissioned artists and craftsmen from Germany, Holland and Italy to decorate and furnish its many rooms and galleries. The poet William Cowper lived in the house for some time during the 18th century. It was presented to the National Trust in 1948, and now houses many treasures from the Victoria and Albert Museum.

HAMPSTEAD, Gt London　　*40 TQ28*

Beautiful old houses and the vast expanse of Hampstead Heath combine to make this north-west suburb of London an extremely pleasant area. It was a popular spa resort in the 18th century, and its old buildings are interesting on two counts – because of their historical associations, and their connections with famous people.

Keats House was the poet's home and is a Regency building that was built the year after the Battle of Waterloo. Manuscripts and relics are on show, and Keats wrote 'Ode to a Nightingale' in the garden. Fenton House is probably the oldest in Hampstead, and dates from about 1693. It is a beautiful brick-built structure with a lovely walled garden and wrought-iron gates, and is situated in Hampstead Grove. It contains pottery, porcelain and furniture.

Many enchanting little streets run through Hampstead, but probably the most attractive is Church Row, leading from Heath Street to the 18th-century Parish Church of St John. John Constable, the famous painter, lived in Hampstead for many years and is buried here.

Hampstead Heath affords views over London and with the surrounding open space makes up a delightful 790-acre area of unspoiled, semi-wild heathland.

Left: The Royal Naval College, Greenwich
Below: The garden front of Ham House

HAMPTON COURT PALACE, Gt London 40 TQ16

No description will prepare the first-time visitor for the magnificence and sheer size of Hampton Court Palace. Built of red brick, it is nearly 700ft long by 400ft wide and contains over 1,000 rooms. Cardinal Wolsey began the palace in 1514 during a phenomenal rise to power which had begun when he was made Chaplain to Henry VII. After Henry VIII had come to the throne, Wolsey's ascent became meteoric and he decided to build for himself a home that was to be the finest private dwelling in the kingdom. By this time the Cardinal's vast wealth was attracting suspicion and jealousy, and in 1529 he attempted to regain Henry's favour by presenting the palace and its contents to the King as a gift. Henry, however, had made up his mind, and the following year Wolsey was imprisoned for high treason.

Hampton Court became Henry's favourite palace and he spent large sums of money improving and enlarging it. Subsequent monarchs used the palace regularly, but no extensive changes were made to the fabric of the building until the reign of William and Mary. They did not like the palace at Whitehall and commissioned Sir Christopher Wren to rebuild Hampton Court, which they intended to be their equivalent of the great French palace at Versailles. The plans to rebuild the palace completely never came to fruition. The western part of Wolsey's original palace was left virtually untouched, and Wren's work consisted of adapting and rebuilding the eastern part of the building. In 1838 Queen Victoria opened the State Apartments to the public. The palace contains an enormous collection of treasures, ranging from domestic utensils to great works of art by such masters as Mantegna and Verrio. Complementing the palace's superb architecture are the grounds which surround it.

Below: Heraldic beasts guard the entrance to Hampton Court Palace
Centre: Sir William Chambers designed the Chinese pagoda in Kew Gardens as a decorative focal point
Right: Deer in Richmond Park

HARROW, Gt London 40 TQ18

Harrow-on-the-Hill stands high above the surrounding plain, and its restored 11th-century church with a prominent 13th-century spire can be seen for miles. The famous public school was founded in 1571 by John Lyon, a yeoman of the parish, and granted a charter by Elizabeth I. Former pupils of Harrow School include Sir Robert Peel, Lord Byron, and Sir Winston Churchill.

KEW GARDENS, Gt London 40 TQ17

This famous institution's facilities for research are unrivalled, but it is not as a purely scientific establishment that Kew is known. The great beauty and strangeness of its charges are part of London legend, and its earthen beds have been laid out to be pleasing to the eye.

The first nine acres of gardens were laid out by George III's mother, Princess Augusta, some 200 years ago, and they really began to flourish during the reign of her son. Their present-day success is largely due to the eminent 19th-century botanist Sir Joseph Banks, a close friend of the king, who worked with head gardener William Aiton to lay the basis for the superb collection that now exists. Royal patronage continued, even after the gardens came into public ownership in 1841. Today's visitors can be thankful for this as they enjoy the conserved wildness of the Queen's Cottage and grounds – a gift from Queen Victoria.

The largest living collection in the gardens is the Arboretum, where many species of trees and shrubs grow harmoniously. The Tropical and Palm Houses protect rare and exotic species from all over the world, while the magnificent flower borders of the herbaceous section are a constant delight. Great cushions of alpines grow amongst sandstone outcrops and beside the stream of the Rock Garden, and the woodland garden around The Mound is a quiet green retreat.

RICHMOND PARK, Gt London 40 TQ27

The herds of red and fallow deer that roam this huge royal park are a reminder that it was originally part of a hunting estate enclosed by Charles I. Most of the park retains its feeling of wild countryside, but several gardens, notably the Isabella Plantation and the grounds of Pembroke Lodge, have been laid out.

RICHMOND UPON THAMES, Gt London 40 TQ17

Standing as it does between two large areas of parkland and being set on an exceptionally attractive reach of the Thames, Richmond has one of the best positions of any of London's towns. It makes good use of this setting, for it has a multitude of beautiful buildings, many of which were built in the 18th century when Richmond was a fashionable resort. All that now remains of the Royal palace that once stood here is a Tudor gateway situated on Richmond Green, a beautiful area surrounded by superb 17th- and 18th-century buildings.

TWICKENHAM, Gt London 40 TQ17

The Parish Church of St Mary dates from 1713 to 1714 and was designed by John James. Interesting monuments and the grave of Alexander Pope are among its main features. Attractive Georgian houses stand in Syon Row and Montpelier Row. At the end of the latter is South End House, where the poet Walter de la Mare died in 1956.

All Hallows Church of 1940 incorporates an original Wren tower, which was moved from the City and re-erected on this site. Splendid woodcarving from the demolished City church of 1694 can also be seen here, including the organ of 1708 and a splendid Royal Arms board. Strawberry Hill is a well-known Gothic-revival house, associated with Horace Walpole, which was completed in 1776. Fine houses in the area include 18th-century Marble Hill, and largely 17th-century York House. The latter is now the town hall. Twickenham is a mecca for Rugby Union supporters. It is here that all the great international fixtures take place, on a pitch purchased in 1907.

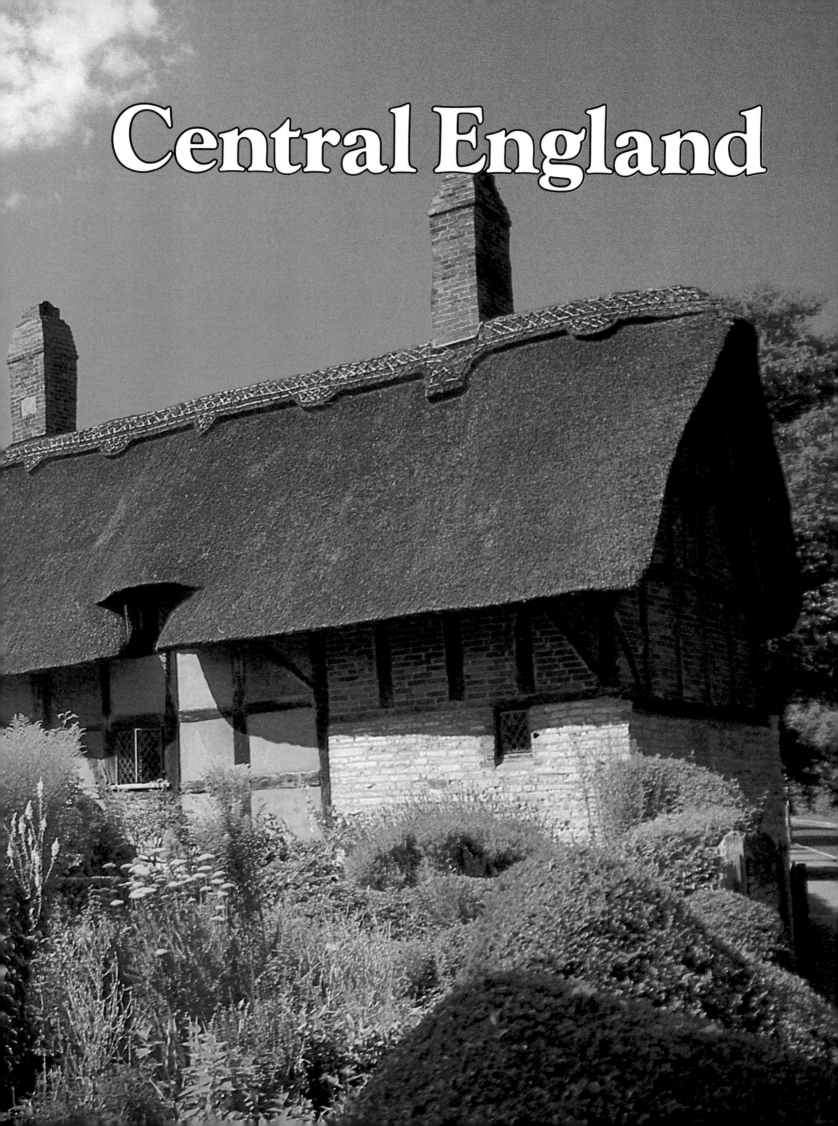

Central England

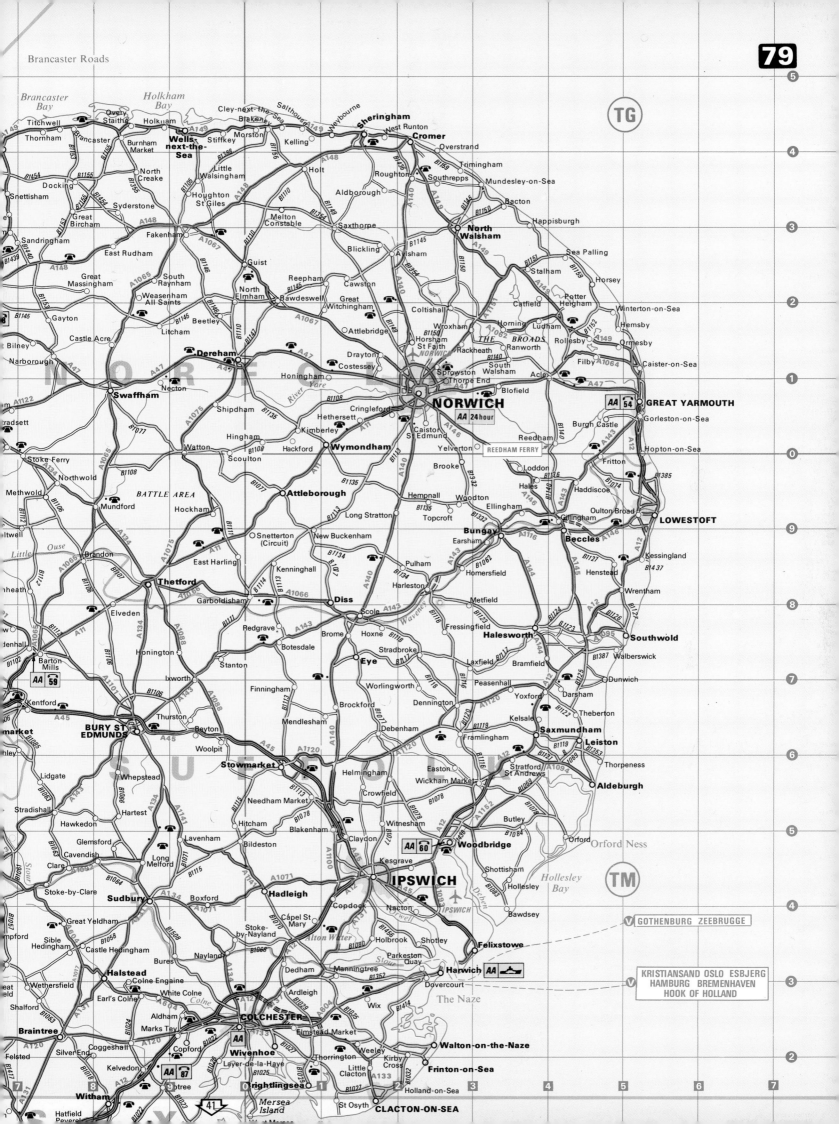

The North Cotswolds
65 miles

MORETON-IN-MARSH

The Roman Fosse Way forms the main street of this pleasant little town, and coaching inns such as the Redesdale Arms and the White Hart recall the importance of this ancient route in a later age.

The handsome Redesdale Market Hall, topped by a Cotswold stone roof and a tall chimney, dates from 1887. Opposite is the 17th-century curfew tower, complete with its original clock and bell.

CHASTLETON

Chastleton House was built by wealthy wool-merchant Walter Jones in 1603. On the top floor are state rooms and a long gallery, which contain many items of original furniture.

ROLLRIGHT STONES

This important Bronze Age monument comprises two configurations of stones. The circle, nicknamed the King's Men, measures 100ft across and is close to the Whispering Knights group and an isolated outlier called the King's Stone.

LONG COMPTON

A little thatched gatehouse tops the churchyard gate at Long Compton. The church itself is of Norman and later date and preserves an old stone figure of a lady in the porch.

SHIPSTON-ON-STOUR

This small country town in the fertile Stour valley was once one of England's most important markets for sheep. Many of the imposing Georgian houses here were built for prosperous wool-merchants, and these are complemented by a number of handsome coaching inns – a legacy from the early days of long-distance stage-coach traffic. An important trunk road – the A34 – still passes through the town. The 19th-century church incorporates the 500-year-old tower of its predecessor.

EBRINGTON

Delightful stone and thatched cottages complement a church with a fine Norman doorway in this lovely Cotswold village.

The Rollright Stones have weathered 4,000 years on an isolated Cotswold hilltop

HIDCOTE BARTRIM

The tiny picture-book hamlet of Hidcote Bartrim boasts a late 17th-century manor surrounded by lovely formal gardens. A number of separate gardens, each with a different theme or colour scheme, are divided by a wide variety of hedges.

MICKLETON

Medford House (not open) is a superb example of Renaissance architecture, and the village itself preserves thatched and timber-framed buildings. The church dates from the 12th century.

LONG MARSTON

King's Lodge in Long Marston has associations with King Charles II, who is said to have come here in disguise after the Battle of Worcester. The bell in the village church hangs in a turret built on great oak beams resting on the floor of the nave.

WELFORD-ON-AVON

Welford-on-Avon's Norman church has an ancient lychgate and stands among charming timber-and-thatch cottages. A maypole stands on the village green.

BIDFORD-ON-AVON

A narrow 15th-century bridge that retains some of its original cutwaters spans the Avon in this peaceful little town. Several houses, including the Old Falcon, are built of layers of blue lias and golden oolite stone, giving a subtle striped effect. At the centre of the town is an attractive square.

CLEEVE PRIOR

This pretty village is named after the priors of Worcester, once lords of the manor here. The tall-chimneyed Jacobean manor house is surrounded by neatly topiaried hedges, and attractive cottages overlook the triangular green.

BRETFORTON

Buildings of particular note here are the 600-year-old Fleece Inn and medieval Grange Farm. The latter, changed greatly from its original form by successive owners, gave shelter to Prince Rupert in 1645. The village possesses several dovecots, some of them very old.

BROADWAY

One of the much-photographed 'show' villages of the Cotswolds, Broadway has a handsome grass-verged main street and a host of lovely old houses built of Cotswold stone. Several of them are now antique shops.

SNOWSHILL

Tucked into a beautiful combe at the edge of the Cotswolds, Snowshill is known for its Tudor manor house, where a fascinating collection of items as diverse as musical instruments, toys and Japanese armour is on display.

BROADWAY TOWER

Lady Coventry built this picturesque folly tower in the 18th century, and it now forms the nucleus of a country park. Its lofty situation at over 1,000ft gives views over several counties.

CHIPPING CAMPDEN

This lovely village is dominated by the Perpendicular tower of its fine church, built by wool-merchants such as William Grevel, whose house in the main street is another of Chipping Campden's treasures. It has a rare two-storeyed carved bay window dating from the late 14th century. Almost opposite is the old Woolstaplers' Hall, which houses a small museum. Further down the street is the Jacobean market hall, now preserved by the National Trust. The Campden Car Collection consists of 22 sports and racing cars.

BOURTON-ON-THE-HILL

A fine example of a Winchester bushel can be seen in Bourton's Norman and later church. The village stands on a hill and is made up of cottages standing in attractively terraced gardens. Bourton House has a superb 16th-century tithe barn.

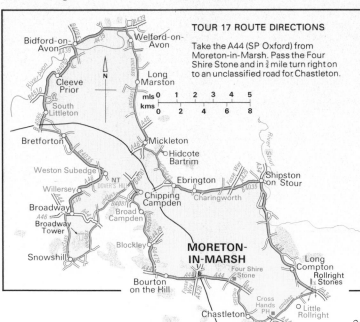

TOUR 17 ROUTE DIRECTIONS

Take the A44 (SP Oxford) from Moreton-in-Marsh. Pass the Four Shire Stone and in ¾ mile turn right on to an unclassified road for Chastleton.

Go through Chastleton and in ½ mile turn left, then cross a cattle grid and turn right on to the A44. Beyond the Cross Hands inn turn left and continue to the Rollright Stones. In ¾ mile turn left on to the A34 and drive through Long Compton to Shipston-on-Stour. Turn left on to the B4035 (SP Campden). In 1¾ miles cross a main road and continue for 1 mile, then go forward on to an unclassified road to Ebrington. At the end of this village keep right, then right again (SP The Hidcotes). In 2¼ miles turn right for Hidcote Bartrim. Return to the T-junction and turn left, then right (SP Mickleton). Meet the main road and turn right on to the A46 into Mickleton. Turn left at the end of the village and in ½ mile continue on an unclassified road through Long Marston and Welford-on-Avon. Keep forward, later cross the River Avon then turn left on to the A439 and drive to Bidford-on-Avon. Turn left on to the A4085 (SP Broadway), cross a bridge and in ½ mile turn right for Cleeve Prior. Continue through South

Littleton and in 1 mile go over a level crossing and turn left for Bretforton. Here join the B4035 and continue to Weston Subedge. Turn right on to the A46 and go through Willersey, then turn right at a T-junction on to the A44 for Broadway. Drive to the end of the green in Broadway and turn left on to an unclassified road for Snowshill, climbing then bearing right into the village. Turn left by the church and at the crossroads at the top of the hill keep forward (SP Chipping Campden, Broadway Tower). In 1¾ miles turn left, go past Broadway Tower and in ½ mile cross a main road (SP Mickleton) then in ¾ mile turn right. In 2½ miles, at a T-junction, turn right on to the B4081 for Chipping Campden. Turn left here on to the B4081 (SP Broad Campden) and in ¼ mile turn left to Broad Campden. Keep right in the village, continue to Blockley and turn left then right on to the B4479. In 1½ miles, at a T-junction, turn left on to the A44. Go through Bourton-on-the-Hill and return to Moreton-in-Marsh.

Ludlow and Wyre Forest
76 miles

KIDDERMINSTER
Carpets have been woven in this busy town for well over 200 years. Kidderminster is also the birthplace of Sir Rowland Hill, whose statue stands in the town centre. The father of the British postal system, he introduced the 'penny post' in 1837 and later became the first Secretary to the Post Office.

WEST MIDLAND SAFARI AND LEISURE PARK
Giraffes, elephants and many other exotic beasts can be seen in this 200-acre wildlife park. Other attractions include a pets' corner, a 'boat safari', bird gardens and a dolphinarium.

BEWDLEY
The River Severn here is spanned by Thomas Telford's handsome balustraded bridge, built in the 1790s. Bewdley is the southern terminus of the Severn Valley Railway, perhaps the best-known standard-gauge steam railway in the country. The town itself shows architecture of many periods and styles, including a 16th-century gabled building that is now the post office, and an 18th-century market hall. Behind the latter is the Shambles – the old butchers' market. It is now occupied by a small but excellent folk museum.

STOURPORT-ON-SEVERN
After the opening of the Staffordshire and Worcestershire Canal, built by the engineer James Brindley in 1766, Stourport became a major canal port. It has survived to the present day as the only example of a purpose-built canal town in England.

GREAT WITLEY
This village is the setting for one of the finest rococo churches in England. It stands in the sadly neglected grounds of ruined Witley Court, a 17th-century mansion that was burnt down in 1937. The interior of the 18th-century church is rich in colour and pattern, from painted ceiling panels and windows to elegant gold and white plasterwork.

TENBURY WELLS
This pretty little market town was briefly turned into a spa in the mid 19th century, when mineral springs were discovered here. The pump room and baths, though long disused, can still be seen. The parish church, largely rebuilt in 1865, contains an unusual crusader's tomb with a tiny effigy holding its heart in its hands.

LUDLOW
One of the loveliest towns in England, Ludlow grew up around its 11th-century castle, an important stronghold in the troubled Welsh border country. It stands high above the River Teme, and its efficiency as a defence post and lookout is confirmed by the far-reaching views from the top of the sturdy Norman keep. Within the castle bailey stand the ruins of one of very few surviving Norman round chapels, and visitors can see both the great hall, where Milton's masque *Comus* was first performed, and the apartments where the 'Princes in the Tower' stayed before setting out on their final journey.

The range of handsome architecture in Ludlow's Broad Street has led to justifiable claims that it is the most attractive street in Britain

TOUR 18 ROUTE DIRECTIONS

From Kidderminster take the A456 (SP Leominster) and pass the West Midland Safari Park before crossing the Severn by Telford's bridge into Bewdley. Leave by the B4194 (SP Ribbesford) and drive along the west bank of the Severn. In 2¾ miles, at a crossroads, turn left on to the A451 into Stourport-on-Severn. Return to the crossroads and continue on the A451 to Great Witley. Drive to the end of the village and turn right on to the A443. In 1 mile branch right on to the B4202 (SP Cleobury Mortimer). Skirt the village of Abberley and at Clows Top crossroads turn left on to the A456 (SP Leominster). Go through Mamble and Newnham Bridge and continue along the Teme valley to the edge of Tenbury Wells, then turn right on to the B4214 (SP Cleehill). At Cleehill turn left on to the A4117 and descend into Ludlow.

From Ludlow return along the A4117 Kidderminster road and turn left immediately beyond a railway bridge into Fishmore Road. Cross the new by-pass and in 1¾ miles bear right, then follow signs to Clee St Margaret. Here, cross a ford and turn left (SP Abdon). At Abdon turn right (SP Ditton Priors) and in 1¾ miles bear right (SP Cleobury North). Skirt the north side of Brown Clee Hill and in 1½ miles turn left and descend to a T-junction. Turn right and in ½ mile turn left on to the B4364 (SP Bridgnorth). Go through Cleobury North and continue on the B4364 to Bridgnorth, turning right on to the A458 to enter the town.

Leave Bridgnorth by the B4363 (SP Cleobury Mortimer). At Kinlet turn left on to the B4363 (SP Bewdley) then at a T-junction turn left on to the B4194. Go through Wyre Forest to Bewdley and turn left on to the A456 to return to Kidderminster.

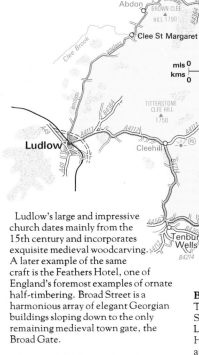

Ludlow's large and impressive church dates mainly from the 15th century and incorporates exquisite medieval woodcarving. A later example of the same craft is the Feathers Hotel, one of England's foremost examples of ornate half-timbering. Broad Street is a harmonious array of elegant Georgian buildings sloping down to the only remaining medieval town gate, the Broad Gate.

CLEE ST MARGARET
Remotely set in the Clee Hills by the Clee Brook, this little village is built mainly of stone and is centred on a church with a Norman nave.

CLEOBURY NORTH
Wooded Burwarton Park adds much to the charm of this village, which boasts a large and picturesque Norman church that was carefully restored by architect Sir Gilbert Scott in the 19th century.

BRIDGNORTH
This delightful town on the River Severn is sharply divided into two parts: Low Town sits beside the river, while High Town is perched above. The two are connected by steps, a winding lane and the steepest funicular railway in England – the brainchild of a local 19th-century businessman. High Town is the oldest part of Bridgnorth, and here stands all that is left of the Norman castle – a fragment of the keep, leaning at a perilous angle of 17 degrees. Beside it is the Church of St Mary Magdalene, a dignified neo-classical structure designed by Thomas Telford. St Leonard's Church is surrounded by a little close of charming old houses. Other striking buildings in the town include the 17th-century town hall, perched on an open arcade, and the fine 16th-century black-and-white Bishop Percy's House. The Hermitage is one of several local caves inhabited until fairly recent times.

SEVERN VALLEY RAILWAY
This famous standard-gauge line runs through 12½ miles of lovely scenery along the Severn valley between Bridgnorth and Bewdley. The railway has one of the largest collections of locomotives and rolling stock in the country. Trains run every weekend and some weekdays during the summer season.

The Shropshire Hills

73 miles

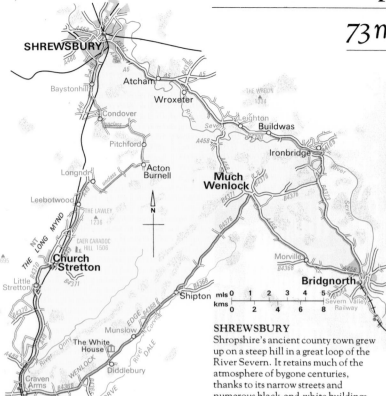

The Severn at Ironbridge is spanned by the world's first iron bridge, built by Abraham Darby III to advertise his ironworks at nearby Coalbrookdale

Much Wenlock's sign echoes Wenlock Priory's Norman tracery

TOUR 19 ROUTE DIRECTIONS

Leave Shrewsbury by the A49 (SP Leominster) and ½ mile beyond Baystonhill turn left on to an unclassified road to reach Condover. Turn left here (SP Pitchford) and in ½ mile bear left. In 1½ miles turn right into Pitchford and continue to Acton Burnell. Turn right (SP Church Stretton), and in 2 miles bear right. Go through Longnor and turn left on to the A49. Turn right on to the B4371 into Church Stretton town centre, and at a crossroads turn left on to the B4370. Go through Little Stretton, turn right on to the A49 and drive to Craven Arms. (Here a detour can be made to Stokesay Castle by continuing on the A49.)

Leave Craven Arms by the B4368 (SP Bridgnorth). Go through Diddlebury, pass the White House at Aston Munslow and continue to Shipton. Bear left here on to the B4378 (SP Much Wenlock) and drive to Much Wenlock. Leave by the A458 Bridgnorth road and drive through Morville to Bridgnorth. Leave by the B4373 and in 5½ miles bear right (SP Wellington). Go down into the Severn Gorge, cross the river and turn left on to the A4169 into Ironbridge. Keep forward beyond Ironbridge on the B4380 (SP Shrewsbury). Go through Buildwas and Leighton to the edge of Wroxeter, then continue on the B4380 for ¾ mile and turn left on to the A5. Go through Atcham, cross the Severn and return to Shrewsbury.

SHREWSBURY

Shropshire's ancient county town grew up on a steep hill in a great loop of the River Severn. It retains much of the atmosphere of bygone centuries, thanks to its narrow streets and numerous black-and-white buildings. A castle was built here by the Normans, though the oldest parts of the present castle – restored by Telford some 200 years ago – date from the 13th century. St Mary's Church, built around 1200, is one of the town's oldest buildings, closely followed by the 14th-century Bear Steps cottages. In the town are statues of two of Shrewsbury's most famous citizens – Charles Darwin, born here in 1809, and Robert Clive, who was mayor of Shrewsbury in 1762. Clive House, his home, is open to the public and contains a collection of china, costumes and military mementoes.

ACTON BURNELL

Edward I held what is said to have been the first English parliament here in 1283. Ruined Acton Burnell Castle dates from the 13th century and was built by Robert Burnell, Bishop of Bath and Wells, partly as a castle and partly as a palace.

THE LONG MYND

This heather-covered mass of ancient grits and shales is largely owned and protected by the National Trust. Where the moorland hills fall towards Church Stretton they are scored by numerous ravines; the lovely Cardingmill valley is especially beautiful.

CHURCH STRETTON

During the late 19th century the district around Church Stretton became known as 'Little Switzerland', and the town itself developed into a popular inland resort. Red-brick and half-timbered Victorian villas mingle with older black-and-white buildings to create a pleasant character complemented by the Church of St Lawrence. Above the Norman north doorway is a Celtic fertility symbol.

STOKESAY CASTLE

Wooden beams, overhanging walls, steep roofs and decorated woodwork make Stokesay a picture-book castle where the imaginative visitor can easily slip into a world of gothic fantasy populated by knights and dragons. Dating from 1280, the castle is really a fortified manor house which owes its superb condition to a singularly uneventful history. Beyond the moat is a church that was damaged during the Civil War and subsequently refurbished during the Commonwealth. Interior furnishings and fittings of that time remain intact.

THE WHITE HOUSE

Many periods are represented in the complex of buildings associated with this mansion, and the house itself has a 14th-century hall and 16th-century cross-wing. A fascinating museum of country life here displays a variety of farm relics.

SHIPTON

Beautiful Shipton Hall is the focal point of this Corve Dale village. Built around 1587 and enlarged during the mid 18th century, it comprises a large range of buildings including a fine stable block which dates from the 18th century.

MUCH WENLOCK

This lovely little town near the great chalk escarpment of Wenlock Edge preserves many fine old buildings including a Norman church and a Tudor guildhall. Wenlock Priory was founded by St Milburga in the 7th century. Nothing remains of the earliest buildings; the beautiful ruins that stand here today date from Norman times, and feature some exquisite carving.

BRIDGNORTH

This unique riverside town is full of interesting buildings from every period of its long history, including a fragment of a Norman castle, two churches and many attractive old cottages and inns. The town also figured importantly in early railway history. The first railway locomotive was built here for Trevithick in 1804, and Bridgnorth station is now, fittingly, the terminus of the Severn Valley Railway, a preserved steam-operated line.

IRONBRIDGE

This little town takes its name from one of Britain's foremost industrial monuments. Completed in 1781, the first iron bridge in the world was built across the Severn Gorge here by Abraham Darby. It was his grandfather's pioneering work in the iron industry that earned this area the distinction of being the cradle of the Industrial Revolution. Much of the industrial heritage of Ironbridge and nearby Coalbrookdale is preserved by the Ironbridge Gorge Museum Trust.

BUILDWAS

Concrete cooling towers looming from Buildwas power station make a controversial counterpoint to the 12th-century remains of Buildwas Abbey, near the River Severn. Stone from the ruin was incorporated in the local church.

WROXETER

During Roman times the important town of *Uriconium* stood here. Excavated remains include the baths and fragments of other buildings. The nearby church incorporates Roman bricks and masonry. Inside are several very fine monuments and memorials.

ATCHAM

Spacious wooded parklands and two fine 18th-century bridges are the main features of this pretty village, which also has a church uniquely dedicated to St Eata. The Mytton and Mermaid Inn is of Georgian origin. Humphry Repton laid out the grounds of nearby Attingham Hall.

Cambridge and the Fenlands
79 miles

TOUR 20 ROUTE DIRECTIONS

Leave Cambridge on the A1303 (SP Bedford). In 2½ miles pass Madingley Post-mill and then the American Cemetery, then turn right on to an unclassified road and go through Madingley. Turn left on to the A604 and in 4 miles branch left on to an unclassified road to go through Swavesey and Over to Willingham. Turn left on to the B1050 and later left again on to the A1123 into Earith. Continue through Needingworth and in 1½ miles turn left on to the A1096 into St Ives.

Follow the A1096 southwards, cross the river and in ¼ mile turn right on to an unclassified road and continue to Hemingford Grey. Turn left and right, drive to Hemingford Abbots and follow signs for Huntingdon to join the A604. In 1 mile branch left, then turn right at a roundabout on to an unclassified road to reach Godmanchester. Turn right on to the B1043 and cross the river by a 14th-century bridge to enter Huntingdon.

Leave Huntingdon on the A141 (SP Kettering), pass Hinchingbrooke House and continue on the A141 through Brampton. Follow signs for London and in 2 miles join the A1 for the outskirts of Buckden. At a roundabout on the A1 take the B661 (SP Kimbolton). Pass Grafham Water and continue on the B661 to Great Staughton, then turn left on to the A45. Continue for 4 miles, crossing the A1, then cross the River Ouse into St Neots.

Leave the town by turning right on to the B1043. In 4 miles join the A1, and in another 3 miles turn left on to the B1042. Continue through Sandy, then at Potton take the B1040 (SP St Ives). Follow this road through Gamlingay to Waresley, then keep forward on to an unclassified road for Great Gransden. Turn right then shortly left into the village. Follow signs to Caxton and turn right then left (SP Bourn). Pass Bourn Post-mill and in 1 mile turn right at a T-junction to drive through Bourn, then join the B1046. Continue through Toft and Comberton to reach Barton, then turn left on to the A603. Drive for 1 mile, then turn right on to an unclassified road (SP Trumpington) and continue through Grantchester, then cross the River Cam and drive to Trumpington. Here join the A1309 and return to Cambridge.

The medieval bridge chapel at St Ives is one of only four in the country

CAMBRIDGE

Peaceful riverside walks, revered museums such as the Fitzwilliam, and lovely old streets all contribute to the magic of Cambridge, but it is the college buildings which dominate the ancient heart of the city. The oldest ones, predating Peterhouse, the first college (founded in 1284) belong to Clare College, part of which occupied the buildings of a 12th-century nunnery. King's College is known for its chapel, a medieval masterpiece that was built long before the rest of the college. Trinity, established in 1546 by Henry VIII and now the largest college, has a library designed by Sir Christopher Wren. Its chapel contains memorials to famous past students including Isaac Newton and Lord Tennyson.

AMERICAN CEMETERY AND CHAPEL

The War Memorial Chapel here is a striking example of modern architecture. Inside is a 540-square-foot map showing Atlantic sea and air routes used by American forces during the Second World War.

WILLINGHAM

Two windmills and the impressive tower of Willingham's 14th-century church are prominent landmarks in the flat farmlands that surround this village. The church nave has a notable 15th-century hammerbeam roof adorned with over 50 carved angels.

ST IVES

A well-known nursery-rhyme recalls the days when people travelled many miles to the important annual fair here, first held in 1110. The history of the town and the Fens around it is illustrated in the Norris Museum. The River Ouse here is spanned by a 15th-century bridge that incorporates one of only four medieval bridge chapels in England.

HEMINGFORD GREY

A moated mansion here dates from the 12th century and is one of the oldest inhabited dwellings in England. The 12th-century church is sited in a bend of the River Ouse.

GODMANCHESTER

The site of this ancient town was once occupied by a Roman military station. Nowadays it is a treasure-house of varied architectural styles, from the homeliness of old timber and thatch to the clean lines of Georgian façades.

HUNTINGDON

A restored Norman building in this historic town was the school where Oliver Cromwell and Samuel Pepys were taught. It is now the Cromwell Museum. The Falcon Inn is thought to have been Cromwell's headquarters during the Civil War.

HINCHINGBROOKE HOUSE

Now restored and in use as a school, this Tudor and later mansion has been home to the Cromwells and the earls of Sandwich.

BUCKDEN

Considerable remains of Buckden Palace, a former residence of the bishops of Lincoln, comprise a fine Tudor tower and an inner gatehouse of about 1490. The church is known for its notable spire and carvings.

ST NEOTS

This ancient market town grew up around a Benedictine priory founded in the 10th century. The large medieval church is of interest, and several 17th-century inns can be seen in the nest of old streets around the market place.

SANDY

Sandy Lodge, a Victorian Tudor building on the outskirts of this small town, is the headquarters of the Royal Society for the Protection of Birds. It stands on a 100-acre reserve which offers a planned nature trail.

BOURN POST-MILL

Although the working parts of this remarkable windmill have been replaced from time to time, the base and outer structure date back to 1636.

GRANTCHESTER

Rupert Brooke immortalized this beautiful village of thatched and lime-washed cottages in his poem 'The Old Vicarage, Grantchester'. He lived here for a while after leaving King's College.

TRUMPINGTON

Inside the elaborate local church is England's second oldest memorial brass. It is dated 1289 and was raised to Sir Roger de Trumpington. Other features of the village include a 16th-century inn and two 18th-century halls.

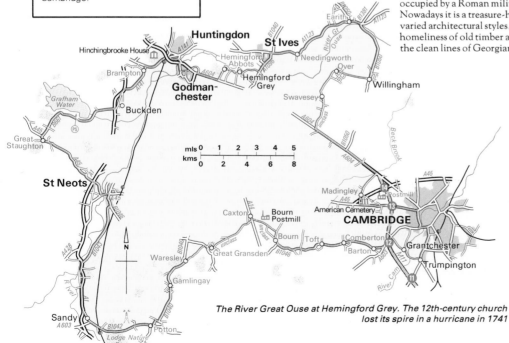

mls 0 1 2 3 4 5
kms 0 2 4 6 8

The River Great Ouse at Hemingford Grey. The 12th-century church lost its spire in a hurricane in 1741

SuffolkVillages
70 miles

HADLEIGH
This former wool town on the River Brett has seen considerable industrial development in the present century, but the town centre retains many fine old buildings including a medieval church. Half-timbered buildings include the splendid 15th-century Guildhall, whose ground floor was once an almshouse. Nearby is the Deanery Tower, which survives from a 15th-century Archdeacon's palace that stood here.

KERSEY
One of East Anglia's prettiest villages, Kersey's main street is lined with beautifully preserved houses and dips steeply down to a picturesque ford. A hilltop overlooking the village is a fitting site for the magnificent 15th-century church.

BOXFORD
This quaint old village takes its name from an attractive stream that runs close to its timber-framed cottages. The church features an unusual wooden porch that may well be the earliest of its kind in the country, and contains an unusual 17th-century font with doors.

SUDBURY
One of the great masters of English landscape- and portrait-painting, Thomas Gainsborough, was born here in 1727. His birthplace is now a museum and art gallery, and he is commemorated by a statue in front of St Peter's Church. Nearby stands Sudbury's remarkable Victorian corn exchange.

BURES
Fine half-timbered houses and an elegant church dating from the 13th to 15th centuries are the main features of this pretty village on the banks of the River Stour. In the church is a font adorned with painted shields, and a private chapel containing a monument dated 1514. St Stephen's Chapel, set on a slope 1 mile north-east of the village, is an ancient thatched building that was once attached to the former Earl's Colne Priory.

St Stephen's Chapel, near Bures, contains beautiful medieval effigies of the earls of Oxford

Many of Kersey's cottages were once the homes of weavers

NAYLAND
Alston Court, an attractive half-timbered courtyard house, is one of many 15th-century buildings to be seen in this River Stour village. John Constable painted the altarpiece in the local church. Nayland marks the western end of Dedham Vale, an area of outstanding natural beauty that stretches eastwards to Flatford Mill. The area is featured in many of Constable's works.

STOKE-BY-NAYLAND
Visitors who are lovers of Constable's paintings will recognize the lofty 120ft tower of Stoke-by-Nayland's handsome church. Entry to the south end of the building is through magnificently carved doors, and inside are many notable monuments. Close by are the timber-framed Maltings and the Guildhall, both superb survivals from the 16th century.

EAST BERGHOLT
This village gained lasting fame as Constable's birthplace. He was born here in 1776, and featured the village in many of his paintings. The flint-and-brick church has an incomplete west tower, and the church bells are hung in a most unusual bell house, built of heavy timbers, in the churchyard.

FLATFORD MILL
Perhaps the most famous and admired of all Constable's landscape subjects, Flatford Mill is picturesquely situated on the River Stour and is now a field-study centre. Both it and nearby Willy Lott's Cottage attract legions of artists every summer.

ROYAL HOSPITAL SCHOOL
An impressive tower with a white stone pinnacle that can be seen for miles around marks the location of the Royal Hospital School, which was founded in 1694 for the sons of seamen. The present group of buildings was occupied when the school moved from Greenwich in the early part of this century.

ERWARTON
Red-brick almshouses dating from 1740 are a striking feature of this pretty village, which also has an Elizabethan hall with an unusual pinnacled gateway. The building is not open to the public.

SHOTLEY GATE
Views of the busy shipping traffic into Harwich and Felixstowe can be enjoyed from this promontory. Close by is the former naval training centre, HMS *Ganges*.

IPSWICH
Modern commercial development has made this major port and agricultural centre into the largest town in Suffolk. In spite of this it has managed to preserve a number of historic buildings. They include the Ancient House, a 16th-century building that features fine pargeting – the East Anglian art of moulding designs into wet plaster. Another typical East Anglian art is displayed in several of the town's churches including St Lawrence's and St Margaret's. This is flushwork – the arrangement of flint and stone to form intricate patterns. Museums in Ipswich include Christchurch Mansion, a 16th-century country house.

TOUR 21 ROUTE DIRECTIONS
Leave Hadleigh on the A1071 (SP Sudbury) and at the edge of the town turn right on to the A1141 (SP Kersey, Lavenham). In 1¼ miles, at a crossroads, turn left on to an unclassified road for Kersey. Follow the Boxford road from Kersey church, and leave Boxford on the A1071 (SP Sudbury). In 2½ miles turn right on to the A134 for Sudbury.
Leave Sudbury on the B1508 (SP Bures) and drive along the Stour valley to Bures. Turn left by Bures church on to an unclassified road (SP Nayland). In 4¾ miles cross a staggered crossroads on to the B1087 for Nayland. Continue on the B1087 along Dedham Vale to Stoke-by-Nayland. Follow the B1068 (SP Ipswich) from here, then 2 miles beyond Higham meet the A12 and turn right then left on to an unclassified road (SP East Bergholt). In 1 mile turn right into East Bergholt, and bear right by the church to reach Flatford Mill. Leave Flatford Mill and bear right along a one-way street. In ½ mile turn right at a crossroads, then in ½ mile meet the B1070 (SP Manningtree). Keep forward and in 1½ miles turn left on to the A137 (SP Ipswich). Go through Brantham and in 1 mile, by the Bull Inn, turn right on to the B1080 (SP Holbrook). Continue through Stutton and through the grounds of the Royal Hospital School. Continue for ½ mile and turn right on to an unclassified road to go through Harkstead, Erwarton and Shotley, turning right on to the B1456 for Shotley Gate. Return along the B1456 (SP Ipswich), passing through Chelmondiston and Woolverstone then later turn right on to the A137 and drive into Ipswich.
Leave Ipswich following signs for Colchester, then join the A1071 (SP Sudbury), passing through Hintlesham to return to Hadleigh.

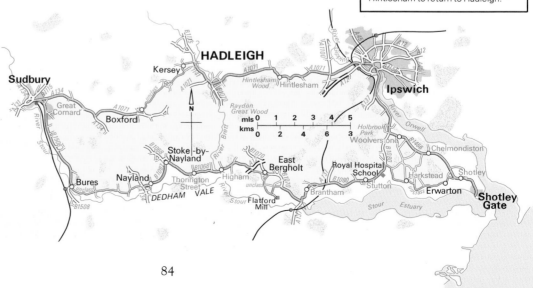

Norfolk Broads and Coast
79 miles

NORWICH

This cathedral and university city stands on a site where there has been a settlement for well over 1,000 years. Its importance in Norman times is reflected in the 12th-century castle, now occupied by the city museum and art gallery, and in the magnificent cathedral. Begun at the end of the century, this great church is one of the finest Norman cathedrals in the country, and is the only one in northern Europe to retain its semicircular east end. The spire, which dominates the entire city, was added in the 15th century. The cathedral's treasures include the oldest bishop's throne still used in England and exquisite carving such as the 800 beautiful roof-bosses and the splendid choir stalls.

Norwich has managed to preserve many of its medieval buildings. Some, such as the 14th-century house known as the Bridewell, and the remarkable Stranger's Hall, have been imaginatively converted into museums. St Peter Hungate Church is now a museum of church art and craftsmanship.

ACLE

This well-known touring centre is within easy reach of the lovely Norfolk Broads and is a good base from which to explore the area. Its unusual church has a picturesque thatched roof and a round tower that dates from the 12th century. East of the village, on the tour route, are several windpumps that have survived from the days when many such machines were built to pump excess water from the reclaimed marshlands.

GREAT YARMOUTH

Amply equipped for the holidaymaker, Great Yarmouth boasts five miles of sandy beach, two piers and a host of amusements. Parts of the old port survive amid the funfairs, including the Old Merchant's House, parts of the town walls and the Elizabethan House which, despite its Georgian façade, contains fine 16th-century interior features such as panelling and plasterwork. It is now a museum. Also open to the public is Anna Sewell House, a 17th-century building that was the birthplace of the authoress of *Black Beauty*. A maritime museum, a model village and the House of Wax are among the resort's other attractions.

CAISTER-ON-SEA

Remains of town walls and a gateway survive from the time when this popular little resort was a Roman settlement. Much more recent is the 15th-century castle whose remains now house a museum of historic cars.

THE BROADS

More than 30 large and very beautiful sheets of water, often linked by navigable channels, are contained in a triangular area between Norwich, Lowestoft and Sea Palling. These, together with many rivers, lakes and canals, provide some 200 miles of waterway for cruising and sailing. Boats can be hired in such centres as Wroxham, Horning and Potter Heigham.

TOUR 22 ROUTE DIRECTIONS

Leave Norwich on the A47 (SP Yarmouth) and go through Blofield and Acle to Great Yarmouth. Leave by the A149 (SP Caister). In 2 miles, keep forward at a roundabout into Caister. Turn left on to the A1064 (SP Acle) and pass the remains of Caister Roman Town on the right. Take the second exit at a roundabout, then in ¾ mile turn right on to an unclassified road (SP Great Ormesby). In 1 mile turn left on to the A149 into Ormesby St Margaret at the edge of the Broads. Turn right by the war memorial on to an unclassified road (SP Scratby), then at a T-junction turn right (SP Hemsby). Drive to the end of Hemsby village and turn left on to the B1159 (SP Mundesley). Continue through Winterton-on-Sea and West Somerton and follow signs for Cromer through Horsey and Sea Palling, then in 1¾ miles turn right and continue through Lessingham and Happisburgh. At the crossroads 1½ miles beyond Happisburgh turn right for Walcott and continue through Bacton, Mundesley, Trimingham and Overstrand to Cromer. Leave on the A149 (SP Norwich) and in 2¼ miles bear left (SP North Walsham). Drive through Thorpe Market to North Walsham and follow signs for Norwich on the B1150. Pass Westwick Park and drive beneath an arched gateway across the road, then continue through Coltishall and Horstead to Norwich.

Horsey's village church has a thatched roof and a typical East Anglian round tower with an octagonal top

Once a smugglers' haunt, West Somerton is now frequented by anglers

WEST SOMERTON

Situated at the weedy eastern end of Martham Broad, this quiet village is an excellent angling base and a good place to see how the marshes were drained. A maze of streams and man-made ditches still carries excess water into the main broads, and two windpumps that were used to pump from one level to another can be seen nearby.

HORSEY

Despite frequent incursions of the sea since it was built, the thatched village church has retained its Norman round tower and a belfry dating from the 15th century. Near the village is Horsey Mere, a wildlife reserve where there is a restored drainage windmill now in the care of the National Trust.

HAPPISBURGH

The name of this pretty little fishing village is pronounced 'Hazeborough'. Offshore shipping is warned away from the treacherous Haisboro' Sands by a lighthouse, but the same drifts provide sun- and sea-bathers with a superb dune-backed beach.

BACTON

This village is an attractive little place that grew up alongside Broomholm Priory, a 12th-century foundation that claimed to possess a piece of the True Cross and became a great centre of pilgrimage. Remains of the priory, which was mentioned by Chaucer, include the gatehouse, north transept, chapter house, and refectory.

OVERSTRAND

Pleasant cliff walks lead from here to the nearby resort of Cromer, and safe bathing can be enjoyed from the sands. The 14th-century Church of St Martin was built after the old parish church fell into the sea.

CROMER

This fishing village, still known for the fine-quality crabs brought in by its fleet, grew popular with holidaymakers during the last century. The cottages of the old town overlook the beach, and the 15th-century parish church, which carries one of the tallest towers in Norfolk, is a reminder of Cromer's history. Three 19th-century fishermen's cottages have been turned into an interesting museum. More modern attractions include a zoo, a boating pool and a golf course.

Inland from Cromer is Felbrigg Hall, a 17th- and 18th-century mansion set in pleasant grounds with lakeside walks.

NORTH WALSHAM

Homely buildings and winding little lanes make this beautiful market town well worth a pause in any journey. Its fine church is given an air of Gothic mystery by a ruined tower that fell in 1724. Inside are a painted screen, a tall 15th-century font cover and various monuments.

HORSTEAD

Horstead church carries a slender west tower that dates from the 13th century. The delightful gabled and weather-boarded village mill stands opposite the miller's house.

Midland Hunting Country
90 miles

MARKET HARBOROUGH
This pleasant old market town has retained much of its character despite modern development. The fine 14th-century broach spire of St Dionysius' Church soars above the quaint old grammar school dating from 1614. It stands on sturdy wooden pillars and features decorative plasterwork. In the High Street is the Three Swans Inn, which has a lovely 18th-century inn sign of delicate wrought iron.

ROCKINGHAM
A hill above the River Welland in this delightful village is the setting for Rockingham Castle. Its commanding site was first fortified by William the Conqueror, but the 11th-century keep was destroyed during the Civil War when the Roundheads captured it. Parts of the Norman castle survive, but much of the present house is Elizabethan. It stands in gardens that are known for an unusual yew walk flanked by topiary elephants.

WELLAND VIADUCT
This 82-arch railway viaduct dates from 1874 and is a notable example of 19th-century industrial architecture. It spans the whole width of the Welland valley.

KETTON
The fine quality stone from local quarries, and highly prized Collyweston roof slates contribute to the harmonious architecture of this attractive village. The church, one of the best in the area, is built of Barnack stone, a durable material greatly valued by medieval masons. The 12th-century west front is particularly fine.

STAMFORD
This lovely old town first grew to prosperity in Saxon times when it was an established ford on the River Welland. In the Middle Ages it had a university and 11 churches, several of which survive to recall its former importance. By the 18th century Stamford had become an important coaching stop on the Great North Road. The town retains something from almost every era of its illustrious past – though much of its medieval work, including most of the town walls and the little castle that stood here, was badly damaged when the town was sacked by a Lancastrian army in 1461. Today, the few surviving medieval houses sit happily side by side with Tudor, Georgian and Victorian buildings, while just outside the town is Burghley House, one of Stamford's chief architectural treasures. It has been described as England's greatest Elizabethan house, and contains a fine collection of paintings. The Burghley Horse Trials are held every September in the park, which was landscaped by Capability Brown.

EMPINGHAM
Dominating this large and attractive village is the handsome tower and spire of St Peter's Church, a well-proportioned building with a good west front. Features of the interior include fragments of ancient glass and considerable remains of medieval colour.

The imposing west gateway of Burghley House, near Stamford, dates from 1801

BURLEY
Burley-on-the-Hill (not open) is considered by many to be the most beautiful country house in the county. Its fine colonnades and exquisitely restrained detail, the work of Joseph Lumley between 1694 and 1705, ornament a small hill that was an ancient earthwork.

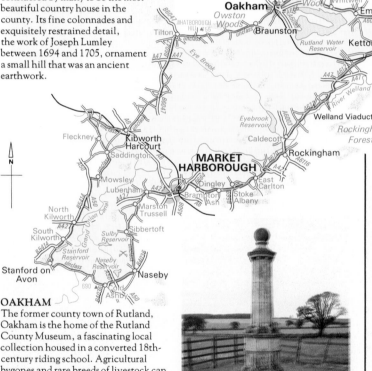

OAKHAM
The former county town of Rutland, Oakham is the home of the Rutland County Museum, a fascinating local collection housed in a converted 18th-century riding school. Agricultural bygones and rare breeds of livestock can be seen at the Rutland Farm Park, just outside the town at Catmose Farm. Oakham is a busy little town, with interesting buildings including a castle with a fine Norman hall, a 16th-century school and a lovely church.

BRAUNSTON
This lovely ironstone village stands on a hillside above the valley of the little River Gwash. Inside its distinctive church are traces of a building dating from the 12th and 13th centuries.

KIBWORTH HARCOURT
Examples of architecture from many periods can be seen in this village. Among the most notable are the Old House of 1678, the 18th-century Congregational Church, and 19th-century Kibworth Hall.

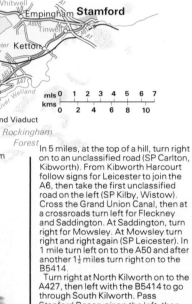
This monument was erected in 1823 to commemorate the Battle of Naseby, fought here on 14 June 1645

STANFORD ON AVON
Divided between Leicestershire and Northamptonshire by the River Avon, this pleasant village has a good church with a pinnacled 15th-century tower. Stanford Hall is impressively sited in open pasture and stands on the site of an earlier house. The present building dates from the reign of William and Mary, and has an imposing façade that adds a touch of grandeur to its pleasing design. Its rooms contain collections of costumes and furniture.

TOUR 23 ROUTE DIRECTIONS
Leave Market Harborough on the A427 (SP Corby). Continue through East Carlton, then turn left on to the B670 for Rockingham. At the edge of Rockingham turn left on to the A6003 (SP Uppingham), cross the River Welland and continue to Caldecott. Keep forward on the B670 and in 4½ miles pass under the Welland viaduct. In 2 miles turn right then left to join the A6121 and continue through Ketton and Tinwell to Stamford.

From Stamford follow signs first for Grantham, then for Oakham, to leave by the A606. Continue through Empingham and Whitwell, near Rutland Water, and in 1 mile turn right on to an unclassified road (SP Exton, Cottesmore). Skirt Exton Park and at Cottesmore turn left on to the B668. Continue through Burley and descend into Oakham.

Follow signs for Melton Mowbray, go over a level crossing and turn left, then left again, on to an unclassified road for Braunston. From here take the Leicester road to Tilton, then join the B6047 (SP Market Harborough).

In 5 miles, at the top of a hill, turn right on to an unclassified road (SP Carlton, Kibworth). From Kibworth Harcourt follow signs for Leicester to join the A6, then take the first unclassified road on the left (SP Kilby, Wistow). Cross the Grand Union Canal, then at a crossroads turn left for Fleckney and Saddington. At Saddington, turn right for Mowsley. At Mowsley turn right and right again (SP Leicester). In 1 mile turn left on to the A50 and after another 1½ miles turn right on to the B5414.

Turn right at North Kilworth on to the A427, then left with the B5414 to go through South Kilworth. Pass Stanford Reservoir on the left, then turn left on to an unclassified road (SP Stanford on Avon). Pass Stanford Hall and Stanford Park, go through Stanford on Avon and in ¼ mile turn left (SP Cold Ashby). Cross the Grand Union Canal and in Cold Ashby turn left on to the B4036. Drive to Naseby, turn left on to an unclassified road for Sibbertoft and pass the site of the Battle of Naseby on the left. At Sibbertoft turn right (SP Theddingworth) and in 1 mile bear right to Marston Trussell. Turn right on to the A427 and return through Lubenham to Market Harborough.

NASEBY
A stone column 1½ miles north of this village marks the field where the Battle of Naseby was fought in 1645. The Cromwellian victory heralded a new era of British government and sealed the fate of King Charles I. The Naseby Battle Museum at Purlieu Farm displays layouts of the battleground and various local relics. In Naseby churchyard is a huge copper ball that is said to have been brought back from the Siege of Boulogne in 1544.

Woodlands of Staffordshire
67 miles

The west front of Lichfield Cathedral, one of its best features, carries 113 carved figures

LICHFIELD
The skyline of this compact city is dominated by 'The Ladies of the Vale' – the three slender spires of the cathedral. The first cathedral here was built around AD700 to house the body of St Chad, and was the mother church of the whole Saxon kingdom of Mercia. The present cathedral, dating from about 1330, was very badly damaged in the Civil War. The west front, richly embellished with carved figures, is among the most striking features of the exterior, while inside the cathedral are mainly Victorian furnishings such as the delicate chancel screen. In the south transept is a bust of Dr Samuel Johnson, author, wit and compiler of the first English dictionary. His birthplace – a tiny house at the corner of Breadmarket Street – is now a museum. Nearby stand statues of Johnson and his companion and biographer James Boswell. Lichfield's many interesting buildings include the imposing 17th-century Bishop's Palace and the pleasant medley of houses in the Close.

WHITTINGTON BARRACKS
The official museum of the Staffordshire Regiment can be visited at Whittington Barracks, themselves evidence of Lichfield's long association with the military.

TAMWORTH
Like Lichfield, Tamworth was an important town in the Saxon kingdom of Mercia. The castle was founded in AD913 by Aethelfleda, the warrior daughter of Alfred the Great who was known as the 'Lady of the Mercians'. The oldest parts of the present castle are Norman, but it also incorporates fine Tudor and later workmanship such as the splendid 16th-century banqueting hall. Tamworth still holds a market – a tradition that goes back 1,000 years or more. Overlooking the stalls in Market Street is a charming little red-brick town hall, built in 1701. Nearby stands a statue of Sir Robert Peel, the 19th-century prime minister who was Tamworth's MP for 17 years.

ALREWAS
Famous for its River Trent eel fishing and basket-weaving industries, this charming little village of thatched black-and-white Tudor cottages is one of the prettiest in the county. Its 13th- and 14th-century church contains a fine font.

TRENT AND MERSEY CANAL
Designed by the great engineer Brindley to service the industrial heartlands of England, this canal was begun in the late 18th century and was the first safe means of transporting fragile goods from the Potteries.

TUTBURY
The ruins of a medieval castle dominate this picturesque little town in the Dove valley. Foundations of a Norman chapel are the oldest part of Tutbury Castle, while the most recent of its towers, Julius' Tower, dates from the 19th century. Tutbury church features some of the finest Norman work in the Midlands, with a splendid west doorway. The Dog and Partridge is a picturesque 16th-century timber-framed building in the main street.

SUDBURY
The Vernon family, owners of Sudbury Hall from its building until 1967, are mainly responsible for the harmonious architecture of this little village, whose brick-and-stone pub of 1671 carries their coat of arms. Sudbury Hall was completed some 20 years later. It has a magnificent long gallery, and its decor includes elaborate plasterwork.

ABBOTS BROMLEY
Grouped around a lovely village green surrounded by half-timbered and Georgian houses and completed by a 17th-century buttercross, Abbots Bromley is best known for its Horn Dance. Performed in early September, the tradition is many centuries old, and probably of pagan origin. The dancers include six men carrying ancient antlers, a boy with a bow and arrow, a man riding a hobby-horse, and a 'fool'.

BLITHFIELD RESERVOIR
The Queen Mother opened this 4,000-million-gallon reservoir in 1953 and today it is a valuable sanctuary for wildlife.

BLITHFIELD HALL
This estate has been the home of the Bagot family and their ancestors for 900 years. The house is of Elizabethan origin, with additions from later periods. Of particular interest is a unique collection of relics from the Stuart period. Herds of black-necked Bagot goats roam the park.

SHUGBOROUGH HALL
This great white mansion, home of the earls of Lichfield, stands in beautiful grounds and contains fine collections of furniture and period bric-a-brac. The grounds are studded with classical monuments and follies such as the Arch of Hadrian, the Doric Temple and the Tower of the Winds.

CANNOCK CHASE
Once the private hunting ground of the kings of England, the 26 square miles of wooded Cannock Chase form a designated area of outstanding natural beauty. Good views are afforded by the hilltops of Seven Springs, which culminate in 795ft Castle Ring; the latter is crowned by the ramparts of a good Iron Age hill-fort.

Sudbury Hall was begun in 1613 and completed in the late 17th century

TOUR 24 ROUTE DIRECTIONS

Follow the A51 (SP Tamworth) from Lichfield to Tamworth, passing Whittington Barracks. Leave Tamworth on the A513 (SP Burton, Alrewas), and at Alrewas turn right on to the A38 (SP Burton). In 1 mile cross the Trent, and continue alongside the Trent and Mersey Canal. In 1¼ miles turn left at a crossroads on to the B5016 for Barton-under-Needwood. Keep forward (SP Yoxall) and in 1 mile, by the Bell Inn, turn right (SP Tutbury). In 3 miles cross a main road and continue to Tutbury. Keep forward into the High Street (A50), cross the River Dove and go over a level crossing, then turn left on to an unclassified road (SP Scropton, Sudbury). Continue for 2 miles beyond Scropton and turn left on to the A515. (A detour to Sudbury can be made by turning right here on to the A515 then left into the village.)

The main route continues on the A515 through Draycott-in-the-Clay. In ¾ mile turn right at a crossroads on to an unclassified road for Newborough. Turn right in Newborough on to the B5234 (SP Abbots Bromley), and later turn right on to the B5014 into Abbots Bromley. Go through the village and in ½ mile turn left on to the B5013 (SP Rugeley). Cross Blithfield Reservoir and pass Blithfield Hall on the right, then in 1¾ miles turn right (SP Stafford).

In 1½ miles, at a crossroads, turn left then left again on to the A51. Cross the River Trent and turn right on to the A513 (SP Stafford). Pass the entrance to Shugborough Hall on the right, and at Milford turn left on to an unclassified road (SP Brocton). Keep forward (SP Stafford) in Brocton, then turn left on to the A34 (SP Cannock). In ¾ mile turn left (SP Hednesford) and climb on to Cannock Chase. Pass a German military cemetery and keep forward into Hednesford. In ½ mile keep forward at a crossroads, cross a railway bridge and turn right on to the A460. Go under a railway bridge, then turn left on to an unclassified road (SP Rawnsley, Hazelslade). In ¾ mile turn left, go over a level crossing and climb through woodland to a crossroads. Turn right into Startley Lane and later turn right on to the A51 and return to Lichfield.

Central England
Gazetteer

ABBEY DORE, Herefs & Worcs 76 SO33
The meadows and orchards of the Golden Valley surround this little village, which is famous for its parish church. In 1174 an abbey was founded here, but after the Dissolution of the Monasteries its buildings were neglected. In 1633 Lord Scudamore commissioned the brilliant craftsman John Abel to rebuild the church. Much of the original fabric was restored; additions by Abel included the fine wooden screen – a good example of his work.

ALDEBURGH, Suffolk 79 TM45
This quiet resort was once a busy port, but coastal erosion and storm damage destroyed much of the town; the 16th-century timber-framed Moot Hall once stood in the town centre but is now almost on the sea wall. Aldeburgh still has its appeal to visitors, however – not least for its musical connections. Benjamin Britten's opera *Peter Grimes* is set here, and he is associated with the annual Aldeburgh Music Festival. *Peter Grimes* was based on a collection of tales entitled *The Borough* by a famous native of Aldeburgh, George Crabbe. He was born here in 1754.

ALTON, Staffs 77 SK04
Stone buildings are a feature of this village, which includes a circular lock-up and the ruins of a 12th-century castle. Nearby Alton Towers is a partly ruined 19th-century Gothic mansion by Pugin, surrounded by fine gardens and a large park which contains model railways, boating lakes, and a paddling pool.

ASHBOURNE, Derbyshire 77 SK14
Wide streets and handsome buildings feature in this market town, which is situated on the edge of the Peak District National Park. St Oswald's Church has a 212ft spire, and a brass records the dedication of the church by the Bishop of Coventry in AD241. The former grammar school is a fine Elizabethan building dating from 1585. Almost opposite is the 17th-century red brick mansion where Dr Johnson used to stay with his friend, the poet John Taylor. The Spalden and Owlfield almshouses are also of note, and the Green Man and Black's Head is an interesting Georgian inn with a gallows sign spanning the road. A curious and very traditional game of football is played every Shrove Tuesday. A white football is put down in the centre of the town, and an unlimited number of players – local men divided into two teams – try to score in the two goals by any means possible.

ASHBY-DE-LA-ZOUCH, Leics 77 SK31
Grecian-style houses, Georgian shops and modern office-blocks blend together in unexpected harmony along the wide main streets of this market town. The ruins of the castle, built by Lord Hastings in the 15th century, are tucked away behind the main street. St Helen's Church contains a finger pillory, a form of punishment used up to the last century for anyone interrupting the sermon. The Countess of Huntingdon, who led a religious revival in the 18th century and died in 1791, is buried in the Hastings Chapel.

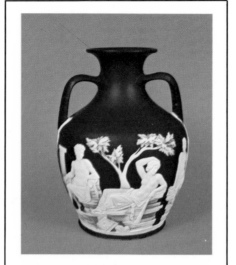
Josiah Wedgwood's Portland Vase can be seen in the Wedgwood Museum at Barlaston

AYLESBURY, Bucks 77 SP81
The busy county town of Aylesbury manages to preserve an old-world charm in the narrow Tudor alleyways and fine 17th-century houses of the town centre. Many of the older buildings are situated in St Mary's Square, three sides of which are occupied by mellow terraces, the fourth by the church and churchyard. The massive tower, topped by a 17th-century lead clock-tower and spire, dates from the 13th century. Aylesbury recalls its own history and that of Buckinghamshire in the County

Set in magnificent grounds, the conservatory at Alton Towers resembles an Oriental palace

Museum, housed in the old grammar school in Church Street. The King's Head Hotel, a splendid old coaching inn dating from the 15th century and now belonging to the National Trust, is a reminder of the town's stage-coach days. Market Square is dominated by the County Hall, built about 1720 but severely damaged by fire in 1970. Among these old buildings are many fine modern additions; the new county council buildings are outstanding.

BANBURY, Oxon 77 SP44
This busy industrial and shopping centre dates back to Saxon times, but only a few buildings constructed earlier than the 17th century survive. The original Banbury Cross of nursery rhyme fame was destroyed in 1602, but a replica was erected in its place in 1859. St Mary's Church was built in the late 18th century. A number of attractive old houses and inns are still to be seen in the town, and the vicarage of 1649 is of particular note. Banbury Cakes, made from puff pastry filled with dried, spiced fruit, can still be bought locally.

BARLASTON, Staffs 76 SJ83
This is the site of the famous Wedgwood pottery and museum. Here can be seen many interesting examples of Josiah Wedgwood's experimental designs, as well as an exhibition of 18th- to 20th-century ceramics. One of the most famous exhibits is the Portland vase, a faithful copy of a priceless Roman vase now in the British Museum. Attractions for visitors to the factory also include a demonstration room and a 'seconds' shop.

BEDFORD, Beds 78 TL04
This thriving industrial and commercial centre on the River Ouse can trace its history back to Saxon times. It was prominent in the reign of King Alfred, and was sacked and burned by the Danes in 1010. A castle built by the Norman Beauchamp family was demolished in 1224, but the mound can still be seen.

Bedford achieved doubtful fame when, at a time of religious persecution, it imprisoned John Bunyan in the county gaol from 1660 to 1672, and again in 1676. A slab in Silver Street marks the site of the prison. Several Bunyan memorials include a statue and the Bunyan Museum, which stands on the site of a barn where he preached.

The town also boasts well-known schools and a cluster of early churches. St Paul's Church was originally of the 12th century but has been greatly restored. It retains a 15th-century pulpit from which Wesley preached.

The Cecil Higgins Art Gallery has a fine collection of ceramics, glass and paintings.

BEWDLEY, Herefs & Worcs 76 SO77
Telford's fine bridge spanning the Severn at Bewdley was built in 1795. Severnside is a beautiful street lined with 17th- and 18th-century houses. An elegant parade of Georgian and earlier buildings lines both sides of Load Street, which is closed off at one end by a large Georgian house and 18th-century St Anne's Church. Bewdley's more distant history is represented by several half-timbered buildings.

BIBURY, Glos   77 *SP10*

William Morris thought Bibury 'the most beautiful village in England'. Most of its stone-built houses have gardens that run down to the River Coln, and the Arlington Row of river-fronted cottages is owned by the National Trust. Near Arlington Mill, which houses a museum, is a bird sanctuary. Bibury Court Hotel is of Jacobean origin, and The Swan is a pleasant coaching inn.

BIRMINGHAM, W Midlands   77 *SP08*

One of the world's most important manufacturing centres, and Britain's second city, Birmingham is first recorded as a small Roman station on Icknield Street. It became an industrial town early in its history and is known to have supplied thousands of sword blades to the Parliamentary forces during the Civil War in the 16th century.

The city's growth brought with it much of the ugliness and squalor associated with 19th-century industrial towns, as well as some imposing public buildings. The town hall, built in 1834, is modelled on a classical temple in Rome. The nearby Council House of 1879 is a typically ornate Victorian building capped by a small dome. The Roman Catholic Cathedral of St Chad, built around 1840, was designed by Augustus Pugin, the architect famous for his work on the Houses of Parliament. The Anglican Cathedral of St Philip is earlier, dating from the 18th century, but it was not created a cathedral until 1905, when Birmingham was made a diocese.

The Bull Ring Centre is the largest of the city's many new developments which sprang up in the 1960s. The 23-acre complex comprises a vast pedestrianized shopping centre, incorporating car parks and a market, linked to road and rail stations. The mass of concrete and glass covers an area which in medieval times served as the village green, and is Birmingham's oldest inhabited area. The new roads built to service the new town are epitomized by the multi-level junction at Gravelly Hill, popularly known as 'Spaghetti Junction'.

In contrast the city preserves its many miles of canal, a network boasting more miles of waterway than Venice. The Gas Street Canal Basin has been landscaped to create a pleasant recreational area, and gaily-coloured narrow-boats once again moor along the banks.

Birmingham's museums include the Museum of Science and Industry and the Railway Museum at Tyseley, outside the city centre, where locomotives and rolling stock are kept. The city's principal museum and art gallery is in the Council House, and displays include a particularly fine collection of pre-Raphaelite paintings, as well as exhibits from ancient Egypt, Rome and Greece.

BISHOP'S CASTLE, Salop   76 *SO38*

This hillside market town stands on the edge of Clun Forest and preserves a number of interesting old buildings, the most picturesque of which is the 16th-century House on Crutches. Its Victorian church retains a Norman tower, and the 18th-century town hall stands over a medieval lock-up.

BLAKENEY, Norfolk   79 *TG04*

This picturesque tidal port is favoured by yachtsmen. Extensive salt-marshes are a feature of the neighbourhood. The church, Early English and later, has two towers of which one may have been a beacon. The nave roof is of the hammerbeam type, and is carved with angels. The Guildhall dates from the 15th century. To the north of the village is Blakeney Point, where there is a large bird sanctuary.

BOSTON, Lincs   78 *TF34*

This ancient seaport on the River Witham lacks the prosperity of former years, although it is still a thriving community. As a port, its decline began when developing links with the New World diverted much of Boston's former trade to west coast ports, and today the harbour remains partially silted up. The American town of Boston derives its title from here, the name being taken to the New World by immigrants who sailed from the port with John Winthrop in 1630.

St Botolph is reputed to have founded a monastery here in 654, and the name Boston is a shortened corruption of Botolph's town. The present St Botolph's Church was completed in 1460. It is an outstanding example of the Perpendicular style, and is one of the largest parish churches in England. The 272ft tower is nicknamed Boston Stump, and is used as a navigational aid for shipping in The Wash. The Guildhall of 1450 is now a museum.

BOURNE, Lincs   78 *TF02*

Bourne is an ancient market town and reputedly the birthplace of Hereward the Wake, the last Saxon to resist the invading Norman army. The Burghley Arms Hotel was the birthplace of Sir William Cecil, Lord High Treasurer to Elizabeth I, in 1520.

BOURTON-ON-THE-WATER, Glos   77 *SP12*

One of the most popular villages in the Cotswolds, Bourton is a cluster of lovely old buildings of Cotswold stone, enhanced by the River Windrush with its grassy banks and little bridges. At the centre stands a lovely church with a 14th-century chancel and a domed Georgian tower. The entire village is reproduced at one-ninth its size in the Model Village, behind the Old New Inn. Other attractions for visitors include the four-acre Birdland Zoo Gardens, where some 600 species of exotic birds can be seen, and the Motor Museum, a collection of cars and motorcycles from their earliest days to the 1950s.

BRIDGNORTH, Salop   76 *SO79*

Shropshire has more than its fair share of lovely old towns, and Bridgnorth vies with the best of them. It is divided into two parts – Upper Town and Lower Town – by a steep ridge which is negotiated by a twisty road, several flights of steps and a funicular railway. In Lower Town is Bishop Percy's House, a fine half-timbered building of 1580 which is possibly the oldest house in Bridgnorth. Upper Town is on the site of the original settlement and though much of it burned down during the Civil War, the High Street is still straddled by its picturesque town hall. The half-timbered upper storey of this building was made from a barn after the old town hall became a battle casualty. Many fine inns can be found in the High Street as it leads to the ancient North Gate, and at the other end are the elegant Georgian houses of East Castle Street. A precariously leaning tower is all that remains of Bridgnorth Castle. Nearby St Mary Magdalene's Church was built by engineer and architect Thomas Telford in 1794.

Bishop Percy's House is the finest example of black-and-white architecture in Bridgnorth. Built in 1580, it is named after Thomas Percy, a famous antiquary and bishop who was born here in 1729

This motorized beer bottle is perhaps the most unusual of many fascinating exhibits associated with the brewing industry in the Bass Museum at Burton upon Trent

BRILL, Bucks   77 SP61

Isolated Brill is a lovely village which stands at 700ft above the Vale of Aylesbury. Its two greens are fringed with charming cottages and almshouses, and its Tudor manor house radiates the warmth of mellow red brick. Brill windmill dates from 1668 and may be one of the oldest post-mills to have survived anywhere in Great Britain.

BURFORD, Oxon   77 SP21

Like so many other wool towns in this part of the country, Burford is centred on a charming street lined with honey-coloured buildings of local stone. The main street descends a steep hillside and crosses the River Windrush via a fine old bridge. Buildings of particular interest include 15th-century almshouses, the Great House of 1690 and a basically Norman church which claims to be the second largest in Oxfordshire. Features of this splendid building include an imposing tower and spire, and a fine Lady Chapel that was built as the Chapel of the Guild of Merchants. In 1649 a group of Cromwellian mutineers were trapped in the building by their own forces, and on capture three of the imprisoned men were shot near the churchyard. A restored Elizabethan house now known as The Priory was once the home of Speaker Lenthall, who defied Charles I in the House of Commons.

BURTON UPON TRENT, Staffs 77 SK22

Numerous breweries in this area testify to the unique qualities of the local water. The town is famous for its beer-making, and the history of the industry is traced in the fascinating Bass Museum, housed in the brewery's Victorian joinery shop. One unusual exhibit is a remarkable old Daimler truck in the shape of a giant beer bottle.

BURY ST EDMUNDS, Suffolk   79 TL86

Edmund, the last king of the East Angles, was killed by the Danes around 870 and was subsequently hailed by his people as a martyr. In 903 his body was moved to Bury, which became an important religious centre. The abbey here was once one of the architectural glories of England, but like many of its contemporaries it was broken up at the Dissolution. Today its former splendour can be judged by extensive ruins. Two gates still stand, and the precincts are made splendid by the Cathedral Church of St James. A large graveyard separates this fine building from 15th-century St Mary's Church, which is known for its magnificent hammer-beam roof and the grave of Mary Tudor. Bury St Edmunds itself is an attractive market town which retains its 11th-century street plan and many fine old buildings. Moyse's Hall dates from the 12th century and contains a museum.

CAMBRIDGE, Cambs   78 TL45

In 1209 a split in the Oxford community resulted in a migration of students and scholars to Cambridge. The first college, Peterhouse, was founded in 1284. King's College, founded by Henry VI in 1441, has an outstanding chapel that overlooks the Cam and is famous for some of the finest Gothic fan vaulting in Europe. Corpus Christi is unique in having been founded by two town guilds, and lovely half-timbered Queens' of 1346 is by far the most picturesque.

The town itself is a delightful collection of old streets and houses alongside the river. There are also several good museums. Extensive art and archaeological collections are housed in the Fitzwilliam, the Scott Polar Research Institute has many relics relating to famous expeditions, and the Sedgwick displays fossils from many parts of the world.

CASTLE HEDINGHAM, Essex 79 TL73

The Norman castle keep, built by the de Veres, is considered one of the finest in England. It dominates the little medieval town, whose fine Norman church shows a late 14th-century screen, a brick tower of 1616, and a double hammerbeam roof. The 12th-century churchyard cross has been restored, and the town's numerous old houses and inns are of interest.

CASTLE RISING, Norfolk   79 TF62

The sea has long withdrawn from this one-time port, but the Norman castle built to protect it still stands. It occupies a Roman site and has a great keep in which a fascinating sequence of rooms, galleries, and minor stairs are reached by a single dramatic staircase. The local Church of St Lawrence is famous for its Norman west front, which has a fine doorway and beautiful arcading, and houses a richly carved square font on a circular shaft. Bede House or Trinity Hospital dates from the 17th century and is an almshouse charity for elderly ladies.

CHELTENHAM, Glos   76 SO92

Cheltenham started life as a typical Cotswold village, but in 1715 a mineral spring was discovered here. A pump room was built in 1738, George III gave the place his personal approval, and within half a century architects were commissioned to design a new town. The result attracted many people of education and means, who came as much for Cheltenham's fashionable elegance and taste as for the vaunted medicinal properties of the water. The architect Papworth was responsible for much that is best in Cheltenham, and Forbes built the famous Pittville Pump Room. Composer Gustav Holst was a pupil at the town's grammar school. Each March Prestbury Park is host to the Cheltenham Gold Cup horse race.

CHIPPING NORTON, Oxon   *77 SP32*

The 'Chipping' of this name means 'market', and for a considerable period the 'market at Norton' was the commercial centre for the Evenlode valley. When the medieval wool trade made the Cotswolds one of the wealthiest parts of England, the town assumed new importance as a gathering place for wool merchants and other traders. Much of the town's attraction today is due to its many survivals from a prosperous past. Among these are numerous 18th-century houses and a 'wool' church that is among the finest in the county.

CIRENCESTER, Glos   *76 SP00*

In Roman times Cirencester was *Corinium Dobunorum*, the second largest town in England and the focus of several major highways. This period of Cirencester's illustrious history is recreated in the Corinium Museum. When the Romans withdrew the town declined, but wool later boosted it and wool money paid for its Church of St John the Baptist, one of the largest of its kind in the country. From the top of the tower there are marvellous views across the town to Cirencester Park, seat of the Earl of Bathurst. In the 3,000-acre grounds is a folly said to have been designed by the famous 18th-century poet Alexander Pope.

COALBROOKDALE, Salop   *76 SJ60*

This place has been dubbed the cradle of the English iron industry, and the original furnace of Abraham Darby (1708) can still be seen. Darby's experiments in the use of coke, instead of charcoal, as a fuel to smelt iron, revolutionized the industry and sowed the seeds of the Industrial Revolution. Many early industrial monuments in the area are preserved by the Ironbridge Gorge Museum Trust. The former Great Warehouse at Coalbrookdale, built in 1838, is now occupied by a museum tracing the history of the iron industry.

COLCHESTER, Essex   *79 TM02*

The town was founded by the Belgic tribe *Catuvellauni*, and the Romans knew it as *Camulodunum*. The Roman walls that encircled the town are still standing, and the Balkerne Gate is one of the original entrances.

The town continued to flourish after the departure of the Romans and was called the fortress on the Colne, or Colchester, by the Saxons. The Normans took stone from existing Roman buildings to build the castle, which has the largest keep in England. An excellent museum at the castle displays a splendid collection of Roman antiquities.

Holly Trees is a Georgian mansion of 1718 which adjoins the castle park, and now contains a collection of costumes and antiquities. The Minories contains interesting items of furniture and paintings. Siege House was Fairfax's headquarters during the Civil War, and bullet holes made by the Royalist attackers can still be seen in the structural timbers. Priory Street follows the town walls and leads to the ruined church of St Botolph's Priory. This is an Augustinian foundation that was built on the site of an earlier church. The remains are built mainly of Roman brick.

The Bliss Tweed Mill, built in 1872, stands near the old wool town of Chipping Norton

COVENTRY, W Midlands   *77 SP37*

'Eleven years of toil, frustration, hope and ecstasy' is how Sir Basil Spence described the building of the remarkable new cathedral he designed, which was completed in 1962. Standing beside it, in stark contrast, are the ruins of the old cathedral. Coventry was the site of munitions factories during the Second World War, and became a prime target for German bombers. The town was virtually reduced to rubble, which accounts for its modern appearance today.

Reminders of old Coventry include the remains of the Charterhouse, founded in 1381, comprising a section of wall which once enclosed a monastery; Ford's Hospital, a courtyard of Tudor almshouses, which were restored after bomb damage; Bird's Hospital, another row of almshouses founded 'for as long as the world shall endure'; and nearby Bablake Old School. Other survivors are the half-timbered

and gabled Golden Cross Inn, the timbered houses of Priory Row, and St Mary's Guild Hall, begun in 1340 and completed in 1550. The Herbert Museum and Art Gallery holds Graham Sutherland's sketches for the tapestry in the cathedral. On Whitley Common are the Coventry Zoological Gardens, and in Much Park Street is the Coventry Toy Museum, with exhibits dating back as far as 1740.

DEDHAM, Essex   *79 TM03*

This quiet, attractive village lies in Constable country, and was one of the artist's favourite subjects. The High Street boasts several fine houses and two old inns; the Sun Hotel is a half-timbered early 16th-century building with stable yard, and the Marlborough Head Inn dates from about 1500. Many of Constable's paintings feature the tower of the 15th- and 16th-century church. Insignia of the Guilds of Weavers and Millers, who generously endowed the church, are among heraldic shields on the nave roof.

DERBY, Derbyshire   *77 SK33*

Derby is an ancient county town on the River Derwent. As long ago as the Norman Conquest the town had six churches and a population in excess of 2,000. More recent times have seen it develop as a manufacturing town.

The cathedral, formerly the parish church, was rebuilt in 1725. It displays a fine 16th-century tower and houses the tomb of Bess of Hardwick.

Painter Joseph Wright was a native of Derby, and some of his paintings are hung in an art gallery annexed to Derby Museum. The museum contains a working model of the former Midland Railway, and the Industrial Museum, housed in the Old Silk Mill in Sowter Road, contains a Rolls-Royce aero-engine collection and an introduction to local industries. The Arboretum contains a plague stone, a reminder of the time when Derby was devastated by the disease. The Royal Crown Derby porcelain works still produces the fine bone china for which it has long been famous.

The tower of St John's Church offers remarkable views across Cirencester to 3,000-acre Cirencester Park

DISS, Norfolk   79 TM18
Diss is an old market town that was built round the edge of a six-acre lake. Its Decorated and Perpendicular church contains two 15th-century chancel chapels built by local trade guilds. Attractive shops, old inns, and a mixture of Tudor, Georgian, and Victorian houses can be seen in the town.

DOWNHAM MARKET, Norfolk 78 TF60
This small market town is situated on the River Ouse, in an area where a drainage scheme was started by Charles I's Dutch engineer Vermuyden. Dutch influence is evident in some of the buildings here. In the market place is an ornate Victorian clock.

DUNWICH, Suffolk   79 TM47
Little remains of the thriving town that once stood here. Its site had been continuously inhabited since Roman times, but centuries of storms, floods and gradual erosion have meant that most of this historic place now lies under the sea. In the little village that stands here today, a small museum portrays the history of the town and displays various objects washed up on local beaches.

EARLS BARTON, Northants   77 SP86
The magnificent Saxon church tower here was built about 1,000 years ago and is one of the finest examples in England. It may have been part of the defences of a nearby Norman castle.

ELY, Cambs   78 TL58
The site on which Ely stands was an island until the Fens were drained in the 17th and 18th centuries. The superb cathedral that dominates the surrounding Fenland was begun in 1083. It is notable for the octagonal lantern tower and choir stalls, both designed by Alan de Walsingham.

The Bishop's Palace dates from the 15th cen-

A detail of Fairford's lovely stained glass

tury and later, and across the green is the Chantry, a 17th- to 18th-century house. The ancient grammar school incorporates a gateway house known as Ely Porta, and the beautiful Prior Crauden's Chapel – in Decorated style – is now the school chapel.

EVESHAM, Herefs & Worcs   76 SP04
Evesham is sited on the River Avon, in the centre of a famous fruit- and vegetable-growing district. The area is particularly beautiful in early spring, when it is a mass of blossom. Ruins of the abbey include a fine Perpendicular bell-tower and a half-timbered gateway on an original Norman stone base. A cross has

been erected in memory of Simon de Montfort, slain in the Battle of Evesham which was fought to the north of the town in 1265. Two interesting churches are All Saints', with the beautiful Lichfield chantry, and St Lawrence's. The Almonry is a 14th- to 16th-century house in Vine Street, now containing a museum. The Tudor Round House (or Booth Hall) is also of interest.

FAIRFORD, Glos   77 SP10
This attractive River Coln town has an old mill on a stretch of river notable for its trout fishing. John Keble was born here in 1792, and the church has 15th- to 16th-century stained-glass windows said to be the finest of their period in England. The British prototype Concorde was first tested on an RAF airfield nearby.

FELIXSTOWE, Suffolk   79 TM33
Towards the end of the 19th century this sheltered spot on the Suffolk coast was developed as a seaside resort. Long before this, a 16th-century stronghold which became the Landguard Fort was defending the sea approach to Harwich. A later period of insecurity, this time generated by Napoleon's hold on Europe, resulted in the building of a Martello tower in 1810. Today Felixstowe Dock is an important tanker terminal, container port and car-ferry terminus.

FINCHINGFIELD, Essex   79 TL63
Possibly the most photographed village in Essex, Finchingfield is a picture-book community complete with a church on a hill, a picturesque windmill, quaint old cottages and a charming green enlivened by the noisy population of its duckpond. St John's Church has a sturdy Norman tower that indicates its origins, but the main body of the building is a mixture of later styles. The fine 15th-century Guildhall is now occupied by a small museum.

Charming cottages, a green, and a church rich in architectural detail from many periods, help make Finchingfield one of England's most photographed villages

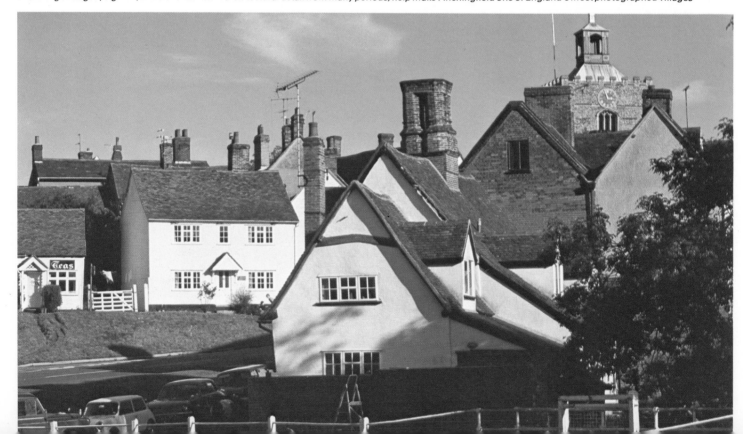

FOTHERINGHAY, Northants   78 *TL09*

A mound here once carried the grim castle in which Mary Queen of Scots was imprisoned before her execution in 1587. Nowadays the mellow old cottages and willow-hung banks of the Nene create a tranquillity in which such macabre associations become difficult to believe. The imposing church was a gift from Edward IV.

FRAMLINGHAM, Suffolk   79 *TM26*

Framlingham's superb Norman castle was started in 1190 and represented an important advance in castle design. Fragments of the Great Hall are incorporated in picturesque 17th-century almshouses within the walls, and the towers carry distinctive Tudor chimneys. Monuments to the Howard family, who took possession in the 15th century, can be seen in the fine Perpendicular church.

GLOUCESTER, Glos   76 *SO81*

Gloucester was once the Roman *Colonia Glevum*, a fortified city guarding the roads into Wales. The fine cathedral is of Norman to early Perpendicular design. The 14th-century east window is of interest, and of particular note are the tomb of murdered King Edward II, the crypt, the choir stalls, the noble central tower and the lovely old cloisters. A cross to the memory of Bishop Hooper, who was martyred in 1555, can be seen in the Close. The timbered Parliament House dates from the 15th century. Local antiquities and Roman relics are exhibited in the City Museum, while 15th-century Bishop Hooper's Lodging contains a museum of English rural life.

GRANTHAM, Lincs   78 *SK93*

Grantham is a town of ancient origin, a railway junction, and a farming and hunting centre. It once served as a staging point between London and Lincoln. Several fine coaching inns are still to be seen, and there is an attractive market square. The magnificent church – one of the most impressive parish churches in the country – carries a 281ft spire, and houses a chained library of 83 books, presented by a local rector in 1598. The famous Angel Inn is partly 14th-century and was where King Richard III signed the death warrant of the Duke of Buckingham in 1483. The Beehive Inn stands in Castlegate, and has a real beehive, complete with bees, as a sign. The town museum contains memorabilia of Sir Isaac Newton, a former pupil of King's School.

GREAT MALVERN,
Herefs & Worcs   76 *SO74*

This well-known inland resort is set on the slopes of the Malvern Hills, dominated by the splendid 1,395ft viewpoint of Worcestershire Beacon. St Anne's Well, one of the medicinal springs that gave the resort its reputation and past prosperity, still gushes from the Beacon's slope. The fine Priory Church contains a great deal of 15th-century stained glass and some fine misericords, including one depicting three rats hanging a cat. Nearby, at Malvern Wells, is St Wulfstan's Roman Catholic Church, where the composer Sir Edward Elgar is buried.

Set on the leafy slopes of the Malvern Hills, Great Malvern overlooks the wide plain of the Severn valley

GREAT YARMOUTH, Norfolk   79 *TG50*

This busy port and holiday resort has managed to retain many historic features. Most of these can be seen in the South Quay area, where there are remains of the town walls and the notable Custom House. Leading from the town wall to the quay are the Rows, a number of narrow lanes where the 300-year-old Merchant's House can be seen. Close by is the 14th-century Greyfriar's Cloister. The Elizabethan House Museum has a largely 16th-century interior disguised by a Georgian façade. The 13th-century building that houses the Tollhouse Museum incorporates ancient dungeons. Close to England's largest parish church is Anna Sewell House, a 17th-century building that was the birthplace of the authoress of *Black Beauty*.

HADLEIGH, Suffolk   79 *TM04*

Many fine Georgian and Victorian houses are preserved in this market town. Older buildings include the fine 15th-century Guildhall, which has two overhanging storeys. Also of note is the Deanery Tower, a remnant of a medieval palace. Features of the 14th- to 15th-century church include a bench-end that depicts the legend of a wolf which found and guarded the decapitated head of St Edmund.

HARWICH, Essex   79 *TM23*

This busy seaport and sailing centre lies at the mouths of the Stour and Orwell. Continental traffic is dealt with at Parkeston Quay. A number of the local houses date from the 16th, 17th, and 18th centuries, and an 18th-century council chamber can be seen in the Guildhall. A unique naval treadmill crane is preserved on the green. Christopher Jones, captain of the *Mayflower*, was one of the famous sailors born here. The Redoubt is a circular 180ft-diameter fort surrounded by a dry moat and built to defend the port against a Napoleonic invasion.

HENLEY-IN-ARDEN,
Warwicks   77 *SP16*

This small town lies in the ancient Forest of Arden district – though little of the forest remains today. Oak-timbered buildings lining the main street date from the 15th, 16th, and 17th centuries and the Guildhall from 1448. The church shows good 15th-century window tracery, and part of an ancient market cross has survived. Beaudesert Norman church has a fine chancel arch and window.

HEREFORD, Herefs & Worcs   76 *SO54*

Once the capital of Saxon West Mercia, this ancient town is at the centre of a rich agricultural district and is especially noted for the production of cider. There has been a cathedral here since the 7th century, but the present building dates mainly from the 12th, with later alterations. Notable relics in the cathedral are the 14th-century *Mappa Mundi*, King Stephen's 800-year-old chair, the best library of chained books in the country, and many monuments and tombs.

A wealth of interesting buildings of all periods is preserved in the city, including the outstanding early 15th-century Old House. In Widemarsh Street is the St John Coningsby Museum, which incorporates a 12th-century chapel and hall with 17th-century almshouses.

Several museums outside the city centre include the Churchill Gardens Museum, the Herefordshire Waterworks Museum and the Bulmer Railway Centre.

HERTFORD, Herts   78 *TL31*

In this ancient county town on the River Lea can be seen sparse remains of its original Norman castle. The present castle dates from 1500 and 1800. Queen Elizabeth I lived here as a child. A number of buildings dating from the 16th and 18th centuries include Shire Hall, by James, the brother of Robert Adam.

IPSWICH, Suffolk   *79 TM14*

Centuries of development have made this major port the largest and one of the most successful towns in Suffolk. It has managed to keep many relics of its eventful past intact. A red-brick gateway bearing royal arms survives from the unfinished Cardinal College of St Mary, which was founded by Cardinal Wolsey – a native of the town – in the 16th century. The Ancient or Sparrowe's House of 1567 stands in the Buttermarket and is noted for its exterior decoration of intricate patterns and features moulded in plaster, an outstanding example of the East Anglian art of pargeting. Original oak panelling and heavy carved beams can be seen by visitors to the bookshop which it now houses. Close by are the Great White Horse Hotel, featured in Charles Dickens' *Pickwick Papers*, and many old streets lined with well-preserved timber-framed houses. Christchurch Mansion was built by a Tudor merchant and is isolated in an oasis of parkland near the centre of town. It contains fine collections of furniture and paintings. Exhibits relating to local history and wildlife can be seen in the Ipswich Museum of Archaeology and Natural History, which stands in the High Street. The number of good churches in the town reflects its former prosperity.

IRONBRIDGE, Salop   *76 SJ60*

Across the River Severn here is a splendid iron bridge, built in 1779 and the first of its kind in the world. This must surely be the most beautiful monument there is to the Industrial Revolution, which had its birth in this area. The streets and buildings of Ironbridge itself cling to the sides of the Severn Gorge.

KENILWORTH, Warwicks   *77 SP27*

Kenilworth Castle stands on a grassy slope and includes a Norman keep. John of Gaunt remodelled the castle as a palace in the 14th century, and the great gatehouse dates from 1570. Much of the action in Scott's *Kenilworth* is set in this area.

KING'S LYNN, Norfolk   *78 TF62*

Two markets were founded here in Norman times, medieval merchants came here to build warehouses on the River Ouse, and 20th-century industry has continued the town's long history of commercial significance. Everywhere are survivals from periods that the settlement has grown through, and its medieval buildings are some of the finest in the country. Traces of the ancient walls show how the town has expanded since the troubled times in which they were built, and the superb Hanseatic Warehouse of 1428 recalls full-sailed barques laden with exotic goods. To complement the two market places there are two guildhalls, both of which date from the early 15th century. The superb Custom House, perhaps the most outstanding building in the town, was built by architect Henry Bell when he was mayor in 1683. The huge parish church contains two memorial brasses that are the biggest and most famous in England. Red Mount Chapel is a 15th-century octagonal building with beautiful fan-vaulting.

Lavenham owes many of its beautiful old buildings to wealth brought by the medieval wool trade

LAVENHAM, Suffolk   *79 TL94*

Easily one of the most outstanding villages in East Anglia, Lavenham has hardly changed in appearance since its heyday as an important wool town in the 14th and 15th centuries. Its dozens of immaculately preserved buildings include timber-framed houses, the Guildhall, and the Wool Hall. Slightly apart from the village is the superb church. It carries a 141ft tower resplendent with shiny knapped flint.

LEAMINGTON SPA, Warwicks   *77 SP36*

In the 18th century it was claimed that mineral springs in this lovely old town were beneficial in the treatment of various complaints. As the high-society fashion for taking the waters blossomed so also did Leamington, and today it boasts many grand old buildings that recall the prosperity of those times. The Pump Room of 1814, rebuilt in 1925, is an excellent focus for the terraces of Regency, Georgian and Victorian houses that grace the streets around it. The Warwick Art Gallery and Museum exhibits paintings and 18th-century glass.

LEDBURY, Herefs & Worcs   *76 SO73*

Black-and-white houses and inns give this delightful little country town its character. The Market Hall is a quaint timbered construction supported by stout wooden pillars. Also of interest are St Katherine's Hospital – a group of almshouses incorporating a Norman hall – and 16th-century Ledbury Park. Features of the large parish church are a detached tower, a fine Decorated north chapel and a number of monuments.

LEICESTER, Leics   *77 SK50*

This county town and university city has been a thriving centre at least since Roman times. Relics from its very early history include Roman pavements and the Jewry Wall site, which includes remains of 2nd-century Roman baths and the wall itself. Various relics from ancient times to the Middle Ages can be seen in the Jewry Wall Museum. Other museums in the city include the museum of the Royal Leicestershire Regiment and the Newarke Houses Museum, which offers a vivid insight into social history from the 16th century to the present day. It is housed in the Chantry House of 1511. Among many interesting churches is St Martin's, which stands on a Saxon site that was previously occupied by a Roman temple, and now enjoys cathedral status. Good Norman work is retained by the Church of St Mary de Castro.

LEOMINSTER, Herefs & Worcs   *76 SO45*

This pleasant country town has produced fine wool since the 13th century, and Hereford cattle are exported all over the world from here. Many black-and-white buildings include the fine Grange Court, built in 1633 by John Abel. Formerly the town hall, this was re-erected on its present site in 1856. The interesting Norman to Perpendicular Priory Church has a double nave, fine Decorated-style windows and a richly carved Norman west doorway. Inside the church is preserved a huge, wheeled ducking stool.

LICHFIELD, Staffs   *77 SK10*

A city of great age and architectural distinction, Lichfield has a fine red sandstone cathedral which carries three tall spires popularly known as 'the Ladies of the Vale'. Inside the building is preserved the 7th-century manuscript book of the *St Chad Gospels*. A house in the town was the birthplace of Dr Johnson and now serves as a Johnson museum featuring, among other relics, his favourite silver teapot. The Swan Inn is also associated with this famous man, and the city celebrates its connection with him annually on the Saturday nearest 18 September.

LONG MELFORD, Suffolk   79 TL84

Perhaps the stateliest village in Suffolk, Long Melford has an impressive main street lined by fine old buildings and dominated by a magnificent church, which dates from the 15th century and occupies the site of a Roman temple. The Lady Chapel of 1496 can almost be considered as separate from the main building, though attached in mortar if not in style to the east end. The well-proportioned tower was added in 1903. A triangular green stands between the church and Melford Hall, one of the finest Elizabethan manors in England. It occupies three sides of a lovely old courtyard and carries a splendid array of turrets.

LUDLOW, Salop   76 SO57

Ludlow stands on the banks of the Corve and Teme, among the gentle Shropshire hills. High above the town's rooftops soars the 135ft tower of the parish church. Mainly of 15th-century date, the church is the largest in the county. The ashes of poet A. E. Housman are interred here. Nearby are the beautiful black-and-white Reader's House and the 17th-century Feathers Hotel. These are the best of many half-timbered buildings preserved in the town. Georgian architecture testifies to the continued prosperity of Ludlow and is at its best in Broad Street, which is lined with many fine dwellings from that period. The town's earliest structure is the castle. From as early as 1085 this occupied a strategic position in the contentious border country known as the Marcher Lands.

MELBOURNE, Derbyshire   77 SK32

Melbourne church is a splendid example of Norman work, especially the beautiful nave. Two of the three towers carried by the building are incomplete. A fine tithe barn stands opposite. Melbourne Hall is of 16th- to 18th-century date, and was once the seat of Lord Melbourne. The gardens contain a superb and well-restored pergola.

MELTON MOWBRAY, Leics   77 SK71

Three famous hunting packs meet here, and the district is often loud with the noise of horns, hounds, and horses. The town is internationally famous for Stilton cheese and pork pies. The history of the town and its products is traced in the Melton Carnegie Museum. St Mary's is arguably the stateliest and most impressive of all the county's churches, and contains some very fine monuments.

MINSTER LOVELL, Oxon   77 SP31

Clustered stone-built cottages and the fine, partly timbered Swan Inn nestle together to form this quaint little Windrush village. Nearby Minster Lovell Hall is a ruined 15th-century building beautifully set between the river and the church.

NEWMARKET, Suffolk   78 TL66

As well as being a famous horse-racing centre, Newmarket is the headquarters of both the Jockey Club and the National Stud. Nearby Devil's Ditch is a seven-mile-long earthwork of ancient origin.

NORTHAMPTON, Northants   77 SP76

One of the largest market towns in England, Northampton is the administrative centre of its county and is noted for its fine churches. Among the best is Holy Sepulchre, a rare round church that was founded in 1110. Inside is a 6ft-tall brass which dates from the 17th century and is one of the largest in England. Other old buildings include 17th-century Hazelrigg Mansion, the 16th-century Welsh House, and the 17th-century Sessions House.

NORTHLEACH, Glos   77 SP11

Northleach stands on high ground, east of the Roman Fosse Way, between the Coln and Windrush valleys. Its attractive stone-built cottages and almshouses are dominated by a magnificent wool church where a fine collection of brasses can be seen.

A collection of antique dolls is on display in the Toy Room of Strangers' Hall, Norwich

Royal Arcade is perhaps the most elegant part of the shopping area in Norwich

NORWICH, Norfolk   79 TG20

Once an important centre of the worsted trade, this county town stands on the River Wensum and boasts a Norman cathedral with one of the finest interiors in the country. Other major features include a fine presbytery and a beautiful cloister. Access to the building is by two fine gates, the Erpingham of 1420 and St Ethelbert's of 1272. The city also boasts no less than 30 parish churches. The largest is St Peter Mancroft, which carries a notable tower, but all the others have particular details that make them worth a visit. Norwich Castle was started about 1130, but its Norman origins have been heavily disguised by 19th-century refacing. Inside is an excellent collection of paintings by the Norwich School of artists. Several of the city's other medieval buildings now house museums, including the Bridewell, Strangers' Hall and St Peter Hungate Church. An old chapel, converted in the 1920s, now houses the well-known Maddermarket Theatre. The Sainsbury Centre for the Visual Arts, at the University of East Anglia, contains Sir Robert and Lady Sainsbury's art collection.

Paintings depicting local hunts can be seen in the Melton Carnegie Museum at Melton Mowbray

NOTTINGHAM, Notts   77 SK54

The growth of this ancient city was influenced by the Saxons, Danes, and Normans, but it was the Industrial Revolution that made it a thriving commercial centre famous for fine machine-made lace. Early prosperity was aided by the natural highway provided by the River Trent, a strategic advantage that may have prompted William the Conqueror to build a strong castle here soon after his invasion of Britain. The present castle was built in the 17th century and restored in the 19th for use as a museum and art gallery. Among several good churches in Nottingham is St Mary's, a splendid example of 15th-century architecture with excellent windows and a glorious Madonna and Child painted by Bartolommeo. Other notable buildings include the 18th-century Shire Hall, the partly medieval Trip to Jerusalem Inn, and a wealth of Georgian domestic architecture. The Brewhouse Yard Museum is a fascinating local history collection and in Castlegate is the Museum of Costume and Textiles. The city's natural history museum is in Wollaton Hall, a 16th-century mansion that stands close to the university campus.

ORFORD, Suffolk   79 TM44

In 1165 Henry II built a moat-encircled castle with an 18-sided keep here in an attempt to establish Norman power over the peoples of East Anglia. Today the building that developed from these early beginnings contains a collection of arms and affords excellent views of the picturesque houses and fishermen's cottages below its walls.

OSWESTRY, Salop   76 SJ22

A long history of periodic sacking by Welsh and English armies, and three disastrous accidental fires, have left Oswestry with few buildings older than the 19th century, although the site has been inhabited for about 2,500 years. Traces of a Norman castle remain, the church retains a lych-gate of 1631, and the Llwyd Mansion is a fine old black-and-white building bearing the crest of the Holy Roman Empire, granted to the Llwyd family for services in the Crusades. Old Oswestry is an Iron Age hill-fort situated 1 mile north.

OXFORD, Oxon   77 SP50

This ancient and world-renowned university town is first mentioned in the Saxon Chronicle of 912, but there was a thriving community here at least 200 years earlier. Organized teaching has existed at Oxford since the 12th century, and the collegiate system became established in the 13th century as the various religious orders consolidated.

The town's street plan forms an intriguing network centred on Carfax, a junction of four streets and the centre of the old community. Perhaps the most notable of the four is High Street, known locally as 'The High'. At the east end is Magdalen, one of the richest colleges in Oxford, and a little closer to Carfax is St Edmund Hall – a unique relic of a residential society founded for graduates in 1220. The High's centrepiece is the University Church of St Mary the Virgin, which is instantly recognizable by its beautiful 14th-century spire. Wren designed the Sheldonian Theatre, at the east end of Broad Street, and the Ashmolean Museum displays art and archaeological collections.

PAINSWICK, Glos   76 SO80

Years ago Painswick was an important centre of the cloth industry. This prosperity is evident in its many old houses and inns, among them the tall-chimneyed Court House (associated with Charles I) and 18th-century Painswick House. The churchyard is famous for its 99 yew trees; there is a tradition that the hundredth one will never grow.

PETERBOROUGH, Cambs   78 TL19

Originally this ancient River Nene town grew up around a medieval monastery. Old features of the town include the cathedral, which was begun in 1118. Its most notable features are the exquisite west front and beautifully painted 13th-century ceilings. Both Catherine of Aragon and Mary Queen of Scots were buried in the cathedral, although the remains of the latter now lie in Westminster Abbey. Other survivors of the past are the Knight's gateway, the Bishop's Palace, Longthorpe Tower and the west gateway, all of medieval origin. The old town hall, or Guildhall, is a fine building dated 1671.

Fine pargeted plasterwork, typical of East Anglia, can be seen in Church Street, Saffron Walden

ROSS-ON-WYE, Herefs & Worcs   76 SO62

High above the roofs of this attractive town rises the splendid 208ft spire of St Mary's Church, which dates mainly from the 13th century. An important feature of the High Street is the 17th-century market hall.

SAFFRON WALDEN, Essex   78 TL53

This delightful town once specialized in the growing of a saffron crocus for use in dyes. A number of fine old houses are embellished by pargeting, or decorative plasterwork. The fine Perpendicular church has an imposing nave, interesting monuments and brasses, and a lofty spire which was added in 1831. The museum exhibits items of anthropological and archaeological interest. Magnificent 17th-century Audley End House lies 1 mile west.

SANDRINGHAM, Norfolk   79 TF62

Included in this 7,000-acre estate, owned by the Royal Family, are a 19th-century house, the farms and woodlands of seven parishes, and a 300-acre country park. The park church, where the Royal Family attend services, is of exceptional note and contains an organ that was the last gift of King Edward VII.

Old Oswestry covers 68 acres and is the finest example of an Iron Age hill-fort in the Welsh border country

SHREWSBURY, Salop   76 SJ41
Superbly set in a huge loop of the Severn, this beautiful and unspoilt town is famous for its half-timbered buildings and picturesque streets. Two notable 18th-century bridges span the Severn into the town centre, and the remains of the castle that defended the vulnerable north-eastern entrance dominate the imposing railway station. Nearby are the 17th-century buildings of old Shrewsbury School. Outstanding churches in Shrewsbury include the Norman and later Abbey Church, 12th- to 17th-century St Mary's, and mainly 18th-century St Julian's, with its ancient towers. Among other outstanding buildings are Rowley's House, now an archaeological museum, and the small complex of 14th-century cottages, shops and lovely old hall called Bear Steps.

SOUTHWOLD, Suffolk   79 TM57
A resort at the mouth of the River Blyth, Southwold offers a sand and shingle beach, bathing, and golfing. The Southwold Museum, in Bartholomew Green, contains interesting displays on local history. Near the magnificent church, in the middle of town, stands a lighthouse.

SPALDING, Lincs   78 TF22
This historic fenland town stands on the banks of the Welland in an area of drained marshland where market gardeners and bulb growers raise crops in soil of almost legendary richness. In springtime the district is glorious with tulips, daffodils, narcissi and hyacinths that form a carpet of blazing colour comparable only with the bulb fields of Holland. Every May the town holds a spectacular Flower Festival that attracts visitors from all over the country. On the eastern outskirts are the beautiful Springfield Gardens, 25 acres of lawns and water features designed to show over a million bulbs to their best advantage. The town itself has many old buildings in charming streets on both banks of the river, including several good examples of 18th-century design. One of the oldest is the greatly restored Ayscoughfee Hall, which dates from the 15th century and now houses a museum of British birds.

STAFFORD, Staffs   76 SJ92
Black-and-white houses to be seen in Stafford include the High House, where King Charles I and Prince Rupert stayed for three nights in 1642. The Swan Hotel has associations with George Borrow, who was an ostler here in 1825. St Mary's Church houses a Norman font and a bust of the famous angler Izaak Walton, who was born here in 1593.

STAMFORD, Lincs   78 TF00
Justly considered one of England's most beautiful towns, stone-built Stamford has a long history that can be traced back as far as the time of Danish settlement. In the 13th and 14th centuries it was important enough to have its own university, and the powerful influence of early Christianity is evident in many fine churches and other ecclesiastical buildings. All Saints' Place is the visual centre of the town

and is noted for its outstanding, multi-period architecture. Browne's Hospital has been described as one of the finest medieval almshouses surviving in England, and includes a beautiful Jacobean hall and a chapel. Close to the River Welland are the ancient Burghley Almshouses. The George Hotel was a coaching inn in the 14th century, and among fine buildings from many periods in St George's Square is a house that has been continuously inhabited since about 1350.

STOKE-ON-TRENT, Staffs   76 SJ84
The Stoke-on-Trent of today came into being when the old town combined in 1910 with Tunstall, Burslem, Hanley, Fenton and Longton, a cluster of towns long known as the Potteries. Pottery was made here in Roman times, and finds can be seen in Hanley at the City Museum and Art Gallery, which has one of the world's largest and finest collections of ceramics. Several museums concentrate on the industrial archaeology of the area. Some of the famous factories can be visited.

The agriculture of days gone by is vividly recalled in Stowmarket's Museum of East Anglian Life

The rich fenlands around Spalding are at their colourful best at tulip-time

STOWMARKET, Suffolk   79 TM05
Poet John Milton visited this busy Gipping valley market town many times to see his tutor Thomas Young, who lived at the vicarage. Most of the buildings are of fairly recent date, like the good Georgian and Victorian houses round the market square and the 18th-century workhouse of Stow Lodge Hospital. Inside the town church, which displays a variety of styles, are an old organ and a rare wigstand. The Museum of East Anglian Life is set in the 70-acre grounds of Abbots Hall.

STOW-ON-THE-WOLD, Glos   77 SP12
'Stow-on-the-Wold where the wind blows cold' is a local saying that aptly describes this, the highest hilltop town in the Cotswolds. It has an enormous market square with stocks, a 14th-century cross and a fine 'wool' church.

STRATFORD-UPON-AVON, Warwicks   77 SP25
William Shakespeare was born here in 1564. His childhood home contains a museum relating to his life, and the old Guildhall that housed his school still stands. A picturesque Elizabethan knot garden can be seen near the foundations of New Place, where he died, and his remains lie in Holy Trinity Church. A lovely thatched and timbered cottage in the nearby village of Shottery is where his wife Anne Hathaway was born, and gabled Hall's Croft was the home of their daughter Susanna. Many of the great man's works are staged in the Royal Shakespeare Theatre, which was built on an Avon-side site in 1932; it incorporates a museum and picture gallery. Among many 15th- and 16th-century buildings preserved in the town are several lovely half-timbered houses and the 14-arch Clopton Bridge over the Avon. Harvard House is dated 1596 and was the home of John Harvard, founder of the American university of the same name.

SUDBURY, Suffolk   79 TL84

Sudbury stands on the River Stour and is famous as the birthplace of painter Thomas Gainsborough. Born in 1727, he lived at 46 Gainsborough Street — now a local arts centre and museum containing a selection of his work — and he is commemorated by a bronze statue on Market Hill. St Peter's Church was built in the 15th century. St Gregory's is much older, having been built on the foundations of an old college by the Archbishop of Canterbury in about 1365.

SUTTON, Cambs   78 TL47

Also known as Sutton-in-the-Isle, this village has a commanding church tower surmounted by a rare double octagon and spire. The Burystead of 1742 retains a former 14th-century chapel.

SWAFFHAM, Norfolk   79 TF80

Legend tells of the 'Pedlar of Swaffham', who travelled to London to throw himself into the Thames but was dissuaded by a man he met on London Bridge. This stranger related a dream in which he found treasure in a remote village garden – a garden that the pedlar recognized as his own. He hastened home to find two pots of gold. An image of the pedlar is now incorporated in the town sign. The triangular market place has a domed rotunda built by the Earl of Oxford in 1783 as a market cross. Features of the local church include a splendid angel-carved double-hammerbeam roof and a fine 16th-century west tower.

TEWKESBURY, Glos   76 SO83

Tewkesbury stands near the confluence of the River Avon with the Severn. The many picturesque old houses and inns in the town include several fine timbered buildings, and an ancient water-mill. The House of the Golden Key and the Ancient Grudge are both sited in the High Street, and are two of the town's finest old houses. The Norman central tower of the magnificent Abbey Church is one of the finest in England, and there are a number of fine chantry chapels, tombs and monuments.

THAME, Oxon   77 SP70

Old houses and an exceptionally wide main street are features of this River Thame market town. The 13th- to 15th-century church houses interesting monuments and brasses, and the old grammar school dates back to 1575. Interesting inns include the Spread Eagle and the picturesque Bird Cage. Remains of Rycote Manor House and the recently restored chapel with its notable 17th-century woodwork, lie 3 miles to the south-west.

THAXTED, Essex   78 TL63

Many old houses survive to remind the visitor that this was once a very prosperous town. The 15th-century church was clearly built by a community with a great deal of money to spend. The timbered Guildhall dates from the 16th century and incorporates an earlier ancient lock-up. Several old almshouses and a tower windmill of 1805 can be seen in the vicinity of the church.

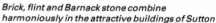

Brick, flint and Barnack stone combine harmoniously in the attractive buildings of Sutton

A carved figure of Swaffham's famous pedlar is featured on a bench-end in the church

TONG, Salop   76 SJ70

A magnificent array of monuments in the 15th-century church has helped this fine building to acquire the nickname 'the village Westminster'. Features include the Golden Chapel of 1515 which displays notable fan vaulting, and a rare ciborium or sacramental vessel. Boscobel House lies 3½ miles east, and it was here that King Charles II hid after the Battle of Worcester in 1651.

WALSINGHAM, Norfolk   79 TF93

The shrine at Walsingham, a place of paramount importance to the pilgrims of the Middle Ages, was founded in the 11th century. Henry VIII had the shrine robbed when he dissolved the monasteries, but in the 19th century the pilgrimages were revived. A new Shrine of Our Lady was built for the Anglican Church in the early 20th century. Remains of what was once a giant concourse of buildings date mainly from the 13th and 14th centuries.

WARWICK, Warwicks   77 SP26

Imposing Warwick Castle is one of the finest medieval strongholds in Europe. It stands on a Saxon site above this compact River Avon town, and its exceptional Norman and later structure hides an interior completely rebuilt during the 17th century. The castle is still occupied, but visitors have access to the state rooms, torture chamber, silver vault, ghost tower, and Avon-side grounds that were landscaped by Capability Brown. Also in the town are the remains of town walls, two gates, and a great number of building styles ranging from half-timbered to the conscious starkness of the 20th century. Lord Leycester's Hospital was founded as a guildhall in 1383 and converted to almshouses in 1571, and the 18th-century Shire Hall is considered an excellent example of its type. Elizabethan Oken's House contains a doll museum, and 17th-century St John's House features both a museum of crafts, costume and furniture, and the Museum of the Royal Warwickshire Regiment. The 18th-century Court House is an Italianate building.

WELLS-NEXT-THE-SEA, Norfolk   79 TF94

Old houses line narrow streets which lead to the quayside of this small resort and port. The beach has good sands at low tide, and bathing may be enjoyed in a creek about 1 mile away. Salt marshes nearby are a haven for wildlife.

WENDOVER, Bucks   77 SP80

Many delightful brick and timber cottages survive here, plus a collection of quaint inns which includes the Red Lion Hotel, where Oliver Cromwell slept in 1642. Bosworth House, in the main street, is of 17th-century origin. Both the local windmill and a watermill have been converted into houses. The ancient Icknield Way crosses the Chilterns nearby on its way from east to south-west England.

WEOBLEY, Herefs & Worcs   76 SO45

Perhaps the most attractive half-timbered village in the area, Weobley includes several cottages which date back to the 14th century. The picturesque Red Lion Inn is of the same age, and so is the church, which carries a lofty spire and contains interesting monuments. Earthworks survive from the former castle.

WILMCOTE, Warwicks   77 SP15

Mary Arden's House, the half-timbered Tudor birthplace of Shakespeare's mother, is the main reason for the large numbers of visitors who come to Wilmcote each year. An interesting farm museum is housed in the outbuildings behind the house.

WINCHCOMBE, Glos   76 SP02

Ancient Winchcombe was once capital of the Kingdom of Mercia. The site of its abbey, founded in AD797 and destroyed by Henry VIII, is being excavated. The 700-year-old George Inn was once used by pilgrims. Just outside the little town is Sudeley Castle, once the home of Catherine Parr.

WISBECH, Cambs   78 TF40

Fruit trees and bulbs are cultivated in the district around this River Nene town, and fruit-canning is an important local industry. The many fine Georgian houses situated on the North and South Brinks, facing the quays and river, include several displaying Dutch characteristics. They form one of the finest riverside vistas in England. Peckover House is one of the most notable; this was built in 1722 and displays rococo plaster decoration. Features of the mainly Norman and Perpendicular church include a double nave and a fine tower dating from about 1520. The Wisbech and Fenland museum portrays the life of the Fens.

WITNEY, Oxon   77 SP30

The name 'Witney' is synonymous with blanket-making, an industry that has grown from the town's close proximity to rich wool country and the availability of ready power from the River Windrush. *Domesday Book* records that two mills stood here, and doubtless there were others even before that. The main street extends for almost a mile to a green set with lime trees and graced with fine houses built with the profits of wool and weaving. Prosperity is similarly mirrored in the 17th-century Butter Cross, which stands on 13 stone pillars and displays both a clock tower and a sundial. The old Blanket Hall of 1720 displays a curious one-handed clock. Witney's church carries a 156ft-high spire that serves as a landmark for many miles.

WOBURN, Beds   78 SP93

This village of thatched red-and-white brick cottages is set in lovely wooded countryside which is overshadowed by the fame of its neighbour, Woburn Abbey. A palatial 18th-century mansion, Woburn is renowned for its collection of paintings and period furniture. It stands in a 3,000-acre park in which is the Wild Animal Kingdom, a game reserve with a dolphinarium among its many attractions.

The tower of Worcester Cathedral overlooks pleasant gardens bordering the Severn at South Quay

WOODBRIDGE, Suffolk   79 TM24

Attractive houses of major historical interest surround the old market square round which this port has grown. Many date from the 16th century, and the entire group is centred on the superb Shire Hall, which features work from the 16th to 19th centuries and picturesque Dutch-style gables. Woodbridge church carries a tall flint-flushwork tower and contains a seven sacrament font. Two old mills, one a rare example which depends on the tide, can be seen here. The port's status as a busy centre of ocean trade declined a long time ago, but today it is a popular sailing centre.

WOODSTOCK, Oxon   77 SP41

The royal demesne of Woodstock was from Saxon to Tudor times the site of a great country manor that served as the playground of royalty. Woodstock House was, unfortunately, a total casualty of the Civil War and has all but vanished. In the town itself is a grand town hall that was built in 1766 by Sir William Chambers with money donated by the Duke of Marlborough. Tradition has it that the famous Bear Inn dates back to 1237. On the edge of the town stands Blenheim Palace, built by the First Duke of Marlborough with money voted to him by Parliament after his victory over the French at Blenheim in 1704. The house was designed by Vanbrugh and the grounds, later landscaped by Capability Brown, cover 2,500 acres and include a vast lake, a Triumphal Way, and a sunken Italian garden. The palace itself is filled with art treasures and fine furnishings. Prime minister and war leader Sir Winston Churchill was born here in 1874, and lies buried in the churchyard at Bladon, a village at the edge of Blenheim Park.

WORCESTER, Herefs & Worcs   76 SO85

County town of Hereford and Worcester, the city is built on both banks of the River Severn, linked by a fine stone bridge built between 1771 and 1780. The cathedral is mainly of the Early English to Perpendicular period, and its 11th-century crypt was the work of Bishop Wulstan. Other notable features include the much-restored 14th-century tower, choir stalls of 1379, Prince Arthur's Chantry of 1504 and the circular Norman chapter house. Among the many monuments is an effigy of King John, considered the earliest royal effigy in England. Picturesque old houses flank Friar Street and New Street. Tudor House, in Friar Street, was once an inn and now contains a museum of domestic life. The Corn Exchange dates from 1848. The Commandery, or Hospital of St Wulstan, includes an interesting old hall with a gallery. The Dyson Perrins Museum of Worcester china is incorporated in the Royal Worcester porcelain works.

Cromwell defeated the Scottish army of King Charles II at the Battle of Worcester in 1651, and a half-timbered house of 1577 in New Street is associated with the King's escape. A timbered house in Trinity Road was visited by Queen Elizabeth I in 1574.

WYMONDHAM, Norfolk   79 TG10

An exceptionally fine timbered 17th-century market cross in this town is perhaps unique. The parish church is part of a Benedictine abbey, which accounts for its two towers at the east and west ends. A fine Norman nave, a remarkable carved hammerbeam roof, and notable Renaissance terracotta sedilia are of particular note. St Thomas à Becket's Well, once visited by pilgrims, is near the church.

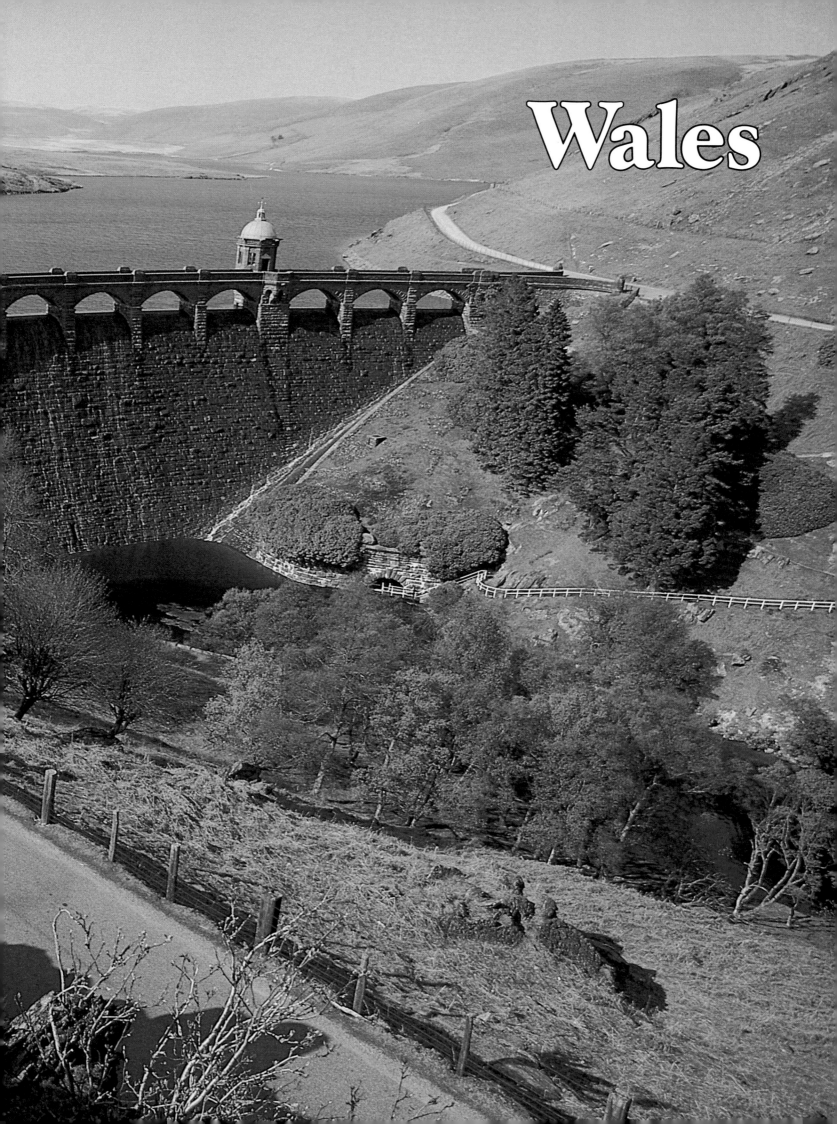

Wales

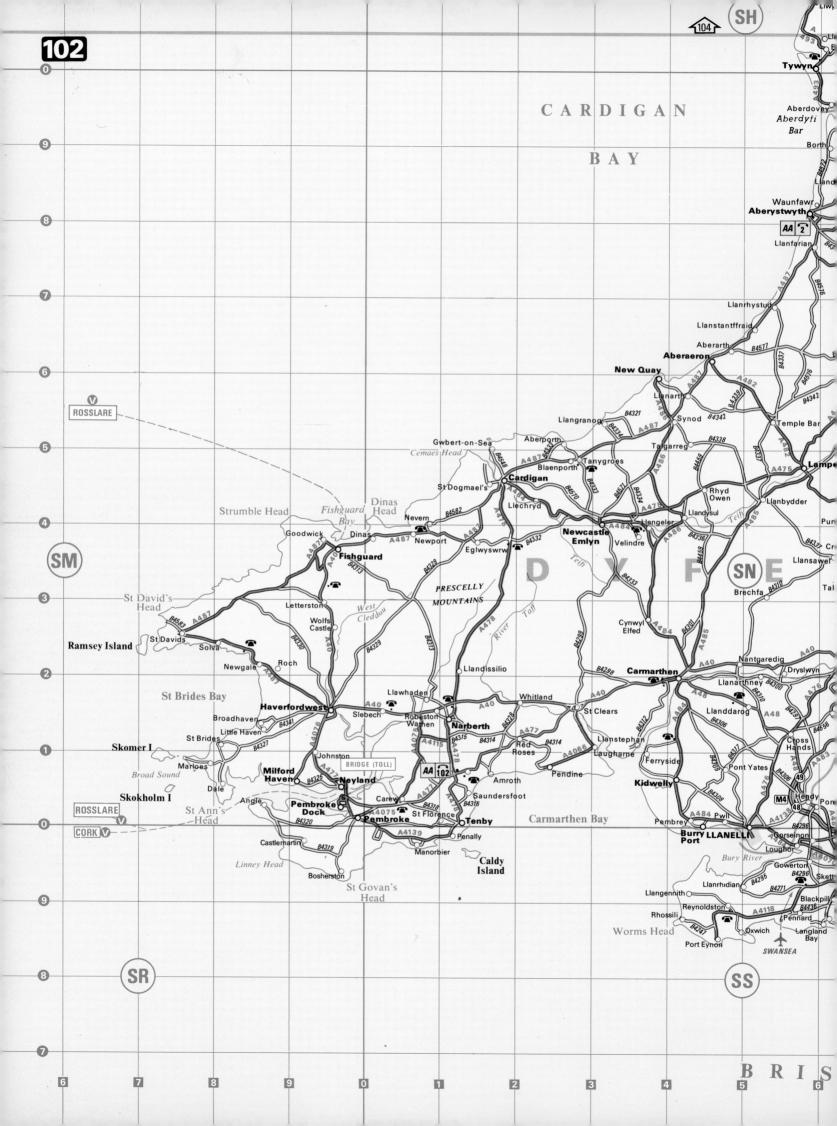

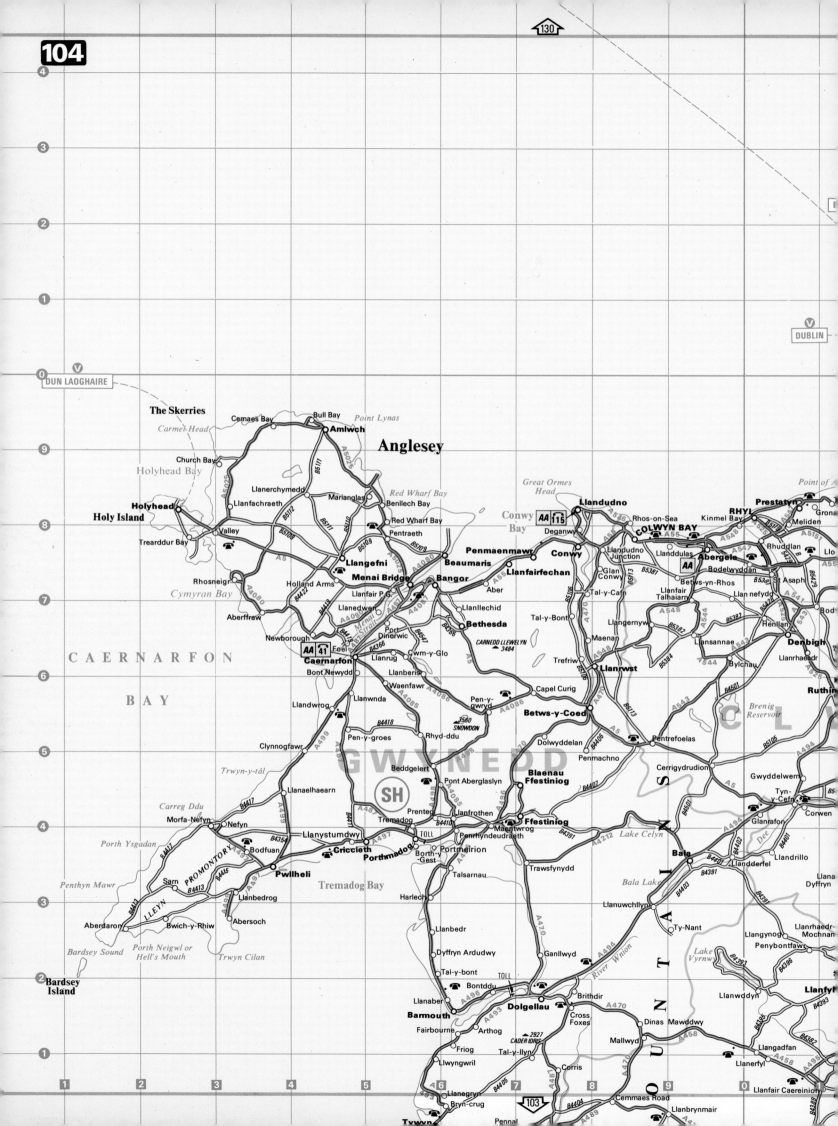

Black Mountain and Tywi Valley
88 miles

LLANDEILO
This attractive little market town stands on the Afon Tywi, the longest river in Wales. Its waters are spanned here by a fine stone bridge that was built in the 19th century. Its central span, at 145ft, is also claimed to be the longest in Wales. The church of St Teilo, from which the town takes its name, originally dates from the 13th century but was almost completely rebuilt in Victorian times.

TALLEY
Neat cottages and an attractive church cluster protectively round the remains of once-famous Talley Abbey, deep in the green folds of the Dyfed hills. Little of the abbey's 12th-century fabric has survived pillaging for building material that has gone on unchecked through the centuries, but an undeniable air of sanctity still exists. A path through the yard of the adjacent church leads to the two placid lakes of Talley.

LLANDOVERY
The fertile flood-plain of the Afon Tywi makes ideal pasture-land, so it is not surprising that Llandovery, like Llandeilo, has a long-established cattle-market where local livestock are gathered for sale. The market is overlooked by the ruined and overgrown keep of a medieval castle, and Llanfair church is built within the ramparts of a Roman fort. The church incorporates Roman tiles.

DOLAUHIRION BRIDGE
Designed by William Edwards and built in 1773, this splendid bridge spans the Tywi in a single graceful arch of 84ft.

CILYCWM
Situated in one of the tributary valleys of the Tywi, Cilycwm is surrounded by some of the wildest scenery in South Wales and is noted for the old wall paintings in its 15th-century church. The village chapel is claimed to have been the first Methodist meeting place in Wales.

TWM SION CATTI'S CAVE
A short nature trail up Dinas Hill leads to the one-time hideout of Twm Sion Catti, a famous early 16th-century outlaw whose modern reputation has a lot in common with England's tales of Robin Hood.

LLYN BRIANNE RESERVOIR
The creation of this huge reservoir in the early 1970s was greeted with mixed feelings, as the area flooded had previously been considered one of the most remote and beautiful in Wales. New roads to the lake have made it easily accessible, and the spectacular scenery that surrounds its great expanse can be enjoyed by all. The last British nesting sites of the red kite lie in closely guarded and highly secret locations in this area.

TOWY FOREST
On the northern slopes of Llyn Brianne, and accessible via the new reservoir road, are the coniferous ranks of Towy Forest. The Afon Tywi has its source some miles to the north in the wild moorlands of central Wales.

Dramatic Carreg Cennen Castle is associated in legend with one of King Arthur's knights.

LLANGADOG
Llangadog was once an important town with a 12th-century native Welsh castle unusual in that it was probably using defensive techniques learned from the Norman conquerors. The overlords, ever wary of opposition, completely destroyed it in 1277. All that remains today is a mound sited about ½ mile south of the village. Carn Goch, the largest Iron Age hill-fort in Wales, lies 3 miles to the south-west.

BLACK MOUNTAIN
West from the A4069 viewpoint the Black Mountain falls away in ridges to the fertile Tywi valley. Geologically, the Black Mountain is made up of very ancient red sandstone in the north and younger millstone grit in the south, the two beds being separated by a band of limestone. It is a lonely, windswept land inhabited only by sheep and indigenous wild animals.

AMMANFORD
Until the late 19th century the Cross Inn at the centre of this town was almost the only building here, but the discovery of a local anthracite coalfield quickly brought the mixed blessing of industrial prosperity. Nowadays the area is dotted with slag heaps from the workings, but the essentially agricultural character of the local countryside remains.

LLANDYBIE
This small town stands on the edge of the local coalfield and is justifiably proud of its splendid early Victorian railway station. The church preserves a medieval barrel-roof and carries an imposing battlemented tower. Inside are a number of interesting monuments. A lane leads eastwards from Llandybie to beautiful river scenery and the waterfall of Glynhir.

CARREG CENNEN CASTLE
A path through a farmyard leads to this imposing pile of walls and turrets perched on a limestone cliff which drops a breathtaking 200ft into the attractive valley below. The existing building dates from the 13th century, but a fortress existed here long before that. The atmosphere of permanence about the castle inspired Dylan Thomas to refer to it, in *Under Milk Wood*, as 'Carreg Cennen, King of Time'.

DYNEVOR CASTLE
The ivy-clad tower of a castle can be seen rising from trees on a hill directly west of Llandeilo. This is Dynevor – or more properly Dinefwr – Castle, which was once the seat of Welsh princes. Ruins comprising the keep and part of the curtain wall are situated in a private park near a 19th-century mansion. The castle is not open to the public.

TOUR 25 ROUTE DIRECTIONS
Leave Llandeilo on the A40 (SP Llandovery). (In ½ mile pass a left turn that offers a detour along the B4302 to Talley Abbey.) The main tour continues to Llandovery. Turn left beyond a level crossing on to the A483 (SP Builth Wells). In ¼ mile, at a crossroads, turn left (SP Rhandirmwyn). In 1¾ miles pass Dolauhirion Bridge, just off the main

tour. (After another 1¾ miles, a detour can be made by turning left to Cilycwm village.) The main route continues through Rhandirmwyn, later passing a footpath to Twm Sion Catti's Cave. Continue to the car park at Llyn Brianne Reservoir. (A narrow but well-surfaced road may be taken from here to the reservoir's farthest arm and Towy Forest.)

Return to Llandovery. Turn right, then left on to the A40 (SP Brecon), and take the next right turn on to the A4069 (SP Llangadog). Drive to Llangadog, then continue to a T-junction and turn left (SP Brynamman). Ascend on to the slopes of the Black Mountain, pass a 1,600ft viewpoint and descend to Brynamman. Turn right for Gwaun-cae-gurwen and right again, just before a level crossing, on to the A474. Go through Garnant and Glanaman to Ammanford, and at the traffic lights turn right on to the A483 (SP Llandeilo). Go through Llandybie to Ffairfach. (Here a detour to Carreg Cennen Castle can be made by turning right on to an unclassified road, then turning right again. Keep left at the edge of Trapp to reach the castle's car park.) The main route continues through Ffairfach to return to Llandeilo, with views to the left of Dynevor Castle.

Old Cardiganshire
75 miles

LAMPETER

Although little more than a village by English standards, Lampeter is one of the largest settlements in the wilderness of mid Wales. Its population is scarcely more than 2,000, but it is a busy market centre and, more surprisingly, a university town. Founded in 1822 by Thomas Burgess, Bishop of St David's and the son of a Hampshire grocer, St David's College became part of the University of Wales in 1971. Lampeter's importance in a former age is recalled by a grassy mound in the college grounds – all that remains of a medieval castle.

ABERAERON

Like Lampeter, Aberaeron also has a connection with Hampshire. A Hampshire curate married an Aberaeron heiress in the late 18th century, and together they planned and developed the prosperous little seaport and shipbuilding centre that Aberaeron became. Today its trade has declined, but it is still a popular resort and yachting centre and preserves its harmonious Regency townscape.

ABERYSTWYTH

Set in a hillside at the mouth of the Afon Rheidol, Aberystwyth is a seaside resort, university town and historic administrative centre. Pleasant gardens now surround the ruins of the 13th-century castle that played such an important part in Aberystwyth's turbulent history before falling into decay after the Civil War. Nearby stands a striking Victorian Gothic building that was constructed as a hotel and later became the first home of the University of Wales. The main campus of the university is now on Penglais Hill, where the National Library of Wales is also to be found. The library contains 5½ million books, and its collection of Welsh writings – the largest in the world – includes the 12th-century *Black Book of Carmarthen*, the oldest manuscript in the Welsh language. Also worth a visit are the Ceredigion Museum and the 'Aberystwyth Yesterday' exhibition – both rich in local-interest items.

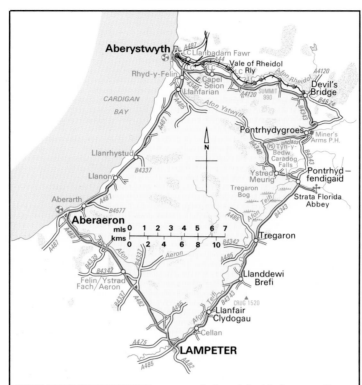

TOUR 26 ROUTE DIRECTIONS

Leave Lampeter by the A482 (SP Aberaeron), and drive to Aberaeron. Here, take the A487 (SP Aberystwyth) and go through Aberarth, Llanon and Llanrhystud. Climb inland and descend through Llanfarian to the Ystwyth valley. Continue through Rhyd-y-Felin and cross the Afon Rheidol to reach Aberystwyth.
 From Aberystwyth return across the Afon Rheidol on the A487 (SP Aberaeron) and in 1¼ miles keep forward on to the A4120 (SP Devil's Bridge). Go through Capel Seion and in 5 miles cross a 990ft road summit before continuing to Devil's Bridge. Leave by the B4343 (SP Tregaron).

Go through Pontrhydygroes and in ¼ mile pass the Miners' Arms pub and bear right (SP Trawscoed). Shortly past the Tyn-y-Bedw picnic site, turn left on to the B4340 and go through Ystrad Meurig to Pontrhydfendigaid. Leave on the B4343 (SP Tregaron). Cross the Afon Teifi and shortly turn left on to an unclassified road to visit Strata Florida Abbey.
 Return to Pontrhydfendigaid, turn left on to the B4343 and drive to Tregaron. From here follow signs for Llanddewi Brefi, B4343, and drive along the Teifi valley to Llanddewi Brefi. Continue on the B4343 (SP Lampeter) to Llanfair Clydogau. Continue through Cellan, and in 2 miles turn right on to the A482 and return to Lampeter.

VALE OF RHEIDOL LIGHT RAILWAY

British Rail's only line still to use steam locomotives runs 12 miles along the lovely Rheidol valley between Aberystwyth and Devil's Bridge. Originally opened in 1902 to carry local lead ore and the occasional passenger, the line's route through the breathtaking scenery of the 'Vale' has ensured its success as a major tourist attraction.

DEVIL'S BRIDGE

A spectacular wooded gorge, tremendous waterfalls, and three bridges stacked on top of each other are to be seen here. The road bridge is the uppermost of the three, and dates from 1901, whilst the oldest, at the bottom, is thought to have been built in the 12th century by monks from Strata Florida Abbey – though legend maintains it was built by the Devil.

PONTRHYDYGROES

The neat cottages in this village were once occupied by employees of the important local lead-mining industry. Ruins of the mine buildings stand on the surrounding hillsides.

PONTRHYDFENDIGAID

A quaint old bridge spans the Teifi here. Once a year the village is the venue of a popular and well-endowed eisteddfod – a traditional Welsh festival of poetry and music.

STRATA FLORIDA ABBEY

Described in the Middle Ages as 'the Westminster of Wales', Strata Florida is now a beautiful ruin set in an idyllic, peaceful valley. Founded in the 12th century, the magnificent abbey fell into decay after Henry VIII's purge on the monastic houses. Low stone foundations and a lovely Norman doorway are all that remain today.

TREGARON

This unspoilt little market town retains much of the character it must have had in the 1850s when it was visited by George Borrow, the author of *Wild Wales*. He walked here from Devil's Bridge, and stayed at the Talbot Inn, which stands in the square and overlooks a statue of Henry Richard. The son of a local clergyman, he was born in 1812 and became Liberal MP for Merthyr. Richard's ardent campaigning for disarmament earned him the nickname 'the Apostle of Peace'.

LLANDDEWI BREFI

This delightful village can trace its history back at least as far as AD 519, when an important synod held here was addressed by St David. The 13th-century church stands on a grassy mound said to have risen beneath the patron saint's feet as he spoke, and a statue of him stands by the west door.

LLANFAIR CLYDOGAU

The church of this scattered little parish stands in a circular graveyard and contains a strangely carved font. Other features of the village include a handsome bridge and an elegant chapel.

Constitution Hill offers fine views of Aberystwyth and the unspoilt coastline that lies beyond the town

The Brecon Beacons

63 miles

TOUR 27 ROUTE DIRECTIONS

Leave Brecon on the A40 (SP Llandovery), cross the River Usk and in 1 mile cross the Afon Tarell. At the roundabout, take the second exit, then take the next left turn (SP Mountain Centre). Climb, and pass the Mountain Centre, then in 1¾ miles turn left at a crossroads on to the A4215 (no SP). In 3 miles descend to the Tarell valley and turn right on to the A470 (SP Merthyr). Pass the Storey Arms at a 1,440ft road summit and continue past the Fawr Reservoirs to Cefn-coed-y-cymmer. (A detour to Cyfarthfa Castle can be made by continuing for 1¼ miles on the A470.)

From Cefn-coed-y-cymmer turn left on to an unclassified road (SP Pontsticill, Talybont). In 1¼ miles pass under a railway bridge and turn left. Continue through Pontsticill and at the end of the village keep left to follow the shores of Pontsticill Reservoir. Continue for 2¾ miles and turn right. Later pass the Talybont Reservoir and in 1¼ miles turn right (no SP) into Talybont village. Cross the canal bridge at Talybont and turn right on to the B4558. Beyond the village keep forward (SP Llangynidr, Crickhowell). Drive to Llangynidr, then 1 mile beyond the canal bridge turn right on to the B4560 (SP Beaufort). Climb through sharp bends, pass a quarry and turn left on to an unclassified road (SP Crickhowell). Keep forward through Llangattock, then turn left on to the A4077 and turn right to cross the Usk into Crickhowell.

Leave Crickhowell on the A40 (SP Brecon) and in 2¾ miles pass a right turn leading to Tretower. Continue on the A40 to Bwlch. Beyond the war memorial turn right on to the B4560 (SP Talgarth). Continue through Llangorse and at the end of the village turn left on to an unclassified road. Drive on towards Brecon, passing a turning leading to Llangorse Lake. Continue for 1½ miles and turn left across a bridge. Go through Llanfihangel Tal-y-Llyn, and in 2½ miles turn left. In ½ mile turn right on to the A40 and follow signs to Brecon.

An ancient dug-out canoe (inset) was discovered in Llangorse Lake (top), a popular boating and fishing spot

BRECON

This sedate little market town is a popular centre for touring the 500-square-mile Brecon Beacons National Park. Nestling below the great sandstone crest of the Beacons, which reaches 2,907ft at Pen-y-fan, its highest point, Brecon stands at the point where the rivers Honddu and Usk meet. The confluence of the rivers is overlooked by a ruined medieval castle that was largely dismantled by the townspeople in the 17th century to prevent its capture by either side in the Civil War. Brecon's other medieval survivals include a small fragment of the town walls and the fine cathedral, which dominates the town from its hilltop site. It was not until 1923 that the church was made a cathedral; before that it was the parish church.

Many centuries of local history are represented in the Brecknock Museum, housed in an imposing neo-classical building that was originally the Shire Hall. Exhibits range from an ancient dug-out canoe found at nearby Llangorse Lake to a large collection of intricately carved love spoons, traditional gifts made by young Welshmen for their sweethearts.

CEFN-COED-Y-CYMMER

The great Cyfarthfa Ironworks were founded here in 1766 by the Crawshay family and Watkin George, one of the foremost of the early ironmasters. Also here is a fine 19th-century railway viaduct of 15 stone arches.

CYFARTHFA CASTLE

Built in 1825 for 'Iron King' William Crawshay, this rather extravagant latterday castle now houses a museum and art gallery.

PONTSTICILL RESERVOIR

Excellent views can be enjoyed from a viewpoint at the south end of this extensive reservoir, which was constructed at the beginning of this century as part of a system designed to supply nearby coalfields.

TALYBONT RESERVOIR

Large numbers of waterfowl and other aquatic wildlife may be seen on this two-mile-long reservoir, which supplies Newport with water.

TALYBONT AND THE MONMOUTHSHIRE AND BRECON CANAL

Winding its way from Brecon to Pontypool, the Monmouthshire and Brecon Canal offers a leisurely route from which to enjoy the scenery of the Usk valley. It was built between 1799 and 1812, principally to supply the iron

THE FAWR RESERVOIRS

Strung out along the west side of the A470 and fed by the Taf Fawr river are the three Fawr reservoirs – namely Beacons, Cantref, and Llwynon. They were constructed between 1892 and 1927 to supply Cardiff with water.

mines of old Monmouthshire (now Gwent), and was originally planned to stretch from Pontypool to Abergavenny. Within months of its commencement the decision was made to extend it to Brecon. Talybont has a modern bridge crossing the canal and makes an ideal centre from which to walk the towpaths and explore the surrounding countryside. East of Talybont the canal passes through the 375-yard Ashford Tunnel.

LLANGYNIDR

A fine bridge dating from about 1600 spans the Usk at Llangynidr, and five of the Monmouthshire and Brecon Canal's six locks are in this village.

LLANGATTOCK

St Catwg's Church, on the edge of the village, carries a massive 15th-century tower and contains some interesting memorials. Old limestone quarries are found to the south, on the slopes of Mynydd Llangattock, where there is also a National Nature Reserve.

CRICKHOWELL

This pleasant little town on the River Usk retains much of the atmosphere of coaching days, when it was an important posting-station on the road between London and the Irish ferry ports of west Wales. The archway leading to the Bear Hotel's former stables still carries a 'post-horses' sign, and a board on the White Hart, on the outskirts of the town, lists tolls once paid by travellers to the Duke of Beaufort. Much earlier, Crickhowell shared the turbulent history of so many Welsh towns when its Norman castle was captured by Welsh and English in turn, before finally being destroyed by the soldiers of Owain Glyndwr in 1403. Fragments of the castle now stand in a small park beside the A40.

TRETOWER

This tiny village is the setting for two of the finest ancient monuments in the Brecon Beacons National Park. One is Tretower Castle. The round keep which is now its most prominent feature dates from about 1230, but it was built within the ruin of an older, square keep – probably the tower from which the village takes it name. Nearby stands Tretower Court, a fine fortified manor house that was the seat of the Vaughan family. One of their number was Henry Vaughan, the 17th-century mystical poet.

BWLCH

Fine views of the Usk valley and the surrounding mountains are a feature of the route as it approaches this little hamlet. The name 'Bwlch' means 'The Pass'.

LLANGORSE AND LLANGORSE LAKE

Restoration and so-called improvement during the 19th century destroyed much of the character of the little local church, but its 15th-century wagon-roof has survived. An ancient inscribed stone has been preserved here. Nearby Llangorse Lake is the largest natural lake in South Wales and a haven for many kinds of flora and fauna.

mls 0 1 2 3 4 5
kms 0 2 4 6 8

BRECON

The Welsh Lake District
60 miles

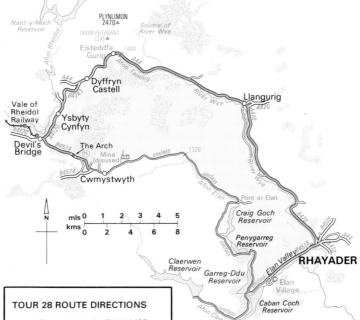

RHAYADER
This attractive country town on the River Wye is full of character and has fascinating shops, where many examples of Welsh crafts can be found, including the products of the famous Dragon Pottery. The Welsh name of the town, Rhouadr Gwy, means 'Waterfall on the Wye', and refers to the small falls here which, before the creation of the Elan valley dams, and the building of the town bridge in 1780, were formidable and spectacular rapids. As Rhayader lies in a vast wilderness of mountain and moorland, it is a popular centre for pony trekking, walking and fishing.

ELAN VALLEY AND CABAN COCH RESERVOIR
Late in the 19th century the Corporation of Birmingham constructed a reservoir system in an area now unofficially known as the Radnorshire Lake District. The new landscape is very beautiful and highly popular, but the scheme called for the drowning of a whole valley complete with attractive waterfalls, meadows, farms, houses and a church. The entire complex supplies Birmingham with an amazing 60 million gallons of water a day and provides a haven for many forms of aquatic and marginal wildlife.

Beneath the placid surface of Caban Coch Reservoir is a house in which the poet Shelley lived for some time. He wrote appreciatively about the splendid scenery in a letter to his friend Hogg.

CLAERWEN RESERVOIR
The Claerwen project, officially opened by the Queen on 23 October 1952, is a vast 600-acre lake held back by a massive dam.

GARREG-DDU RESERVOIR
A unique submerged dam separates this reservoir from Caban Coch Reservoir.

PEN-Y-GARREG RESERVOIR
Some 124 acres of lake, unbroken except where a tiny fir-covered islet rises at the centre, backs up the Elan valley from yet another of the project's great dams. This and the other reservoirs can be fished for trout by permit-holders.

CRAIG GOCH RESERVOIR
Topmost of the Elan valley reservoirs, Craig Goch has a surface area of about 200 acres. Plans are being made to increase the capacity of the lake by allowing it to back up the valley all the way to the source of the Afon Elan.

CWMYSTWYTH
Ruins of mine workings, buildings and cottages in the neighbourhood of this desolate village illustrate the 19th century's insatiable desire for mineral wealth, but the village itself – no longer a centre of the mining industry – has settled into attractive retirement. Beyond Cwmystwyth, off the Pontrhydygroes road, is a pile of rubble that once stood as the proud mansion of Hafod, built by Thomas Johnes in the late 18th century. The building was twice burnt down, and each blaze destroyed many priceless works of art and irreplaceable manuscripts.

TOUR 28 ROUTE DIRECTIONS
Leave Rhayader on the B4518 (SP Elan valley), continue to the edge of Elan Village and then continue forward on an unclassified road to Caban Coch Dam and Reservoir. Continue to the Garreg-Ddu viaduct, turn left across it, and continue to an AA telephone box, then turn right to reach Claerwen Dam. Return across Garreg-Ddu viaduct and turn left. From the end of Garreg-Ddu Reservoir ascend to Pen-y-garreg Dam and Reservoir and continue alongside Craig Goch Reservoir. Ascend and turn left (SP Aberystwyth) and continue to Cwmystwyth. Keep forward to join the B4574 (SP Devil's Bridge) for Devil's Bridge, passing under The Arch. Leave Devil's Bridge village by crossing the bridge on the A4120 (SP Ponterwyd) and continue to Ysbyty Cynfyn. Continue and turn right on the B4343 (SP Dyffryn Castell). Meet the A44 and bear right to reach Dyffryn Castell. Ascend to Eisteddfa Gurig and continue to Llangurig following the River Wye. Leave Llangurig on the A470 for the return to Rhayader.

THE ARCH PICNIC SITE
Thomas Johnes of Hafod erected an arch over the road here in 1810 to commemorate the Golden Jubilee of George III. Three Forestry Commission trails lead from the picnic site into wild countryside.

DEVIL'S BRIDGE
The Afon Mynach meets the Afon Rheidol here, and together they plunge 300ft down a gorge in a series of spectacular falls. The gorge is spanned by three bridges, one above the other. The lowest and oldest bridge gave the place its name, for legend tells that it was built by the Devil. There are picnic sites and nature trails, and steps down to the bottom of the falls.

Devil's Bridge is the eastern terminus of the Vale of Rheidol Light Railway, a narrow-gauge line that is the only British Rail line to operate steam locomotives. It is an unfailing tourist attraction, and its Devil's Bridge terminus is a charming miniature, boasting all the usual station facilities and set amid dense rhododendron thickets.

YSBYTY CYNFYN
Several stones of the prehistoric circle in which this immaculate, evergreen-shrouded church stands have survived in place. Many gravestones in the churchyard bear Cornish names and are reminders of the days when West Country miners came to Wales in search of better opportunities. A path leads from the church to a wooded gorge featuring a waterfall and the 'Parson's Bridge', so called because it was built for the convenience of a travelling parson who held services both here and at Llanbadarn Fawr.

DYFFRYN CASTELL AND PLYNLIMON
A path leads from here to the slopes of 2,470ft Plynlimon. On wet days the vast expanse of bog and moor on its flanks tends to be depressing, but the views afforded by its summit on a fine day are spectacular enough to make the ascent easily worth the effort. On a clear day the view encompasses virtually the whole of Wales, from Snowdonia in the north to the Brecon Beacons in the south. Plynlimon is the source of the Severn, the Wye and several other rivers.

LLANGURIG
Small and beautiful Llangurig is delightfully set in the upper Wye valley. The church of St Gurig owes much of its appearance to J. W. Lloyd of Llandinam, who commissioned Sir Gilbert Scott to restore the building. Lloyd, famous for his inconstancy, began his career as a curate in Llangurig but later became a Catholic and eventually aspired to become a Knight of St Gregory. In later life he returned to the Anglican faith. Stained-glass windows show scenes from the life of St Gurig, relate incidents associated with the royal families of Wales, and depict members of the Lloyd family.

Pen-y-garreg is the smallest of the Elan valley's chain of reservoirs

The Uplands of Mid Wales
56 miles

LLANIDLOES

This popular touring centre is a historic and attractive little market town at the confluence of the Severn and Clywedog rivers. The striking black-and-white Market Hall, supported on oak pillars, dates from the late 16th century and is the last of its kind to survive in Wales. The first floor houses a folk museum. The church has a beautiful north arcade said to come from ancient Abbey Cwmhir, 12 miles to the south-east, and also – again from the abbey, which was demolished at the Dissolution – a splendid hammerbeam roof.

The town hall houses a small market on the ground floor, and in China Street Perllon-dy (Orchard House) is an early 17th-century timbered building now used as a craft shop, gallery and restaurant.

LLYN CLYWEDOG RESERVOIR

Excellent views of the reservoir can be enjoyed from the dam, whose curving 237ft wall is the highest of its kind in Britain. The reservoir was opened in 1968 and is a popular sailing venue.

HAFREN FOREST

Comprising large plantations between Clywedog Reservoir and the slopes of Plynlimon, this forest was started by the Forestry Commission in 1937, and is named after the Welsh equivalent of 'Severn'. A picnic site is situated in the forest opposite the extreme western arm of the reservoir.

DYLIFE

A few haphazard ruins, spoil tips and an air of desolation are all that remain of an enormous lead-mining community that once flourished at Dylife. Huge numbers of men lived and worked here under awful conditions until the 1870s, but all that is left now is an inn and a tiny group of houses set back off the road. A little east of Dylife the infant Afon Twymyn plunges down spectacular Ffrwd Fawr waterfall.

LAKES GLASLYN AND BUGEILYN

Care should be taken to stay on the footpath access to these two lakes, as the area is made dangerous by deep peat bogs and several precipitous drops. This is a wild and lonely landscape, once extensively mined for lead, but now inhabited only by sheep, birds and the occasional fox. Glaslyn lies on private land, and Bugeilyn (which means 'Shepherd's Lake') is situated in the foothills of the Plynlimon range. Small flint arrowheads, presumably once used by people now buried in nearby prehistoric cairns, have been found washed out of the peat.

MACHYNLLETH

Machynlleth is the focal point for the lower Dyfi valley, and although it is a small town, it has played an important role in Welsh history. Its architecture is delightful – unusual for a Welsh town – and fine period houses from medieval times to the 18th and 19th centuries line the broad, tree-lined streets. Dominating the centre of the town is a huge clock-tower, with several old coaching inns standing about the road

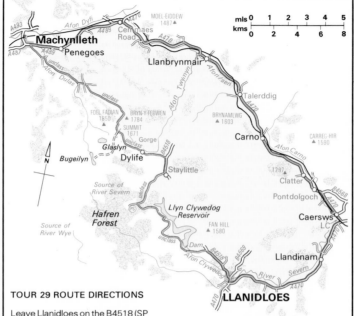

TOUR 29 ROUTE DIRECTIONS

Leave Llanidloes on the B4518 (SP Llyn Clywedog). Cross the River Severn and turn left to follow the Clywedog valley. After 2 miles, with views of 1,580ft Fan Hill on the right, turn left on to an unclassified road. Cross the valley and ascend to Clywedog Dam, from where there are excellent views of Llyn Clywedog Reservoir. Continue with the reservoir on the right and Hafren Forest on the left. Drive to a T-junction and turn right (SP Llanbrynmair). After 2¼ miles reach the edge of Staylittle, and turn left on to the B4518, then after ¾ mile turn left (SP Machynlleth) on to an unclassified road, which is unguarded and must be driven with care. After a short distance pass high above the deep gorge of Afon Twymyn, and continue through Dylife. (About 2 miles later, pass a track leading left from the route, offering a detour to lakes Glaslyn and Bugeilyn.)

Continue towards Machynlleth and shortly reach a 1,671ft road summit. Views south and east here take in extensive moorland, with 1,850ft

Foel Fadian to the left and 1,784ft Bryn-y-Fedwen to the right. Descend, with impressive views north-west to Cader Idris and Aran Fawddwy, then drive down a long descent and keep forward at all road junctions to reach Machynlleth. Leave Machynlleth on the A489 (SP Newtown) and continue to Penegoes. Follow the Dyfi valley to Cemmaes Road and turn right on the A470 (SP Newtown). Continue along the Twymyn valley to Llanbrynmair. Continue through the wooded gorge of the Afon Iaen to reach a road and rail summit at Talerddig, where there is a natural arch beside the road. Continue to Carno, then drive along the broad valley of the Afon Carno and pass through Clatter and Pontdolgoch to reach Caersws. Continue on the A470 and after ¾ mile, at a T-junction, turn right (SP Llangurig) and shortly go over a level crossing, then follow the River Severn to reach Llandinam. Remain on the A470 for the return to Llanidloes.

The coniferous plantations of Hafren Forest clothe Plynlimon's eastern slopes

junctions around it.

In Maengwyn Street is an ancient stone building where Owain Glyndwr held a Welsh parliament, and where in 1404 he was proclaimed King of Wales. Now the Owain Glyndwr Institute, it houses the Tourist Information Centre. An old slate quarry 2½ miles north of the town is now the fascinating Centre for Alternative Technology, a working demonstration of the self-sufficient life.

PENEGOES

A tradition that the head of a Welsh chieftain, executed in this village, is buried under a local tree has proved so tenacious that in 1950 there was a serious proposal to dig for the skull. Penegoes once had a tiny curative bath that was fed from a spring whose waters were said to bring relief from rheumatism. Richard Wilson, painter of landscapes, was born here in 1714.

LLANBRYNMAIR

Roughly divided into half old and half new, this small, scattered village enjoys a rural setting threaded by little rivers and was the site of an important castle in the 12th century. Only the castle mound survives today. The local church is sited in the old part of the village and contains ancient oak timbers. Abraham Rees, preacher and scholar, was born in the village in 1743. In 1778 he embarked on the preparation of information for Chambers' Encyclopaedia, a mammoth task that took nine years to complete and won Rees election as a Fellow of the Royal Society.

CARNO

Opposite Carno's church, which contains an ancient cross-incised slab that saw many years' service as a gatepost, is the Aleppo Merchant Inn. This unusual title was given to the pub by a retired sea-captain who had been in charge of a ship of that name. A Roman fort was situated here, and later in history several fierce battles between the ruling princes of north and south Wales were fought near Carno.

CAERSWS

Standing within a great loop of the River Severn, and protected by a tributary of the Afon Carno, Caersws was chosen by the Romans as the site of a fort which stood at the hub of a road system that linked their camps at Llandrindod Wells, Brecon Gaer, Pennal and Chester. The main road runs through the remains, traces of which can be clearly seen. The village today is an excellent centre for touring the upper Severn valley.

LLANDINAM

The village lies on the banks of the River Severn, and is a pleasant place noted chiefly as the birthplace of David Davies, whose statue stands near the pretty iron bridge which spans the river. Davies rose from humble beginnings to become one of Wales' wealthiest industrialists. He developed the coal industry and founded Barry Dock as a coal-exporting port. The statue of him is by Alfred Gilbert, the sculptor of Piccadilly Circus's Eros.

North Wales Valleys and Coast
70 miles

LLANDUDNO
Created in the 1850s, Llandudno is one of the finest planned seaside towns in Britain. Elegant hotels and guest-houses line its spacious boulevards, and its two beaches – separated by Great Orme's Head – are ideal for bathing. Great Orme's Head itself is a huge crag of weathered limestone and is a place of considerable contrasts. Its lower slopes are carpeted with formal gardens interspersed by entertainment facilities, while its summit, which can be reached by cable railway, is covered in sheep-cropped turf.

CONWY
Set between the mountains of Snowdonia and the Conwy estuary, this is one of the most memorable walled towns in Europe. The grey towers and turrets of the splendid 13th-century castle look down on a tight mesh of narrow streets still enclosed by walls that have stood almost intact for 700 years. Most of the ancient buildings that once stood here have disappeared, but a notable survivor is Aberconwy, a 15th-century merchant's house. Many visitors are drawn to Conwy's picturesque quayside, where the 'smallest house in Great Britain' may be found.

BODNANT GARDENS
The finest garden in Wales, and one of the best in Britain, Bodnant occupies a superb terraced site on the east side of the Conwy valley. It is best seen in early summer when its celebrated azaleas and rhododendrons are in bloom. The gardens were first laid out in 1875.

LLANRWST
This ancient market town, situated in the green valley of the Afon Conwy, is best known for the lovely three-arched bridge that spans the river here. Other notable buildings include the church, which retains its elaborate rood loft and screen, and Ty Hwnt i'r Bont, a 17th-century house that once served as a courthouse. On the outskirts of the town is Gwydir Castle, a Tudor mansion built for the powerful Wynne family, and nearby is Gwydir Chapel, which is noted for its 17th-century painted ceiling.

PENTREFOELAS
Mountain scenery starts to give way to moorland near this hamlet. An 8ft-high inscribed pillar known as the Levelinus Stone marks the spot where Llywelyn ap Sysyllt, a prince of Gwynedd, fell in battle in 1023.

DENBIGH
Another of the great fortresses built in North Wales during the Middle Ages stands here. It was built by Henry de Lacy, Earl of Lincoln, during the late 13th century and still has an air of gaunt strength. Inside the walls that surround the medieval town are the remains of an incomplete church, begun in 1579 by the Earl of Leicester, and popularly known as 'Leicester's Folly'. In the lower part of the town are the remains of a friary founded in about 1284. Denbigh's most famous son is Henry Morton Stanley, the journalist who found Dr Livingstone in Africa.

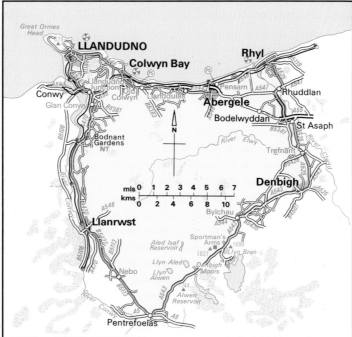

Gwydir Chapel at Llanrwst is noted for its charming painted ceiling

TOUR 30 ROUTE DIRECTIONS

Leave Llandudno on the A546 (SP Conwy). After 2 miles, at a roundabout, take the first exit on to the A55 (SP Betws-y-coed). (A detour may be made from the main tour to Conwy by crossing the Afon Conwy from this roundabout.) Continue on the main tour through Llandudno Junction. After ¾ mile, at a roundabout, take the third exit, the A470. Drive through Glan Conwy and in 2 miles pass the entrance to Bodnant Gardens. Continue to Llanrwst, and take the B5427 (SP Nebo), then at a T-junction turn right on to the B5113. Pass through Nebo and continue to Pentrefoelas. Turn left on to the A5, and in ¼ mile turn left again on to the A543 (SP Denbigh). Continue past Alwen Reservoir and across the Denbigh Moors, then go through Bylchau to Denbigh.

From Denbigh take the A525 (SP Rhyl) and drive through Trefnant to St Asaph. Follow signs for Rhyl, and in ¾ mile keep forward at a roundabout. (A detour may be made from the main route by turning on to the A55 (SP Conwy) to Bodelwyddan.) The main route continues through Rhuddlan to Rhyl. Leave Rhyl promenade on the Abergele road, shortly turning right on to the A548. Continue through Pensarn, then at a roundabout turn left into Abergele. Follow the B5443 Conwy road through Llanddulas, then join the A55 to enter Colwyn Bay. Continue on the Conwy road. After ¾ mile, at a roundabout, take the second exit, the A546. Cross Little Orme's Head and return to Llandudno.

Conwy Castle is a remarkably fine example of 13th-century defensive architecture

ST ASAPH
A small town even by Welsh standards, St Asaph is in fact a city. Its cathedral, the smallest in England and Wales, was rebuilt in 1482 after standing as a shell for many years, and was extensively restored in the 19th century. Apart from the cathedral and the 15th-century Church of St Kentigern, there are few buildings of note in the town, but it is a charming place nonetheless.

BODELWYDDAN
The 202ft spire of the parish church here is one of the best known landmarks in North Wales. No less than 14 kinds of marble were used in building the church, which was begun in 1856.

RHUDDLAN
It was here, in 1284, that Edward I confirmed his sovereignty over the newly conquered kingdom of Wales. The king also held a parliament here, and Old Parliament House stands on the site of the original buildings. Richard II was imprisoned briefly in the great castle on his way to Flint, where he conceded the throne to Henry Bolingbroke. The castle was slighted after the Civil War, and is now a dignified ruin.

RHYL
Rhyl has three miles of safe, sandy beaches and is the most popular resort on the North Wales coast. It offers every conceivable kind of seaside attraction, including leisure parks, botanical gardens, sports facilities and the famous Royal Floral Hall.

ABERGELE
Caravan sites and chalets are visible proof of Abergele's popularity as a seaside resort. Also a market town of long standing, it has a Tudor church with a 16th-century screen pitted with initials and dates carved by schoolboys when the building was used as a school in Tudor times.

COLWYN BAY
Fine parks are a feature of this Victorian seaside town. Colwyn Bay began to grow little more than a century ago and, unlike some of its neighbours, it has retained the dignity of a more elegant age.

The Lleyn Peninsula
66 miles

PWLLHELI
A considerable port and shipbuilding centre in the days of sail, Pwllheli was a free borough as early as the 14th century, when, together with Nefyn, it was given by the Black Prince to Nigel de Loryng, who had helped him win the Battle of Poitiers. Today Pwllheli is best known as a holiday resort and the principal town of the Lleyn Peninsula. It was also here that one of the first post-war holiday camps, Butlin's, was established, on the site of a former naval base to the east of the town.

LLANYSTUMDWY
David Lloyd George, the famous liberal prime minister who was MP for Caernarfon for 50 years from 1890, was brought up and educated in this little village. He also died near here, in 1945, at a Jacobean mansion called Ty Newydd. The village remembers its most famous son in a small museum of Lloyd George mementoes, and in a simple memorial designed by the Welsh architect Clough Williams-Ellis.

YR EIFL
Englishmen know the triple peaks of this 1,849ft mountain as 'The Rivals', but a more accurate translation of the Welsh name is rendered 'The Fork'. Footpaths lead to the summits. One of the finest Iron Age hill-forts in Wales, with mighty stone walls defending an interior crowded with hut circles, is sited on the eastern peak. It is possible that the complex was inhabited until about AD 400.

TOUR 31 ROUTE DIRECTIONS
Leave Pwllheli on the A497 (SP Criccieth) and drive through Llanystumdwy to Criccieth. Take the B4411 (SP Caernarfon) and drive to the junction with the A487, turning left on to this road. Drive through Bryncir and Llanllyfni to Penygroes, then turn left on to an unclassified road (SP Clynnog, Pwllheli). In 2 miles, at a T-junction, turn left on to the A499. Go through Pontlyfni and Clynnog-Fawr, then in 3½ miles turn right on to the B4417 (SP Nefyn). Pass a lay-by under the slopes of Yr Eifl and descend through Llithfaen to Nefyn. Turn right on to the Aberdaron road and go through Morfa Nefyn, continuing on the B4417 through Edern and Tudweiliog. Continue to a junction with the B4413 and turn right to reach Aberdaron. From here, take an unclassified road to Rhiw, continuing on the Abersoch road to pass Plas-yn-Rhiw before continuing to Llangian. Turn left here, then ascend and turn right to descend into Abersoch. From Abersoch follow the A499 along the coast to Llanbedrog, then continue through low-lying countryside and join the A497 to return to Pwllheli.

Sunset over Criccieth Castle, a dramatically sited fortress that has helped guard the coast since 1230

CRICCIETH
The Victorian appearance of this little grey town belies its long history. The site of Criccieth Castle, probably fortified in pre-Roman times, was already old when the present castle was built in 1230. It shared the turbulent history of many Welsh castles, and was already in decay before the Civil War. Now in the care of the Department of the Environment, the castle ruins stand on a headland overlooking sand and pebble beaches to the east and west.

LLANLLYFNI
The Afon Llyfni flows to the north of this Victorian quarrymen's village from its source at Llyn Nantlle Uchaf, among derelict slate workings. Of the several old chapels in Llanllyfni, only Ebenezer has retained its 19th-century interior.

PENYGROES
This colourful quarrymen's town grew from its sister community of Llanllyfni with the development of the slate industry during the 19th century.

CLYNNOG-FAWR
This small coastal village has a magnificent 16th-century church dedicated to St Beuno, who founded a monastery here in AD 616. An ancient coffer in the church is still known as *Cyff Beuno*, or St Beuno's Chest. St Beuno's Chapel, connected to the church by a passageway, is believed to have been the saint's burial place. It was restored in 1913.

NEFYN
At one time it was claimed that Nefyn sent more of its men to sea than almost any other British town. In 1284 Edward I celebrated his conquest over the Welsh here, and in 1353 the Black Prince made the town one of the ten royal boroughs of North Wales. Today, Nefyn enjoys a genteel retirement from politics and makes the most of the resort possibilities offered by its fine sands.

MORFA NEFYN
Rugged headlands shelter a long sweep of sandy beach at Morfa Nefyn, and an unclassified road leads right from the tour route to the picturesque hamlet of Porth Dinllaen. This small community was once considered as a rail terminus point for Ireland; some might think it had a lucky escape.

ABERDARON
Set in the area known as the 'Land's End' of the Lleyn Peninsula, Aberdaron was the last mainland settlement visited by pilgrims on their way to Bardsey Island, 2 miles offshore. Colonized by monks, the island in early times was a celebrated place of pilgrimage, and numerous pilgrims and holy men came here to die. A café in Aberdaron is reputed to be where pilgrims were fed while they waited for boats to cross Bardsey Sound. The large church dates from the 12th century, and stands on the site of a church founded some 600 years earlier by St Hywyn.

RHIW
The scattered cottages and 18th-century church of this village do little to obstruct views of the magnificent south Lleyn coast. The village itself is windswept and exposed, but 1,000ft Mynydd Rhiw shelters the house and gardens of nearby Plas-yn-Rhiw from the Atlantic weather. This charming house was built in the 16th century and modernized in Regency times. The house and its grounds (open only by appointment), together with large areas of beautiful coastline, were given to the National Trust in 1952.

LLANGIAN
Neat cottages with well-tended gardens full of flowers have helped this lovely place win the coveted 'Best-kept Village in Wales' award.

ABERSOCH
This affluent, fashionable resort owes much of its popularity to its sheltered position and mild climate. A sandy beach known as the Warren, one of the finest on the Lleyn Peninsula, runs parallel with the Abersoch–Llanbedrog road. In recent years Abersoch has become an increasingly popular sailing resort.

LLANBEDROG
Excellent sandy beaches and attractive cliff walks have assured Llanbedrog's popularity as a resort. The parish church is embowered in trees and preserves a medieval screen. Fragments of ancient glass can be seen in the east window. Above the village is a hill which features a ruined mill and offers good views.

Historic Anglesey
80 miles

MENAI BRIDGE

This little town, called Porthaethwy in Welsh, takes its English name from Thomas Telford's suspension bridge over the Menai Strait. Completed in 1826 – a remarkably early date for such a bridge – the 1,000ft-long bridge still carries traffic across the strait on to the Isle of Anglesey. Set at the Anglesey end of the bridge, Menai Bridge is of interest to the tourist for its Museum of Childhood and for the Tegfryn Art Gallery, which stands in pleasant grounds near the shore of the Menai Strait.

BEAUMARIS

Guarding the northern entrance to the Menai Strait, Beaumaris Castle was built around 1295 and is a fine example of medieval military architecture. The town that has grown around it is the chief administrative centre of the island, and has some fine old buildings, including a church that was begun at the same time as the castle. Tudor Rose House, dating from the 15th century, serves as a reminder that the Tudors were an Anglesey family.

RED WHARF BAY

More than ten square miles of sand are revealed here at low tide, so it is not particularly surprising that the bay was once famous for its cockles. During the last century a small local shipyard built boats for the Amlwch copper trade.

BENLLECH

Perhaps the most popular seaside resort on the island, Benllech offers two miles of golden sand and safe bathing.

AMLWCH

At the height of the copper boom Amlwch was big enough to boast a staggering 1,025 ale houses. Today the harbour, which once accommodated 30 large ships at a time, is used only by pleasure craft.

CEMAES BAY

Cottages cluster round a small harbour in this quaint little fishing village. Spectacular cliff walks lead in both directions from the bay, and on the headland to the west is Wylfa nuclear power station.

HOLYHEAD

Overlooked by the stern outline of Holyhead Mountain, this is Anglesey's largest town and has been a point on the principal route from London to Ireland since Roman times. A number of prehistoric monuments nearby are evidence of even earlier settlement in the area. It was in the early days of Christianity, when missionaries began to colonize Anglesey, that Holyhead first became an important centre, and it was in this period that its church was founded. Most of the present church dates from the 14th century, though it stands within the walls of a Roman fort. Today, Holyhead is a busy ferry terminal, with regular sailings to Dun Laoghaire.

TREARDDUR BAY

This fashionable Anglesey resort has fine sandy beaches broken up by occasional rocky outcrops.

BARCLODIAD-Y-GAWRES

The carved stones of this megalithic passage grave are among the finest of their kind in Britain.

ABERFFRAW

Aberffraw is a grey, somnolent village which has little to show of its historic past. Between the 7th and 13th centuries it was the capital of the Kingdom of Gwynedd. A rocky islet nearby features an ancient church which is accessible at low tide.

MALLTRAETH

In about 1800 a high embankment was built here to stop the incursion of the sea. Before this the estuary of the Cefni penetrated far inland, nearly cutting Anglesey in two. The village is known for its fine sands and salt marshes.

NEWBOROUGH

Former inhabitants of Llanfaes, ousted by Edward I, founded this English-sounding village in 1303. A national nature reserve covers 1,566 acres of duneland and rocky coast to the south of the village, and Newborough Forest has been planted to stabilize the dunes.

BRYN-CELLI-DDU

This is a magnificent prehistoric passage grave of a type more usually found in Ireland. It consists of a passage leading to a polygonal chamber beneath a large mound.

PLAS NEWYDD

Rebuilt by architect James Wyatt in the 19th century, this mansion overlooks the Menai Strait and is famous for the Rex Whistler mural in its dining room.

LLANFAIR PG

The famous name of this village is the longest in Britain, containing 59 characters: Llanfairpwllgwyngyllgoger-ychwyrndrobwyllllantysiliogogogoch. The name came about when the already long names of two neighbouring villages were combined. The little station here, reopened several years ago, sells tickets that have become famous as the longest in the world.

Llanfair's other claims to fame include the Britannia Bridge, a tubular structure built in the 19th century by George Stephenson to carry the railway across the Menai Strait, and recently adapted to carry the A5 on an upper deck. Also near the village is the Marquess of Anglesey Column, which commemorates Wellington's aide at the Battle of Waterloo.

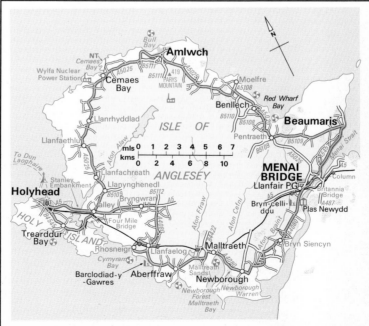

TOUR 32 ROUTE DIRECTIONS

Drive from Menai Bridge on the A545 to Beaumaris. Turn inland on the B5109 (SP Benllech) and at Pentraeth turn right on to the A5025 to continue past Red Wharf Bay to Benllech. Continue for 2 miles, then at the roundabout take the first exit. Drive on to Amlwch, and continue through Cemaes Bay, Llanrhyddlad, Llanfaethlu, Llanfachreath and Llanynghenedl to Valley. Turn right at traffic lights on to the A5 and cross the Stanley Embankment to Holy Island. Drive to Holyhead, then return along the A5 and shortly branch right on to the B4545 to Trearddur Bay. Cross Four Mile Bridge and return to Valley. Turn right at traffic lights on to the A5, go through Bryngwran and in 1 mile, at a crossroads, turn right on to the A4080. At Llanfaelog turn right to Rhosneigr, then continue on the A4080 to Barclodiad-y-Gawres. Continue through Aberffraw, Malltraeth and Newborough, then 2 miles beyond Bryn-Siencyn pass a left turn leading to Bryn-celli-ddu. Continue on the A4080, passing the entrance to Plas Newydd. Go through the outskirts of Llanfair PG and return on the A4080 to Menai Bridge.

Wales Gazetteer

ABERAERON, Dyfed   *102 SN46*
This handsome little seaside town on the banks of the Afon Aeron was founded and built by a couple who inherited a fortune in the 18th century. The development, which included the construction of harbours, quays, stores, a town hall, and numerous dwellings, continued well into the middle of the 19th century and resulted in an extremely pleasing Georgian-style town with a charm enhanced by the Welsh habit of highlighting architectural details with brightly coloured paint. Aberaeron's days as a busy seaport and shipbuilding centre are long gone, and today it is an elegant and unspoilt holiday resort.

Aberaeron's 19th-century cottages date from the time when it was a busy seaport

ABERDYFI, Gwynedd   *102 SN69*
Aberdyfi basks with its head in the sun and its feet in the waters of the Dyfi estuary, and boasts a very agreeable climate. It has good sands, but its original business was not with tourism, but rather with seafaring and shipbuilding. At one time it had several shipyards, the last being where Pennelig Terrace now stands. Aberdyfi's last boat was built in 1880.

ABERGAVENNY, Gwent   *103 SO31*
This busy market town is held to be the gateway to Wales, and is certainly a natural entrance to the Brecon Beacons National Park. The Romans had a fort here called *Gobannium*, and the foundations of this are thought to lie under the castle mound. The castle was founded early in the 11th century. The few remains date from the 13th and 14th centuries and consist of two broken towers, the gateway and fragments of wall. The town museum is situated in the castle grounds. Other interesting buildings in the town include the Old Court, a house dating from 1500 built into the old town walls. St Mary's Church was originally the church of a Benedictine priory founded in the 11th century, but today only the tithe barn and prior's house remain of the priory buildings. Treasures in the church include 24 medieval choir stalls and a huge wooden figure of the patriarch Jesse.

ABERYSTWYTH, Dyfed   *102 SN58*
Seat of government and a holiday resort with a shopping area that serves a large locality, Aberystwyth grew to real importance with the establishment of its Norman castle by Edmund Crouchback in 1277. It is still a place of significance, and opposite the ruins of the castle is a Victorian hotel building that was bought in 1870 to form the nucleus of the University of Wales. Modern university buildings stand east of the town on Penglais Hill and include the National Library of Wales, which houses an incomparable collection of early Welsh manuscripts. Also of interest are the varied exhibits of the Ceredigion Museum. Notable among the many superb 18th- and 19th-century buildings preserved in the town are the fine houses that stand in Laura Place.

BALA, Gwynedd   *104 SH93*
Behind Bala's cheerful and unassuming tree-lined High Street is Tomen-y-Bala, the mound of a Norman castle. The town stands at the eastern end of Llyn Tegid, or Bala Lake, the largest natural lake in Wales. Along its south-eastern bank runs the steam-powered Bala Lake Railway.

BANGOR, Gwynedd   *104 SH57*
Visitors expecting the 'dreaming spires' of a university city are likely to be disappointed. Old Bangor should be enjoyed for what it is, a delightfully undistinguished maze in which the Cathedral of St Deiniol (claimed to be the oldest bishopric in Britain) crouches with unassuming modesty. The handsome buildings of the University College of North Wales were officially opened in 1911. On the seaward side Bangor's streets dip down to the city shore and a superb Victorian pier.

Scrapped steam locomotives and old rolling stock stand in a metal-breaker's yard on Barry Island

BARMOUTH, Gwynedd   *104 SH61*
A popular resort offering traditional attractions, Barmouth is squeezed between dark cliffs and the seashore. Its lengthy and spacious promenade is one of the finest frontages along the Welsh coast. A dominating feature of Barmouth is its railway bridge, spanning the wide estuary and made almost entirely of wood. The quaintness of the town becomes apparent away from the main street, up the steep alleyways, and at Panorama Walk. Here, in 1895, the National Trust acquired its first property, a modest four acres of clifftop.

BARRY, S Glam   *103 ST16*
In the 19th century Barry's population expanded from 500 to a staggering 12,665, and side by side with the development of docks that were to become among the largest in the world came the popularization of the Barry Island holiday resort. Nowadays the resort has everything for the holidaymaker, including funfairs, gardens, etc. Park Road leads to Porthkerry Country Park, passing the scant remains of Barry Castle on the way.

Beddgelert nestles among some of the Snowdonia National Park's most spectacular mountains

BEAUMARIS, Gwynedd *104 SH67*
The biggest attraction of Beaumaris is undoubtedly the castle, an unfinished masterpiece that was the last in a chain built by Edward I to subjugate the Welsh people. A measure of the success with which this aim was achieved is the fact that the castle has never seen any military action and was never completed. The town contains much of interest, including the early 17th-century Court House and 15th-century Tudor Rose House.

BEDDGELERT, Gwynedd *104 SH54*
Perhaps the only genuine alpine resort in Snowdonia, Beddgelert is completely surrounded by mountains and echoes their permanence in the solid stone of its architecture. Its name (meaning 'Gelert's Grave') refers to the legend that Welsh hero Llywelyn the Great killed his dog Gelert because he thought that it had savaged his son. In fact the dog had just saved the baby boy from wolves. Historians have debunked this story, which has since been blamed on an inventive local innkeeper.

BETHESDA, Gwynedd *104 SH66*
Bethesda is a quarrymen's village which takes it name from the Nonconformist chapel that was established here. Several impressive chapels exist apart from the one which gives the town its name, but Bethesda's fame rests firmly with the quarry that has been gouged out of the flanks of towering Elydir Fawr. The largest open-cast slate quarry in the world, it is 1 mile long, covers an area of 560 acres, and is up to 1,200ft deep.

BETWS-Y-COED, Gwynedd *104 SH75*
This famous village suffers from a surfeit of visitors in high summer, but it is still an enchanting spot where it is possible to get away from traffic and people along well-defined riverside and woodland walks. The pleasant mountain resort is celebrated for its waterfalls – notably the Swallow, Conwy and Machno.

BLAENAU FFESTINIOG, Gwynedd *104 SH74*
There is little need to explain the reason for the existence of this largish town on such an inhospitable hillside – slate abounds everywhere. It has been used to build houses, pave paths, build garden walls, and even in death there is no escape from it; tombstones are often made of slate. Huge waste tips of slate threaten to engulf the town at some points. Recently, the defunct slate industry has given birth to an unlikely new industry – the tourist trade. Llechwedd Slate Caverns, an award-winning enterprise, now attract increasing numbers of visitors who are taken on a tram ride through underground tunnels and into massive chambers where life-size models and period equipment help to recreate the atmosphere of slate mining a century ago. Visitors are also able to inspect the pillaring techniques which allowed tier upon tier of caverns to be mined. Almost opposite the Llechwedd Slate Caverns is another tourist enterprise – the Gloddfa Canol Mountain Tourist Centre, which has opened the world's largest slate mine.

Intricately carved love spoons are on display in the Brecknock County Museum at Brecon

BRECON, Powys *103 SO02*
Streets lined with Georgian and Jacobean houses add much to the beauty and character of Brecon, a mid-Wales town that was raised to the status of cathedral city in 1923. It is an ideal centre from which to explore the Brecon Beacons National Park. The cathedral is situated on the northern outskirts and was originally the church of a Benedictine priory. Dating mainly from the 13th and 14th centuries, the building is cruciform in plan and displays a number of outstanding architectural features. Several priory buildings, including a fine tithe barn, have been restored. Remains of Brecon Castle are now part of the Castle Hotel, and fragments of the medieval town walls can be seen at Captain's Walk, an area where, it is said, French prisoners exercised during the Napoleonic wars. St Mary's Church is a greatly restored medieval building. The Brecknock County Museum stands in Glamorgan Street, and the Museum of the South Wales Borderers is sited in The Watton.

BRIDGEND, M Glam *103 SS97*
This large industrial town is split into the districts of Nolton and Newcastle by the River Ogmore. Newcastle derives its name from the town's 12th-century castle.

BUILTH WELLS, Powys *103 SO05*
The Welsh name for this market town is *Llanfair yn Muallt* – St Mary's in Builth – and it originated as a settlement around a Norman castle of which nothing is now left except a mound behind the Lion Hotel. Edward I used the castle to control the Welsh, who made their last stand for independence here in 1282 when Llywelyn the Last passed through the town and was killed nearby. Builth rose to popularity in the 18th century when spas became fashionable.

CAERLEON, Gwent *103 ST39*
Associations with the Romans and King Arthur make this small town one of the most historic in Wales. It was *Isca Silurum*, chief fortress of the Second Augustan Legion, from AD75 to the 4th century AD. The fort measures 540 yards by 450 yards and held about 6,000 foot soldiers and horsemen. It included barracks, baths, shops and temples. In AD80 an amphitheatre was built, 267ft long and with a seating capacity of 6,000. It can still be seen. In the Prysg field, some 300 yards north-west of the church, are the excavated foundations of the barrack blocks. In the town centre, where the legionary commander's building would have been, is the Legionary Museum – part of the National Museum of Wales.

CAERNARFON, Gwynedd *104 SH46*
Workaday Caernarfon is a comfortable small town which has become the most important tourist centre in Snowdonia. It has an illustrious history that stretches back to Roman times, when a settlement called *Segontium* was founded nearby. Above the jumbled roofs of the town rise the massive towers of Edward I's 13th-century castle, acknowledged as the finest of its type in Britain. A gesticulating statue of Lloyd George, who was Caernarfon's MP for many years, stands opposite the castle balcony from which newly invested Princes of Wales greet their subjects.

Caernarfon Castle guards the mouth of the Afon Seiont, a popular mooring place

CAERPHILLY, M Glam   *103 ST18*

Caerphilly is renowned for its cheese and its castle. The cheese-making has largely disappeared from the town, but the castle remains as the second largest in Britain after Windsor. With its land and water defences, it covers 30 acres. The Romans built a fort at Caerphilly in about AD75 some 200 yards north-west of the present castle. Gilbert de Clare, Lord of Glamorgan, started building the castle in 1268. In 1270 the partly-built structure was destroyed by Llywelyn ap Gruffydd, Prince of Wales, but work was resumed the next year. The best view of the town itself is from Caerphilly Common, an 800ft-high ridge.

CAERWENT, Gwent   *103 ST49*

Here, under peaceful fields and old cottages, lie the remains of *Venta Silurum*, once a town of some 3,000 people. The Romans built *Venta* to show the natives (the *Silures*) just what the Roman way of life was like. Some of the normally belligerent Silures obviously liked what they saw, for they moved down from their hill-top fort of Llanenellin and settled into life in a Roman city. The wall surrounding the city still stands for much of its length, and is most impressive in the south, where it is over 15ft high in places. This wall was strengthened with bastions as a defence against raiders coming from the sea in the 14th century. The town of Caerwent stands within the Roman walls, and the main street marks the approximate line of the Roman central avenue. Caerwent church contains several reminders of the Roman past in its porch, and displays an interesting mosaic from the occupation.

CARDIFF, S Glam   *103 ST17*

Cardiff displays the mixture of dignity and pragmatism to be expected from the capital city and cultural centre of Wales. Massive expansion resulted in the city becoming the world's principal coal port by the start of the 20th century, and much of its present-day appearance can be directly attributed to this era. One family particularly involved in the city's growth was the Butes, who built the vast docks, sank a fortune into the development of the city as a living and working community, and restored the castle. The latter, an appealing mixture of genuine period remains and 19th-century reconstruction, was the brainchild of the third Marquess, working with

Above: The exotic ceiling of the Arab room in Cardiff Castle typifies Burges' extravagant style

Below: Renaissance-style City Hall is one of Cardiff's most distinguished civic buildings

This memorial to Sir Thomas Picton, British soldier, can be seen at Carmarthen Museum

architect William Burges. Inside the perimeter walls the handsome Norman keep surmounts a motte surrounded by a defensive moat. In direct contrast, and well distant in a 'gothick' complex, are 19th-century living quarters that reveal the full expression of romantic medievalism so loved by Bute and the famous Burges. Cardiff's principal buildings stand quite close to the castle in Cathay's Park and include the City Hall and County Hall, the University College and the National Museum of Wales. The Llandaf district is situated north-west of the city centre and can be reached through some of Cardiff's elegant parks. Here, in a village-like setting, is the city's cathedral, an historic building which was almost destroyed by the ravages of time but is now fully restored to its old splendour. Other interesting features of the city include the famous Cardiff Arms Park rugby ground.

CARDIGAN, Dyfed   *102 SN14*

The beautiful Afon Teifi flows into the sea at Cardigan. The salmon and sea trout that thrive in its tree-shaded waters are fished for from coracles, small traditional craft that have continued to use the river while relative newcomers have been forced elsewhere by the silting of Cardigan's port. The town is no longer of major maritime significance, but the observant visitor will find many reminders of its seafaring past. A fine 17th-century six-arched bridge spans the Teifi beneath the remains of a Norman castle. Today the town has a mainly Victorian character.

CARMARTHEN, Dyfed   *102 SN42*

Excavations have revealed that Carmarthen was a Roman settlement of some importance. It was then known as *Moridunum*, and was the farthest west of the large Roman forts. The Normans arrived in 1093 and built a castle on a mound above the river. This was at one time the principal residence of the princes of South Wales, and was thus the frequent object of sieges. Much of the site is now taken up by Carmarthen's most imposing building, the County Hall, which was designed by Sir Percy Thomas and displays a high, steep-angled roof. The most venerable of Carmarthen's buildings is St Peter's Church, at the top of Priory Street. It dates from the 13th and 14th centuries and includes some 16th-century work in the south aisle. At Abergwili, on the eastern outskirts of the town, is the fine County Museum.

CHEPSTOW, Gwent *103 ST59*
Spectacularly perched above a bend of the Wye are the extensive remains of Chepstow Castle, a massive fortification that was begun in stone only a year after the Norman invasion of England. A path through pleasant gardens leads from the castle into the quaint old town, which includes many old houses built along switchback streets.

CHIRK, Clwyd *105 SJ23*
An interesting section of the Shropshire Union Canal in this well-kept village includes a long, damp tunnel which opens into a wide basin before the canal is carried high across the Ceiriog valley. Outside Chirk behind superb 18th-century wrought-iron gates is Chirk Castle, a 13th-century border fortress in a commanding position above the Ceiriog valley. Unlike many of its contemporaries this stronghold has been continuously inhabited since it was built, and considerable structural changes have been made to suit the tastes of successive owners.

CONWY, Gwynedd *104 SH77*
Three bridges span the Afon Conwy estuary for access to this walled town, which is squeezed between the mountains and the sea. The oldest of the bridges was built by Thomas Telford in 1826 to carry traffic previously forced to use the ferry. In 1848 Stephenson built a tubular railway bridge across the estuary, and in 1958 a new road bridge took the load from Telford's original. All three bridges seem to lead straight into Edward I's magnificent castle, which, along with the town walls, is a supreme example of 13th-century defensive architecture. The original medieval street plan is preserved within the walls, but only a few old buildings survive. Outstanding amongst these are Aberconwy, which was built in 1400, and the lovely Tudor house of Plas Mawr.

COWBRIDGE, S Glam *103 SS97*
Often called the capital of the Vale of Glamorgan, this old market town lies 12 miles west of Cardiff. Its original charter dates from the 14th century and a new charter was granted in 1887. Remains of the 14th-century town walls survive on the south side, but only the Porth Mellin survives of the three gates that once existed. The Church of the Holy Cross has a 13th-century embattled tower, an interesting structure of buttresses and stairways.

DENBIGH, Clwyd *104 SJ06*
Overlooking the town's attractive streets are the ruins of Edward I's great castle. It was begun in 1282 with the construction of town walls that have remained remarkably intact to the present day. Perhaps the most impressive feature of the fortress is its tripartite gatehouse. Inside the town walls are remains of St Hilary's Tower, which formed part of the original garrison chapel, and Leicester's Folly. The latter is part of a church that was to have replaced the Cathedral of St Asaph, but was never completed. In the lower part of the town are the remains of a Carmelite friary, which was founded in 1284 by Sir John Salesbury.

The Afon Mynach tumbles beneath the three bridges that span the narrow gorge at the popular beauty spot known as Devil's Bridge

DEVIL'S BRIDGE, Dyfed *103 SN77*
Cwm Rheidol narrows to form a spectacular 500ft-deep wooded gorge at Devil's Bridge, where the Afon Mynach adds its own 300ft of impressive waterfalls to the grandeur of the Afon Rheidol's Gyfarllwyd Falls. Excellent views into the gorge can be enjoyed from the road bridge, but the full scenic splendour of the area can only be fully appreciated by a descent into the valley bottom. A flight of 91 steps known as Jacob's Ladder zig-zags down to river level, where a small bridge and platform afford views of five separate waterfalls. Of the three bridges stacked on top of each other at Devil's Bridge the oldest is – naturally – the lowest, and is thought to have been built in the 12th century by monks from Strata Florida Abbey. Legend has it that the devil built it as a complex trick to win a soul. The second bridge was built in 1753, and an iron bridge was built above the other two early this century.

DOLGELLAU, Gwynedd *104 SH71*
Granite and boulder stone from the surrounding mountains are the principal materials from which Dolgellau is built. Its narrow, twisting streets are set in a fine position beside the Afon Wnion, and to the south green slopes rise to the craggy summits of Cader Idris. St Mary's Church was built in 1716 against a plain medieval tower. Wooden columns support the nave roof, and the interior is lit by windows with excellent stained glass. Beautiful Precipice Walk, which lies north of the town and is approached from the Llanfachreth road (off the A494), affords superb views throughout its seven-mile length round the rugged slopes of Foel Cynwch. Gold for the Queen's wedding ring came from old mines in the tree-clad hillsides above Dolgellau's rooftops.

FISHGUARD, Dyfed *102 SM93*
Lower Town, as the oldest part of Fishguard is called, is a delightfully unspoilt fishing village. It was chosen as the setting for the film version of Dylan Thomas' *Under Milk Wood*, and is connected to Upper Town by a steep hill. The square in Upper Town features a Market Hall and the attractive Royal Oak Inn. During the 18th century Fishguard witnessed the signing of a treaty that ended the last invasion of British soil. In reality the so-called 'invasion' was a fiasco perpetrated by a motley band of French soldiers and convicts bent on pillage.

FLINT, Clwyd *105 SJ27*
It is hard to believe that ships could once tie up against the walls of Flint Castle. The town declined as a port during the last century when the Dee changed its course and its main channel silted up. Immortalized by Shakespeare, the castle is now a sad ruin separated from the town by the main road and a railway, looking out over the Dee estuary with industrial chimneys as neighbours.

GROSMONT, Gwent *103 SO42*
This small old-world town, set amid beautiful scenery by the River Monnow, was a borough until 1860. Inside its massively towered church is a huge, flat-faced stone knight of ancient origin. The castle here was one of three erected in the vicinity to protect the border between England and Wales, the others being Skenfrith and White Castle.

HARLECH, Gwynedd *104 SH53*
Dominating this granite-built town from a craggy hilltop are the ruins of a 13th-century castle. This was constructed on a rectangular plan, with two concentric sets of walls and circular towers at the corners. The battlements can be reached by a staircase in the southern angle of the curtain wall and afford fine views of the surrounding countryside. The large flat plain between the castle and the sea was once covered in water, and the castle's site was a rocky headland at the very brink of the ocean.

HAVERFORDWEST, Dyfed *102 SM91*
More English than Welsh, this important market town is situated above the Western Cleddau on the slopes of a steep hill which is surmounted by a ruined castle, standing in a prominent position above the town and overlooking the river. It was founded before 1120 by the First Earl of Pembroke, Gilbert de Clare, and rebuilt in the 13th century by William de Valence, a later earl of Pembroke. The keep was built into the living rock and commands splendid views. The castle remains now house a museum and Pembrokeshire Coast information centre.
   The Church of St Mary is one of the finest in South Wales. It was originally built in the middle of the 13th century, and contains an effigy of a pilgrim from the time of Henry VII – thought to represent a traveller from the shrine of St James of Compostela because of the scallop shells in his satchel. The church also contains armorial memorials, a brass of 1651 and a fine lancet window.

The high moorland of the Black Mountains stretches away to the south of the Wye valley near Hay-on-Wye

LAMPETER, Dyfed   *102 SN54*

Neat rectangular fields bounded by hedges cover the gentle hills around Lampeter like a giant patchwork quilt. The town itself preserves a distinctive Welsh character coloured by its own personality. Small shops interspersed with dapper private houses, two Georgian hotels, and a proud Victorian town hall occupy the main street under the eye of the parish church. The latter was rebuilt in 1869, but contains memorials from earlier ages. Lampeter is best known for St David's College, which was founded in 1822 so that Welsh students (prohibited by expense from attending Oxford or Cambridge) could have a university education. Although integrated with the University of Wales in 1971, the college remains a complete university in miniature.

LAUGHARNE, Dyfed   *102 SN31*

Overlooking the Taf estuary here is the Boathouse, once the home of the poet Dylan Thomas. The house stands on a narrow cliff walk near the castle, close to a shed in which he wrote some of his later poetry. He is buried in Laugharne churchyard, and a simple cross marks his grave. Although Thomas always denied that Laugharne was the inspiration for *Under Milk Wood*, the townsfolk of Laugharne seem happy to act the parts, and every three years the play is performed in the town.

Laugharne itself is charming, with modest Georgian houses and a white-painted tower that belongs to the town hall in the main street. Built in 1746, the town hall preserves a charter granted by the Normans in 1307. Local government is still conducted under the terms of this charter, and meetings of the Court Leet and Court Baron are presided over by an official known as the Portreeve.

HAY-ON-WYE, Powys   *103 SO24*

Book-lovers will be in their element here, for Hay has more than its fair share of bookstores. Many of them belong to a single business that is the largest second-hand book concern in the world. Narrow streets winding through the old town are full of fascinating small shops, and on market day are alive with bustling activity. William de Braose, one of the most ruthless of the Marcher Lords, built a castle here to replace one burned down by King John. Folk hero Owain Glyndwr destroyed the later castle during the 15th century, but a fine gateway, the keep, and parts of the wall remain.

HOLYHEAD, Gwynedd   *104 SH28*

This, the largest town in Anglesey, is a major ferry terminal for Ireland and is constantly busy with the jostling of travellers, seamen, and holidaymakers. The old parish church of St Cybi is built within the walls of a Roman fort, and the flank of Holyhead Mountain – which towers over the town – is scattered with the remains of prehistoric huts.

KIDWELLY, Dyfed   *102 SN40*

Kidwelly lies off the Tywi estuary, with the vast Towyn Burrows and Pembrey Forest stretching away to the south. As a borough it is one of the oldest in Wales, the first charter having been granted by Henry I. The older and formerly walled part lies on the west bank of the Gwendraeth Fach below the castle. The newer town has a prominent church and is situated on its east bank. The two are linked by a bridge which, although considerably widened, dates from the 14th or 15th centuries. Kidwelly's church was originally the church of a Benedictine priory founded in 1130 by Bishop Roger of Salisbury, who also built the castle. Kidwelly Castle, after careful restoration, is now the best preserved of old Carmarthenshire's nine strongholds.

KNIGHTON, Powys   *103 SO27*

The Offa's Dyke long-distance footpath was officially opened here in 1971. The dyke itself, built by a king of Mercia in the 8th century, runs through the town. Built largely of local stone, Knighton occupies a delightful hillside position in the Teme valley and has scant remains of a Norman motte-and-bailey castle. Knighton's railway station stands on the Central Wales line and is a little gem of Victorian-gothic railway architecture. Knighton's livestock sales are famous.

Knighton's Victorian clock-tower provides an attractive centrepiece to this little border town

LLANBERIS, Gwynedd   104 SH56

This former slate-workers' village is now known as the starting point for one of the three main walks to the summit of Snowdon. Close to the village is the lower terminus of the Snowdon Mountain Railway. Across Llyn Padarn from Llanberis is the vast Dinorwic Slate Quarry, now a museum of the slate industry. The narrow-gauge railway which used to carry slate from the Dinorwic quarry to Port Dinorwic on the Menai Strait is now one of Wales' famous steam-hauled lines.

LLANDDEWI BREFI, Dyfed   102 SN65

A great synod was held here in AD519 to debate the Heresy of Pelagius, which denied the biblical doctrine of original sin. One of those refuting Pelagius was St David, beneath whom the ground is said to have risen so that those around could hear what he was saying. The village's 13th-century church stands on a mound which tradition holds to be the same miraculous eminence.

David Davies is commemorated in his home town of Llandinam by a bronze statue

LLANDINAM, Powys   103 SO08

Green hills rising to the lower slopes of mountains spread from the Severn valley site of this pretty village. Close to a handsome iron bridge that spans the river is a statue of Llandinam's most famous native, David Davies, who was born here in 1818. After starting from a modest beginning as the son of a humble local farmer, Davies worked to become a railway contractor, then went on to make a fortune with the construction of Barry Docks. He became one of the great industrialists and entrepreneurs of the Victorian age. The local church has been greatly restored and stands on the site of a hill-fort which is still faintly visible. Ancient carvings preserved in the church include one depicting Adam and Eve.

LLANDOVERY, Dyfed   103 SN73

Llandovery's name means 'Church amid the waters' and derives from its position at the confluence of the Bran, Gwydderig and Tywi. The town has been a place of some significance at least since Roman times, and Llanfair-ar-y-Bryn church stands within the ramparts of a Roman fort. A reminder of the town's later connections with cattle droving is the building which houses Lloyds Bank. Until 1909 this was the Black Ox Bank, founded in 1799 by a drover named David Jones. The nearby Market Hall is a low 19th-century building capped by an extraordinary pepper-pot turret. Llandovery College, a public school founded in 1848, was created for the express purpose of providing an education entirely in the Welsh language. Overgrown remains of a Norman castle surmount a mound above the cattle market.

LLANDRINDOD WELLS, Powys   103 SO06

After the ubiquitous grey stone and slate so characteristic of Welsh towns and villages, Llandrindod Wells comes as a cream and strawberry surprise. From whichever direction this delightful town is entered, the visitor meets its full impact at first glance with complete amazement. Suddenly he is in the midst of towers, turrets, cupolas, balconies, oriels, colonnades, ornamental ironwork, loggias, balustrades – almost every architectural extravagance imaginable. The effect is magnificent, and everywhere there are gardens, parks, green banks and commons.

The town grew up around healing springs that rise here, but it took a long time to do so. The year 1670 is usually accepted as the start of Llandrindod's emergence as a spa, but it did not reach its heyday until the second half of the

Graceful Dolauhirion Bridge, dating from 1773, spans the Afon Tywi north of Llandovery

19th century. The coming of the railway in 1866 took Llandrindod into its golden years. Spa treatment went out of fashion however, and Llandrindod declined. This was by no means the end of Llandrindod, for in 1974 it took on a new lease of life as capital of the newly-formed county of Powys. An interesting museum here preserves an ancient boat recovered from the Afon Ithon near the Roman fort called Castell Collen, plus a collection of dolls from all over the world. There is also a gallery illustrating the Victorian spa, with period costumes and chemists' equipment. The Automobile Palace Veteran Cycle Collection displays cycles and tricycles dating from the mid 19th century.

Llanddewi Brefi's church was orginally built with transepts that have long since disappeared

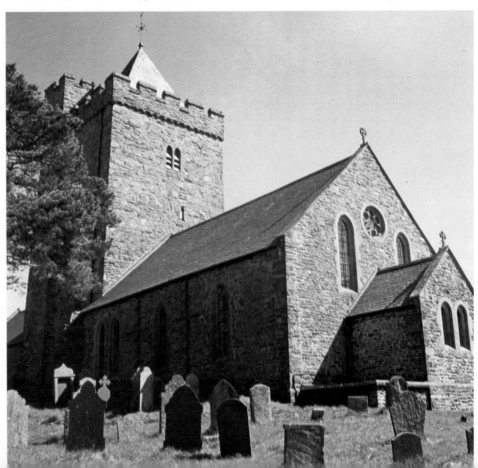

LLANDUDNO, Gwynedd   *104 SH78*

Justifiably known as the 'Queen of Welsh Resorts', Llandudno developed in the 1850s from a cluster of fishermen's cottages to a Victorian seaside resort which is a classic of its kind. The town was the brainchild of Liverpool surveyor Owen Williams, who planned the great sweep of the Promenade and the majestically wide streets. Great Orme's Head, with its gardens, cable railway, an ancient church and windswept grassy slopes, separates the resort's two superb beaches.

LLANELLI, Dyfed   *102 SN50*

Set on the Afon Loughor, Llanelli became industrialized during the early 19th century, when Alexander Raby moved into the district known as the Furnace and established the first ironworks. He was later responsible for building the first modern dock and the Dafen works, which opened in 1847. The once flourishing port, which was mainly concerned with the shipment of coal, is now virtually closed. In Parc Howard stands Bryncaerau Castle, now a museum containing a collection of Llanelli pottery and a history of the tinplate industry. The castle also houses an art gallery specializing in the work of local painters.

LLANFAIR CAEREINION, Powys   *104 SJ10*

The river at the foot of the hillside on which this quiet little greystone town is built has two names – Banwy and Einion. In the local church, which was rebuilt in 1868, is the 14th-century stone figure of a knight.

In recent years Llanfair Caereinion has gained fame as the headquarters of the restored Welshpool and Llanfair Light Railway, a narrow-gauge steam-hauled line that is now a major tourist attraction.

LLANGOLLEN, Clwyd   *105 SJ24*

This small town's world-wide reputation as a centre of Welsh culture and music comes from the International Eisteddfod, held here for one week in July. During this time the small streets are transformed by a riot of colourful national costumes and chatter of foreign tongues, while the surrounding hillsides echo to the sound of great international choirs and poets performing in a huge 1,000-seat marquee. Plas Newydd is a black-and-white house on the edge of the town which was, for many years, the home of the 'Ladies of Llangollen'. This eccentric pair of spinsters, who arrived here in 1779, entertained a string of celebrities and generated endless gossip with their lifestyle. The house and grounds are attractive additions to the landscape.

LLANIDLOES, Powys   *103 SN98*

Tree-lined streets, a happy blend of old and new architecture, and a few attractive shopfronts combine to form Llanidloes' unique character. The 16th-century Market Hall in the centre of the town is a rare survivor of a type of building that was once common all over the country. Its arcaded lower floor is open to the street and once sheltered market stalls. The floor above now houses a folk museum.

This Victorian puppet theatre (left) is one of many traditional seaside entertainments to be found in Llandudno. The pier (above), which dates from the same period, serves as a landing stage for steamers

LLANTRISANT, M Glam   *103 ST08*

Both church and castle command dominating hilltop sites above the steep attractive streets of Llantrisant. The Royal Mint was moved here in 1967.

LLANTWIT MAJOR, S Glam   *103 SS96*

Once this quiet place was one of the most important and influential centres of learning in British Christendom. The school founded here by 5th-century St Illtud attracted scholars from distant parts and fostered some of the greatest minds of early Welsh history. A faint echo of the foundation survives in the 13th- and 15th-century Church of St Illtud – a remarkable structure formed by two churches joined end to end. Inside is a richly-carved Jesse Tree. Other features of the town include an old dovecot and monastery gateway, a medieval town hall, the Old Swan Inn, and the imposing Great House.

MACHYNLLETH, Powys   *103 SH70*

On market days Machynlleth's Maengwyn Street is packed with stalls selling a wide variety of wares. On the north side of the same street is the Owain Glyndwr Institute, which stands on the site of a building where Welsh revolutionary Owain Glyndwr held Wales' last independent parliament in 1404. On the other side of the street is the timbered Court House, with an inscription dated 1628.

MANORBIER, Dyfed   *102 SS09*

A small seaside village overlooking Manorbier Bay, Manorbier has a sandy beach and safe bathing. The parish church is of Norman origin and carries a 13th-century tower. The chancel, south transept and south aisle date from the 15th century. Manorbier Castle is a moated Norman structure which dates from the 12th and 13th centuries and is thought to have been more of a baronial residence than a fortress.

MERTHYR TYDFIL, M Glam   *103 SO00*

Although Merthyr Tydfil has been a market town since the 12th century, it was not until the 19th century that the potential of the town's natural iron resources was realized. By 1831 it was the largest town in Wales, and four large ironworks had been set up by pioneers Josiah Guest, Richard Crawshay and their contemporaries. After the First World War heavy industry moved out of the town to areas near the ports, and Merthyr Tydfil was left in a desperate situation with half the population unemployed. Various parliamentary acts later helped to ease the town's economic crisis, and the community is now supported by light industries and some coalmining. Cyfarthfa Castle was built in 1825 for William Crawshay and is now a museum and art gallery.

MILFORD HAVEN, Dyfed   *102 SM90*

Milford Haven is situated on steeply sloping ground on the northern shores of a drowned valley also called Milford Haven. The present town dates back to the late 18th century, when it was developed as a naval dockyard. It suffered a setback when the naval dockyard was removed to Pembroke Dock in 1814, but later became a successful deep-sea fishing port.

The Haven itself is a 12-mile-long – and in some places 2-mile-wide – drowned valley which is a superb natural harbour. The Haven's main industry today is the refining of oil, with four great oil refineries and one of the largest oil-fired power stations in Britain around its shores.

MONMOUTH, Gwent   *103 SO51*

Strategically placed where the rivers Wye and Monnow meet, this ancient town played a vital role in subjugating South Wales from the Roman period till the Middle Ages. The outstanding reminder of these troubled times is a unique fortified bridge which has spanned the Monnow and guarded the town since 1260. The once-powerful castle preserves an interesting 12th-century building among its remains. Nearby is the Great Castle House, a 17th-century structure noted for its fine interior decorations.

MONTGOMERY, Powys   *103 SO29*

Montgomery's superficially Georgian character is shown in the red-brick town hall that dominates Broad Street, an aptly named thoroughfare almost as wide as it is long. Away from the centre the 18th century has less hold, and fine examples of Tudor and Jacobean architecture make surprise appearances round secretive corners or at the tops of quaint slopes and steps. The parish church of St Nicholas was built just before Henry III granted Montgomery's Royal Charter in 1227. Its best features include a 15th-century nave roof, a double screen, and monuments to the Herbert family. Poet George Herbert was born in the now-ruined castle, built by Henry III.

NEATH, W Glam   *103 SS79*

Best known today as an industrial town where steel and tin-plate are made, Neath still preserves some evidence of its long history. The ruins of a medieval abbey can still be seen, and the remains of Neath Castle include the 13th-century gateway, its two towers, and parts of the curtain wall. The site of the old Roman fort of *Nidium*, mentioned in the *Twelfth Journey of Antonius*, was discovered in 1949 during the excavation of a building site. Gnoll House was once the home of Sir Humphrey Mackworth, a great industrialist who founded the copper industry in the last century. This mansion is now the town's war memorial, and the 250 acres of Gnoll Woods are public parkland.

NEVERN, Dyfed   *102 SN04*

Not only is Nevern one of the most attractive and beautifully set villages in Wales, it also possesses a magnificent 13ft-high Celtic cross, carved with intricate patterns and obscure inscriptions. Also in the churchyard is an avenue of Irish yews leading to the rugged old church itself, which contains other carved stones.

NEWPORT, Gwent   *103 ST38*

In 1801 Newport had a population of 1,100, which grew to nearly 70,000 by the end of the 19th century as the docks exported the coal and iron products from the Gwent valleys. Today it is one of the major metal-exporting ports in Britain. Access to the docks is gained by one of Britain's largest sea locks, measuring 1,000ft by 100ft. Before the coming of the Normans this was the port or market town of the *Cantref of Gwenllwg*, of the ancient kingdom of *Morgannwg*. Newport Castle was built in about 1126 and stands beside the Usk near Newport Bridge.

Stow Hill commands a good view of the town and the Bristol Channel, and is surmounted by St Woolos' Cathedral, which has stonework of many centuries and a good Norman interior. Over 500 acres of parks and pleasure grounds in Newport include Tredegar Park, which is set in woodlands on the western edge of the town.

NEWTOWN, Powys   *103 SO19*

Robert Owen, a social reformer who became known as the father of trade unionism, was born in Newtown and is buried in the churchyard of the old parish church. Some of the reasons why Owen was such an assiduous campaigner for workers' rights can be understood by a visit to the Newtown Textile Museum, and a museum dedicated to his memory is situated over the Midland Bank. The 15th-century rood screen from the old church has been preserved in a handsome 19th-century successor. Newtown has recently become part of a designated development area, with extensive new building, including two new bridges over the Severn, a theatre, and pleasant parkland.

PEMBROKE, Dyfed   *102 SM90*

Small, but undoubtedly capital of the arm of land called 'Little England Beyond Wales', Pembroke's name is a corruption of the Welsh *Penfro*, meaning 'land's end'. In about 1090 the Norman Lord Arnulf de Montgomery founded what was to be one of the most powerful castles in Britain here. It was built on a spot which had superb natural defences: a butt of rock with steep and treacherous slopes protected on three sides by water. The castle was one of a chain built by the Normans to seal off from the Welsh the area that was to become known as 'Little England'. The present castle at Pembroke was begun in about 1190. Underneath the structure is a huge limestone cavern called the Wogan. This was linked to the castle by a winding stair and has an opening to the river. The old town walls can be traced in several places, especially at the Park and Mill Bridge.

Arnulf de Montgomery founded a priory here in 1098, and this is separated from the castle by a tidal inlet. The priory fell into ruins after the Dissolution, but in 1878 restoration of the church was begun, and today this building is in something like its original condition. St Deniol's has a chapel which displays windows decorated with the symbols of freemasonry and contains monuments to several local families.

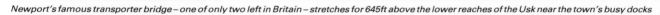

Newport's famous transporter bridge – one of only two left in Britain – stretches for 645ft above the lower reaches of the Usk near the town's busy docks

PONTYPOOL, Gwent   *103 SO20*

An industrial town in a predominantly coal-mining and tin-plate district, Pontypool was the first town in Britain to successfully produce tin-plate, in 1720. The town is also famous for its Japanese-type lacquer ware, which has been made here since the 17th century.

PONTYPRIDD, M Glam   *103 ST09*

Set in the southern Rhondda valley at the confluence of the Taff and the Rhondda, Pontypridd's principal industries are coal and iron. Anchor chains for Nelson's fleet were produced here, and these are still manufactured for large ships. In Ynysangharad Park are statues of Evan and James James – the father and son clothmakers who wrote the Welsh national anthem *Hen Wlad Fy Nhadau* ('Land of My Fathers'). A memorial tablet adorns their house in Mill Street.

PORTHCAWL, M Glam   *103 SS87*

Ranking as one of the leading resorts on the south coast of Wales, Porthcawl is situated on a low limestone promontory midway between Cardiff and Swansea, overlooking the Bristol Channel. The harbour is the central point of this attractive town, with its numerous hotels, boarding houses and shops. The large funfair of Coney Beach is modelled on Coney Island in New York, and stretches along Sandy Bay.

PORTHMADOG, Gwynedd   *104 SH53*

Travellers have to pay a toll to cross the one-mile-long embankment which was built here in the early 1800s to reclaim 4,500 acres of sea and sand. The building of the embankment created a good harbour and Porthmadog became one of the most important ports along the Welsh coast. Its prosperity was assured with the building of the Festiniog narrow-gauge railway in 1836, for it became the point from which the slate quarried at Blaenau Ffestiniog was exported. Porthmadog attracts thousands of visitors every summer.

PORTMEIRION, Gwynedd   *104 SH53*

Set on a wooded peninsula overlooking Traeth Bay between Porthmadog and Penrhydeud-raeth, Portmeirion is the work of the distinguished Welsh architect Clough Williams-Ellis. He had long been a campaigner against the spoiling of Britain's landscape, and in 1926 he set out to prove that the development of an old estate did not necessarily mean wrecking it. In the heart of the Welsh countryside he erected a 17th-century-style Italianate village after the fashion of Portofino or Sorrento. Portmeirion contains a castle, lighthouse, watch-tower, campanile, and grottos intermingled with 18th-century English cottages, and each building has been sited to the best advantage of natural slopes and heights. The estate also encompasses Gwylt Gardens, which is considered one of the finest wild gardens in Wales and contains rhododendrons, hydrangeas, azaleas, and a collection of exotic plants.

PRESTEIGNE, Powys   *103 SO36*

This charming little town was once the capital of the old county of Radnorshire and is full of period atmosphere. Broad Street has some fine Georgian houses, and the Radnorshire Arms is a lovely Jacobean half-timbered building which has a priest hole. The church has a 16th-century tapestry in the north aisle, some medieval glass in the Lady Chapel, and the old jail bell inscribed 'Prosperity to the benefactors, 1725'.

RAGLAN, Gwent   *103 SO40*

One of the most visually impressive strongholds in Wales, Raglan Castle was erected on the site of an 11th- or 12th-century motte-and-bailey structure. The present building dates from 1430 to the early 17th century and the Great Yellow Tower of Gwent is one of its oldest parts. The 14th- to 15th-century village church contains mutilated effigies of the Somersets, damaged during the seige of the castle by Cromwell's troops.

RUTHIN, Clwyd   *104 SJ15*

Ruthin Castle was founded by King Edward I in 1281 on the site of an earlier stronghold. Five round towers originally guarded the inner ward, but only the remains of three of them are left, together with the ruined double-towered gatehouse. St Peter's Church has a fine oak roof presented by King Henry VII in gratitude to the men of Wales who supported him in his successful fight for the English crown against Richard III at Bosworth Field in 1485. On the west side of the market square is half-timbered Exmewe Hall, which was used as a grandstand when bull-baiting was held in the square. The old Court House and prison, which now houses a bank, was built in 1401.

ST DAVID'S, Dyfed   *102 SM72*

To Welshmen this is the most hallowed spot in Great Britain, for it was here, in the 6th century, that Dewi Sant (St David) was born and grew up to become the special saint of Wales and all Welshmen. The cathedral, almost hidden in the vale of the little River Alun, was begun in 1180 by Peter de Leia. In 1240 the central tower collapsed, causing considerable damage to the choir and transepts. More damage was done by a severe earthquake in 1248. Even today the piers of the nave lean quite considerably from the vertical. The cathedral fell into disrepair after the Reformation, but was eventually restored in the 19th century by Sir Gilbert Scott.

ST FAGANS, S Glam   *103 ST17*

Attractive thatched cottages are charming features of this village, but St Fagan's is best known for the amazing collection of buildings that has been gathered round its castle to form the National Folk Museum of Wales. Complete buildings of many different periods have been rescued from all over Wales and painstakingly rebuilt in the grounds. Even the furnished interiors are authentic, and some of the buildings still fulfil their original functions.

Tenby developed into a major holiday town after the arrival of the railway in 1853. The grand hotels built on the headland overlooking South Beach date from this time

Two ruined keeps are all that remain of Tretower Castle, which was built after the Norman Conquest

SWANSEA, W Glam   103 SS69

Almost three centuries of intensive industrialization have left indelible scars upon the Swansea landscape, but not all of Swansea is built over or barren – over 900 acres of parkland bring the country into the city. In 1919 the former Technical College became a university which has since expanded to occupy several buildings in the town.

TENBY, Dyfed   102 SN10

Narrow streets with houses and shops built against the ruins of the 13th-century town walls impart a distinctive charm to this pleasant resort. From medieval times the sheltered harbour to the north served as an important link with Bristol and Ireland, and the town is ideally situated on a narrow, rocky promontory on the west side of Carmarthen Bay. Ruins of the 13th-century keep and walls of Tenby Castle can be seen on Castle Hill. The keep now contains a museum. Extensive remains of the town walls survive, including the five-arched main gateway. On Quay Hill is the Tudor Merchants' House, a good example of 15th-century architecture displaying a gabled front and corbelled chimney breast. The ground floor is now a National Trust information centre which includes an exhibition of the Tudor period. Adjacent Plantagenet House is of the same date. St Mary's, the largest parish church in Wales, dates from the 13th century.

TINTERN, Gwent   103 SO50

Ruins of a famous Cistercian abbey form the main attraction offered by this picturesque village, which is situated in a loop of the River Wye. Tintern Abbey was founded in 1131 by a member of the de Clare family, and enlarged in the 13th and 14th centuries. The walls of its roofless church, which was consecrated in 1288, stand almost intact, and a fine rose window over 60ft high is set in the east wall.

TRETOWER, Powys   103 SO12

A sturdy keep surrounded by the ruins of a previous keep is all that remains of Tretower Castle, which was usurped as a habitation in the 14th century by nearby Tretower Court. The latter is considered a very fine example of a fortified mansion.

TYWYN, Gwynedd   102 SH50

Tywyn stands in the plain of the lower Afon Dysynni, surrounded by the foothills of the Cader Idris range. The older part of the town lies about 1 mile inland. The Norman church is dedicated to St Cadfan of Brittany, who founded the first church here in the 6th century. A 7th-century carved stone here stands 7ft high and bears the earliest Welsh inscription in existence. In more recent times Tywyn has gained fame as the terminus of the Talyllyn narrow-gauge railway.

WELSHPOOL, Powys   105 SJ20

Many of the narrow streets which characterized this town until recently have been sacrificed to commercial interests, but enough remain to kindle an imaginative picture of Welshpool as it was. Opposite the town hall is a half-timbered building with a Jacobean staircase, one of several such examples in the town. Severn Road leads to a splendid Victorian railway station incorporating many gables, end towers, and a platform canopy resplendent with wrought-iron arcading. The Powysland Museum stands in Salop Road, while on the west side of the town is the new terminus of the Welshpool and Llanfair Light Railway, a narrow-gauge line which runs from here to Llanfair Caereinion.

Outside the town is magnificent Powis Castle, a 13th-century stronghold that has slowly been transformed into a huge mansion. The castle is of special interest because it has been continuously occupied, and its present form has evolved through the centuries as a response to the tastes of its owners.

These Victorian porcelain dolls can be seen in Wrexham's enchanting Doll and Toy Museum

WREXHAM, Clwyd   105 SJ35

Wrexham has changed in character over the years from a border market town to the administrative, commercial and shopping centre for a concentrated industrial area. Towering 136ft high, the 18th-century Church of St Giles qualifies for inclusion among any list of notable churches of England and Wales. Also worth a visit is Wrexham's Doll and Toy Museum, a fascinating collection of more than 3,500 items including dolls' house furniture, mechanical toys and Victorian clothes.

On the eastern outskirts of the town is Erddig, a fine mansion magnificently restored in recent years by the National Trust. The domestic outbuildings such as the laundry, bakehouse and sawmill, are all in working order.

Beautiful terraced gardens complement the mansion of Powis Castle, near Welshpool

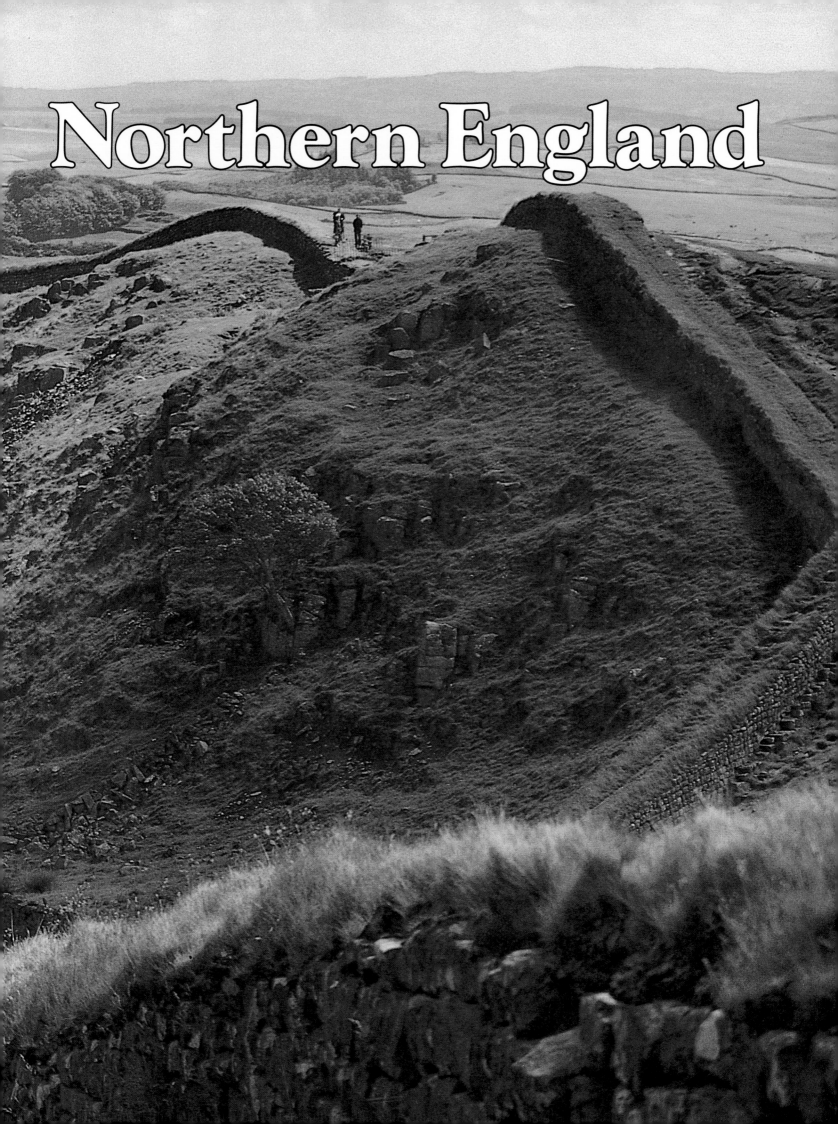

Northern England

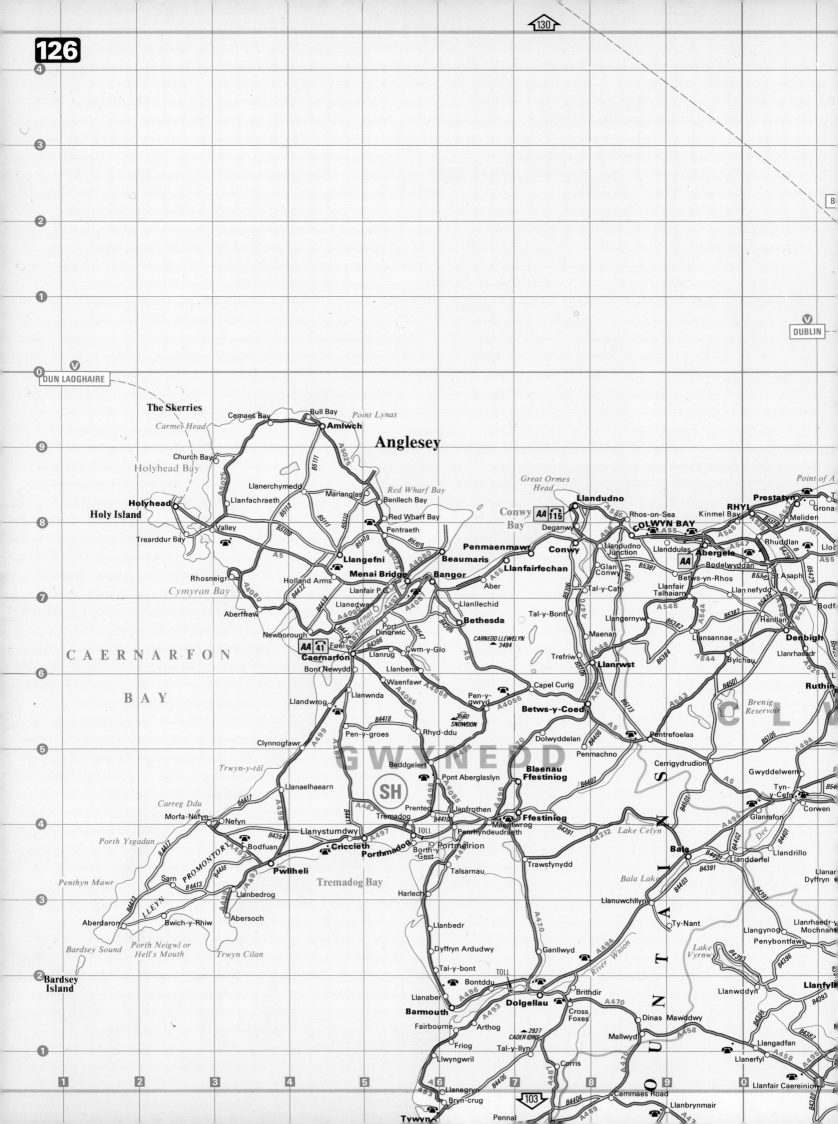

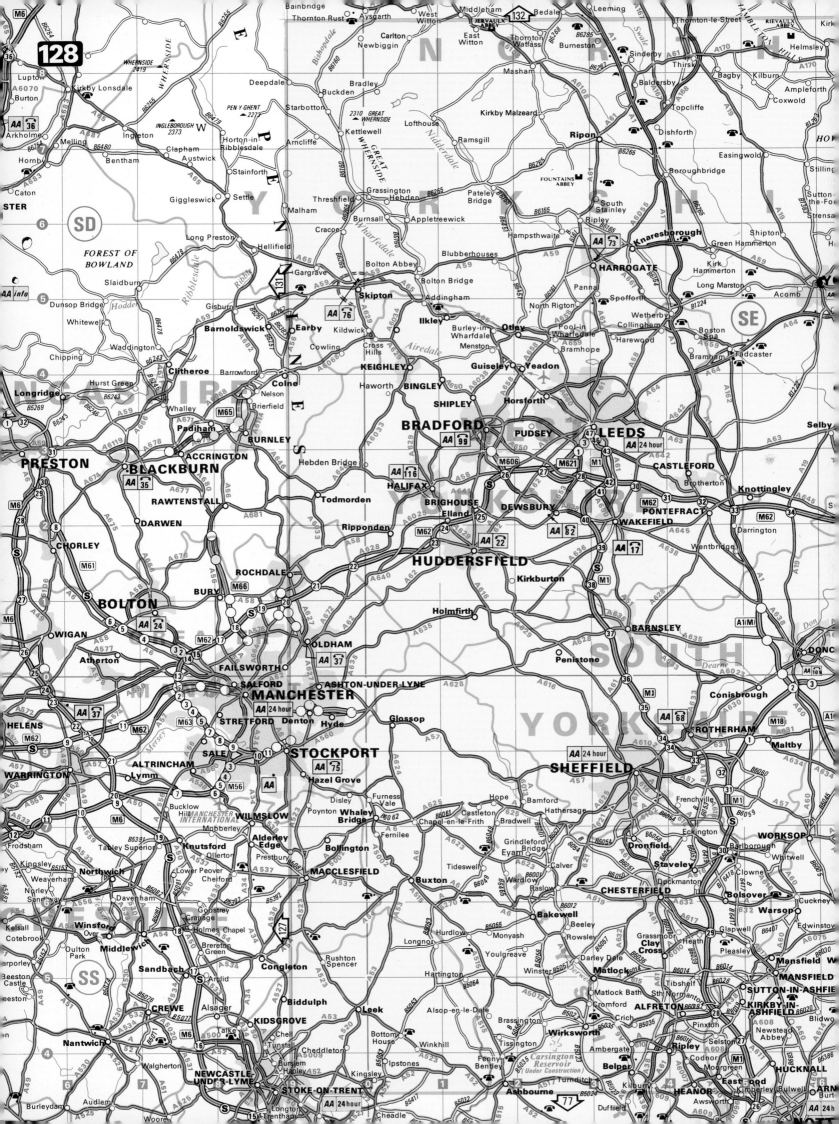

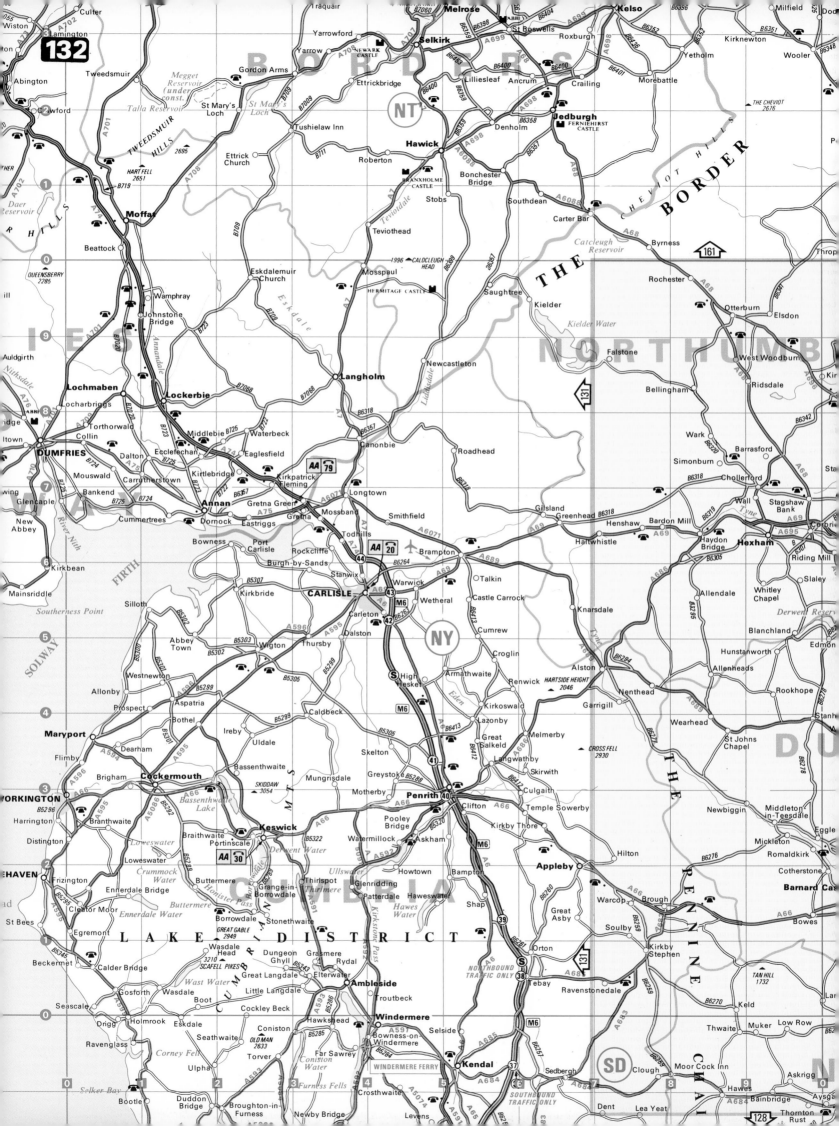

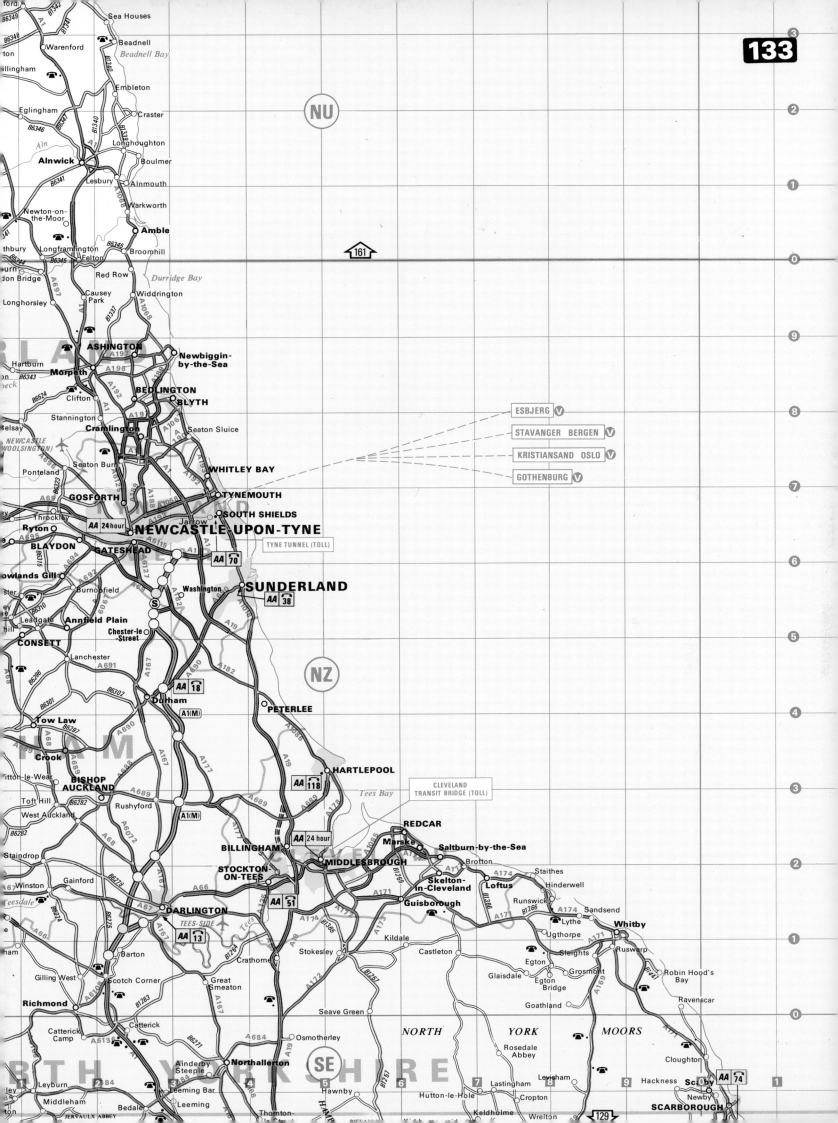

High Peak and Cheshire Plain
67 miles

CONGLETON
This solid, north country market town on the River Dane is an important cattle market and textile centre, and a dormitory town for Manchester and the Potteries. The town was granted a charter in 1272, and many relics of its long civic history are displayed in the Victorian town hall. St Peter's Church is a staid 18th-century building but is full of carved woodwork, including a Jacobean pulpit. A few half-timbered houses remain, among them three old inns, including the Bear's Head Hotel, named after the sport of bear-baiting which survived in Congleton longer than anywhere else in the country.

LITTLE MORETON HALL
Beautiful carved gables and a distinctive black-and-white exterior of Elizabethan wood- and plasterwork have made this splendid 16th-century manor house one of the most famous examples in Britain. The dazzling effect of symmetrical timber patterns against brilliant white is increased by the reflection of the house in its own lovely moat. Inside are a long wainscoted gallery, a great hall and a chapel.

RUDYARD
Rudyard Kipling's parents courted and became engaged in this lovely village, and when their talented son was born they named him after it. Attractive woodlands to the north border a two-mile reservoir formed in 1793 to provide water for the Trent and Mersey Canal. Today the banks of this attractive lake are skirted by a five-mile footpath dotted with secluded picnic spots near the water's edge. A section of the path follows the trackbed of an

Ramshaw Rocks are a distinctive Peak District landmark

abandoned railway, and its route passes caverns, unusual rock formations and the remains of Roman copper workings.

MEERBROOK
Wild upland country popular with climbers and fell-walkers surrounds this tiny moorland village. A curious feature of the area is its naturalized colony of red-necked wallabies, which numbers some 30 animals.

RAMSHAW ROCKS
These jagged gritstone crags tower above the A53, and form part of a more extensive ridge of exposed millstone grit known as the Roaches. The whole outcrop is very popular with climbers.

FLASH
Situated at 1,518ft, Flash claims to be the highest village in England and is itself dominated by 1,684ft Oliver Hill to the north.

BUXTON
The highest town in England, Buxton's fame and popularity is mainly due to the natural spas found here. The Romans knew of them, but it was not until 1750 that Buxton was developed as a second Bath. The pleasing Georgian architecture which resulted includes the Crescent, built near the original spa, St Ann's Well. As much as 280,000 gallons of the health-giving water flows each day from nine springs.

GAWSWORTH
Spacious lawns and gardens watered by five lakes grace the grounds of Gawsworth Hall, a beautiful black-and-white timber-framed house dating from Tudor times. Also in the park are rare traces of a tilting ground, where knights once displayed their prowess in jousts and mock battles. Features of the village itself include the fine Old Rectory and an attractive church, both dating from the 15th century.

MARTON
A famous oak tree in this village is said to be the largest in England. The local church is a quaint timbered structure dating from the 14th century.

CAPESTHORNE HALL
A chapel which adjoins this lovely 18th-century house may be the earliest surviving work of the architect John Wood of Bath. The house itself contains various relics, including pictures, ancient vases, old furniture and Americana.

JODRELL BANK
Manchester University made the name of Jodrell Bank internationally famous by building a giant steerable radio telescope here in 1957. Now known as Mark I, the instrument has a 250ft reflector and is still one of the largest of its type in the world. The Mark II was built in the early 1960s and has a 125ft reflector with an advanced form of digital control. Regular presentations of the stars and planets are given in the Planetarium, and there are fascinating working models of both the telescopes on view.

One of the powerful radio telescopes at Jodrell Bank

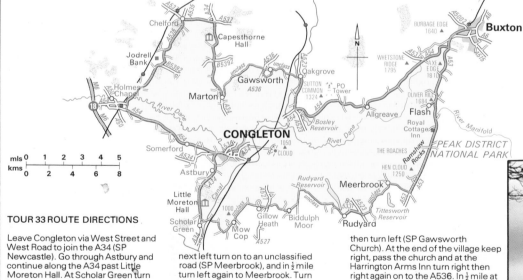

TOUR 33 ROUTE DIRECTIONS

Leave Congleton via West Street and West Road to join the A34 (SP Newcastle). Go through Astbury and continue along the A34 past Little Moreton Hall. At Scholar Green turn left on to an unclassified road (SP Mow Cop). In ¼ mile turn left, and continue to climb Mow Cop. Pass a church and in 1 mile turn right (no SP) into Mow Lane. Descend through Gillow Heath to the main road and turn left, then in 300yds turn right on to an unclassified road (SP Biddulph Moor). At Biddulph Moor turn left (SP Leek). Take the next right turn, then, at a T-junction, turn left. In 1 mile turn right to Rudyard. Continue on the B5331 (SP Leek), and at a T-junction turn right on to the A523. Take the

next left turn on to an unclassified road (SP Meerbrook), and in ½ mile turn left again to Meerbrook. Turn right (SP Blackshaw Moor, Leek), and in ½ mile turn left on to the A53 (SP Buxton) and pass Ramshaw Rocks. (On the way to Buxton a detour can be made by turning left to Flash along an unclassified road.)
Continue to Buxton, then return along the A53 (SP Congleton). In 1½ miles turn right on to the A54. Go through Allgreave, skirt Bosley Reservoir, then turn right on to the A523 (SP Macclesfield). Continue for 2 miles to Oakgrove and turn left on to an unclassified road to Gawsworth,

then turn left (SP Gawsworth Church). At the end of the village keep right, pass the church and at the Harrington Arms Inn turn right then right again on to the A536. In ½ mile at a crossroads, turn left to Marton, then right on to the A34 (SP Manchester). In 3½ miles pass the entrance to Capesthorne Hall, and 1 mile further along the A34, at traffic lights, turn left on to the A537 (SP Chester). Continue to the Chelford roundabout and turn left on to the A535 (SP Holmes Chapel) to reach Jodrell Bank. Keep forward on the A535 and in 3½ miles, near Holmes Chapel, turn left into Manor Lane (no SP). Continue to the A54 and turn left to return to Congleton.

BEVERLEY

This ancient market town grew up around the monastery that was attached to its minster, which is one of the most beautiful churches in Europe. The medieval twin-towered building is renowned for its stonework – the canopy of the exquisite Percy Tomb is perhaps the finest 14th-century example of its kind. Almost as impressive is St Mary's, originally a chapel to the minster, and also a delightful example of English Gothic architecture. It has a particularly impressive ceiling of 40 painted panels depicting all the kings of England up to Henry VI. The town itself boasts a fine art gallery and museum, and also the East Yorkshire Regiment Museum. Lairgate Hall is famed for its Adam ceiling and hand-painted Chinese wallpaper.

SKIDBY WINDMILL

Well-preserved Skidby Windmill was built in 1821, and is the only surviving example of a working tower-mill in north-east England. Its black-tarred tower and white cap form a striking combination that makes it a prominent local landmark. An agricultural museum is being established inside.

HULL

Properly known as Kingston-upon-Hull, this city has virtually been rebuilt since the Second World War, when it was severely damaged by bombs. The third largest port in Britain, Hull also supports the country's largest fishing fleet. The docks stretch for seven miles along the north bank of the Humber. The modern town includes many parks and gardens and a fine shopping precinct. A few old buildings survive: Maister House is a good Georgian house owned by the National Trust, and a museum in the old High Street occupies a 17th-century mansion where William Wilberforce was born in 1759. His great achievement was the 1833 Act abolishing slavery in the British Empire. Other museums are the Town Docks Museum, and the Transport and Archaeological Museum.

SPROATLEY

This village is in the heart of the Holderness area, where vast flat fields, golden with corn in summer, stretch to the horizon or lap the fringes of small copses. Its 19th-century ivy-clad church contains an inscribed 13th-century coffin lid.

BURTON CONSTABLE HALL

Grand 18th-century state rooms and 200 acres of parkland landscaped by Capability Brown are features of this attractive Elizabethan house. Lakes covering some 22 acres provide plenty of scope for boating, and a model railway runs through the grounds.

HEDON

At one time this small town was a major port connected to the Humber estuary by canals. It was rich enough to start building the magnificent 'King of Holderness' in the 12th century, and subsequent work on this church shows the prosperity to have lasted at least until the 15th century.

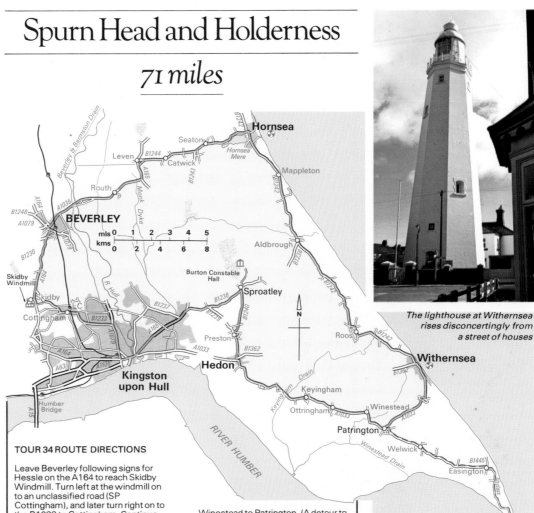

The lighthouse at Withernsea rises disconcertingly from a street of houses

TOUR 34 ROUTE DIRECTIONS

Leave Beverley following signs for Hessle on the A164 to reach Skidby Windmill. Turn left at the windmill on to an unclassified road (SP Cottingham), and later turn right on to the B1233 to Cottingham. Continue on the B1233, keeping forward at two roundabouts, then turn right on to the A1079 and drive into Kingston-upon-Hull. Leave on the A165 (SP Hornsea, Bridlington). In 3½ miles keep forward at a roundabout, then at the next roundabout take the third exit, the B1238 (SP Aldbrough). In 1½ miles reach Sproatley. Bear right, and at the end of the village turn left on to an unclassified road to reach Burton Constable Hall. Return to Sproatley and turn right to return along the B1238, then branch left by the war memorial on to the B1240 to Preston. At Preston turn left to reach Hedon. Turn left here on to the A1033 (SP Withernsea) to go through Keyingham, Ottringham and Winestead to Patrington. (A detour to Spurn Head can be made here by following the B1445 to Easington, and continuing through Kilnsea.) Leave Patrington on the A1033 to Withernsea. At the Spread Eagle pub in Withernsea, turn left into Hull Road, then turn right by the old lighthouse on to the B1242 (SP Roos, Hornsea). Go through Roos and in ½ mile turn left, then in ¼ mile turn right to Aldbrough. Continue on the B1242 through Mappleton to Hornsea. Leave Hornsea on the B1244 (SP Beverley), pass Hornsea Mere and go through Seaton and Catwick to Leven. Turn left on to the A165 then in 1 mile, at a roundabout, take the second exit, the A1035, to return to Beverley.

Battered wooden sea defences face the east wind at Spurn Head

PATRINGTON

Hedon's superb church has a rival here in the 'Queen of Holderness', a magnificent cruciform building in the Decorated style. Its tower and spire are considered outstanding, and excellent craftsmanship of many kinds can be seen inside.

SPURN HEAD

Between the North Sea and the Humber estuary is Spurn Head, a narrow hook of sand and shingle. Many migrant species of bird rest in the sanctuary at the end of the peninsula, and their comings and goings are watched from a special observatory.

WITHERNSEA

This quiet resort offers donkey rides, a reasonable sand and shingle beach, paddling and boating pools, a playground and various amusement arcades. Sports facilities include bowling greens, a putting course, and an open-air swimming pool.

HORNSEA

Hornsea is famous for its pottery, which is made in Marlborough Avenue. There are guided tours of the factory, and a playground, pony-rides, an aviary, a model village and a mini-zoo to keep the children occupied. Hornsea itself is a popular resort, with gardens separated from the beach by a promenade.

The North Yorkshire Moors
73 miles

SCARBOROUGH

In the mid 17th century it was discovered that a stream here had curative properties, and Scarborough began to develop as a spa. The next century saw the arrival of the bathing machine, and since then Scarborough has steadily grown as a resort. Its twin bays are divided by a headland that was used as a Roman signal station, and it was here that the Normans built their castle. North Bay is backed by lovely gardens, and is popular for its rock pools, while South Bay is more sheltered and sandy, with good bathing. Around the old harbour stand picturesque 18th-century buildings including the Customs House, King Richard III's house and some splendid old pubs. The town also has several grand Victorian buildings such as the Medicinal Baths. Wood End was the holiday home of the Sitwells, a famous literary family, and Anne Brontë is buried in St Mary's churchyard. Scarborough Zoo and Marineland, the largest amusement park in the region, is in Northstead Manor gardens.

FYLINGDALES MOOR AND RADAR STATION

The huge white domes of Fylingdales Early Warning Station seem a constant reminder of doom in the lonely desolation of the surrounding moor. At one time the area was inhabited, and the intrusive evidence of advanced technology contrasts strangely with prehistoric burial mounds and the Wade's Causeway, which is Roman.

FYLINGTHORPE

This residential area of Robin Hood's Bay boasts the fine 17th-century Old Hall, which was built by the Chomley family of Whitby Abbey.

ROBIN HOOD'S BAY

Considered one of the most picturesque villages in England, this charming collection of old houses, shops and inns was once a favourite haunt of smugglers. It is difficult to establish any real connection between the village and the folk hero after whom it is named, but it may be that the famous outlaw leader came here to escape by boat to Europe.

HAWSKER

It is thought that the well-preserved 10th-century cross shaft at Old Hall in Hawsker may mark the site of a medieval church. The intricate design of interlaced knotwork and bird figures is typical of traditional Norse design.

WHITBY

For centuries Whitby has been home to a fishing fleet, and naturally there is a strong maritime tradition in the town. Captain Cook learnt his seamanship on colliers sailing from here. Cook is remembered in Whitby Museum, along with Captain Scoresby, who invented the Crow's Nest and was one of the great whaling captains of the 18th century. Terraces of old cottages climb the steep banks of the River Esk, and on top of East Cliff are the remains of an abbey, dissolved in 1539 and battered by the weather and by German shells in the First World War.

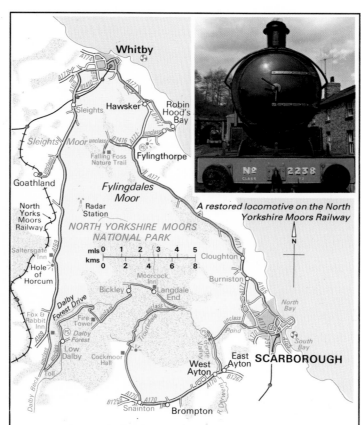

A restored locomotive on the North Yorkshire Moors Railway

TOUR 35 ROUTE DIRECTIONS

Leave Scarborough by following signs for North Bay, and join the A165. In 1 mile, at a roundabout, take the A165 to Burniston. At the junction with the A171 turn right (SP Whitby). Continue to Cloughton and bear left with the A171 to Fylingdales Moor. Continue on the A171 for 9½ miles, and turn right on to an unclassified road (SP Fylingthorpe, Robin Hood's Bay) to reach Fylingthorpe. Continue to Robin Hood's Bay. Leave the village on the B1447 (SP Whitby) and drive to Hawsker, then turn right on to the A171 and continue to Whitby. Leave Whitby on the A171 (SP Teesside) and in 2¼ miles turn left on to the A169 (SP Pickering). (A detour can later be made by turning right on to an unclassified road to Goathland.) Follow the A169 past the Hole of Horcum and in 4 miles, by the Fox and Rabbit Inn, turn left on to an unclassified road (SP Thornton Dale). In 2 miles turn left (SP Low Dalby (Forest Drive)) on to a Forestry Commission road. Continue to Low Dalby and turn left (SP Bickley) on to the Forest Drive. Continue to a fire tower and turn left. In 2 miles leave the Forestry Commission roads, and at a T-junction turn right (SP Scarborough). Go through Langdale End and in 1 mile turn sharp right (SP Troutsdale, Snainton). At a T-junction in Snainton turn left on to the A170 (SP Scarborough). Continue through Brompton to West and East Ayton. Immediately after crossing the Derwent into East Ayton turn left on to an unclassified road. In 2 miles turn right (SP 'Private'). Keep forward for 3 miles to a T-junction and turn right to re-enter Scarborough.

The gigantic, unearthly globes of the radar station at Fylingdales

GOATHLAND

All around this greystone moorland village are lovely walks leading past streams that suddenly plunge over rocky lips as spectacular waterfalls. Three superb examples in the immediate neighbourhood are Nelly Ayre Force, Mallyan Spout, and Thomason Force, and dozens of others can be visited by the rambler willing to venture a little farther. The village itself is well known for the Plough Stotts, a traditional group who perform sword-dances in the area. A well-preserved stretch of Roman road can be seen to the south, and the North Yorkshire Moors Railway is close by.

NORTH YORKSHIRE MOORS RAILWAY

Steam transport enthusiasts have restored and reopened the old British Rail link that connected Grosmont with Pickering, and in doing so have provided a superb mobile viewpoint from which 18 miles of beautiful national park countryside can be enjoyed in comfortable conditions.

HOLE OF HORCUM

This vast natural hollow in the Yorkshire moorlands shelters the farms of High and Low Horcum, forming a lush oasis of pasture in the wilderness of Levisham Moor.

DALBY FOREST DRIVE

Some 10 miles of well-surfaced roads offer the motorist a route through the beautiful woodlands of Dalby and Bickley Forests, where conifer plantations and stands of mature deciduous trees provide a vast haven for many species of wildlife. Red squirrels inhabit the conifers, the glades are full of wild flowers in spring and summer, and there is constant activity from such common woodland birds as jays, nuthatches, and the tiny goldcrest. A footpath which starts just beyond Staindale leads left to a curious formation of layered limestone known as the Bridestones. Planned amenities include numerous parking places, picnic sites and forest trails while many footpaths allow an uninhibited appreciation of the area. The Forest Drive is likely to be closed during periods of very dry weather, when the fire risk is abnormally high.

BROMPTON

The Church of All Saints here is remembered as the place where the poet William Wordsworth was married, on 4 October 1802. His bride was Mary Hutchinson, who lived at Gallows Hill Farm, just east of the village. Brompton was also the home of Sir George Cayley, the 'father of aviation', who carried out many early experiments with flying machines in the last century.

WEST AND EAST AYTON

Situated on either side of the River Derwent, the twin villages of East and West Ayton are linked by an attractive four-arched bridge which dates from 1775. The ruined pele tower of Ayton Castle makes a good counterpoint to the tower of East Ayton's church, on the other bank.

York and the Howardian Hills
68 miles

YORK
York offers more medieval architecture than almost any other town in Britain. In York, however, medieval building is fairly modern compared with some of the city's most ancient treasures, such as the Roman Multangular Tower, and parts of the city walls. Constantine the Great was proclaimed Emperor of Rome here in AD306, and the city boasts 2,000 years of history. The most famous of its buildings is York Minster. Begun in 1220, this took 250 years to complete, and the fine stone-carving and stained-glass windows are as awe-inspiring today as they must have been to the pilgrims of the Middle Ages who came here to worship. The great east window is the size of a tennis court. Close to the minster is a maze of narrow old streets, of which the Shambles is the most famous. The town walls still stand, and a walk round them serves as a good introduction to the old city. Among the many interesting places to visit in York are the Elizabethan King's Manor, Merchant Adventurers' Hall, the Yorkshire Museum and Gardens, the Castle and the National Railway Museum.

KIRKHAM
Ruined Kirkham Priory stands in a lovely setting by the River Derwent. The buildings include a beautiful 13th-century gatehouse and a lavatorium where the monks used to wash.

CASTLE HOWARD
One of the most spectacular houses in Britain, Castle Howard dates from the 17th and 18th centuries and is considered to be the greatest achievement of the architect Vanbrugh. A central dome forms the focal point of the house and is echoed in the 1,000-acre grounds by a circular mausoleum designed by Hawksmoor. Other garden follies include the lovely Temple of the Four Winds, and the huge gatehouse is crowned by a pyramid. The house gained recent fame as the setting for the television serialization of Evelyn Waugh's novel *Brideshead Revisited*.

SLINGSBY
Misnamed and never completed, the 17th-century house known as Slingsby Castle is a picturesque ruin that adds an air of gothic mystery to the countryside round the village.

HOVINGHAM
The stone cottages of this lovely little village cluster round the green under the Saxon tower of All Saints' Church and the stately presence of Hovingham Hall. The latter (not open) is an unusual building in distinctive yellow limestone, with a gatehouse that was designed as an indoor riding school.

GILLING EAST
It is thought that the architect Vanbrugh may have designed the west front of Gilling Castle, though most of the building is much too old for him to have had any hand in its construction. The keep dates from the 14th century, and a well-preserved ribbed plaster ceiling helps to make its dining-room one of the finest in England.

BRANDSBY
Features of this harmonious hillside village include a woodcarver's shop, an 18th-century hall, and an unusual church with a stone cupola. Neat terraces of cottages complete the picture.

STILLINGTON
The 18th-century writer Laurence Sterne was vicar here for a time, and the lovely old church in which he served features a 12th-century priest's door.

BRAFFERTON
Brafferton church was extensively restored in Victorian times, but still displays good 15th-century work.

BOROUGHBRIDGE
Three large monoliths known ominously as the Devil's Arrows stand a few hundred yards to the west of Boroughbridge. The largest rises to 22½ft and it is thought that the group may be some 3,000 years old.

ALDBOROUGH
This pretty village stands on the site of *Isurium*, the northernmost town to be built without military motives during the Roman occupation. Remains revealed through excavation include sections of a boundary wall, two tessellated pavements, and a wide variety of coins, pottery, and artefacts on display in the small site museum. In the village itself are a maypole, on the village green, and a cross that probably commemorates the Battle of Boroughbridge, which was fought here in 1322. St Andrew's Church incorporates Roman stonework, and contains fine woodwork and a good 14th-century brass.

EASINGWOLD
An unusual bull-ring can be seen in the market place of this pleasant town of red-brick houses and cobbled lanes. The local church contains an ancient parish coffin.

RASKELF
The 15th-century tower of St Mary's Church is made of wood and is said to be unique in Yorkshire. Parts of the church date back to Norman times.

York is one of the best-preserved walled cities in Europe. Its tremendous wealth of lovely buildings is watched over by the towers and turrets of the magnificent minster, the city's chief glory

TOUR 36 ROUTE DIRECTIONS
Leave York on the A1036 (SP East Coast, Malton). In 3 miles, at a roundabout, take the first exit, the A64 (SP Malton). (A short detour can be made after 9 miles by turning right off the A64 on to an unclassified road (SP Kirkham Priory) to Kirkham.) The main route continues on the A64. One mile beyond the Kirkham turning, turn left on to an unclassified road (SP Welburn, Castle Howard). Pass through Welburn, and at a crossroads turn right to Castle Howard. Leave Castle Howard and continue to the edge of Slingsby. (For a detour to Slingsby keep forward at the village crossroads.) The main tour turns left here on to the B1257 (SP Helmsley). Continue to Hovingham and turn left (SP Coulton, Easingwold). Drive through Hovingham High Wood and at a crossroads turn right (SP Gilling). In 1½ miles, at a T-junction, turn right on to the B1363 to reach Gilling East. Return south along the B1363 to Brandsby. Continue through Stillington, pass the church and keep forward on to an unclassified road (SP Easingwold), then in 3½ miles meet the A19 and drive forward into Easingwold. At the crossroads in Easingwold, turn left on to an unclassified road to reach Raskelf. In Raskelf bear left, then right (SP Boroughbridge), drive to Brafferton and turn right. In 1 mile cross the River Swale and turn left. In 2¾ miles turn left then immediately right, then in 1 mile, at a T-junction, turn left. Continue to a roundabout and take the first exit, the B6265, and enter Boroughbridge. Here turn left and keep left (SP York). At the far end of the town branch left on to an unclassified road to Aldborough. At the battle cross, bear right, then pass the church to reach the B6265 and turn left. Drive to Green Hammerton and join the A59 for York.

The Lancashire Plain
74 miles

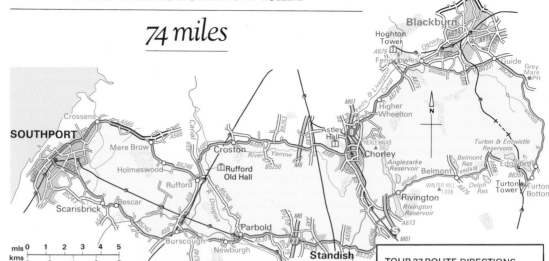

SOUTHPORT

Southport is a traditional seaside resort, a mixture of Victorian elegance and modern entertainment. Race-horses train in the early morning on the sands where donkeys give children rides later in the day. The neat gardens and parks contrast with amusement areas like Happiland and Pleasureland. The shops and booths of the front complement the broad boulevard of Lord Street behind. Sports are well catered for, from skateboarding to golf. The Royal Birkdale Golf Club is known throughout the country, and has been host to Ryder Cup competitions. There is an excellent zoo in Princes Park, the Steamport Transport Museum is rapidly becoming the largest of its kind, and the Atkinson Art Gallery has both permanent and temporary exhibitions. Church Town, the old part of Southport, has thatched cottages, old pubs and the superb Victorian Botanic Gardens.

RUFFORD OLD HALL

This superb timber-framed Tudor building stands in 14½ acres of beautiful grounds and is one of the finest structures of its kind surviving in England today. Built by the Hesketh family in the 15th century, it was slightly extended during Victorian times but has not been spoilt by 19th-century restoration. The exterior is a startling combination of decorative black timbers infilled with brilliant white plaster, and the great hall carries an extremely ornate hammerbeam roof. Inside the house can be seen a rare 15th-century screen. One wing of the house is occupied by the Philip Ashcroft Museum of folk crafts and antiquities.

CROSTON

Picturesque countryside following the twisting course of the River Yarrow makes a fine setting for this tiny village. Among its most notable buildings are 17th-century almshouses and a 15th-century church containing a curious memorial brass.

ASTLEY HALL

Charmingly set in nearly 100 acres of wood and parkland, this fine 16th-century and later house has a drawing room with lovely tapestries depicting scenes from the legend of the Golden Fleece. Throughout the house are fine collections of furnishings, pottery and paintings, and special exhibitions are frequently mounted in its rooms.

CHORLEY

Industry is this old textile centre's way of life. It was once known for cotton-weaving and calico-printing, but in recent years these traditional concerns have been largely replaced by a variety of modern enterprises. The town stands at the edge of farming country close to the foot of the Pennines, in an area dominated by the imposing height of 682ft Healey Nab which rises to the east.

HOGHTON TOWER

The ancestral home of what is claimed to be the oldest baronetcy in England, this fine 16th-century mansion

Some of the timbering on Turton Tower dates from the 19th century

occasionally opens its state rooms, ballroom, Tudor wellhouse and dungeon to the public. The gardens can also be visited at certain times. In 1617 King James I stayed here, and is said to have been so taken with a loin of beef prepared by the house kitchen that he drew his sword and knighted the joint. Ever since then, it is said, that particular cut has been called sirloin.

TURTON TOWER

The core of this L-shaped building is a 15th-century pele tower, a type of fortified dwelling that was once common in the north of England. Two wings were added in the 16th century, and the house now contains fine collections of paintings and furnishings, plus a fascinating folk museum.

RIVINGTON

Rivington Pike rises to a 1,190ft summit above this attractive little moorland village. It is crowned by an 18th-century stone tower and commands excellent views over miles of countryside. In the village itself is a good church housing a fine screen and a 16th-century pulpit. Rivington Hall, which stands in 400-acre Lever Park, was rebuilt in 1744 and contains a general interest museum.

STANDISH

This colliery town stands on the line of a Roman road and features a good church that was rebuilt in the 16th century. Inside the building, particularly in the roof, are good examples of woodwork. The 19th-century spire is a prominent local landmark, and the church has fine stained glass of the same period. The old village stocks are preserved on the steps of a modern town cross.

PARBOLD

Parbold Hall is a splendid stone-built Georgian house (not open) with a Venetian-style doorway. Excellent views of the surrounding countryside can be enjoyed from the summit of Parbold Hill, which is crowned by the impressive 19th-century building of Christ Church.

SCARISBRICK

Designed by the architect Pugin in 1837, ornate Scarisbrick Hall is an excellent example of the opulence favoured in the Victorian period. It is Gothic in style and was the architect's first major work, taking four years to complete. The 150-room house is now occupied by a school, and is open on application.

TOUR 37 ROUTE DIRECTIONS

Leave Southport on the A565 (SP Preston). In 3 miles turn right on to the B5246 (SP Rufford). Go through Rufford and turn left on to the A59 (SP Preston). Turn left and in ½ mile pass Rufford Old Hall. After 1 mile, turn right on to the A581 (SP Chorley). Continue to Croston, turn right, and in ¼ mile turn left at a war memorial. In 1 mile, at a T-junction, turn right on to the A581. Cross the M6, meet the A49 and turn left. Turn right on to the A581, pass Astley Hall and continue to Chorley. At traffic lights in Chorley, turn left on to the A6 (SP Preston). In 1 mile cross a railway bridge, and at a roundabout take the second exit, the A674 (SP M6, Blackburn). Go through Higher Wheelton and in 2 miles, meet a roundabout. (A detour can be taken here by taking the first exit, the A675, to Hoghton Tower.) The main route takes the second exit. In ½ mile, at a T-junction, turn right to Feniscowles, then turn right on to the A6062 (SP Darwen). In ½ mile go under a railway bridge and immediately turn right on to an unclassified road, then turn left. In 1 mile, keep forward at the crossroads by the Black Bull pub. Meet the A666 and keep forward on to the B6231 (SP Accrington) to Guide. Turn right by the King Edward VII pub on to the B6232 (SP Bury), keep left and in 2 miles, by the Grey Mare pub, turn right (SP Edgworth). Keep forward at the crossroads in Edgworth to Turton Bottoms, then at a T-junction turn sharp right on to the B6391 (SP Darwen). (Turton Tower stands to the left.) Continue on the B6391 to a T-junction and turn left on to the A666 (SP Bolton). In ½ mile turn right (SP Belmont), then take the next right turn and keep forward to Belmont. At a T-junction, turn right on to the A675. Take the next left turn (SP Rivington), and at a T-junction turn right, then meet another T-junction and turn left to Rivington. Follow signs for Adlington and at a T-junction turn left (SP Horwich), and in ¾ mile turn right on to the A673, then take the next left turn (SP Blackrod). In 1 mile meet the A6, keep forward and in ½ mile turn right. In 1 mile, at a T-junction with the B5239, keep forward (SP Standish). In 1½ miles turn right on to the A5106, then in 200yds turn left on to the B5239 to Standish. At the traffic lights in Standish keep forward on to the A5209. In 1½ miles turn right (SP M6), and at a roundabout take the second exit to Parbold, then continue to Burscough. Join the A59 (SP Southport) and in ¾ mile turn right on to the B5242. Continue through Bescar, and at traffic lights turn right on to the A570 to Scarisbrick, then continue on the A570 to Southport.

Hadrian's Wall
53 miles

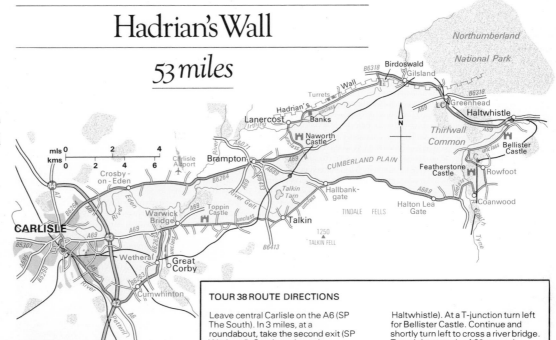

CARLISLE

Carlisle's position just south of Hadrian's Wall has meant that during its long history its possession has been continually contested by the English and Scots. A castle was built here by William Rufus, the Conqueror's son, in 1092. The outer walls, impressive keep, main gate and Queen Mary's Tower can still be seen. The tower contains the Border Regiment and King's Own Royal Border Regiment Museum. The Norman cathedral has notable stained glass, fine wood-carving and a painted barrel-vault ceiling. In the grounds stands a 13th-century pele tower known as the Prior's Room, and nearby is a 15th-century tithe barn. Between the castle and the cathedral is Tullie House, a Jacobean town house with Victorian extensions that is now occupied by the museum and art gallery. In Greenmarket is the Guildhall, a splendid half-timbered building where Carlisle's eight trade guilds once met.

GREAT CORBY

In 1611 the Howard family extended the old pele tower that had been guarding Great Corby since the 13th century, adding a long range that transformed it into a great L-shaped house. The present aspect of Corby Castle, set amid lovely grounds in a particularly scenic area, owes much to further extension work carried out in the 19th century.

TALKIN

This village has a lovely little church that has managed to preserve surprising evidence of its Norman origins. Work from that early period can be seen in the nave, bellcote and chancel, and there are even traces in the pulpit and altar rail.

FEATHERSTONE CASTLE

Beautifully situated in large grounds beside the River South Tyne, this fine house (not open) is built round a courtyard and dates from the 13th century.

BELLISTER CASTLE

In the 16th century the ruined tower attached to this three-storey building (not open) was known as a bastell house, which perhaps gives a clue to the origin of the name. The house itself dates from 1669.

HALTWHISTLE

William the Lion founded this old mining town's church in 1178, and as it stands today the building is a particularly fine example of Early English architecture. There is no tower, and the sanctuary preserves three carved coffin lids which are thought to date from the 14th century.

HADRIAN'S WALL

Between AD122 and 139 the Roman Emperor Hadrian ordered that a defensive wall should be built to discourage the independent Scottish tribes from marauding into the largely pacified territory to the south. Today this major engineering achievement still stands as a remarkable monument to the Roman occupation of Britain. It

Part of Hadrian's Wall at Gilsland

stretches 73 miles from Wallsend-on-Tyne to Bowness-on-Solway. Its course was plotted from one natural advantage to the next, and it was built of the materials most readily to hand – stone in the east and turf in the west. Along it stood 20 or so major forts, with mile-castles and signal towers in between.

TOUR 38 ROUTE DIRECTIONS

Leave central Carlisle on the A6 (SP The South). In 3 miles, at a roundabout, take the second exit (SP Wetheral). Continue through Wetheral, and in 1½ miles, at a T-junction, turn right on to the A69 (SP Newcastle). (A detour can be made by turning right immediately after crossing the River Eden on to an unclassified road to reach Corby Castle.) Continue on the A69 through Warwick Bridge, then at a crossroads turn right (SP Castle Carrock) and in 50yds turn left. After 2½ miles branch left (SP Talkin), and in 1 mile keep left. At the crossroads with the B6413, keep forward and go through Talkin. After ¼ mile turn right (SP Hallbankgate). At Hallbankgate turn right on the A689 (SP Alston). Continue through Halton Lea Gate and in 1 mile turn left (SP Coanwood). At the crossroads beyond Coanwood, turn left (SP Haltwhistle). In Rowfoot turn left (SP Featherstone Park) to Featherstone Castle. Continue, cross a bridge and keep forward (SP Haltwhistle). At a T-junction turn left for Bellister Castle. Continue and shortly turn left to cross a river bridge. Turn right on to the A69 to reach Haltwhistle town centre. Return along the A69 (SP Carlisle), follow the railway for 2¾ miles and drive over a level crossing to reach Greenhead. Leave Greenhead, bear left, and then in 50yds turn right on to the B6318 (SP Gilsland). In ½ mile pass a section of Hadrian's Wall. At the T-junction in Gilsland, turn right, then in ¼ mile turn left. In another mile turn left again (SP Birdoswald, Lanercost) to reach Birdoswald. Continue to Banks, then bear left and continue to Lanercost. Cross the river, then immediately turn left to Naworth Castle. At the castle entrance bear right and in ½ mile, at a crossroads, turn right on to the A69 (SP Carlisle) to reach Brampton. Follow the A69 through Brampton, then keep forward on to the B6264 (SP Carlisle Airport). Go through Crosby-on-Eden and in 3½ miles turn left on to the A7 for Carlisle.

BIRDOSWALD

Large and impressive outer defences of a Roman fort known as *Camboglanna* overlook the River Irthing near here. Excavations have uncovered two gates and an interval tower. Well-preserved sections of Hadrian's Wall extend to the east and west. Close by are substantial remains of Harrow's Scar milecastle.

BANKS

A turret on the Roman wall here was once manned by troops garrisoned at the nearest milecastle. A footpath leads east to the Pike Hill signal tower. Many relics of the Roman occupation, various other antiquities, fine paintings, and sculpture can be seen in the LYC Museum and Art Gallery.

LANERCOST

Extensive remains of a priory that was built with stones taken from the Roman wall can be seen here, including parts of a gatehouse showing 16th-century adaptations. The 12th-century nave serves as the parish church.

NAWORTH CASTLE

Pleasantly designed round a central courtyard, this 14th-century castle (open by arrangement) features a great hall, an oratory and fine tapestries.

BRAMPTON

An unusual eight-sided moot hall stands in the cobble-flanked main street of Brampton, and the local church is the only ecclesiastical building known to have been designed by the inventive 19th-century architect, Philip Webb. The interior of the building is lit by a superb stained-glass window by the Victorian artist Burne-Jones.

Lanercost Priory was built for Augustinian monks in the 12th century

The Eastern Pennines
58 miles

BARNARD CASTLE
Eighty feet above the River Tees stand the ruins of the castle which gave this town its name. Since its destruction by Oliver Cromwell in the Civil War the castle has been a ruin, although until then it had been a powerful stronghold built by the Balliols, one of whom was crowned King of Scotland in 1292. Barnard Castle's greatest treasure, however, is the Bowes Museum. Set in its own park, it contains a priceless collection of art treasures personally accrued by John and Josephine Bowes. The town is an excellent touring centre, with many pleasant walks nearby. Beside the Tees, to the south of Barnard Castle, stand the romantic ruins of 12th-century Egglestone Abbey.

STAINDROP
Strongly associated with the Neville family of nearby Raby Castle, this long village is strung out along a single main street and has a fine green. The local church was once the family church of the Nevilles and contains fine monuments spanning many generations. It is of Saxon origin, and carries a tower that was added in the 12th century, but its south aisle, porch and nave all date from the 15th century.

RABY CASTLE
This impressive pile stands in a 270-acre deer park and exactly matches the popular conception of what a castle should look like, right down to its moat and nine great towers. It is known to have been in existence in one form or another from 1016, but its present distinctive appearance is largely due to 14th-century rebuilding and extension. Inside are fine collections of furniture, paintings and ceramics, and among the many fine chambers is a curious octagonal drawing room. The kitchens display 14th-century rib-vaulting and preserve a smoke-driven spit, while outside in the stables is a collection of carriages.

Caldron Snout is one of many spectacular falls on the River Tees

TOUR 39 ROUTE DIRECTIONS

From Barnard Castle follow signs for Bishop Auckland, and at the edge of the town turn left to follow the A688 to Staindrop. Turn left by Staindrop church and in 1 mile pass the entrance to Raby Castle. Continue along the A688 for ½ mile and turn left on to an unclassified road (SP Cockfield). In ½ mile keep straight on (SP Butterknowle), and in another 2¼ miles turn left on to B6282 for Copley and continue to Woodland. Meet a T-junction and turn left, then after 300yds turn right on to an unclassified road (SP Hamsterley). After 3 miles turn left (SP Wolsingham), then in ¾ mile, at a T-junction, turn left again to cross Bedburn Beck. After a short distance pass a left turn that leads into Hamsterley Forest, and drive through woodland before emerging into open countryside. Cross the River Wear and continue to the edge of Wolsingham. Turn left on to the A689 (SP Stanhope) and continue through Frosterley and along the A689 to Stanhope. Leave Stanhope on the A689 (SP Alston) and continue to Eastgate. Leave Eastgate along the A689 to reach Westgate. Continue through Daddry Shield to St John's Chapel. Turn left on to an unclassified road (SP Middleton-in-Teesdale) and climb to Langdon Common. Descend into Teesdale and at a T-junction turn left on to the B6277. In ½ mile reach the Langdon Beck Hotel. (A short detour can be made here by turning right. Drive along a rough track to the picnic area at Cow Green Reservoir. A footpath leads from here to the waterfall of Caldron Snout.) Continue along the B6277 and after 2½ miles pass the High Force Hotel. A footpath opposite the hotel leads to the High Force waterfall. Continue along the B6277 through Newbiggin to reach Middleton-in-Teesdale. Leave Middleton-in-Teesdale and turn right (SP Scotch Corner). Cross the River Tees and in ½ mile keep left (SP Barnard Castle). Continue for ¾ mile, rejoin the B6277, and continue through Mickleton and Romaldkirk to Cotherstone. Recross the Tees and return to Barnard Castle.

WOLSINGHAM
A good base from which to explore beautiful Weardale, this typical County Durham town of stone houses holds a precarious balance between the needs of industry and the preservation of its charm. The result is the type of contrast seen between giant steelworks on the outskirts and the historic 12th-century tower of St Mary's Church, nearer the centre of the town.

FROSTERLEY
A local stone known as Frosterley marble is much prized for building and monumental sculpture, but centuries of quarrying have almost exhausted the supply. Many of the county's churches have fonts, memorials, pillars and various other features fashioned from the stone, which is not really marble but a grey limestone that becomes black and reveals hundreds of tiny fossils when polished.

STANHOPE
Stanhope churchyard features the fossilized stump of a tree that grew some 150 million years ago. The church itself dates from 1200 and contains a number of fascinating relics, including a Saxon font, two wooden plaques and a painting thought to be Flemish. Close to the churchyard is the old town cross.

WESTGATE
Both Westgate and nearby Eastgate derived their names from the entrances to Old Park, which was once the hunting residence of the bishops of Durham. The village has a 19th-century church and an attractive water-mill, and was once well known as a cock-fighting centre.

CALDRON SNOUT
More of a tiered cascade than a proper waterfall, beautiful Caldron Snout tumbles 200ft down a natural staircase of hard dolerite rock.

HIGH FORCE
Here one of England's loveliest waterfalls plunges 70ft over the menacing black cliff of the Great Whin Sill, to be caught in a deep pool surrounded by shrubs and rocks.

MIDDLETON-IN-TEESDALE
Strong Quaker influence is evident in the no-frills orderliness of this stern little town. This is because the local lead-mines – the mainstay of Middleton's economy until they were closed at the start of this century – were run by members of that denomination. The local church dates from the 19th century and shares its churchyard with various remains of a predecessor.

ROMALDKIRK
Attractive cottages, a stream, a green and a fine cruciform church combine to make this one of the prettiest villages in Teesdale.

COTHERSTONE
Dramatic scenery surrounds this pleasant village, which stands at the point where Balder Beck meets the River Tees. Near the watersmeet are slight remains of a Norman castle.

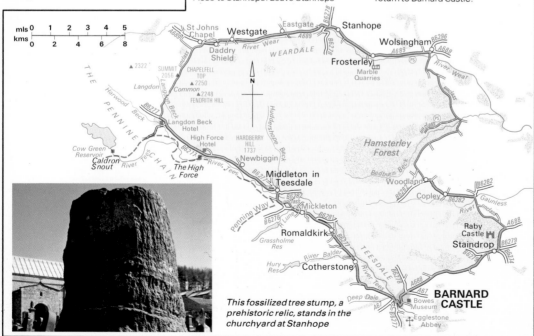

This fossilized tree stump, a prehistoric relic, stands in the churchyard at Stanhope

Forests of the Scottish Border
90 miles

BELLINGHAM
The focus of life in North Tynedale, this small market town once had a flourishing iron industry but nowadays is best known as a gateway to the great moors and forests of Northumberland. Its ancient Church of St Cuthbert has a unique roof, barrel-vaulted with six-sided stone ribs instead of the usual timber, probably as a precaution against fire. In the churchyard is a well whose waters are traditionally held to have healing powers.

BORDER FOREST PARK AND NORTHUMBERLAND NATIONAL PARK
The Border Forest Park incorporates three forests and is the largest area of its type in Britain. In the east its vast landscapes merge with the open- moorland horizons of the Northumberland National Park, which extends from Hadrian's Wall to the Cheviots, making a staggering 600 square miles of beautiful, wild and unspoiled countryside. Both parks are crossed by the 250-mile Pennine Way footpath and the Kielder, Redesdale, and Wauchope forests offer many planned walks and nature trails.

KIELDER
This and several other villages were developed as the area's forestry industry became established, and nowadays they make handy bases from which to explore the local countryside. Kielder Castle is an 18th-century shooting lodge that is now a Border Forest Park information centre.

HERMITAGE CASTLE
Romantically associated with Mary Queen of Scots, this brooding castle punctuates the desolate moorland landscape with four great towers and grim walls that entirely suit their windswept situation. It was a stronghold of the Douglas family in the 14th century, and much later became the property of Mary's lover Bothwell.

BEWCASTLE
Several ancient remains can be seen in the bleak open moorland that surrounds Bewcastle. In the village churchyard is the famous Bewcastle Cross, which dates from the 7th century and is intricately carved with runic inscriptions and patterns.

HADRIAN'S WALL
This great wall runs across the country from Solway to Tyne. Built in the 2nd century AD, it was already derelict by the 4th century. The ruins of forts are dotted along the route of the wall, and there are several museums featuring relics from the days when 15,000 Romans manned the wall.

BANKS
Notable Roman sites in the area around Banks include Coombe Crag, Pike Hill and Boothby Castle Hill, and there is a milecastle with a section of the Roman wall here. A converted farmhouse on the route of the wall contains the LYC Museum and Art Gallery, which has a permanent exhibition of Roman and Cumbrian folk art, crafts, and antiquities.

TOUR 40 ROUTE DIRECTIONS
Leave Bellingham on the B6320 (SP Hexham) and in ½ mile turn left and cross a river. Take the next right turn on to an unclassified road (SP Kielder). In 4 miles cross a river, then turn right and continue to Stannersburn. Enter Kielder Forest, pass Kielder Reservoir and go through the village of Kielder. Continue for 3 miles and cross the Scottish border, then in 3½ miles turn left on to the B6357 (SP Newcastleton). In 6½ miles, at the junction with the B6399, bear left with the B6357 to Newcastleton. (A detour can be made at this junction by turning right on to the B6399 and in 4 miles turning left on to an unclassified road to Hermitage Castle.)
At the far end of Newcastleton village the main route turns left on to an unclassified road (no SP). Cross a river and turn right (SP Brampton). At the Dog and Gun Inn turn left (SP Carlisle). In 4 miles turn right, and in another ¾ mile keep forward on to the B6318. Take the next left turn on an unclassified road to Bewcastle. At Bewcastle turn right (no SP) and cross a river. In 5 miles cross the B6318 and in 2½ miles, at a T-junction, turn left (SP Birdoswald) to Banks. Continue through Birdoswald and in ½ mile turn right on to the B6318 (SP Gilsland). In 1 mile turn right to Gilsland, then turn left on the B6318 and in 2 miles turn left on to the A69 to Greenhead. Turn left on the B6318, and in 5 miles pass the Twice Brewed Inn. Continue past Housesteads and through Carrawbrough to Chollerford. At the roundabout take the first exit, the B6320 (SP Wark, Bellingham) and go through Wark then continue to Bellingham.

Housesteads is one of the best-preserved forts on Hadrian's Wall

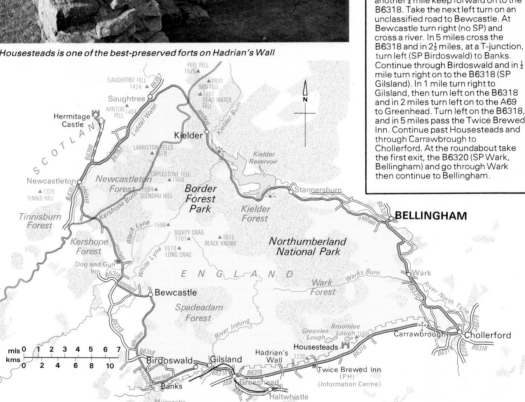

BIRDOSWALD
The Roman fort of *Camboglanna* occupies a five-acre ridge-top site overlooking the gorge of the River Irthing near Birdoswald. Access to the remains, which include a particularly well-preserved angle tower and postern gate, is controlled by the farmer.

GILSLAND
Sulphur and chalybeate springs brought brief fame to this small place as a spa resort, but it is much better known for its excellent Roman remains. Hadrian's Wall runs south of the village and includes the fascinating and well-preserved Poltross Burn milecastle.

TWICE BREWED INN
Slightly away from the site of the original building, this famous inn now houses a useful Northumberland National Park information centre.

HOUSESTEADS
The best-preserved fort on Hadrian's Wall can be seen here. Once known as *Borcovicium*, it follows the typical Roman pattern of rectangular walls with rounded corners, and was built to house up to 1,000 infantrymen. The ramparts and gateways of the fort can all be clearly seen, and buildings uncovered in extensive excavations here include granaries, a hospital, latrines and the commandant's house. Outside the fort are remains of Roman civilian buildings, and some of the slopes below are terraced – probably for cultivation to support the inhabitants of the fort. Relics found during excavations in the area are displayed in a well-laid-out museum. Close to Housesteads the wall reaches its highest point as it follows the craggy ridges of Great Whin Sill. To the west of the fort is Housesteads milecastle.

CARRAWBROUGH
One of the very few Mithraic temples found in Britain has been excavated here. Probably dating from the 3rd century, it was a very small building containing three dedicatory altars to the deity Mithras, and a figure of the Mother Goddess. Close by is the Roman fort known as *Brocolitia*.

CHOLLERFORD
Housesteads may be the best preserved of the Roman wall's forts, but *Cilurnum* (or Chesters), on the River North Tyne near Chollerford, is by far the most interesting and best excavated. It was a large stronghold housing 500 troops. Digging has revealed fascinating details of the fort itself, plus the remains of a bath house and central heating system. Relics from this and other sites in the area can be seen in the interesting local museum.

141

Northern England
Gazetteer

ALNWICK, Northumb   *133 NU11*
The splendid castle of this attractive and historic town was founded by the Percy family in the 12th century, but was ruined during a violent phase of border warfare and was not restored to military effectiveness until the 14th century. The gateway is guarded by an impressive barbican, and the outline of its massive keep, walls and towers completely dominates the town. St Michael's Church echoes the castle with its battlemented tower and is said to preserve some of the best 15th-century workmanship in the county. Among the treasures inside are numerous fine monuments and a Flemish carved chest that dates from the 14th century. Remains of Alnwick Abbey stand on the northern outskirts of the town and include a well-preserved 14th-century gateway.

AMBLESIDE, Cumbria   *131 NY30*
This popular tourist centre of grey slate houses stands near the northern end of Lake Windermere and is popular with anglers, fell-walkers and climbers. The beautiful scenery of the lake shore is best appreciated from the water, and regular boat tours can be joined at Waterhead.

APPLEBY, Cumbria   *131 NY62*
Appleby, situated in the valley of the River Eden, lies in a district of great natural beauty and is an excellent touring centre. It is also known for its annual horse fair, a colourful spectacle that takes place in the town every June.

The castle, sited at the top of the main street, was once the home of Lady Anne Clifford, and is one of many historic buildings in northern England that this famous benefactress restored after Civil War damage. Lady Anne died in 1678, and her tomb is in St Lawrence's Church at the lower end of the main street. St Michael's Church, in Bongate, was restored by Lady Anne and has a hog-back gravestone which probably dates back to early Norman times and is the oldest stone monument in the borough. St Anne's Hospital was founded by Lady Anne in 1651 as an almshouse.

The handsome octagonal tower and spire of All Saints' Church, Bakewell, are a careful Victorian reconstruction of the original work

---

Gypsy families from all over the country converge on Appleby every June for the traditional horse fair – the largest such gathering in the world. Today luxurious trailers replace the gaily-painted horse-drawn caravans of the past

BAKEWELL, Derbyshire   *128 SK26*
A busy cattle market and the largest town in the Peak District National Park, Bakewell stands on the wooded banks of the Wye. Many of its attractive stone buildings bear witness to a historic past, and its beautiful 12th-century church is famous for the superb Saxon cross preserved in its churchyard.

Haddon Hall lies two miles south-east of Bakewell. Medieval architecture can be seen at its best in the peaceful lines of this romantic old house. Among its many treasures is a chapel with a Norman font and lovely 15th-century wall paintings, and a long gallery with a painted ceiling and outstanding panelling.

BAMBURGH, Northumb   *161 NU13*
Grace Darling was born in this unspoilt fishing village in 1815, and is buried in the graveyard of the mainly 13th-century church. She became famous in 1838 when she sailed with her father from a lighthouse on nearby Longstone Island, in the teeth of a gale, to rescue survivors from the wrecked ship *Forfarshire*. The RNLI has founded a local museum to her memory. Immediately obvious to the visitor is Bamburgh's huge Norman castle, once the seat of the kings of Northumbria and now restored to its original magnificence.

BARNARD CASTLE,
Co Durham   *132 NZ01*
The town of Barnard Castle stands in a picturesque setting on a clifftop overlooking the River Tees and is an ideal base from which to explore the lovely countryside of Teesdale. The first castle here was built in the 12th century by Guy de Balliol, but this was rebuilt by his nephew and adapted throughout the centuries by various owners. Today the extensive remains include the three-storey keep and parts of a 14th-century great hall.

Close to the town is the fascinating Bowes Museum. Built in the style of a French château, it contains one of the finest art collections in Britain, featuring fine European paintings, furniture, porcelain, tapestries, jewellery and dolls. To the south of Barnard Castle are the lovely ruins of Egglestone Abbey, dating from the 12th century.

BARNSLEY, W Yorks   *128 SE30*
Mentioned in *Domesday Book*, Barnsley was an early coal-mining area and is still the administrative centre of the Yorkshire coalfield. The town hall is an imposing building, and the nearby College of Technology is a good example of modern architecture. In St Mary's Church is an 18th-century organ by Snetzler.

BARROW-IN-FURNESS,
Cumbria   *131 SD26*
Situated at the southern end of the Furness peninsula, this town is a major engineering and shipbuilding centre, and includes the building of Polaris submarines among its achievements.

North of the town are the exceptional pink-sandstone remains of 12th-century Furness Abbey. A great deal of the building remains, including one end of the church, the east side of the cloister and the chapter house.

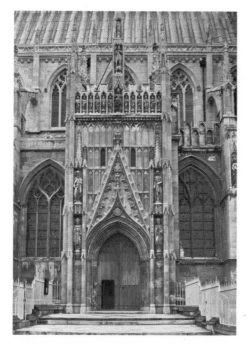

The beautiful north porch of Beverley Minster carries carved figures of Christ and the Disciples

BERWICK-UPON-TWEED, Northumb   *161 NT95*

A busy seaport and now England's northernmost town, Berwick was alternately held by Scottish and English forces during the bitter border struggles that began with the Romans and continued until the 15th century. Remains of a castle built here by the Normans include three towers and ancient sections of wall. During Elizabethan times the town walls were restored, and they have survived as a complete circuit round old Berwick.

The parish church, one of the few to be built during Cromwell's Commonwealth, is of exceptional architectural interest and was extended in the 19th century. In 1717 Vanbrugh built Britain's earliest barracks here, and today these incorporate the Museum of the King's Own Scottish Borderers. Relics from the town's past and collections of paintings and ceramics can be seen in Berwick Museum.

BEVERLEY, Humberside   *129 TA03*

Medieval Beverley Minster is claimed to be one of the most beautiful Gothic churches in Europe. Its lovely twin bell-towers can be seen for miles across the flat Humberside pastures, and its interior is packed with treasures including the magnificent Percy Tomb, the great east window and a wealth of fine woodwork. At the far end of the main street is St Mary's Church, a beautiful building that was started in the 12th century as a chapel for its more famous neighbour. One of its more notable features is a 15th-century ceiling painting of the English kings. Evidence that much of the town's expansion took place in the 18th and 19th centuries can be seen in the many Georgian houses and shopfronts that survive. The market cross dates from about 1714, and the Guildhall of 1762 displays fine plasterwork and wood carving.

BISHOP AUCKLAND, Co Durham   *133 NZ22*

The chief charm of this busy mining town is Bishop's Park, which can be reached from the market place through a gatehouse dating from 1760. The 800-acre park belonged to the bishop's palace, the official country residence of the bishops of Durham from the 12th to the 13th century.

BLACKBURN, Lancs   *127 SD62*

Textiles have been made here since the Flemish weavers first settled here in the 14th century and although Blackburn was initially involved in woollens and cotton, its later diversification helped the town to overcome the worst effects of the cotton-trade depression. The Lewis Textile Museum illustrates the history and development of the industry. Much of this history belongs to Blackburn as James Hargreaves, the inventor of the spinning jenny, was one of the town's weavers.

The cathedral, formerly St Mary's Church, was rebuilt in 1820–26 and enlarged between 1937 and 1950.

BLACKPOOL, Lancs   *127 SD33*

Until the seaside-holiday vogue of the 18th century the town was little more than a cluster of cottages, but it has developed from these small beginnings to become one of the premier resorts in Great Britain. Everything is geared up to the boisterous, funfair atmosphere of high summer, and the natural asset of a beautiful sandy beach is supplemented by three fine piers and the famous 519ft tower. In the latter are a ballroom that is often the scene of dance festivals and beauty contests, an aquarium and butterfly farm, and various facilities for children. The traditional heart of the seven-mile Promenade is the famous Golden Mile, a bewildering collection of novelty shops, ice-cream vendors and seafood stalls. Blackpool Zoo is the most modern in Britain.

BOLTON, Gt Manchester   *127 SD70*

Bolton, the home of fine spinning and weaving, has been known as one of the great Lancashire cotton centres for many years. Two very important inventions of the Industrial Revolution were made by inhabitants of the town: Samuel Crompton, a native, conceived the 'mule' spinning frame; Arkwright, a local barber, designed the water frame. Crompton also pioneered the making of textile machinery, plus subsidiary industries like bleaching, dyeing and fabric finishing. Local connections with the industry are recalled in the Tonge Moor Textile Museum.

BOLTON ABBEY, N Yorks   *128 SE05*

Woodlands and pastures in a bend of the River Wharfe make a fittingly peaceful setting for the remains of this once-powerful 12th-century priory. Most of the structure lies in ruins, but the nave has served as a parish church for hundreds of years, and the old gatehouse was incorporated into a mansion during the 19th century. The little river can be crossed by stepping stones or a footbridge here, and attractive riverside walks extend from the ruins to the Strid gorge.

BRADFORD, W Yorks   *128 SE13*

Bradford, a centre of the wool and worsted industry for some time, is now a cathedral and university city. Its parish church became a cathedral in 1920, and the Institute of Technology was raised to university status in 1966. The town hall and wool exchange were both built in the Victorian Gothic style by a local firm.

Cartwright Memorial Hall, housing a museum and art gallery, is set in Lister Park which also contains botanical gardens. Another museum is housed in partly 14th-century and partly Elizabethan Bolling Hall. Composer Frederick Delius was born in Bradford in 1862.

Ruined Bolton Priory stands in a magnificent setting beside the River Wharfe

Many of Buxton's most dignified buildings, including the Crescent (above), date from the 18th century, but the beautifully restored Opera House (left) is a legacy of the Edwardian era

BRIDLINGTON, Humberside *129 TA16*
Protected by the great white cliffs of Flamborough Head, this popular resort offers good bathing, sailing, fishing and a variety of traditional seaside entertainments. Around the harbour there is still an atmosphere of the old fishing village the town used to be, and fishing boats run trips out into the bay. Sewerby Hall, north of Bridlington, is a fine Georgian mansion now housing an art gallery and museum. There is a small zoo in the grounds.

BRINKBURN, Northumb *133 NZ19*
Set in a loop of the River Coquet, this quiet village has a beautiful priory church founded by Augustinian canons in 1135. The buildings have been sensitively restored and display fine lancet windows and the original altar stone.

BROUGHAM, Cumbria *131 NY52*
Pronounced 'Broom', this village on the River Eamont includes the remains of a 12th-century castle built on the site of a Roman fort. The little Church of St Ninian nearby is noted for its old woodwork, and was restored in 1660 by Lady Anne Clifford, who also restored the Chapel of St Wilfred.

BUXTON, Derbyshire *128 SK07*
Situated just outside the Peak District National Park, this is the highest town in England and an ideal base from which to tour the moors and dales of the Peak District. The town itself is built round a spa whose medicinal properties were discovered by the Romans and exploited to the benefit of the town towards the end of the 18th century. The growth of the town during this period was largely due to the efforts of the Fifth Duke of Devonshire, who built the beautiful Crescent and Pump Rooms opposite the town's hot springs. Spa treatment is available from the Royal Devonshire Hospital, which was originally built as the Great Stables and has a superb dome that was added in 1879. The Pavilion concert hall, theatre, and ballroom stand in 23 acres of lovely gardens featuring a boating lake, bowling and putting greens, tennis courts, and a children's play area. Fine collections of fossils and minerals are among many interesting exhibits in the local museum.

CARLISLE, Cumbria *131 NY45*
During the Roman occupation, Carlisle, then known as *Luguvalium*, was a strategic centre of the frontier that separated the peoples of the south from the wild northern tribes. Continued excursions from Scotland prompted William Rufus to build the town's sturdy castle in 1092; Queen Mary's Tower, a later addition, contains a fascinating museum devoted to the Border Regiments. During the Civil War the six western bays of Carlisle's small medieval cathedral were demolished to repair the town wall, but two surviving bays of the nave display Norman workmanship. The choir was restored in the 13th century and features a magnificent east window. In the cathedral grounds is a 13th-century pele tower known as the Prior's Tower. The city's early 15th-century Guildhall is now a museum of guild, civic and local history. Tullie House Museum occupies a fine Jacobean mansion and its comprehensive collections include exhibits relating to Hadrian's Wall.

CASTLETON, Derbyshire *128 SK18*
This large Derbyshire village grew up around the Norman castle which Sir Walter Scott immortalized in his novel *Peveril of the Peak*. The great keep which now dominates the ruins was added in 1176 by Henry II.
Castleton is particularly well known for the four limestone caverns nearby: the Peak cavern, the Speedwell Mine, the Treak Cliff Cavern and Blue John Mine – named after the semi-precious stone, Blue John, which has been prized since Roman times.

CHESTER, Cheshire *127 SJ46*
Founded nearly 2,000 years ago by the Romans, Chester is the only city in England to have preserved its medieval walls in their entirety. They contain parts of the original Roman defences. Chester, or *Deva* as it was once known, remained a principal military station and trading town until the Romans withdrew from Britain at the beginning of the 5th century. For five centuries the site was deserted, but it gradually regained its position as a place of importance, and the medieval town flourished as a port until silting of the Dee during the 15th century brought a decline

in its trade. The city continued as a commercial centre, however, and its fortunes largely revived during the rich 18th and 19th centuries. Much survives from all periods of Chester's history, but the source of its distinctive character is undoubtedly the galleried tiers of shops known as The Rows. The beautifully restored sandstone cathedral dates mainly from the 14th century. It incorporates extensive Benedictine monastic remains, and is especially noted for its richly carved woodwork, the Lady Chapel, the refectory, and the cloisters. Black-and-white buildings abound in Chester – God's Providence House, Bishop Lloyd's House and Old Leche House being outstanding – and there are also many timbered inns. Several interesting museums and a famous zoo are among the city's other attractions.

The ornate clock above Eastgate in Chester was erected to commemorate Queen Victoria's Diamond Jubilee

CHESTERFIELD, Derbyshire *128 SK37*
This ancient market town dates back far enough to be mentioned in *Domesday Book*. In 1266 it was the scene of a battle in which the Earl of Derby was defeated by the forces of the Crown, and during the Civil War the Earl of Newcastle and his Royalist troops claimed a victory here over the Parliamentarians.

The railway through Chesterfield was built under the supervision of George Stephenson, who lived north-east of the town at Tapton House and died here in 1848. His grave can be seen at Trinity Church. Chesterfield owes a good deal to this great man; it was he who discovered the rich seam of coal lying under the town and formed a company to work it. His association with the town is commemorated by the Stephenson Memorial Hall.

The only remaining Tudor building in the town can be seen near All Saints' Church, famous for its twisted spire.

CHILLINGHAM, Northumb *133 NU02*
During the summer months the grounds of Chillingham Castle are accessible for people wishing to see the remarkable Chillingham wild cattle. The animals in this herd are the descendants of wild oxen said to have been trapped when the park was created in 1220.

CLITHEROE, Lancs *127 SD74*
After the Civil War the small Norman keep of Clitheroe Castle was presented to General Monk, and today it still stands in a dominant position on a limestone knoll above the town. Inside is an important collection of fossils from the surrounding district. The town itself is an industrial centre that grew to prosperity through cotton.

Sinister Pendle Hill, associated with the notorious trial of several Lancashire women who were said to be witches and accordingly executed, rises to 1,831ft on the east side of Clitheroe.

COCKERMOUTH, Cumbria *131 NY13*
The town grew up around the Norman castle built at the junction of the rivers Derwent and Cocker, and although much of the castle was destroyed during the Civil War, an underground dungeon has survived.

William Wordsworth was born in the town in 1770 and his old home attracts many visitors each year. A stained-glass window in All Saints' Church commemorates the poet.

CONISTON, Cumbria *131 SD39*
This cluster of whitewashed cottages at the tip of lovely Coniston Water is a bright spot in a landscape dominated in the west by the 2,631ft Old Man of Coniston. A little farther north is the 2,555ft peak of Dow Crag, whose testing faces are popular with climbers. Features of the village itself include Coniston Old Hall, with its typical round Lakeland chimneys, and the Ruskin Museum. John Ruskin, the 19th-century writer and artist, loved this area and is buried in the local churchyard. The lake itself is famous as the place where Sir Donald Campbell died while trying to better the world water-speed record in 1965.

CORBRIDGE, Northumb *132 NY96*
A 17th-century bridge crosses the Tyne in this pleasant old market town, and the main street is lined with attractive houses and gardens. The church's Saxon tower is of interest, and the churchyard contains a 14th-century pele tower. A Roman arch can also be seen in the church. An unusual cast-iron cross in the market place dates from 1814.

Roman remains of *Corstopitum* and a museum displaying relics of the occupation here, can be seen 1½ miles west. A Roman cavalry force was stationed here until AD140, when the fort was rebuilt to form a military base and depot for operations in Scotland.

CRASTER, Northumb *133 NU21*
Craster is known for its oak-smoked kippers and splendid cliff scenery. The former can be sampled at many places in the district, and the latter is best appreciated from a 1¼-mile walk leading to Dunstanburgh Castle. The great rocky promontory that juts into the sea here would be impressive in any circumstances, but crowned with the picturesque ruins of the castle it is magnificent. Remains of this essentially 14th-century structure cover 11 acres and are enclosed by massive defensive walls. Above the village is the Georgian house of Craster Tower, which incorporates the remains of a medieval building.

CRICH, Derbyshire *128 SK35*
Here in this small hill village, vintage tramcars from all over the world have been restored to working order and are on display in a fascinating museum which occupies a disused quarry. An air of authenticity is created by a period setting comprising the reconstructed façade of Derby's Georgian Assembly Rooms and a collection of Victorian street furniture.

High above the village is Crich Stand, a 950ft-high hill crowned by a lofty monument to the Sherwood Foresters – the Nottingham and Derby regiment.

Beautifully preserved trams from all over the world are kept at the Crich Tramway Museum

This 18th-century mill at Cromford was built by Richard Arkwright, father of the cotton industry

CROMFORD, Derbyshire *128 SK25*
The world's first mechanized water-powered textile factory was built here by Richard Arkwright in 1771. Two of his mills still stand here, and he also built many of the village cottages to house his millworkers. A fine old bridge that spans the River Derwent carries a rare 15th-century bridge chapel.

DARLINGTON, Co Durham *133 NZ21*
This town is of Anglo-Saxon origin, and was once involved in the wool industry. As the profitability of wool began to drop, Darlington became a pioneering railway centre concerned with the manufacture of wagons, locomotives, tracks and signals. The historic North Road Station, opened in 1842, is now a museum whose exhibits include the original *Locomotion No. 1*, the engine that opened the world's first passenger line in 1825.

DONCASTER, S Yorks 128 SE50

Doncaster, known as *Danum* under the Romans, became a Saxon settlement before the Norman occupation. It is now well known as a busy industrial town. Of its older buildings the Mansion House, by James Paine, is a fine example and one of the three mansion houses in England originally intended as mayoral residences (the other two are in London and York). It was built from 1745 to 1748, and the ballroom has an ornamental ceiling and white marble fireplaces. Both the museum and art gallery are of interest, and the former exhibits many Roman relics.

Cusworth Hall, 1½ miles south-west, is an 18th-century house now housing a museum of South Yorkshire life which includes special sections for children.

DOUGLAS, Isle of Man 130 SC37

Douglas is the chief town of the Isle of Man, and a popular holiday resort with extensive sands and a fine promenade running along the wide bay. Horse-drawn trams, known locally as 'toast-racks', are still a feature of the resort.

The House of Keys is the site of the Manx Parliament, the Tynwald, whose Scandinavian origins are earlier than those of Westminster. It stands on Prospect Hill. The nearby Manx National Museum displays local antiquities, natural history and folklore.

DURHAM, Co Durham 133 NZ24

Durham grew up around its cathedral, set on a high rock and surrounded on three sides by the River Wear. Nothing remains of the original Saxon cathedral, and the present Norman building – one of the largest English churches – was begun in 1093 by Bishop William of Calais. The nave was completed early in the 12th century, and the Galilee porch, containing the tomb of the Venerable Bede, a little later on. The castle, like the cathedral, is also built on a neck of land that once guarded the city approaches. It has a notable crypt chapel and a richly carved doorway. Durham University has grown up around the cathedral and

The pretty limestone village of Fenny Bentley in the southern Peak District

castle, and occupies most of the buildings in the city centre. It is England's oldest residential university after Oxford and Cambridge.

The Gulbenkian Museum of Oriental Art is unique as the only museum in Britain devoted solely to this subject, and the many fascinating and beautiful items exhibited include Chinese jade, Tibetan paintings and sculpture, and Egyptian antiquities.

EDWINSTOWE, Notts 128 SK66

An attractive village on the River Maun, Edwinstowe is near the older parts of Sherwood Forest and the Dukeries. Robin Hood and Maid Marian are said to have been married in the 13th-century church. A mausoleum to the Ward family can be seen here, and interesting old oak trees nearby include the Major Oak, said to have sheltered Robin Hood.

EPWORTH, Humberside 129 SE70

This town is situated in the low-lying Isle of Axholme and was the birthplace of John Wesley, the founder of the Methodist Church. His father, Samuel Wesley, was the rector of Epworth. Their home was rebuilt after a fire in 1709, and still contains furniture associated with the Wesley family.

EYAM, Derbyshire 128 SK27

This is the famous plague village, three-quarters of whose inhabitants were killed by the disease in one year. An annual commemoration ceremony is conducted here on the last Sunday in August. The village church dates from the 13th to 15th centuries and contains an elaborate sundial. An Anglo-Saxon cross with its original cross-head stands in the churchyard.

FENNY BENTLEY, Derbyshire 128 SK15

Features of this pleasant village include the successful amalgamation of a 15th-century manor house with the remains of an ancient tower, and a good Derbyshire church. Inside the latter is a macabre monument with shrouded effigies of Thomas Beresford, his wife, 16 sons, and five daughters.

FLEETWOOD, Lancs 131 SD34

This large fishing port lies on the Wyre estuary overlooking Morecambe Bay, and is a popular resort offering four miles of sandy beach, a large indoor swimming pool and attractive seafront gardens. A wonderful panoramic view of the Lake District mountains can be enjoyed from Mount Pavilion.

GAINSBOROUGH, Lincs 129 SK89

Gainsborough is associated with George Eliot's *Mill on the Floss*, in which it appears under the name of St Ogg's. A triple-arched bridge spans the River Trent and links the town with Nottinghamshire on the opposite bank.

Gainsborough Old Hall is one of the largest medieval buildings open to the public in England. During its history Richard III, Henry VIII and the latter's fifth wife, Catharine Howard, stayed at the house.

GAWSWORTH, Cheshire 127 SJ86

The fine village church with its Perpendicular tower has many quaint gargoyles and a notable range of monuments to the Fittons of Gawsworth Hall. This Elizabethan half-timbered manor house has a tilting ground and a carriage museum as well as fine collections of armour, furniture and pictures.

GRANGE-OVER-SANDS, Cumbria 131 SD47

This quiet seaside resort on Morecambe Bay is backed by lovely wooded fell scenery that sweeps right down to the sea. The mile-long promenade offers bracing walks, and the mild local climate has proved ideal for the ornamental gardens which flourish throughout the town. To the west of Grange, near Cark, is Holker Hall. Originally built in the 16th century, this house contains fine furniture and exquisite woodcarvings by local craftsmen.

Commemorative plates from American Methodist chapels are on display in Epworth's Old Rectory

Left: Wordsworth wrote some of his best-known poems at Dove Cottage, Grasmere, where he lived for nine years

Right: Hornsea Mere, Yorkshire's largest freshwater lake, is surrounded by reed-beds and woodland, making it a haven for many species of water bird including large flocks of coot

GRASMERE, Cumbria 131 NY30

This tiny stone village is beautifully set between the tranquil waters of Grasmere Lake and the jagged heights of Helm Crag and Nab Scar. Close by is a beautiful natural arena where the famous Grasmere Sports are staged every August, perpetuating such traditional events as Lakeland wrestling and the guides footrace. Important sheepdog trials are held in the village at about the same time.

At one end of the village is Dove Cottage, where Wordsworth lived from 1799 to 1808. Later it became the home of the writer Thomas de Quincey, who occupied it for 26 years. A Wordsworth museum which now adjoins the house preserves several manuscripts and first editions of the poet's work.

GRASSINGTON, N Yorks 128 SE06

The lovely area in which this Upper Wharfedale village stands is rich in mineral deposits and has been occupied since very early times. Many Iron Age camps and barrows survive, and during the Roman occupation the area was extensively mined for lead ore. The village itself is a popular tourist centre with a cobbled market square and a medieval bridge.

GRIMSBY, Humberside 129 TA20

Grimsby has one of the largest fish markets in the world and its docks, where catches from Arctic waters are landed, are a national centre for the trade. There is an interesting museum near the town hall exhibiting model ships, paintings and ceramics.

HARROGATE, N Yorks 128 SE35

One of the chief towns in Yorkshire's old West Riding, Harrogate achieved early fame as a spa resort. Its mineral springs were discovered in the 16th century, and the Royal Pump Room was built as the country's first public baths in 1842. From that time onwards the town's popularity steadily increased, resulting in a wealth of dignified stone buildings and beautiful gardens that have earned Harrogate the nickname 'the Floral Resort of England'. The Valley Gardens are particularly notable, and the Harlow Car Trial Gardens are used for experimental horticulture. An interesting museum of local history, Victoriana, and costumes is housed in the Pump Room.

HAWORTH, W Yorks 128 SE03

Situated on the edge of rugged moors, this bleak village is famous for its associations with the Brontë family. The parsonage in which the family lived now houses the Brontë Parsonage Museum and has retained many of their personal relics. Emily Brontë, who died here in 1848, and her sister Charlotte were both buried at St Michael's Church.

HEBDEN BRIDGE, W Yorks 128 SD92

Built almost entirely of local stone, this pleasant mill-town is a fine example of the effects of the Industrial Revolution in Yorkshire. The nearby hilltop village of Heptonstall was the original weavers' settlement, but increasing mechanization led to the establishment of mills in the valley, where there was running water to power their machinery. The terraces of cottages that crowd the valley sides were built to house mill-workers.

HELMSLEY, N Yorks 128 SE68

Helmsley is a delightful stone-built town, with a ruined 12th-century castle built by Walter l'Espec, founder of nearby Rievaulx Abbey. Founded in 1131, the abbey is now a beautiful ruin. It is best seen from Rievaulx Terrace.

HEXHAM, Northumb 132 NY96

This attractive old town on the River Tyne is an excellent centre for walkers exploring the Roman wall. The interesting priory church is larger than some cathedrals and contains a rare Saxon crypt. Ranged around the pretty market square nearby are the Moot Hall – once the gatehouse of a 12th-century castle – and the 14th-century Manor Office, which served as the town gaol until 1824.

HOLY ISLAND (LINDISFARNE), Northumb 161 NU14

Missionaries were brought to Lindisfarne from Iona by St Aidan in the 7th century. About 150 years later their monastic foundation was sacked and destroyed by Danish marauders, but in 1082 the Benedictine order built a fine priory on the same site. Its gaunt ruins still stand today, and various relics found during excavations can be seen in a local museum. The island's restored 16th-century castle contains antique oak furniture.

HORNSEA, Humberside 129 TA24

Hornsea has become very well known through its pottery. More can be learned about the processes and skills involved from a conducted tour of the factory. Behind the narrow streets and clustered houses of the old village is Hornsea Mere, a two-mile-long lagoon.

Mill-workers' cottages built of local stone line the steep valley sides at Hebden Bridge

HULL, Humberside   *129 TA02*

Properly known as Kingston-upon-Hull, this major industrial and commercial centre is an international port and a fishing base for deep-sea vessels. It suffered badly during the Second World War, but its rebuilding has included a fine shopping precinct scattered with flower-beds and interspersed with parks and gardens. Despite extensive new developments, the city centre still has a few old buildings including one of the largest parish churches in England. The Town Docks Museum relates to fishing and shipping, and the Transport and Archaeological Museum mounts interesting displays. Paintings, sculptures and visiting exhibitions can be seen in the Ferens Art Gallery.

JARROW, Tyne & Wear   *133 NZ36*

Jarrow, part of industrial Tyneside, is the unlikely site of the monastery in which the Venerable Bede lived and died. St Paul's Church, now standing in its place, shows examples of Saxon work and preserves Bede's chair and a dedication plate of the year 684. Much later, Jarrow gained fame for the Jarrow Marchers, who walked to London to protest about the intense poverty caused locally by shipyard closures during the depression of the 1930s.

KEIGHLEY, W Yorks   *128 SE04*

This manufacturing town on the River Aire retains its broad main street and several attractive public buildings. A Victorian mansion called Cliffe Castle houses the town's museum and art gallery. Keighley is the northern terminus of the Keighley and Worth Valley Railway, a revived steam line that runs to Oxenhope via Haworth and is famous for its large collection of old locomotives.

The age of stylish rail travel is recalled on the Keighley and Worth Valley Railway

KENDAL, Cumbria   *131 SD59*

Kendal, known as the 'Auld Grey Town' because of its many greystone buildings, has been an important Cumbrian market town for hundreds of years. Its oldest remains are the ruins of the Norman castle, which later became the birthplace of Catherine Parr, sixth wife of Henry VIII. Many picturesque old yards are scattered throughout the town, recalling its days as an important wool-town producing the famous Kendal Green cloth. Abbot Hall, an 18th-century mansion, now houses an art gallery and collections of glass, furniture, silver and porcelain. Its stable-block is occupied by the Museum of Lakeland Life and Industry.

Three miles south of Kendal is Sizergh Castle, home of the Strickland family for over seven centuries. An ancient pele tower is incorporated into the house, and the extensive grounds are particularly beautiful.

KESWICK, Cumbria   *131 NY22*

This touring centre beside Derwent Water is close to some of Lakeland's finest scenery and attracts thousands of visitors every year. In Victorian times it was beloved of poets and artists, including Wordsworth, Coleridge, Southey, Ruskin and Walpole. Many of their works and personal possessions are preserved in the fascinating Fitz Park Museum, which also features an impressive scale model of the Lake District. Both Coleridge and Southey lived in Greta Park at different times, and there is a memorial to John Ruskin close to the town on the spectacular viewpoint of Friar's Crag. Moot Hall is a handsome building that was reconstructed in the early 19th century. One mile west of Keswick, in a magnificent setting, is Castlerigg Stone Circle. Measuring over 100ft in diameter, it contains 38 stones and probably dates from the Bronze Age.

KIRKBY LONSDALE, Cumbria *131 SD67*

One of the finest old bridges in England, Devil's Bridge, crosses the River Lune here. The town was used in Charlotte Brontë's novel *Jane Eyre* under the name of Lowton and the authoress herself was a scholar at the Clergy Daughters' School at Cowan Bridge. The church, built on an Anglo-Saxon site, has some good Norman work.

KNUTSFORD, Cheshire   *121 SJ77*

This attractive residential town was the home of the novelist, Mrs Gaskell, who featured it in many of her novels including *Cranford*. She is buried behind the Unitarian Chapel of 1688. The parish church dates from the 18th century, and the Sessions House from 1818.

Tatton Park, set in an extensive park to the north, is a fine late 18th-century mansion that includes among its attractions a museum of veteran cars, sporting trophies and curiosities; 54 acres of ornamental gardens laid out by Humphry Repton, and a priceless collection of paintings and furniture.

LANCASTER, Lancs   *131 SD46*

The old county town of Lancashire, lying in the shadow of the Lakeland mountains, has origins stretching back over 700 years. Perched up on Castle Hill are the town's two oldest foundations – the castle and the priory. Much of the castle has survived and includes Shire Hall, where there is an impressive collection of heraldry. The 14th-century parish church standing next door incorporates the Saxon Benedictine priory that formerly occupied the site. One of the town's many Georgian buildings is the old town hall, now housing the Lancaster Museum. Another interesting museum occupies the elegant 17th-century house known as the Judges' Lodgings. Different aspects of childhood in Lancashire are depicted here, and the museum features the Barry Elder Doll Collection.

Keswick lies between beautiful Derwent Water and the snow-capped peak of Skiddaw

LEEDS, W Yorks   128 SE33
Fabrics, footwear, and engineering items are made in this important university city, which still retains some of its old buildings. Several churches are numbered among these, including St Peter's, which has a restored pre-Conquest cross, and St John's, noted for its wealth of 17th-century woodwork. The Corn Exchange dates from 1861 to 1863 and two other impressive local buildings are the town hall of 1853 and the more recent civic hall of 1933.

Two canals meet in the city, the Leeds and Liverpool and the Aire and Calder. Containers on the latter, known as Tom-Pudding boats, are towed by tugs in strings of up to 19.

Lincoln's majestic cathedral soars above the rooftops of the medieval town

LINCOLN, Lincs   129 SK97
Historic Lincoln rises majestically from the north banks of the River Witham, on a slope crowned by the magnificent triple-towered cathedral. The 11th-century origins of this beautifully situated church are largely hidden by extensions and additions from subsequent periods, and its many ancient treasures include the best preserved of four existing copies of *Magna Carta*. Other interesting churches in the city are St Benedict's and St Peter at Gowt's, both of which include a great deal of Saxon work. Newport Arch, the only surviving Roman gateway to span an English street, is a relic of the ancient walled city of *Lindum Colonia*. The Close, also known as Minster Yard, contains a superb collection of buildings including a fine tithe barn of 1440 and the ancient Bishop's Palace. Lincoln Castle was founded by William the Conqueror in 1068 and over the centuries has grown into the impressive structure that now occupies some six acres. Its main features include 14th-century Cobb Hall, which was once a place of punishment, the Observatory Tower, and a fine Norman keep.

LIVERPOOL, Merseyside   127 SJ39
A settlement has existed here for some time – the north bank of the Mersey bore a community as long ago as the 1st century AD. This had grown into a thriving fishing village by 1200, and was granted a charter by King John. Much later the town expanded with the onset of heavy trade with the West Indies, and also became connected with the slave trade. However, it was not until the introduction of steamships in the 1840s that Liverpool began to take on its present form. Its famous dockside frontage extends for seven miles and forms one of the finest systems to be found anywhere. The landing stage is the largest floating quay in the world. Rising to 295ft is the 17-storey Royal Liver Building which has two towers surmounted by the legendary liver birds.

The new Anglican cathedral by Sir Giles Gilbert Scott was begun in 1904 and displays notable stained glass and a fine organ. In striking contrast is the new Roman Catholic Cathedral of Christ the King, consecrated in 1967. It features a stained-glass lantern-tower and a white-marble altar. Sir Edwin Lutyens conceived a plan for this building in 1933, but the only part of his design to reach fruition was the remarkable crypt. John Wood of Bath designed the town hall, which James Wyatt later enlarged by adding the dome. The restored museum and Walker Art Gallery are also notable. The old parish church of St Nicholas, rebuilt in 1952, except for the tower of 1815, stands in a memorial garden facing Pierhead.

LOUTH, Lincs   129 TF38
Louth has been a busy cattle-market town for centuries, but the new industries mushrooming in the area are gradually overshadowing this traditional role. Fine houses can be seen in Westgate and Upgate, but the town's best feature is its Gothic parish church which has a tower nearly 300ft high and is considered one of the finest in England. The poet Tennyson attended Louth Grammar School, and his first book was published here.

LYTHAM ST ANNE'S, Lancs   127 SD32
No less than four championship courses make this popular seaside resort a mecca for golfing enthusiasts, and the British Sand Yachting Championships are held here every May. The residential part of the resort is laid out on garden-city lines, with many beautiful parks and gardens between streets of pleasant houses. In and between these gardens are many good half-timbered buildings, including attractive 18th-century Lytham Hall. A collection of industrial engines and a model railway make up the Motive Power Museum in Dock Road.

MACCLESFIELD, Cheshire   128 SJ97
Steep, cobbled streets criss-cross this pleasant silk-manufacturing town which retains some of its 18th- and 19th-century mills. The museum in West Park has a good collection of Egyptian antiquities, oil paintings and sketches as well as a small silk exhibition. There are fine views of the Pennines from St Michael's churchyard, and many interesting monuments can be seen in the church.

MALTON, N Yorks   129 SE77
Once the site of a Roman station, this market town is situated on the River Derwent at the foot of the Wolds. Both St Michael's and St Leonard's churches contain Norman work, and Malton Lodge is an interesting old mansion. Old Malton, a mile to the north-east, has a mostly Early English church – the surviving remains of an ancient priory.

The great 18th-century mansion of Castle Howard, seat of the Howard family, lies six miles west. It was built by Vanbrugh and stands in a magnificent park containing numerous statues, a domed temple, and a splendid mausoleum designed by Nicholas Hawksmoor. The building contains numerous art treasures in its palatial interior.

The Flamingo Park of Kirby Misperton Hall is sited north of Malton, and covers 350 acres incorporating the Yorkshire Zoo.

The great mansion of Castle Howard, near Malton, was built by Vanbrugh for the Earl of Carlisle

MANCHESTER, Gt Manchester *127 SJ89*

This great cotton and university city is linked to the sea by the 36-mile Manchester Ship Canal, which was completed in 1894, and includes fine modern docks.

The mainly Perpendicular cathedral was formerly the parish church, and displays a fine tower and notable woodwork. Bomb damage included the destruction of the Lady Chapel and one of the two organs. The city as a whole suffered greatly during the last war, and many of its notable buildings sustained irreparable damage. Of surviving buildings, the interesting 15th-century Chetham's Hospital is particularly notable for its famous library – claimed to be the first public library in Europe. Important manuscripts and more than 3 million books are housed in the Ryland's Library.

Road and railway are carried across the Tyne at Newcastle by Stephenson's High Level Bridge

Gladstone's statue in Albert Square, Manchester. Behind is the Albert Memorial

MASHAM, N Yorks *128 SE28*

Masham's former importance as a market town can be judged from the huge square, which is dominated by a traditional maypole. In the churchyard of St Mary's are important remains of a Saxon cross, and the mainly Norman church is crowned by a 15th-century spire.

Four miles west of Masham is Jervaulx Abbey. Cistercian monks chose this beautiful riverside site as the perfect setting for their abbey in the 12th century. Although it was destroyed in the 15th century, enough remains to show the exquisite proportions of their achievement.

THE MATLOCKS, Derbyshire *128 SK36*

Matlock is situated on the eastern edge of the Peak District National Park, in a high area of gritstone moors and ridges. During the 19th century it became fashionable to take the waters here, and a great hydropathy centre was built at Matlock Bank. Regency visitors popularized the medicinal springs of Matlock

Bath, and although the resort later declined, today it draws more visitors than ever. Its Petrifying Wells are very famous and are hung with various objects such as bottles and bowler hats, left by visitors to turn to stone.

Picturesque ruins of 19th-century Riber Castle dominate nearby 853ft Riber Hill, and the grounds have been turned into an animal reserve. Here, near-natural surroundings are provided for comprehensive collections of European birds and animals. Special features include a colony of lynx, and many breeds of domestic animals that have died out elsewhere.

MIDDLEHAM, N Yorks *133 SE18*

Once the chief town of Wensleydale, this scenic village is now an important horse-breeding and training centre and a good touring base. Its impressive ruined castle was the seat of the powerful Neville family, who controlled much of the area from the massive keep that still stands behind well-preserved 13th-century curtain walls.

MIDDLESBROUGH, Cleveland *133 NZ52*

Since 1850, when iron ore was discovered in the Cleveland Hills, iron and steel have been the town's main industry. The large red-brick Roman Catholic cathedral is an impressive building, but Middlesbrough's best feature is the iron transporter bridge, which was built in 1911 and is one of only two such bridges in Britain. Good displays of natural history items and local antiquities can be seen in the Dorman Museum.

MORECAMBE, Lancs *131 SD46*

This popular resort is situated on the spectacular shores of Morecambe Bay, which stretches for nearly five miles and has lakeland mountains as a distant backdrop. The bay is well known for its shrimps. As well as an abundance of seaside amusements, Morecambe has a gigantic entertainment complex and a vast oceanarium and aquarium.

NANTWICH, Cheshire *127 SJ65*

Noted for cheeses and once famous for its salt-works, Nantwich has a fine 14th- and 15th-century church with an octagonal tower and beautifully carved stalls. Welsh Row is a particularly good place to see some of the many black-and-white houses in the town, and the local almshouses date from 1638. Churche's Mansion is half-timbered and dates from 1577, and the timbered Crown Inn is most attractive.

NEWARK-ON-TRENT, Notts *129 SK75*

Overlooking the Trent at Newark is the town's ruined castle, dominated by its towered gatehouse. King John died here in 1216, and the castle was besieged three times during the Civil War. The splendid parish church features a lofty 252ft tower and spire, and a treasury has recently been established in the crypt, where church plate from all over Nottinghamshire is on display. The recently restored Olde White Hart, with its overhanging façade, is a fine example of 14th-century architecture. Newark Museum, housed in part of the old grammar school, is devoted to local history, archaeology and natural history, while the Millgate Museum, in an old warehouse by the river, consists of a fascinating folk collection.

NEWCASTLE UPON TYNE, Tyne & Wear *133 NZ26*

The old county town of Northumberland, Newcastle upon Tyne was once a station on the Roman Wall, known as *Pons Aelii*. It is now an important university and manufacturing city.

The cathedral shows mostly Decorated and Perpendicular work. It is noted for its rare crown spire, resembling that of St Giles' in Edinburgh. Several interesting chapels include one in the crypt, and the organ, rebuilt in 1811, is housed in a case dating from 1710. The castle displays a restored 12th-century keep, and the Black Gate houses a collection of local antiquities. Roman remains can be seen in the Museum of Antiquities, which is situated in the University Quadrangle.

NORTHWICH, Cheshire   127 SJ67

This important salt-producing town has suffered from subsidence caused by salt-mining beneath its streets, and many buildings are leaning at unnatural angles. St Helen's Church, at Witton, to the east of the town, carries a fine tower showing gargoyles, plus old screenwork and a splendid oak tie-beam roof adorned with nearly 400 bosses. A little to the north-west is the unique electrically controlled Anderton vertical canal lift. This is used to transfer barges from the River Weaver to the Trent and Mersey Canal.

PICKERING, N Yorks   129 SE78

Terraces of sturdy cottages lead off the hilly main street of this old market town, which is ideally placed for exploring the Yorkshire Moors. The ruins of a medieval castle overlook one end of the town from a grassy mound, and the parish church is famous for its fine 15th-century wall-paintings. For a comprehensive picture of local history, visit the Beck Isle Rural Life Museum.

Pickering is the terminus of the North Yorkshire Moors Railway, which operates a service to Grosmont. There are locomotive sheds and a viewing gallery at the station.

PONTEFRACT, W Yorks   128 SE42

Once known as Pomfret, Pontefract includes the historic ruins of a Norman castle. These include a round tower and dungeons, plus a small museum. King Richard II was murdered here, and the castle was besieged on three separate occasions during the Civil War. This turbulent period also saw the partial destruction of All Saints' Church. The tower survived with its interesting octagonal lantern, and contains a remarkable double-spiral staircase. The parish church of St Giles was rebuilt in the 17th century but retains a 14th-century arcade. The butter-cross dates from 1734, and an old pump in the market place was given by Queen Elizabeth I.

Left: The White Bull Inn at Ribchester incorporates pillars said to have come from a Roman temple

Right: Founded in 1132, Fountains Abbey, near Ripon, grew to become the wealthiest Cistercian house in England by the 13th century. Today it is a magnificent ruin

RIBCHESTER, Lancs   127 SD63

A Roman fort known as *Bremetennacum* stood on this site for 300 years. Many finds from excavations here can be seen in the local Roman Museum. Among the exhibits are gold coins, pieces of pottery, brooches, oil lamps, and a replica of a rare bronze parade helmet found here. The priceless original is in the British Museum. Two Roman columns support the oak gallery in 13th-century St Wilfred's Church.

RICHMOND, N Yorks   133 NZ10

Dramatically situated overlooking the River Swale, this attractive and historic town makes an excellent base from which to explore the lovely countryside of Swaledale. The dominant feature of the town is its massive Norman castle with 11th-century curtain walls round a splendid keep. In its shadow are streets of lovely old buildings, all illustrative of important phases in Richmond's past. The cobbled market place is one of the largest in the country and is approached along little alleyways known as wynds. Greyfriars Tower is the remnant of an abbey that was founded here many centuries ago, and facing the market place is one of the strangest churches in England. Dedicated to the Holy Trinity, its main body and medieval tower are divided from each other by shops and offices actually built into its structure. The most outstanding Georgian building in the town is the Little Theatre of 1788, beautifully restored and the oldest theatre in the country to have survived in its original condition.

RIPLEY, N Yorks   128 SE26

Much of this attractive village was rebuilt during the 19th century, but it is largely unspoilt and retains an ancient market cross and stocks in its cobbled square. Ripley Castle, home of the Ingilby family since 1350, shows workmanship of mainly 16th- and 18th-century date and stands in beautiful grounds landscaped by Capability Brown. Oliver Cromwell stayed at the house on the eve of the Battle of Marston Moor in 1644, and armour from the opposing Royalist army is on display.

RIPON, N Yorks   128 SE37

The main features of Ripon's lovely 12th-century cathedral include a Saxon crypt that may be the earliest Christian survival in England, and a beautiful 15th-century screen. Every night Ripon's market square is the scene of a 1,000-year-old custom, when the town Hornblower or 'Wakeman' strides out in his tricorn hat and sounds his ancient horn at each corner of the 18th-century obelisk in the square. Years ago this sound indicated that the Wakeman had begun his night watch over the town. The half-timbered Wakeman's House dates from the 13th century and now contains a museum.

Three miles away are the lovely ruins of Fountains Abbey. Generally considered to be the finest in England, the remarkably well-preserved ruins of this 12th- to 15th-century Cistercian abbey clearly demonstrate the layout of a medieval monastic foundation.

The ruined curtain walls and towers of Pickering Castle mostly date from the 14th century

ROWSLEY, Derbyshire   *128 SK26*

This charming little greystone village stands on a tongue of land at the confluence of the rivers Wye and Derwent. Sir Joseph Paxton designed the earlier of two obsolete but charming station buildings here, and the beautiful Peacock Inn was originally a 17th-century manor house.

Three miles away is Chatsworth House, popularly known as the Palace of the Peak. This magnificent mansion was built in the 17th century for the First Duke of Devonshire and is noted particularly for its superb state apartments, great art collection and lovely grounds, where Britain's tallest fountain can be seen.

SANDBACH, Cheshire   *127 SJ76*

Old black-and-white houses, notably the gabled Old Hall, which now serves as an inn, are a feature of this salt-mining town. Two remarkable carved crosses which may date from the 7th century stand side by side in the market place. A public right of way runs through the arches of the church's 19th-century tower.

SCARBOROUGH, N Yorks   *133 TA08*

An important conference centre and one of the most popular seaside resorts in Yorkshire, this charming old town overlooks two sandy bays divided by the massive bulk of a 300ft headland. In Roman times this excellent vantage point was the site of a signalling station, and the foundations of that ancient structure still exist amongst the magnificent 12th-century castle ruins that stand here today. Views from the 100-acre site, which is accessible through a 13th-century barbican, extend across the red roofs of the medieval old town to the harbour far below. The Natural History Museum, Art Gallery, and Medicinal Baths are housed in notable Victorian buildings, and a museum of general interest can be visited in Wood End, the one-time holiday home of the Sitwell family. Resort facilities and amusements offered to the visitor include a zoo, fine promenades and well-tended seafront gardens.

Skipton Castle's mighty gateway was restored by the great benefactress Lady Anne Clifford in the 17th century

SHEFFIELD, S Yorks   *128 SK38*

Although the Industrial Revolution transformed Sheffield into the capital of the steel industry, its famous cutlery trade dates back to Norman times. The complete story of Sheffield's industrial past is illustrated at the Abbeydale Industrial Hamlet where there is an original 18th-century water-powered steelworks. A fine collection of the city's second famous product, Sheffield Plate, can be seen in the City Museum. The Botanical Gardens and Meersbrook Park are pleasant open spaces. A 16th-century yeoman's house portraying domestic life of the period is preserved in the latter.

SKEGNESS, Lincs   *129 TF56*

In 1863 a rail service was begun at Skegness, with trains running to and from the teeming towns of the industrial Midlands. The result was a boom in seaside tourism, and the holiday crowds of today continue to enjoy the excellent sands and bathing facilities that prompted the transformation of this one-time fishing village into one of the east coast's most popular resorts. Magnificent seafront gardens border a long promenade where Lord Tennyson and his brothers strolled to take the bracing sea air. At the southern end of the beach is Gibraltar Point, where there is a nature reserve and bird observatory.

SKIPTON, N Yorks   *128 SD95*

Skipton is dominated by a medieval castle that was restored by Lady Anne Clifford in 1658. Founded in Norman times, the building was subsequently extended and was strong enough to resist a three-year siege before falling into the hands of Cromwell's Parliamentarian army in the Civil War. Opposite the massive castle gateway is the Craven Museum, where exhibits and displays illustrate the geology and folk history of the district. An old four-storey corn mill, on a site where similar buildings have operated since the 12th century, houses the George Leatt Industrial and Folk Museum, where working water-wheels and a collection of carts and horse-traps can be seen.

SOUTHPORT, Merseyside   *127 SD31*

Particularly well known for its beautiful gardens and annual flower show, this attractive and elegant resort is also noted for its wide range of sporting facilities.

Amenities for holidaymakers include six miles of excellent sands, a pier and a model village. The Victorian heyday of seaside holidays is recalled by old salt-water swimming baths and a room of the Botanic Gardens Museum. The rapidly expanding Steam Transport Museum boasts a fine collection of locomotives, buses, traction engines and various commercial vehicles.

SOUTHWELL, Notts   *129 SK65*

Cathedral status was attained in 1884 by Southwell's minster church, whose twin west towers are a fine example of Norman work. The church is also noted for its Norman nave and the chapter-house – famous for its wonderful foliage carving. The brass lectern was retrieved from the lake at Newstead Abbey, where it was thrown during the Dissolution in the 16th century. Ruins of the old Archbishops' Palace stand near the minster. The Saracen's Head Inn is famous as the place where King Charles I surrendered to the Scots army in 1647.

TIDESWELL, Derbyshire   *128 SK17*

Although this ancient town was granted a market as early as the 13th century, the only notable building to have survived is the superb Church of St John the Baptist, popularly known as The Cathedral of the Peak. Local wells and springs are dressed in a traditional ceremony held every June.

Scarborough's South Bay is overlooked by Castle Cliff, the site of a Roman signalling station

A gaily painted funfair awaits the holiday crowds as the season opens at the popular resort of Skegness

TISSINGTON, Derbyshire   *128 SK15*

Greystone houses line two sides of the attractive triangular green on which this exceptionally beautiful village is centred; the third side is occupied by a fine Norman and later church. Features of the latter include a good Norman font, an unusual 18th-century double-decker pulpit and various monuments. Traditional Derbyshire well-dressing ceremonies are enacted at five wells on Ascension Day.

WAKEFIELD, W Yorks   *128 SE32*

For over 700 years Wakefield was the capital of Yorkshire's woollen industry, but the Industrial Revolution brought about its demise as a major cloth town, and now engineering is its chief industry. As a result of this, Wakefield escaped heavy industrialization and several Georgian houses dignify its streets, but the focal point of the old town is the cathedral church of All Saints, which boasts the tallest spire in the county. Kirkgate, one of the remaining medieval streets, leads to the Old Bridge, where a 14th-century chapel is preserved.

WARKWORTH, Northumb   *133 NU20*

At the top of the main street in Warkworth are the impressive remains of a 12th-century castle. The mainly Norman Church of St Lawrence has an outstanding stone spire, and the famous Warkworth Hermitage is a rock-cut chapel, with two living chambers, dating from the 14th century.

WHITBY, N Yorks   *133 NZ81*

Ruins of an abbey founded here by St Hilda in 657 can be seen above the town on the East Cliff. Below the abbey ruins the River Esk divides the old part of the settlement from the more recent West Cliff area, which is connected to the harbour via a rock-cut passage. Whitby has always had a strong sea-going tradition and has been the home of many famous maritime figures, including Captain Cook, whose house in Grape Street is identified by a plaque. One of the finest buildings here is St Mary's Church, which stands at the top of a spectacular flight of 199 steps and contains superb 18th-century craftsmanship. The museum in Pannet Park illustrates fascinating episodes from the town's long history. Local craftsmen have been making ornaments and jewellery from jet for hundreds of years.

WORKSOP, Notts   *128 SK57*

Visitors wishing to explore the Dukeries – known as such because at one time several dukes and earls owned estates in the area – will find Worksop a good base.

Norman workmanship can be seen in the nave of the church which is part of an old priory dating from the 12th century. The gatehouse also survived, and is notable for its double archway – at one time the upper room housed the country's first elementary school. Worksop Museum contains archaeological and natural history exhibits, including two Bronze Age beakers found 4½ miles south-east in Clumber Park.

YORK, N Yorks   *128 SE65*

Capital of a British province under the Romans in AD71, this ancient centre is still the chief city of northern England and preserves many fascinating reminders of its historic past. The earliest surviving building is the Roman Multangular Tower, though parts of the city walls date from the same period. The walls complete a three-mile circuit round the medieval boundaries of the city and are among the finest examples of their type in Europe. York's chief glory is its magnificent minster, which towers over the little streets and houses of the old town. It is the largest Gothic cathedral north of the Alps, and its fine windows contain more than half of all the medieval glass surviving in England. York has many lovely old churches: Holy Trinity is of 13th-century date and contains good box pews; All Saints' has medieval glass and carries a beautiful 15th-century tower; and St Mary's Castlegate has a rare Saxon dedication stone. Many of the city's buildings have been standing for 500 years and more, including the lovely Guildhall, the Merchant Adventurers' Hall and Chapel Taylors' Hall and the lovely timbered front and picturesque courtyard of William's College. Relics from the Roman occupation can be seen in the Yorkshire Museum, and close to the 13th-century fragments of York Castle is the Castle Museum of Yorkshire life. Close by, in the old Debtors' Prison, are collections of dolls and militaria, and the National Railway Museum preserves rolling stock and about 25 great old locomotives such as the *Mallard*.

The Shambles at York is one of the most famous medieval streets in the country, and is visited by thousands of tourists every year

Scotland

MULL

Kerrera

Oban

AA 84

Loch Spelve

Loch Scridain

A849

Lochbuie

162

Kilchrenan

Kilbride

Taychregga

Iona

Fionnphort

Kilninver

A816

Bunessan

Loch Bùie

Malcolm's Point

Loch Scammadale

NM

Easdale

Loch Avich

V

Luing

Kilmelford

Portinnish

Firth of Lorne

Loch Nell

Colonsay-Oban 2½

Arduaine

Scarba

B8002

B840

Kiloran Bay

Ford

Kilchatton

A870

Gulf of Corryvreckan

Kilmartin

Furnace

A871

Scalasaig

Crarae

Colonsay

A866

Glendebadel Bay

Crinan

B8025

Kilmichael

Fyne

Corpach Bay

B841

Lochgair

Oronsay

Ardlussa

Tayvallich

Cairnbaan

Shian Bay

A846

Lochgilphead

Loch Righ Mór

A83

Loch

Rubh' a' Mhail

Loch Tarbert

Lagg

Loch Sween

Ardrishaig

L Gilp

Otter Ferry

JURA

B8025

Achahoish

Glend

PAPS OF JURA

SOUND OF JURA

Kilmory

Kilfinan

A8003

Ardnave Point

Point of Knap

L Caolisport

Tighnabruaich

Ardnave

Loch Gruinart

Port Askaig

Feolin Ferry

B8024

Rhubo

An Clachan

V

Kames

Sanaigmore

B8018

Ballygrant

A846

Craighouse

Kilberry

KNAPDALE

Tarbert

Millhouse

Saligo Bay

B8017

Blackrock

Kilberry Head

B8024

West Tarbert Pier

Ardlamont Point

Kilchoman

Bridgend

Kennacraig

Loch Indaal

Bowmore

Kilchiaran

A846

(Macbrayne Wed. & Sat 2)

Whitehouse

Isle of

B8016

Port Askaig - Kennacraig (Western Ferries Ltd) 2¾

V

A83

Skipness

Sound of

Port Charlotte

ISLAY

V

Claonaig

Skipness Point

Rhinns of Islay

A847

Claggain Bay

Clachan

Loch Ciaran

Rubha na Faing

Laggan Point

A846

Ardmore Point

V

Cock of Arran

Portnahaven

ISLAY (PORT ELLEN)

NR

Gigha I

Ballochroy

Lochranza

Laggan Bay

Port Ellen - Kennacraig 2

Ardminish

V

Rhunahaorine

A841

GOAT FELL 2866

Ardbeg

A846

Sound of Gigha

Tayinloan

ISLAND

Port Ellen

Mull of Oa

Grogport

Pirnmill

OF

Rubha nan Leacan

Barr Water

Carradale

B880

Glenacardoch Point

Machrie Bay

Brod

Dippen

A841

Glenbarr

Machrae

Bellochantuy Bay

KINTYRE

Kilbrannan

Blackwaterfoot

Bellochantuy

Saddell

B842

ARRAN

Wh

Machrihanish Bay

Kilchenzie

A83

Ardnacross Bay

Brown Head

MACHRIHANISH

Kilmory

A84

Machrihanish

B843

Campbeltown

Brennan Head

K

B842

Johnston's Point

Polliwilline Bay

Mull of Kintyre

Southend

Scotland: narrow roads with passing places.

156

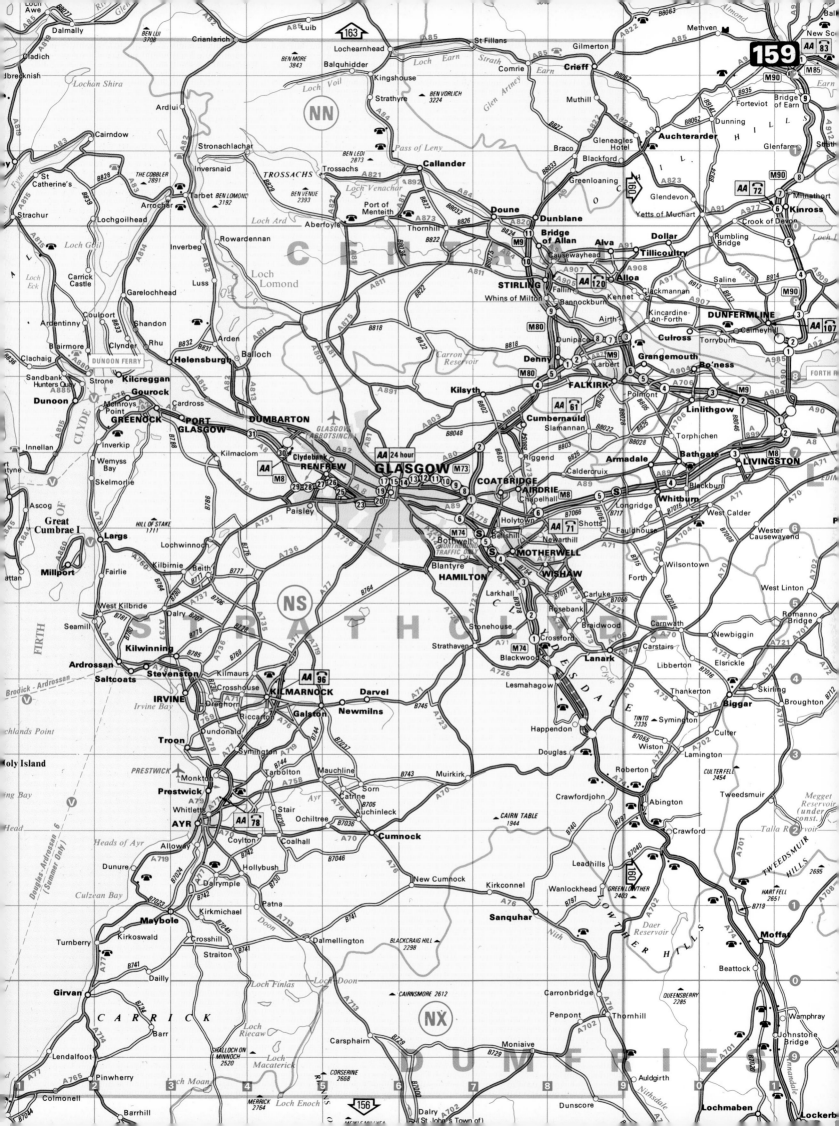

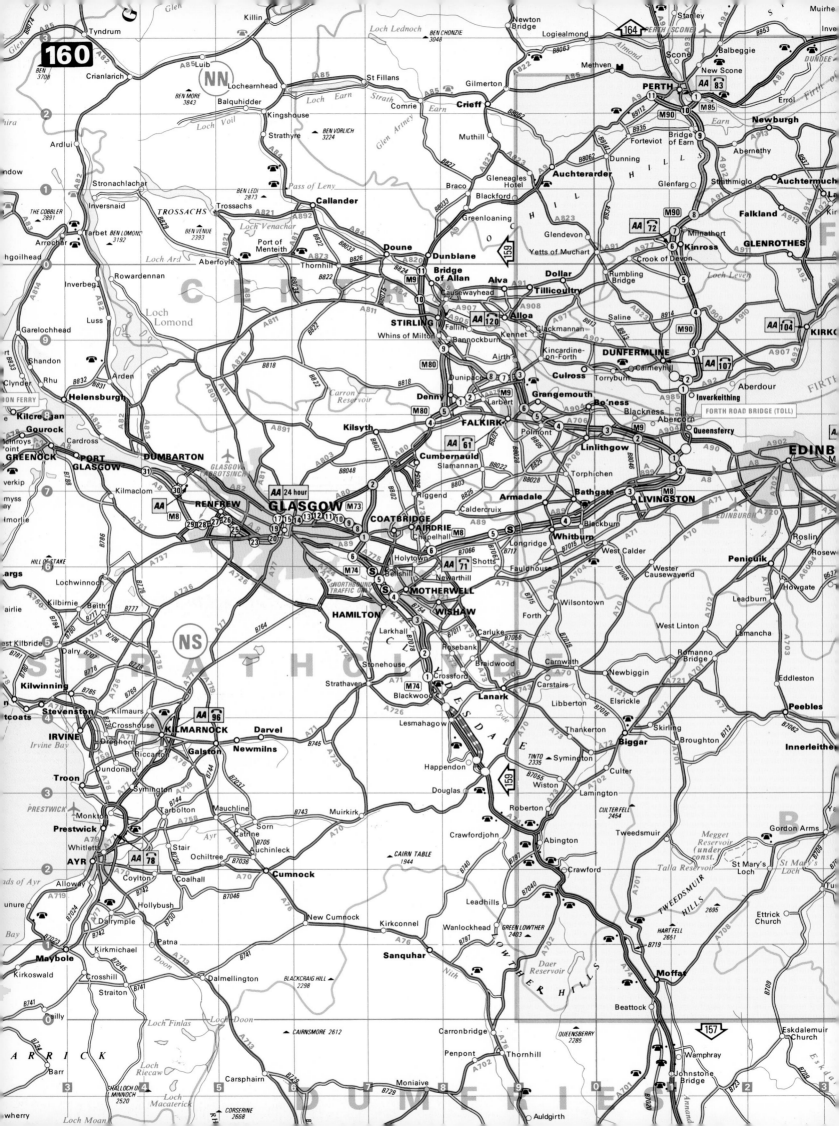

164

TAY ROAD BRIDGE (TOLL)

Scotland: narrow roads with
passing places.

UNDEE
Barry
Carnoustie
Monifieth
Broughty Ferry
Buddon Ness
Tayport
Newport-on-Tay
rmit
NO
St Andrews Bay
Leuchars
ny
Dairsie
Guard
Bridge
St Andrews
Ceres
Kingsbarns
Craigrothie
Fife Ness
Upper
Largo Ward
Crail
Largo
Kilrenny
Anstruther
Pittenweem
Lundin
Links
St Monans
Leven
Earlsferry
Elie

FORTH

North Berwick
TANTALLON CASTLE
Gullane
Whitekirk
Aberlady
East
Linton
Dunbar
Barns Ness
Longniddry
Haddington
FAST CASTLE
St Abb's Head
Macmerry
Cockburnspath
St Abbs
Pencaitland
Garvald
Coldingham
East Saltoun
Gifford
Kingside
Grantshouse
Eyemouth
Humbie
LAMMERMUIR HILLS
Cranshaws
Ayton
Blackshiels
Longformacus
Preston
Mordington
Oxton
Carfraemill
Duns
Chirnside
Westruther
Allanton
Berwick-upon-Tweed
Lauder
Greenlaw
Swinton
Norham
Tweedmouth
Stow
Gordon
Eccles
Ladykirk
VEHICLE CROSSING RESTRICTED TO
LIMITED PERIOD AT LOW TIDE
NU
NT
Hume
Coldstream
Ancroft
Beal
Holy I
Galashiels
Earlston
Birgham
Cornhill-
on-Tweed
Holy Island
Burrows Hole
Clovenfords
Smailholm
Ednam
Wark
Etal
Lowick
Bamburgh
MELROSE
Kelso
Sprouston
Ford
Milfield
Doddington
Belford
Sea Houses
Dryburgh
St Boswells
Roxburgh
Kirknewton
Warenford
Beadnell
Selkirk
Yetholm
Wooler
Chatton
Beadnell Bay
NEWARK CASTLE
Chillingham
Ettrickbridge
Lilliesleaf
Ancrum
Crailing
Morebattle
Embleton
Craster
THE CHEVIOT
2676
Eglingham
Denholm
Jedburgh
FERNIEHIRST
CASTLE
Longhoughton
Hawick
Powburn
Glanton
Alnwick
Boulmer
Roberton
River
Lesbury
Alnmouth
BRANXHOLME
CASTLE
Bonchester
Bridge
Aln
Warkworth
Stobs
Southdean
Carter Bar
Newton-on-
the-Moor
Teviothead
Byrness
Amble
Mosspaul
CALDCLEUGH
HEAD
Thropton
Rothbury
Longframlington
Felton
Broomhill
HERMITAGE CASTLE
Saughtree
Catcleugh
Reservoir
Rochester
Weldon Bridge
Red Row
Durridge Bay
132
Longhorsley
Causey
Park
Widdrington
Kielder
Otterburn
Elsdon
Newcastleton
Falstone
West Woodburn
Hartburn
ASHINGTON
Newbiggin-
by-the-Sea
Kielder Water
NORTHUMBERLAND
BORDERS
THE
BORDER
CHEVIOT HILLS

Western Dales and Solway Plain

112 miles

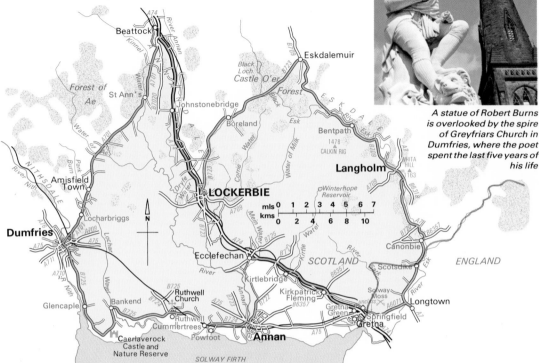

A statue of Robert Burns is overlooked by the spire of Greyfriars Church in Dumfries, where the poet spent the last five years of his life

LOCKERBIE
Lamb Hill in Lockerbie takes its name from the annual lamb fair which has been held here since 1680. Horse-trading was also an important part of life in Lockerbie for centuries, but although the settlement had always stood in a rich farming area, it was the arrival of road and rail transport which marked its growth into a town. Many local families grew rich on the China tea trade, and several fine mansions in the area survive as a reminder of this prosperity. Many of Lockerbie's buildings are constructed of red Permian sandstone from the nearby Corncockle Quarry, which is famous for its fossilized dinosaur footprints.

BEATTOCK
Beattock stands in hilly country on the Evan Water, in lovely upper Annandale. Close by are four prehistoric forts, and farther north along the Evan valley are the picturesque ruined towers of Blacklaw, Mellingshaw, and Raecleuch.

AMISFIELD TOWN
Amisfield Tower is the ancestral home of the Charteris family, who have been associated with the area since the 12th century. It was built in the 16th century and is one of the most beautiful buildings of its type in Scotland.

DUMFRIES
Towards the end of his life Robert Burns made his home in Dumfries, where he died in 1796. The house where he died, now called Burns House, is a museum in his honour. Not far away is St Michael's churchyard, where the poet, his wife and five sons are buried. The focal point of the town, however, is the 18th-century Midsteeple, comprising the old municipal buildings, courthouse and prison. The Dumfries Museum is housed in an 18th-century windmill in Church Street, and displays collections covering local history, archaeology, geology and natural history. In Old Bridge House is another museum where period rooms illustrate life in the past. The Old Bridge itself is the most famous of the five which cross the River Nith here.

CAERLAVEROCK CASTLE AND NATURE RESERVE
A fortified building has stood here since the early 13th century, but the triangular structure that now occupies the site dates mainly from the 15th century. In 1683 the interior was completely reconstructed, and the building has survived to the present day as a particularly fine example of a Renaissance mansion. The 6,200-acre estate is now a nature reserve with outstanding hide facilities and an observatory tower.

RUTHWELL CHURCH
The 18ft cross at Ruthwell church dates from the 8th century and is one of the most remarkable Dark Age monuments to have survived in Europe. This archaeological treasure is preserved in a special apse. It is heavily inscribed with early written phrases in the Northumbrian dialect.

ROUTE DIRECTIONS TOUR 41
Leave Lockerbie on the A74 (SP Glasgow) and continue for 13 miles, then turn left on to an unclassified road for Beattock. Turn left, and in 1 mile turn right on to the A701 (SP Dumfries). Continue through St Ann's and Amisfield Town to Dumfries. At a roundabout, take the Stranraer road, then turn left (SP Carlisle). At the end of the road turn left, then right (SP Glencaple) to continue along the B725 through Glencaple. In 3 miles pass Caerlaverock Castle, which lies ¼ mile to the right. Continue to Bankend and turn right (SP Ruthwell). After 4¾ miles turn right on to the B724. (In ½ mile an unclassified left turn offers a detour to Ruthwell church.) Continue along the B724 through Cummertrees, then in 3 miles join the A75 to enter Annan. Cross the River

Annan and at traffic lights turn left on to the B722 (SP Eaglesfield). In 2 miles turn left on to an unclassified road (SP Ecclefechan), then after 2½ miles cross the Mein Water and turn right to Ecclefechan. In the village turn right and continue to the A74 (SP Carlisle). Continue along the A74 and after 8 miles branch left (SP Gretna Green) to Springfield. (A short detour can be made here by turning right for Gretna and Gretna Green.) Continue along an unclassified road (SP Longtown), cross Solway Moss and in ¾ mile turn left on to the A6071 to Longtown. Return along the A6071, then turn right on to the A7 (SP Galashiels) to Canonbie and then Langholm. Leave on the B709 (SP Eskdalemuir) and go through Bentpath to Eskdalemuir. Turn left here on to the B723 (SP Lockerbie) for the return to Lockerbie.

ANNAN
This town on the north shore of the Solway thrives on fishing. Shrimps, which are canned here, are its most famous product. Once an important shipbuilding centre, where many famous tea-clippers were built, Annan is still busy with coastal shipping.

ECCLEFECHAN
In 1795 the famous essayist Thomas Carlyle was born in the local Arched House, which now contains a collection of his personal possessions.

GRETNA
For 100 years Gretna Hall and the smithy at Gretna Green were the first places over the Scottish border where English runaway lovers could be married without parental consent. Until 1940 the village blacksmith was able to perform the ceremony.

LONGTOWN
This village actually lies in England, but has a distinctly Scottish feel. To the north is Netherby Hall, made famous by the romantic elopement of the Graham heiress with Lochinvar in Sir Walter Scott's *Marmion*.

LANGHOLM
This angling resort and wool centre still holds its annual border-riding ceremony, which was instituted in the 19th century. A monument to General Sir John Malcolm stands on 1,163ft Whita Hill, which rises to the east.

ESKDALEMUIR
Situated at the northern end of lovely Eskdale, this hamlet lies in an area that abounds with prehistoric remains. The Eskdalemuir Observatory, which dates from 1908, lies 3 miles north.

The Old Blacksmith's Shop at Gretna Green is a popular tourist attraction

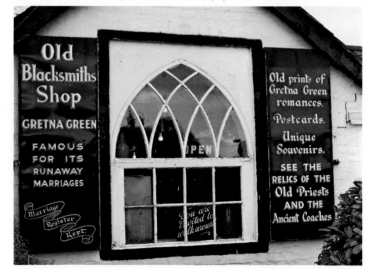

Wigtown Bay and Galloway

88 miles

KIRKCUDBRIGHT
This is an old Royal Burgh on the estuary of the River Dee, some of its streets unchanged since the 18th century when it was a lively and important port. Today, the charm of the ancient town attracts artists and craftsmen, who exhibit in one of the pretty whitewashed cottages beside the harbour. Dominating the port is the mass of McLellan's Castle, built in 1583. Two interesting museums are the E. A. Hornel Museum in Broughton House and the Stewartry Museum, which exhibits local antiquities.

GATEHOUSE OF FLEET
This town was the inspiration for Scott's otherwise fictitious town Kippletringan, in *Guy Mannering*. To the north-west the Water of Fleet runs through a beautiful glen, and to the south are the contrasting features of Fleet Bay and Fleet Forest.

CARDONESS CASTLE
This section of the drive follows one of the most beautiful roads in the south of Scotland. The picturesque ruins of the 15th-century tower house at Cardoness stand in a superb situation overlooking Fleet Bay, Murray's Isles, and the islands of Fleet.

CARSLUITH CASTLE
An unusual feature of this roofless 16th-century tower house is its L-shaped plan, brought about by the addition of a staircase wing in 1568.

NEWTON STEWART
In the 18th century this lovely Galloway market town was a centre for the weaving, spinning and carpet-making industries. Nowadays these local skills are turned to the production of mohair rugs and scarves. Between Newton Stewart and Minnigaff the River Cree is spanned by a fine granite bridge built in 1614 by John Rennie. Galloway Forest Park lies to the north.

MURRAY'S MONUMENT
This obelisk on 2,329ft Cairnsmore of Fleet commemorates Dr Alexander Murray, a local shepherd boy who became Professor of Oriental Languages at Edinburgh University. Near the monument a sparkling burn forms two waterfalls known as the Grey Mare's Tail.

NEW GALLOWAY
This noted angling centre on the River Ken is Scotland's smallest Royal Burgh. It received its charter in 1633. Kells churchyard, a little to the north of New Galloway, features the grave of a Covenanter who was shot in 1685.

15th-century Cardoness Castle stands on a commanding hilltop beside the Big Water of Fleet

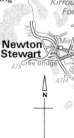

THREAVE CASTLE
Built in the 1360s by Archibald the Grim, Third Earl of Douglas, this castle is beautifully sited on an island in the River Dee. The locally forged and nationally famous Mons Meg cannon was used by James II to overcome the rebellious Douglas family here in 1445; it can now be seen in Edinburgh Castle. In 1640 the stronghold was captured by Covenanters, who sacked it and vandalized its interior.

THREAVE ESTATE
Threave Estate includes the house and grounds, and is the National Trust for Scotland's School of Practical Gardening. The house is not open to the public, but the Wildfowl Refuge and lovely gardens are. Visitors flock here in the spring to see the estate's vast and very beautiful display of daffodils.

CASTLE DOUGLAS
Once the commercial capital of its county, this pleasant old town is beautifully sited near the shores of Loch Carlingwark. There is a flourishing cattle market, where Ayrshire and Galloway cattle are sold. A fine park on the shores of the loch offers many amenities.

DALBEATTIE
In the 19th century the shiny grey granite of which this lovely place is built was shipped from quays on the Urr Water to all parts of the world. South of the town are the green ranks of Dalbeattie Forest, while 2½ miles north is the Mote of Urr – one of the finest Saxon fortifications in Britain.

PALNACKIE
This attractive whitewashed village stands on a creek of the Rough Firth, an inlet of the Solway Firth. About 1 mile south on an unclassified road is 16th-century Orchardton Tower, one of only two circular tower houses in the whole of Scotland.

Dundrennan's houses incorporate stonework from the ruined abbey there

DUNDRENNAN
Stone from the ruins of 12th-century Dundrennan Abbey was used to build many of the houses in this village. The foundation itself has sad associations with Mary Queen of Scots, for it was here that she spent her last night on Scottish soil before sailing from Port Mary to England and eventual imprisonment.

TOUR 42 ROUTE DIRECTIONS
Leave Kirkcudbright on the A755 via Bridge Street and cross the River Dee following signs for Gatehouse of Fleet. In 4½ miles turn left on to the A75 (SP Stranraer). Continue through Gatehouse of Fleet and past Cardoness Castle. Continue on the A75, passing Carsluith Castle on the left, and enter Creetown. Leave on the A75, and in 3½ miles go through Palnure, then in 4 miles, at a roundabout, take the third exit, the A714, to enter Newton Stewart. Leave Newton Stewart following signs for New Galloway, A712, cross the Cree Bridge, and enter Minnigaff. Drive for 1 mile beyond the village and turn left on to the A712 (SP New Galloway). Continue past Murray's Monument and in 4½ miles pass Clatteringshaws Loch, then in 6 miles turn right on to the A762 into New Galloway. Continue on the A762 (SP Kirkcudbright), pass Loch Ken and continue through Laurieston to Ringford. At Ringford turn left on to the A75 (SP Dumfries). In 4 miles, shortly after crossing the River Dee, pass a track that leads left to Threave Castle. Continue along the A75 towards Castle Douglas. (Before reaching the town a detour can be made by taking an unclassified right turn to Threave Estate.) On the main route, continue to Castle Douglas. Leave on the A745 (SP Dalbeattie), and in 5 miles join the A711. Cross the Urr Water to reach Dalbeattie. Return along the A711, re-cross the Urr Water, then turn left and continue along the A711, passing through Palnackie, Auchencairn and Dundrennan to complete the return journey to Kirkcudbright.

Kintyre

74 miles

TARBERT
This port on the east coast of Kintyre is built on the isthmus between East and West Loch Tarbert. The harbour is popular with yachts en route for the Crinan Canal, and is a stopping place for travellers on the way to the isles of Islay, Jura and Gigha or south Kintyre and the Clyde. The south quay is the centre of the town's fishing industry, and all around the harbour stand attractive whitewashed fishermen's cottages. The remains of Tarbert Castle stand just outside the town.

KENNACRAIG
Situated on beautiful West Loch Tarbert, Kennacraig is a terminus for the car ferries that operate between the mainland and the islands of Islay and Jura. It is also a good base from which to explore the coast of the loch.

TAYINLOAN
A vehicle ferry crosses the Sound of Gigha from here to the island of Gigha.

ISLE OF GIGHA
Although only 6 miles long by 1½ miles wide, this flat little island off the Kintyre coast has an impressive rocky shoreline and several interesting features. Among these is Achamore House, which dates from 1884 and contains various works of art and 18th-century English furniture. The gardens were the inspiration of Sir James Horlick, who gave them to the National Trust. They seem to justify Gigha's claim to be the most fertile of all the Scottish islands. High belts of trees protect azaleas, rhododendrons, hydrangeas and a host of ornamental shrubs, from the keen Atlantic winds.

CAMPBELTOWN
Fishing and farming are the chief concerns of Campbeltown, which was founded in James IV's reign in an attempt to bring civilization to the natives. It was created a Royal Burgh in 1700. Although not a pretty town, it has plenty of life, not being dependent on summer visitors. Its recreational facilities include golf, music, drama, tennis and fishing. The museum in Hall Street displays exhibits on local fauna and flora, fishing and archaeology.

The most exposed areas of the Kintyre peninsula receive the full force of Atlantic gales and are treeless peat moss

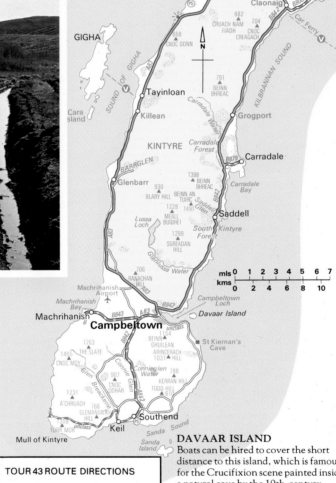

TOUR 43 ROUTE DIRECTIONS

Leave Tarbert on the A83 (SP Campbeltown) and drive to Kennacraig. Continue on the A83 through Tayinloan, Killean and Glenbarr to Campbeltown. (Two detours can be made from Campbeltown. To visit Machrihanish leave on the A83 southbound, then join the B843 and drive 5½ miles to Machrihanish. To visit the Mull of Kintyre, leave by the same road and later take the B842 and drive south to Southend. From here follow a narrow and hilly unclassified road through Keil to the Mull of Kintyre.)
  On the main route, leave Campbeltown with the B842 northbound and continue through Saddell. (Later reach the B879 right turn, which offers a detour to Carradale.) The main route continues on the B842 through Grogport and Claonaig. (A detour can be made to Skipness by keeping forward on to the B8001 in Claonaig.) On the main tour leave Claonaig, turn left on to the B8001 then at Kennacraig turn right on to the A83 to return to Tarbert.

DAVAAR ISLAND
Boats can be hired to cover the short distance to this island, which is famous for the Crucifixion scene painted inside a natural cave by the 19th-century artist Archibald Mackinnon. It was designed so that the only illumination required is a shaft of light from a hole in the rock. It was retouched by a local artist in the mid 1950s.

MACHRIHANISH
One of the main attractions in this former salt-producing village is its beach, which offers 3½ miles of sand on an otherwise rocky coast. Among the resort developments prompted by this natural asset is an excellent golf course that was laid out in 1876. Services from the nearby airport link with Glasgow and the isle of Islay.

SOUTHEND
This small resort offers two sandy beaches facing Sanda Island across the narrow waters of Sanda Sound. Pleasantly isolated coastline is accessible by a short walk in either direction.

Decorative headstones stand in the graveyard of the ruined chapel at Skipness

KEIL
Tradition has it that a ruined chapel here marks the place where St Columba landed to begin his 6th-century mission in Scotland. He and his disciples were pledged to convert the Picts to Christianity; local evidence suggests that the site was a pagan place of sanctity long before the chapel was built. The impressions of two right feet on a flat stone, known as St Columba's Footprints, may have been carved to mark the place where pagan chiefs took their initiation vows.

MULL OF KINTYRE
The southernmost tip of the peninsula and Scotland's closest point to the Irish coast, this wild headland offers some remarkable views. Rathlin Island rises from the sea a mere 12 miles away, and behind it is the dark line of the Northern Irish coast. An early lighthouse built near the South Point in 1788 was later remodelled by Robert Stephenson.

SADDELL
This village on Kintyre's rocky east coast is famous for the ruins of Saddell Abbey. Set in woodland planted with rhododendrons, it is thought to have been founded in 1160 by Somerled, Lord of the Isles. At the head of the bay is Saddell Castle, a battlemented tower built in the 16th century.

CARRADALE
Situated opposite the Isle of Arran on the east coast of the peninsula, this small resort stands on a sheltered bay and has a fishing harbour. Close to the pier are the remains of Aird Castle, and the narrow spit of Carradale Point carries an oval vitrified fort.

SKIPNESS
Features of this charming little place include the remains of an ancient chapel and a large 13th-century castle. From Skipness views extend seaward across the Sound of Bute to Arran.

The Howe of Fife
109 miles

ST ANDREWS
A splendid city, one of the most beautiful towns in Scotland and a favourite resort, St Andrews boasts a long, distinguished history, a university, and ruins of both a castle and a cathedral. The castle was built on a promontory in the 12th century, and rebuilt in the 14th century. It was notorious for its Bottle Dungeon, cut from solid rock. It is said that no-one ever came out alive. The cathedral was Scotland's largest and finest until 1559, when Reformers inspired by John Knox destroyed it. Later, Cromwell gave permission for it to be used as a quarry, and today many stones from it can be seen in the fabric of the town's houses. Near the ruins is the tower of St Rule's, the church in which the relics of St Andrew were kept while the cathedral was being built. The university is also of great antiquity. It was founded in 1412 as Scotland's first university. The oldest buildings include a 17th-century library.

THE ROYAL AND ANCIENT GOLF CLUB
Written records of the Old Course, which is the oldest in the world, date back to the 15th century. The Royal and Ancient was founded in 1754 and is the ruling authority on the game throughout the world.

TAYPORT
This one-time ferry port has a good church that was rebuilt in the 18th century. Some 47 acres of local countryside now form the Tentsmuir Nature Reserve.

WORMIT
The two-mile railway bridge across the Tay here was built in 1885 to replace the famous one that collapsed, with great loss of life, during gales in 1879.

HILL OF TARVIT
Standing in spacious grounds overlooking the Howe of Fife, this fine mansion contains collections of furniture, paintings, tapestries and porcelain. It occupies the site of a 17th-century house and is now partly in use as a nursing home.

CUPAR
Cupar is a Royal Burgh and the market centre for the fertile Howe of Fife. Its parish church has a good 15th-century tower, and the mercat cross in the town is picturesquely adorned with the figure of a unicorn.

NEWBURGH
Situated on the south shore of the attractive Firth of Tay, this small Royal Burgh is near the ancient remains of Lindores Abbey. Close to the water is 18th-century Mugdrum House, opposite a tiny island which preserves the 1,000-year-old Mugdrum Cross.

ABERNETHY
One of the main features of this one-time Pictish capital is the remarkable 12th-century round tower of its parish church. This type of construction is more commonly found in Ireland, and this example is one of only two in Scotland.

LOCH LEVEN
Romance and beauty mingle with an interesting history to make the very special atmosphere which surrounds Loch Leven. Its 14th- or 15th-century castle, set on an island, was the prison of Mary Queen of Scots until she made a sensational escape. The loch is often the venue for fishing competitions, and in winter its ice provides ideal conditions for curling.

FALKLAND
Old weavers' cottages and charming cobbled streets characterize this lovely little Royal Burgh, but it is chiefly known for the historic Falkland Palace. This was a favourite seat of the Scottish Court from the reign of James V, who made considerable improvements to the building before his death in 1542.

ELIE AND EARLSFERRY
Sailing, fishing and fine sandy beaches are offered by these twin resorts. They lie between Chapel Ness and Elie Ness, and are known for their good golf courses.

ST MONANS
Old houses cluster near the water's edge in this lovely little fishing port, and the beautiful Old Kirk of St Monance stands almost on the foreshore. This lovely old foundation dates from the 14th century but was restored in 1828.

PITTENWEEM
The ruined priory in this picturesque little Royal Burgh dates back to the 12th century and the tower of the parish church is dated 1592.

CRAIL
The oldest Royal Burgh in the East Neuk district, this picturesque fishing town was once the haunt of smugglers. A curious weather vane depicting a salmon tops the 16th-century Tolbooth.

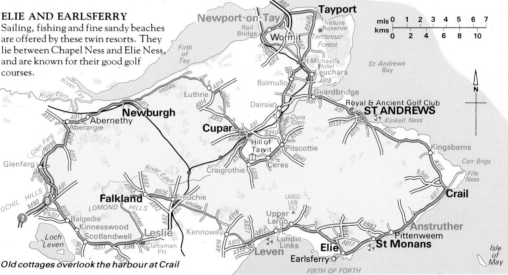

Old cottages overlook the harbour at Crail

TOUR 44 ROUTE DIRECTIONS
Leave St Andrews on the A91 (SP Tay Bridge) and pass the Royal and Ancient Golf Club before reaching Guardbridge. Turn right on to the A919 to reach Leuchars, then in 1¼ miles by the St Michael's Hotel turn right on to the B945 for Tayport. Leave Tayport on the B946, continuing through Newport-on-Tay and Wormit. Shortly branch left (SP St Andrews), and in 1 mile, at a roundabout, take the second exit, then in 1½ miles turn right on to the A92 to return to the St Michael's Hotel. Meet crossroads and turn right (SP Cupar), continue through Balmullo then in 2 miles join the A91 to enter Dairsie. Turn left (SP Pitscottie), cross the River Eden, then turn right and continue to Pitscottie. Turn left and immediately right on to the B939 (SP Kirkcaldy) and continue through Ceres to Craigrothie, then turn right on to the A916, which passes the entrance to Hill of Tarvit Mansion, then join the A92 for Cupar. Leave Cupar on the A91 (SP Kincardine) then turn right on to the A913 (SP Perth). In 1¾ miles turn right (SP Luthrie). At a junction with the A914 turn left, then in ½ mile turn right for Luthrie. After a further 1 mile bear left, meet a T-junction and turn left. At the junction with the A913, turn right into Newburgh. Continue on the A913 to Abernethy, then past Aberargie turn left on to the A912. In 2 miles bear right on to the B996. Drive through Glen Farg, then turn right on to the B996 to Glenfarg village. In 2½ miles, turn right on to the A91, then left on to the B919 (SP Glenrothes). In 1¾ miles reach Balgedie and join the A911 for Kinnesswood and Scotlandwell. Turn left and drive to Leslie, and at the Clansman pub turn left to Falkland. At a T-junction in Falkland turn right on to the A912, then in ¼ mile turn left on to the B936 (SP Freuchie). Keep forward at the crossroads in Freuchie, then turn right on to the A92 and immediately left (SP Kennoway). In 4½ miles turn left into Kennoway. Meet a main road and turn right, then immediately left (SP Leven) and continue to the outskirts of Leven. Turn left on to the A915 (SP St Andrews) and go past Lundin Links and through Upper Largo. Follow the A921 (SP Crail) and in 2½ miles turn right on to the A917 for Elie. Continue on the A917 (SP Anstruther), passing St Monans, then drive through Pittenweem and Anstruther to Crail. Return to St Andrews on the A918.

DUNDEE

Dundee has been a Royal Burgh since 1190, and several battles for Scottish Independence have been fought here over the centuries. Cowgate Port is the only surviving fragment of the town walls, and the 15th-century Old Steeple of St Mary is all that remains of the great medieval church which stood here. In Camperdown House there is a fascinating golf museum, and the City Museum and Art Gallery and Barrack Street Shipping and Industrial Museum are both worth a visit. Dundee Law, once a volcano, is the highest point in the city, and offers excellent views of the town. In the past shipbuilding and whaling were the most important industries here. The soil around Dundee is particularly good for growing fruit, giving rise to the city's reputation for fine preserves. Associated with this is the famous Dundee Marmalade, which was first made in 1797 and is still enjoyed on breakfast tables all over the world.

CARNOUSTIE

As well as being a flourishing industrial area, Carnoustie is a popular holiday resort with sandy beaches and a championship golf course that is considered one of the best in the world. The deep dunes of Barry Links offer lovely coastal walks south to the sandy promontory of Buddon Ness.

ARBROATH

This is the home of the famous 'smokies', haddock smoked over an oak fire, a process which lends a mouth-watering smell to the town's streets. A popular resort with safe bathing, Arbroath has played an important role in Scottish history, for it was here, at Arbroath Abbey, that Robert the Bruce signed Scotland's Declaration of Independence in 1302. The ruins of the abbey include a circular window, known as 'the O of Arbroath', which was once lit as a guide to seamen.

ST VIGEANS

One of the finest collections of early Christian and medieval memorial stones in Scotland is housed in St Vigeans' Cottage Museum. Many of these beautiful monuments take the form of Celtic crosses, often carved with elaborate interlacing decorations on the front and groups of animals, figures and symbols on the back.

AUCHMITHIE

Perched on a rocky sandstone cliff 150ft above a sandy beach, this precarious and exceptionally picturesque little fishing community can trace its history back to the 11th century. The cliffs extend north-east to impressive Red Head and Lang Craig, which overlook Lunan Bay. Dickmont's Den and the Forbidden Cave are two notable examples of the many caves in the area.

INVERKEILOR

The main feature of this tiny place is its isolation from the rush of 20th-century life. Remarkable 'singing sands', whose grains vibrate against each other when walked on, lie to the east, and also nearby is 15th-century Ethie Castle.

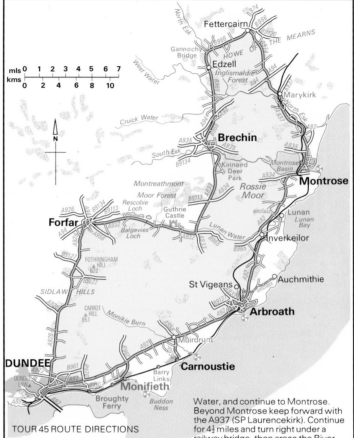

TOUR 45 ROUTE DIRECTIONS

Leave Dundee on the A92 (SP Aberdeen) and drive to Muirdrum. (A detour can be made here by turning right on to the A930 to reach Carnoustie in 2 miles.) Continue on the A92, and in 5 miles turn right under a railway bridge to enter Arbroath. Leave Arbroath on the A92. (Just north of the town a detour can be made by taking an unclassified left turn to St Vigeans.) Continue on the A92. (In ¾ mile another detour can be made by turning right on to an unclassified road for Auchmithie.) On the main route, continue on the A92 through Inverkeilor, cross the Lunan Water, and continue to Montrose. Beyond Montrose keep forward with the A937 (SP Laurencekirk). Continue for 4¼ miles and turn right under a railway bridge, then cross the River North Esk to reach Marykirk. Turn left on to the B974 (SP Fettercairn), reach a junction with the A94, then turn right and left to stay on the B974. In 3¼ miles turn right to reach Fettercairn. Leave Fettercairn and turn left on to the B966 (SP Edzell) to reach Edzell. Continue for 3½ miles, then turn right on to the A94 (SP Perth) and in ¼ mile turn left to continue along the B966 to Brechin. Leave Brechin on the A933 (SP Arbroath) then in 7 miles meet the A932 and turn right (SP Forfar). Continue to Forfar. Leave Forfar on the A929 (SP Dundee) for the return to Dundee.

The route crosses the North Esk at Gannochy, with views of lovely Glen Esk

Brechin's slender round church tower is of a kind usually seen in Ireland

MONTROSE

Here the South Esk River forms a two-square-mile tidal lagoon known as the Montrose Basin, which is popular with many different species of wader all the year round and is a wintering place for pink-footed geese. The town itself is a pleasant market and holiday centre popular with sailors, golfers, and anglers. A fine sandy beach is complemented by a grassy belt that runs parallel to the spacious High Street and is known as The Links. Leading from the High Street to the town's charming old heart are narrow, twisting 18th-century closes lined by quaint old houses.

FETTERCAIRN

Set among woods and fields at the edge of the Howe of the Mearns, this 18th-century village boasts a great 19th-century royal arch that was built to commemorate an incognito visit made by Queen Victoria and Prince Albert. The village square has a 17th-century cross which is notched to show the length of the Scottish ell, a measurement that is roughly the same as the English yard.

EDZELL

From the south this little inland resort is approached through a fine 19th-century arch raised to the memory of the Thirteenth Earl of Dalhousie. Early 16th-century Edzell Castle lies to the west of the main village, and was visited by Mary Queen of Scots.

BRECHIN

The old red sandstone town of Brechin is built on the steep banks of the South Esk River. Adjoining the cathedral is one of two round church towers in Scotland. It dates from the 10th or 11th centuries. It is 87ft high, and was used as a watchtower and place of refuge.

FORFAR

Malcolm III is thought to have held a parliament here in the fertile Vale of Strathmore in 1057, and although his castle was destroyed, the site is marked by a 17th-century octagonal turret, once the town cross. Inside the town hall designed by William Playfair is the Forfar bridle – an iron gag used to silence those about to be executed in medieval days.

In the Heart of the Grampians

84 miles

PITLOCHRY
In a beautiful setting of lochs, rivers, mountains and woods, Pitlochry has become a popular holiday resort, and also supports a famous tweed mill and two distilleries. An interesting attraction at nearby Pitlochry Dam is the fish ladder and observation point, where visitors can watch salmon in spring and early summer on their way to spawn in the upper reaches of the river. In recent years Pitlochry has become known for its summer festival season, when plays and concerts are staged in the modern Pitlochry Festival Theatre.

LINN OF TUMMEL
Once known as the Falls of Tummel, the Linn of Tummel is a well-known feature where running water lends its own particular enchantment to lovely countryside. Nearby Queen's View is named in memory of a visit by Queen Victoria.

FORTINGALL
Old thatched cottages and the attractive River Lyon are the main scenic features of this lovely little village, which is separated from the north end of Loch Tay by the wooded bulk of Drummond Hill. A huge yew standing in the local churchyard is thought to be the oldest living tree in Britain. Its girth was measured at 56ft in 1772, and the village tends its one remaining live stem with great care. Earthworks to the south-west of the village are often referred to as the Roman outpost of *Praetorium*, but they are more likely to have survived from a medieval fortified homestead.

INNERWICK
Isolated amongst the picturesque hills of Glen Lyon, this lonely village has a church which preserves an ancient bell.

BRIDGE OF BALGIE
The attractive Bridge of Balgie is situated on the Glen Lyon road at a point where it meets the steep (1 in 6) mountain road to Killin.

BEN LAWERS
At 3,984ft this grand old mountain of the Breadalbane district is the highest for many miles around. About 8,000 acres of its flanks and summit are protected by the National Trust for Scotland, and the abnormally large number of Alpine plant species growing on its lower slopes makes it an area of considerable scientific interest. Views from the summit, which can be reached quite easily, extend over the whole of the Breadalbane country and much of the Grampian range.

LOCH TAY
Overlooked at its western end by Ben Lawers and surrounded on all sides by breathtaking scenery, this superb loch was a favourite place of the poet Sir Walter Scott. He composed a beautiful word picture that captures the essence of its loveliness in his poem *The Fair Maid of Perth*. Below Ben Lawers the 120-mile-long River Tay flows towards Aberfeldy, carrying the greatest volume of water of any British river and providing an inland route for the famous Tay salmon.

The River Tay leaves Loch Tay at Kenmore, and is spanned by an elegant bridge of 1774

Finlarig Castle, near Killin, was once a stronghold of the Clan Campbell

TOUR 46 ROUTE DIRECTIONS

Leave Pitlochry on the Perth road and in ½ mile turn right (SP Festival Theatre). Cross the New Aldour Bridge and turn right, then in ½ mile turn right on to the A9. In ½ mile turn right again on to the unclassified Foss Road. Continue alongside Loch Faskally to reach the Linn of Tummel. Continue along the south bank of the River Tummel and Loch Tummel, then after 12 miles turn left on to the B846 (SP Aberfeldy) to pass through White Bridge. Continue on the B846 to reach the Coshieville Hotel. Turn right on to an unclassified road and continue to Fortingall, then in ½ mile turn right (SP Glen Lyon) and drive through Glen Lyon to Innerwick. Continue for 1 mile, then turn left towards Loch Tay. Cross the Bridge of Balgie, continue past Ben Lawers Mountain Visitor Centre, then after 2 miles turn right to join the A827 and drive along the north side of Loch Tay to Killin. At the end of Killin cross the River Dochart, then keep right and

take the next turning left on to an unclassified road (SP Ardeonaig). Continue through Ardeonaig and Acharn, and in 1½ miles turn right on to the A827 (SP Aberfeldy). To the left of the route at this point is Kenmore. Continue to Aberfeldy. At Aberfeldy turn left on to the B846 (SP Kinloch Rannoch), cross Wade's bridge and continue to Weem. Turn right on to an unclassified road (SP Strathtay) and follow the north bank of the river to Strathtay. (A detour can be made from Strathtay by turning right across the Tay to Grandtully.) On the main route, continue for 1½ miles and turn left to join the A827 (SP Ballinluig). Continue to Logierait and turn left on to an unclassified road (SP Dunfallandy). In 4 miles turn right across the New Aldour Bridge and turn left for the return to Pitlochry.

KILLIN
During spring and summer this all-year-round resort offers fishing and walking, while in the winter months it provides après-ski facilities for people who come to ski on the slopes of Ben Lawers. The town is situated at the eastern end of mountain-encircled Glen Lochay, on the excellent game-fishing rivers Dochart and Lochay. One of two small islands near Dochart Bridge is the traditional burial ground of the Clan MacNab, and their 17th-century seat, Kinnell House, faces the village from the south side of the river. This mansion later came into the hands of the Breadalbane family. In its grounds is a well-defined circle of standing stones. Just north of Killin is ruined Finlarig Castle, a one-time Campbell stronghold described by Scott in *The Fair Maid of Perth*.

KENMORE
Robert Burns admired the lovely views from an 18th-century bridge that spans the Tay here where the river leaves Loch Tay, and set his impressions down in verse. This little snippet of local history is recorded in the parlour of the hotel, a venerable establishment first licensed over 400 years ago. William and Dorothy Wordsworth left their beloved Lake District long enough to visit Kenmore, and nowadays the village is a charming and popular resort. Nearby, in a bend of the River Tay, stands 19th-century Taymouth Castle. Once the seat of the Breadalbanes, it was visited by Queen Victoria in 1842 and now houses a school.

ABERFELDY
A five-arched bridge that spans the River Tay in this little market town and touring centre was built by General Wade in 1733. The General built roads and bridges all over Scotland after the Rising of 1715, so that troops could be rushed to trouble spots with the minimum loss of time. Of all his works, this bridge at Aberfeldy is thought to be among the finest still standing.

WEEM
Weem Hotel, said to date back to 1527, displays a sign commemorating a visit by General Wade in 1733. Menzies Castle stands in fine grounds just west of the village, and monuments to the Menzies can be seen in the local church. This stronghold was the clan's chief seat. Overlooking the village is the 800ft viewpoint of the Rock of Weem.

GRANDTULLY
Grandtully Castle dates from the 16th century and is the ancestral home of the Stewarts of Innermeath. Canoe slaloms are held in the village, whose name is pronounced 'Grantly'.

LOGIERAIT
Interesting sculptured stones can be seen in the churchyard here, together with reminders of the macabre body-snatching exploits of Burke and Hare in the shape of several mortesafes. These were once placed over new graves and locked in order to prevent this gruesome crime, which was once common in Britain.

The Isle of Skye

142 miles

The gaunt ruin of Caisteal Maol overlooks Kyleakin's busy little harbour

KYLE OF LOCHALSH
This busy fishing and shipping village at the western end of Loch Alsh is best known as the main ferry port for Skye. The island lies a few hundred yards away, across the waters of Kyle Akin, and the crossing takes only a few minutes.

KYLEAKIN
Ruined Caisteal Maol stands on the shore a little to the east of this island port. It is thought that its small Highland keep may have been built by the daughter of a Norwegian king, but it is known to have served for centuries as a lookout post and fortress against Norse raiders. During most of this time it was a stronghold of the Mackinnons of Strath.

BROADFORD
Broadford is a convenient touring centre for south Skye. It stands by Broadford Bay on a junction of roads from the ferry ports of Armadale, Kylerhea, and Kyleakin, and is overlooked by the granite screes of the Red Hills. Prominent in the range is 2,400ft Beinn na Caillich, the site of the largest hill cairn in Scotland.

CUILLIN HILLS
Unrivalled for scenic splendour anywhere in Britain, the Black and Red Cuillins are the most famous landscape features of this outstanding island. A six-mile arc of black peaks, 15 of which exceed 3,000ft in height, curves across the south-west part of the island as the Black Cuillin range; on the other side of Glen Sligachan, in spectacular contrast to its jagged neighbours, are the softly rounded summits and glowing pink granite of the Red Cuillins.

SLIGACHAN
Well known for its salmon and sea trout, this hamlet stands on the River Sligachan near the head of the loch of the same name. The U-shaped glacial valley of Glen Sligachan extends south into the Black Cuillins, with the 3,167ft peak of Sgurr nan Gillean prominent to the left. Several high peaks and spectacular Loch Coruisk can be reached via a path through the glen.

PORTREE
The capital of the island, Portree is the hub of Skye's road system and makes a fine touring centre. Its harbour lies on Portree Bay, which is sheltered by high cliffs. Steamers leave from here for the lovely wooded island of Raasay. James V visited Portree in 1540, and the little port has associations with Bonnie Prince Charlie, who hid for four days on Skye.

THE STORR
This ten-mile backbone of rock extends all along Skye's wild Trotternish peninsula. It is dominated by the 2,360ft Storr Plateau, and its most distinctive feature is perhaps the Old Man of Storr, a slim pinnacle of rock rising to 160ft.

QUIRAING
This strange wilderness of rocks is one of the most peculiar sights on Skye. It is a remarkable group of stone stacks and pinnacles bearing such descriptive names as Needle Rock, the Table, and the Prison, and including a grassy natural amphitheatre and a rugged group known as Leac nan Fionn.

FLODIGARRY
Flora Macdonald, known for her part in Bonnie Prince Charlie's escape after Culloden, spent the early years of her marriage here.

DUNTULM
Crumbling Duntulm Castle dates from the 15th century and was once the seat of the Macdonalds of Sleat and Trotternish. A groove has been worn into the rock on the shore below the castle by the keels of the Macdonald galleys.

SKYE COTTAGE MUSEUM AND FLORA MACDONALD MONUMENT
Traditional Highland furniture and relics from the island's past can be seen in a well-restored Black House here. This type of dwelling was traditional in the islands, though few good examples now survive. Close by is the old burial ground of the Macdonalds, Martins, Macarthurs and Nicolsons. In 1790 Flora Macdonald was buried here, wrapped in a sheet in which Bonnie Prince Charlie had slept at Kingsbridge. Over her grave is a great Iona cross inscribed by Dr Johnson.

UIG
Situated on a fine bay, this picturesque little hamlet of scattered crofts faces across Loch Snizort and its islands to the Vaternish peninsula. The steamer pier is used by car ferries to the Outer Hebrides. In 1746 Flora Macdonald and Bonnie Prince Charlie landed here after a much more difficult and dangerous voyage from those islands.

DUNVEGAN
Until 1748 the only entrance to the massive pile of moated Dunvegan Castle was by a sea gate. Seat of the Macleod chiefs, it dates from the 16th to 19th centuries and is claimed to be the oldest continuously inhabited castle in Scotland. Views from the ramparts extend across island-studded Dunvegan Loch to the distant ranges of Harris. Its greatest treasure is a fragment of silk which is known as the fairy flag and was probably woven on the Island of Rhodes in the 7th century.

DUN BEAG
Extensive remains of a 2,000-year-old Pictish broch stand here. Once a 40ft look-out post and refuge, the ruins include 12ft-thick walls, several rooms and parts of a stone staircase.

CARBOST
The well-known Talisker Whisky Distillery is sited here, on the west shores of Loch Harport.

PORT-NA-LONG
This tiny weaving village has become famous for Harris Tweed.

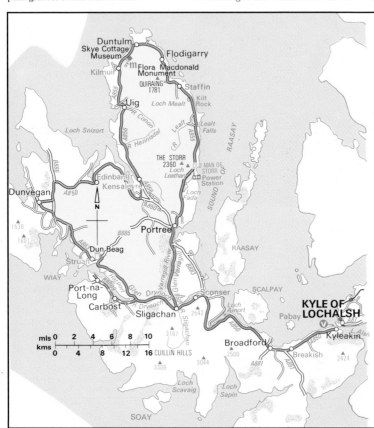

TOUR 47 ROUTE DIRECTIONS

Take the Skye ferry from Kyle of Lochalsh to Kyleakin. Drive along the A850 and pass through Breakish to reach Broadford. Continue towards Portree past the Cuillin Hills, and go through Sconser and Sligachan to Portree. Turn right on to the A855, and pass the reservoirs of Loch Fada and Loch Leathan, on the right, with the precipices of the Storr on the left. Continue through Staffin on the A855, passing the Quiraing, to Flodigarry and Duntulm. Continue along the coast road to Flora Macdonald's burial place and the Skye Cottage Museum. Go through Kilmuir and down Idrigill Hill, and keep left on to the A856 to Uig. Continue to Kensaleyre on the shore of Loch Eyre, and in another ½ mile turn right on to the B8036. After another 1½ miles, at a T-junction, turn right on to the A850 to follow the shores of Loch Snizort Beag and Loch Greshornish to Edinbane and Dunvegan, with fine views of the Outer Hebrides.

From Dunvegan take the A863 (SP Sligachan), which affords good views of the Cuillins ahead, and on the approach to Struan, pass Dun Beag on the left. Cross high ground above Loch Harport and descend to Glen Drynoch. (A detour can be made from the main route here by turning right on to the B8009 and driving first to Carbost, then to Port-na-Long.) On the main route continue to Sligachan and turn right on to the A850 for the return to Kyleakin, where the ferry is taken back to Kyle of Lochalsh on the mainland.

Around Loch Ness
119 miles

A backdrop of distant mountains adds beauty to this peaceful stretch of Glen Moriston

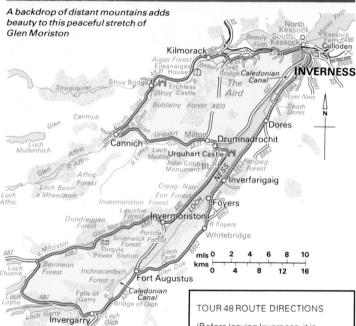

INVERNESS
Standing beside the broad waters of the River Ness, this attractive and historic town is the unofficial capital of the Highlands. It is the focal point of the Highland road system, and is now served by a modern airport. In Victorian times, when exploring the Highlands became a fashionable and popular pastime, a steamer service ran up the east coast to Inverness. Although the present Inverness Castle is Victorian, it stands on the site of the first stone castle here, in which Macbeth is thought to have lived. The castle overlooks a statue of Flora Macdonald who helped Bonnie Prince Charlie to escape after the Battle of Culloden. A clock-tower is all that remains of a fort built by Cromwell beside the River Ness. Abertarff House, one of the oldest houses in the city, has an ancient spiral staircase, and is the headquarters of the Highland Association, which promotes the Gaelic language and culture. The Town House is famous as the place where Lloyd George called the only cabinet meeting to be held outside London, in 1921.

CULLODEN
In 1746 the last battle to be fought in the United Kingdom took place here between Bonnie Prince Charlie's Jacobites and a Hanoverian army under the Duke of Cumberland. The Prince was defeated after 40 minutes by sheer weight of numbers, and subsequent atrocities earned the English leader the title Butcher Cumberland. Culloden Moor has altered since those bloody days. A plantation of new trees partly screens it from view, a road cuts through the battlefield itself, and a huge memorial cairn marks the site where so many men died. There is a museum and information centre in Old Leanach Farmhouse, which stood here while the battle raged around it.

A memorial cairn on Culloden Moor commemorates the famous battle

CALEDONIAN CANAL
Created by the famous Scottish engineer Thomas Telford in the early 19th century to provide a link between the Irish Sea and the North Sea, this 60½-mile waterway uses 22 miles of canal to link several lochs and virtually splits Scotland in two. Without it, the sailing boats of the day would have had to risk the often stormy passage round Cape Wrath.

KILMORACK
South-east of this village is 19th-century Beaufort Castle, seat of the Chief of Clan Fraser. Nearby are the ruins of an earlier stronghold. Although the castle is not open to the public, it can be seen from public paths that cross the Beauly River.

CANNICH
Cannich is a charming stone-built Highland village in a beautiful woodland setting at the south end of Strath Glass.

DRUMNADROCHIT
Situated on the River Enrick and the west side of Loch Ness, this village is a popular centre for walking, angling, climbing, and pony-trekking.

URQUHART CASTLE
Possibly built by the Lord of the Isles, ruined Urquhart Castle overlooks Loch Ness from a lonely promontory and is one of the largest castles in Scotland. It dates from the 14th century, and was largely destroyed before the 1715 Rising. Many sightings of the Loch Ness Monster have been reported from this part of the loch.

LOCH NESS
One of a chain of lochs connected by the Caledonian Canal in the Great Glen, Loch Ness extends from Inverness to Fort Augustus and in places is over 700ft deep. It is world-famous as the reported home of the Loch Ness Monster, or 'Nessie', as it has become known, and is occasionally kept under surveillance by teams from various scientific foundations. Sightings of the creature have been reported since the 7th century, but these have swelled from a trickle to a flood since the road along the wooded west shore was opened in 1933.

INVERMORISTON
This small town at the east end of Glen Moriston faces Loch Ness and is bordered to the north by the Hills of Invermoriston.

INVERGARRY
South of this little hamlet, on the shores of Loch Oich, are the impressive ruins of Invergarry Castle. It was once the seat of the MacDonells of Glengarry and replaced castles destroyed in 1654 and 1689. Bonnie Prince Charlie stayed here before and after the Battle of Culloden, and the Duke of Cumberland had the building burned in reprisal.

FORT AUGUSTUS
Wooded hill country surrounds this hamlet, which stands at the south-west end of Loch Ness in the Great Glen. It takes its name from a Hanoverian outpost that was built against the Jacobite Highlanders after the first Rising in 1715. General Wade built the first fort in 1730 and it was named after William Augustus, the Duke of Cumberland, who was later to become known as the Butcher of Culloden. In the second Rising of 1745 the Highlanders actually captured the fort and managed to hold it until the Prince's defeat at Culloden marked the end of the Jacobite cause. The Great Glen Exhibition in Fort Augustus relates the history and traditions of the area.

FOYERS
This village on the eastern shores of Loch Ness is best known for the beautiful Falls of Foyers. The uppermost of these drops 30ft and the lower 90ft, but their scenic impact was considerably reduced when they were starved of water by the opening of Britain's first hydro-electric scheme in 1896.

INVERFARIGAIG
A permanent Forestry Commission display and several marked trails have been provided here to help the public understand the industry and wildlife of the area. Close to the village, on the east side of Loch Ness, is a steamer pier.

DORES
Dores stands in Strath Dores at the point where it meets Loch Ness, and is well situated for walking and angling. Aldourie Castle lies 2 miles north, off the B862. The first castle was built here in 1626, but the earliest work evident today dates from the 18th century.

TOUR 48 ROUTE DIRECTIONS

(Before leaving Inverness, it is possible to make a 6½ mile detour to Culloden on the A9 (SP Perth). After 1 mile reach a roundabout and take the second exit, then at another roundabout take the third exit. Continue for ½ mile and branch left on to the B9006 (SP Croy) and continue to Culloden.)

On the main tour, leave Inverness on the A9 (SP Dingwall) and after 1 mile cross the Caledonian Canal. In 9 miles cross Lovat Bridge, branch left on to the A831 (SP Cannich) and continue to Kilmorack. Continue through Crask of Aigas and past Eileanaigas House, and later cross Struy Bridge and drive along Strath Glass to Cannich. Continue on the A831 (SP Drumnadrochit) and drive past Loch Meiklie and through Milton to Drumnadrochit. Turn right on to the A82 and pass Urquhart Castle on the left, then drive along the shore of Loch Ness to Invermoriston.

Turn right on to the A887 (SP Kyle of Lochalsh) and cross Torgyle Bridge before meeting the A87. Turn left (SP Fort William) and continue on the A87, passing the Falls of Garry, to Invergarry. Turn left on to the A82, cross the Caledonian Canal, and continue to Fort Augustus. Leave on the B862 (SP Errogie) to reach Whitebridge, then in 1 mile turn left on to the B852 (SP Foyers) to reach Foyers. Continue on the B852 through Inverfarigaig and Dores. Join the B862 for the return to Inverness.

Scotland Gazetteer

ABERCORN, Lothian   *160 NT07*

Abercorn is a tiny hamlet on the shores of the Forth, notable for Hopetoun House – seat of the Hope family, earls of Hopetoun and later marquesses of Linlithgow. Works by Rubens, Rembrandt and Titian hang in the Yellow Drawing Room, and the elegant furniture in the State Room was made by Thomas Chippendale. The mansion lies amid parkland with formal gardens in the style of Versailles surrounding the house.

ABERDEEN, Grampian   *164 NJ90*

The Royal Burgh of Aberdeen is the third largest city in Scotland and an important university and cathedral centre. Aberdeen University combines two medieval colleges – Marischal (1593) in Broad Street and King's (1494) in High Street, Old Aberdeen. Marischal College houses an anthropological museum. King's still has its 16th-century chapel. Also in Old Aberdeen is the Cathedral of St Machar, founded in 1136.

The 16th-century Provost Ross's House in Shiprow is one of the city's oldest buildings and is a fine example of early Scottish domestic architecture. Aberdeen Art Gallery and Museum in Schoolhill has some good English and French paintings, Epstein bronzes, and a Henry Moore sculpture. The house of Sir George Skene, Provost of Aberdeen from 1676 to 1685, stands in Guestrow and now contains a museum of local history and rural life. The municipal buildings in Castle Street incorporate the tower and spire of the 14th-century Tolbooth, which was the scene of public executions until 1857.

ABERDOUR, Fife   *160 NT18*

This little resort on the Firth of Forth is a popular yachting centre. St Fillan's Church, Norman with 16th-century and later restoration, has a leper window blocked by the Pilgrim's Stone. Overlooking the little harbour are the ruins of Aberdour Castle, which was built in the 14th century. Remarkable wall paintings have survived, and a lovely circular dovecot stands in the grounds.

ABERLADY, Lothian   *161 NT47*

The largest motor museum in Scotland is situated in this seaside village. Historic motor cars, motorcycles and commercial vehicles form the main collection and there is also a section of British military vehicles. Aberlady Bay has been designated a nature reserve.

ALLOWAY, Strath   *159 NS31*

The thatched cottage in which Scotland's national poet was born in 1759 is now a Robert Burns Museum and the Auld Brig described by Burns still spans the River Doon here. It is possible that the bridge dates from the 13th century, and above it is a Burns monument that was built in the 19th century. Bibles belonging to the poet and Highland Mary are kept inside the memorial. A roofless building near by is the haunted Kirk Alloway mentioned in one of his works.

ANNAN, Dumf & Gall   *157 NY16*

Sited on the River Annan and the Solway Firth, this pleasant touring centre is noted for its shrimps and is within easy reach of beautiful countryside. Lovely Kinmount Gardens offer walks amongst superb arrays of shrubs, flowers and trees, and views from the area take in Bowness in Cumbria and the Lake District peak of Skiddaw.

ANSTRUTHER, Fife   *161 NO50*

On either side of the harbour stand the Royal Burghs of Anstruther Easter and Anstruther Wester, each boasting pretty churches with unbuttressed 16th-century towers. The village is well known for its herring catch. Anstruther Easter has a 16th-century manse, and St Ayles House, once used by monks from Balmerino Abbey, now houses an interesting fisheries museum which includes a marine aquarium. Sea-angling, golf and good beaches may also be enjoyed in this popular area.

AVIEMORE, Highland   *163 NH81*

In the 1960s the village of Aviemore, situated in the heart of the British winter sports area, became transformed into one of Scotland's major inland resorts. This amazing change was brought about by the building of the Aviemore Centre, a massive complex of shops, restaurants, luxury hotels, and entertainment facilities. Superb sporting facilities include ice-rinks for skating and curling, a go-kart track, a dry ski slope and a swimming pool.

Steam-hauled trains operate on a revived railway which runs along the Spey valley to Boat of Garten, some five miles away.

AYR, Strath   *159 NS32*

As well as being a popular resort with miles of safe, sandy beach, this Royal Burgh is also a fishing port and flourishing centre of industry. Here the spirit of Burns is never very far away. The poet was christened at the Auld Kirk, his statue stands near the station, and relics of his life and work can be seen in the Tam O'Shanter Museum. Ayr's famous Twa Brigs over the River Ayr were built in the 13th and 18th centuries respectively, but the later structure has been replaced by a modern road bridge. The town's oldest building is 16th-century Loudon Hall, which was restored in 1938.

BALLATER, Grampian   *164 NO39*

The Ballater Highland Games are internationally famous and have been drawing large audiences for over 100 years. Traditionally held in August, they include many old Scottish sports and the arduous Hill Race to the summit of Craig Cailleach.

BALLOCH, Strath   *159 NS38*

Although this town actually stands on the River Leven, it has a steamer pier on the shore of Loch Lomond. Popularly known as the Queen of Scottish lakes, the 24-mile-long loch is the largest expanse of fresh water in Britain. Five of the islands in the south-eastern corner of the loch are included in a national nature reserve, and much of the east shore is cloaked by the lovely Queen Elizabeth Forest Park.

BALQUHIDDER, Central   *159 NN52*

Best known as the burial place of Robert Campbell or MacGregor (Rob Roy), Balquhidder is beautifully situated at the eastern end of Loch Voil. Rob Roy was a famous freebooter immortalized by Scott in his novel of the same name. The churchyard of the ruined kirk also contains the tombs of Rob Roy's wife and two of his sons. Near the family grave the walls of a 13th-century or earlier church can be traced.

BANFF, Grampian   *164 NJ66*

Built on a series of cliff terraces rising high above the old harbour, this ancient seaport stands at the mouth of the River Deveron and has become a popular holiday resort. Among its many fine buildings is the notable Duff House, which was built by William Adam in 1735 and eventually given to the town by the Duke of Fife. Its beautiful grounds now form a public park. Banff Museum has a local history section including a collection of British birds.

The lower slopes of the Cairngorms near Aviemore make ideal nursery runs for skiers

BANNOCKBURN, Central   *159 NS79*

The Battle of Bannockburn, fought in 1314 for the possession of Stirling Castle, established Robert the Bruce on the Scottish throne. Bruce won against odds of nearly three to one, and earned the fear of his enemy as well as the respect of his people. An open-air rotunda encircles the Borestone, in which Bruce's standard is said to have been set, and the part of the battlefield just west of Bannockburn is owned by the National Trust for Scotland.

BLACKNESS, Central   *160 NT07*

At one time Blackness was an important seaport, but it is now no more than a village. Blackness Castle, built during the 15th century but with later additions, was one of the most important fortresses in Scotland, and one of the four castles which by the Articles of Union were to be left fortified. It was used in the 17th century as a prison for Covenanters. The House of the Binns, a mansion built in 1478, was once linked to the castle by an underground passage. The mansion has been occupied continuously for over 350 years, and is still a family home although it is now owned by the National Trust for Scotland.

BLAIR ATHOLL, Tayside   *163 NN86*

Blair Atholl's position at the meeting point of several glens once made it strategically important as the key to the Central Highlands, and the Duke of Atholl built his castle here in 1269. The imposing pile of Blair Castle stands in a fine sweep of parkland, and has been altered over the years. It was renovated in the mid 18th century and restored in 1868 by David Bryce, an architect noted for his revival of the Scottish baronial style. Features of the castle include a lovely tapestry room, Jacobite relics and fine collections of furniture and armour.

BLAIRGOWRIE, Tayside   *164 NO14*

The 19th-century Brig o' Blair spans the River Ericht to link the town to Rattray, on the edge of Strathmore. Blairgowrie is an angling resort and the centre of a prosperous strawberry- and raspberry-growing area. Part of the Lornty spinning mill of 1755 can still be seen.

BLANTYRE, Strath   *159 NS65*

Dr Livingstone was born in a tenement here in 1813. His birthplace in Shuttle Row was built in 1780 and has been restored as a national memorial and museum containing personal relics and exhibitions illustrating his life. The explorer's statue stands on the tower of the Livingstone Memorial Church. Blantyre is also of interest to industrial archaeologists, since one of Scotland's first cotton-spinning mills was established here in 1785.

BOAT OF GARTEN, Highland   *163 NH91*

The curious name of this mountain village is derived from a ferry that used to cross the Spey from here before the present bridge was built in the 19th century. It is the northern terminus of a five-mile steam-hauled railway which runs along Strath Spey to the winter sports and recreation centre of Aviemore.

Rob Roy's grave at Balquhidder is flanked by those of his wife and two sons

BO'NESS, Central   *160 NS98*

Borrowstounness, to give the town its full name, was Scotland's third port in the 19th century but lost trade as Grangemouth, a few miles along the Firth of Forth, was developed. Bo'ness is now an industrial town and has associations with James Watt, who experimented with his steam engine at nearby Kinneil House in 1764. A museum is housed in the stable block, where the industrial history of the town and a display of local pottery can be seen.

Parts of Braemar Castle, including this spiral staircase, were rebuilt in the mid 18th century

BOTHWELL, Strath   *159 NS75*

The Battle of Bothwell Brig was fought near here in 1679, resulting in the defeat of the Covenanters and a five-month sentence of imprisonment in Greyfriars churchyard at Edinburgh for 1,200 of their number. A monument commemorates the defeat.

Bothwell Castle stands to the north-west of the town in a lovely setting on the Clyde. It was built during the 13th and 15th centuries and was one of the largest and finest stone castles in Scotland. The castle has had a turbulent past, and though now ruined is still a most impressive sight.

BRAEMAR, Grampian   *164 NO19*

First popularized by Queen Victoria, Braemar is a Royal Deeside summer and winter resort on the banks of Clunie Water, which flows into the Dee north of the village. The Royal Highland Gathering is held here every September.

Braemar Castle, on a bluff overlooking the Dee, was built by the Second Earl of Mar in 1628; it was attacked and burnt in 1689 by the Farquharsons, and after the 1715 Jacobite Rising was garrisoned by English troops to keep the Highlanders in check. It was rebuilt around 1748 with a round tower, a barrel-vaulted ceiling and a spiral stairway.

BRECHIN, Tayside   *164 NO56*

Rising steeply from the banks of the South Esk River, this lovely old town of red sandstone buildings stands against a backdrop of hills that gradually rise to the eastern Grampians. The old cathedral is now a parish church, and parts of the original 12th-century building still exist. It was partly rebuilt in the 19th century, but the lovely Maison Dieu Chapel is preserved as a fine example of 13th-century work.

BRIDGE OF ALLAN, Central   *159 NS79*

Popular as a spa for over 150 years, Bridge of Allan still has its pump room and baths. Robert Louis Stevenson was among those who took the waters at the Airthrey mineral spring. Now a touring centre, the town lies on Allan Water.

Keir Gardens, 2 miles to the north-west, are the delightful grounds of a mansion in which the composer Chopin once stayed. Rhododendrons, water gardens and herbaceous borders are the main features of the gardens.

BRODICK, Isle of Arran, Strath   *158 NS03*

Steamers from Ardrossan on the mainland call at this village on sandy Brodick Bay. Brodick Castle is the ancestral mansion of the dukes of Hamilton, and now houses a magnificent art collection. The 600-acre grounds include a formal walled garden laid out in 1710.

BROUGHTY FERRY, Tayside   *164 NO43*

Originally an old fishing village, Broughty Ferry has developed into a popular holiday resort. Broughty Castle stands on a rocky headland and houses a fascinating whaling museum, and 16th-century Claypotts Castle is one of the most complete examples of an old tower house in existence. Exhibits in the Ochar Art Gallery include many works by 19th-century Scottish artists.

BUCKIE, Grampian *164 NJ46*
High above the rooftops of this straggling port is the elegant and very prominent steeple of St Peter's Catholic Church, acting as a landmark from both sea and land. The harbour here is the busiest on the Moray Firth, and many of the town's long maritime associations are recorded in the Buckie Museum and Art Gallery. Various seafaring exhibits and over 400 pictures of fishing vessels can be seen here.

CALLANDER, Central *159 NN60*
Callander's excellent position near the Trossach Hills and Loch Katrine makes it an ideal touring centre and resort, and it is a natural gateway to the Highlands. A road to the northwest leads through the beautiful Pass of Leny, where the River Leny rushes through a narrow gorge in a fine display of natural power. Close by is the Kilmahog Woollen Mill, where blankets and tweed cloth are made by hand.

CAMPBELTOWN, Strath *158 NR72*
The chief town of southern Kintyre, Campbeltown stands at the head of a sheltered bay and has a rocky shore that is popular with sea anglers. Nowadays it is a resort known for its good facilities and unusually mild climate, but at the end of the 19th century it was a bustling centre of commerce and industry with 30 distilleries and a herring fleet of 500 boats.

About 3½ miles south-east, near Achinhoan Head, is St Kieran's Cave, which is a mere 25ft above high-water mark and may be the earliest Christian chapel in Scotland.

CARRBRIDGE, Highland *163 NH92*
The award-winning visitors' centre in this Highland resort is claimed to be the finest in Europe. It offers all kinds of information about the Highlands, including an exciting audio-visual display that covers some 10,000 years of history. In winter Carrbridge is a popular skiing centre, and its hotels and guest-houses also cater for the many visitors who come here to hike or fish in the summer months.

CASTLE DOUGLAS
Dumf & Gall *156 NX76*
This market town and one-time commercial capital was founded in the 18th century around the village and loch of Carlingwark. On the loch shores traces of prehistoric crannogs – artificial island dwellings – have been found. The loch and its shores form a civic park, offering sports such as boating, golf and tennis.

Threave House, 1½ miles south-west, is a Scottish baronial mansion, now belonging to the National Trust for Scotland, which opens its gardens to visitors. A school for gardeners and a wildfowl refuge have also been created here. Some 2 miles west of the town on an islet in the River Dee is ruined, mainly 14th-century Threave Castle, which was once a stronghold of the Black Douglases. This black-haired branch of the family was so called to distinguish it from the Red Douglases. A gallows knob over the doorway of the castle was the means by which the Douglases dispatched their enemies.

CAWDOR, Highland *163 NH84*
Shakespeare's Macbeth became Thane of Cawdor, and Cawdor Castle is traditionally the scene of Duncan's murder. The castle retains a central tower dating from 1454, a drawbridge with its gateway and iron yett, and some 16th-century building which has been altered at a later date. It is one of Scotland's finest and most picturesque medieval buildings, and is set in a designated conservation area.

CLACKMANNAN, Central *160 NS99*
This town stands on the Black Devon River, which flows south into the Forth estuary at Clackmannan Pow. An old tolbooth in Clackmannan is near the ancient Stone of Manau and the stepped town cross. Clackmannan Tower stands 79ft high on a hill to the west of the town. Robert the Bruce may have built the stronghold, which before the partial collapse of its 14th-century tower was one of the most complete tower-houses in Scotland.

CRATHIE, Grampian *164 NO29*
Crathie, a tiny hamlet close to the Balmoral Estate, is famous for its parish church. Queen Victoria laid the foundation stone in 1895, and the Royal Family attend services here when in residence at Balmoral.

In 1852 Prince Albert bought the beautiful Royal Deeside estate for £31,000, and had the existing castle (not open) rebuilt in the romantic Scottish baronial style. Later, Queen Victoria added Ballochbuie Forest to the grounds, and since 1855 Balmoral has been the private holiday home of the Royal Family. It is beautifully situated in a curve of the River Dee in the district of Mar, near Balmoral Forest.

CRICHTON, Lothian *161 NT36*
Crichton Castle stands south-west of the actual village and is more elaborate than is usual in Scotland. It overlooks the River Tyne from a high and desolate site, and the Italianate lines that were the legacy of the Earl of Bothwell in the 16th century are certainly out of keeping with the dour practicality of conventional castle design. The medieval church features a quaint bellcote.

CRIEFF, Tayside *159 NN82*
Beautifully situated in a hillside position overlooking Strath Earn, Crieff is a popular touring centre in one of Tayside's most scenic areas. The town itself is old, with many interesting features. Close to the town hall is an octagonal cross of 1688, and the old market cross incorporates a 10th-century cross-slab made of red sandstone and decorated with Celtic patterns. Iron stocks that were last used in 1816 are kept in the 17th-century Tolbooth.

CROMARTY, Highland *167 NH76*
Birthplace of geologist Hugh Miller in 1802, Cromarty is a small Black Isle seaport of Easter Ross which guards the narrows of Cromarty Firth. A passenger ferry crosses the narrows to Dunskeath. Hugh Miller's cottage dates from about 1650 and houses a geological collection.

Left: Fishing boats are repaired at Buckie's harbour

Below: The baronial splendour of Balmoral Castle, near Crathie

CULROSS, Fife   159 NS98

One of the best examples of a 16th- to 17th-century small town in Scotland, Culross stands in Torry Bay and was once famous for its girdles, or baking plates. The National Trust for Scotland has splendidly restored many of the old houses, with their crow-stepped gables and red pantiled roofs. Culross is associated with both St Serf and St Kentigern, and the 13th-century church preserves its choir and central tower, which is built over the rood-screen and pulpitum. Interesting 17th-century alabaster effigies of the Bruce family can be seen inside. Culross Palace features old painted ceilings and a terraced garden, and was built between 1597 and 1611 by Sir George Bruce of Carnock, who developed the town's sea-going trade in salt and coal. The delightful Tolbooth faces the estuary and dates from 1626, and the snuffmaker's house of 1693 carries the inscription 'Who would have thocht it, noses would have bocht it'.

DINGWALL, Highland   167 NH55

Created a Royal Burgh in 1226, Dingwall is the one-time county town of old Ross and Cromarty, and lies near the mouth of the River Conon. Dingwall's harbour was the work of Telford, and traces of the old castle can still be seen. The town arms – a starfish – adorn the Tolbooth of 1730, and in front of this is the shaft of a former mercat cross.

DIRLETON, Lothian   161 NT58

The village green and early 17th-century church are overlooked by the beautiful sandstone ruins of Dirleton Castle rising from sheer rock. Built by the Norman de Vaux family in 1225, the castle was altered in the 15th to 17th centuries. The ruins contain a flower garden, a 17th-century bowling green surrounded by yew trees, and a 16th-century dovecot.

DOLLAR, Central   160 NS99

The fine Dollar Academy was erected in 1818 by W. H. Playfair, and is one of the town's proudest possessions. A mile north between the Burn of Sorrow and the Burn of Care stands ruined Castle Campbell, in Dollar Glen. This romantic wooden glen, with its paths and bridges, makes a wonderful setting for the castle, which was once known as Castle Gloume or Gloom, and includes a fine 14th-century square tower joined to a 16th-century wing. Also of interest are the courtyard, great hall, and the great barrel roof on the third floor. John Knox preached here in 1556.

DOUNE, Central   159 NN70

James Spittal, wealthy tailor to James IV, built the picturesque bridge over the Teith in 1535 after being refused passage by the ferryman because he had no money on him.

Doune Castle is one of Scotland's best-preserved medieval castles. Built in the early 15th century by the Regent Albany, the castle overlooks the swift-flowing Rivers Teith and Ardoch. The Regent Albany was executed in 1424, and Castle Doune passed into the hands of the Stuarts of Doune, earls of Moray, in the 16th century.

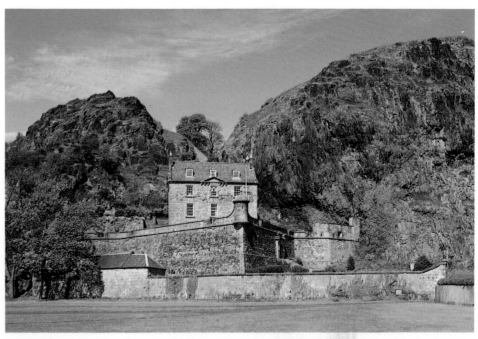

Dumbarton's Castle Rock was first fortified over 1,500 years ago, but the present castle buildings are Georgian

DRYBURGH, Borders   161 NT53

One of a famous group of 12th-century Border monasteries was founded in this tiny village by David I. Although Dryburgh was repeatedly attacked by the English and badly damaged in 1544, the cloister buildings have survived in a remarkably complete state. The church itself has not been so well preserved but its west front, parts of the nave, and the chapter house can still be seen.

DUFFTOWN, Grampian   164 NJ33

This pleasant town was laid out by James Duff, the Fourth Earl of Fife, in 1817. In the middle of the square is a Tolbooth tower, and there is a small local history museum in the town.

Balvenie Castle nearby was originally built by the Comyn family. This great moated stronghold later came into the hands of the Black Douglases and subsequently the Atholls who demolished the entire south-east front and replaced it with a three-storey Renaissance tower house known as the Atholl Building. The area is well known for its many whisky distilleries, including the famous Glenfiddich plant, to the north of the town.

DUFFUS, Grampian   164 NJ16

Gordonstoun School, where the Duke of Edinburgh and the Prince of Wales were once pupils, stands to the north-east of Duffus. St Peter's Kirk, in Duffus, is ruined but displays a fine 16th-century vaulted porch. The church was founded by a member of the Freskyns, ancestors of the Murrays, and several other Scottish families. Facing the church is the shaft of the old parish cross, probably dating from the 14th century.

The massive ruins of Duffus Castle, a fine motte-and-bailey structure, stand on a mound 1½ miles south-east of the village. A water-filled moat still surrounds the building, and the Norman motte is crowned by a fine 14th-century tower.

DUMBARTON, Strath   159 NS37

Known as Dunbreaton – Gaelic for 'Fort of the Britons' – from the 5th century to 1018, Dumbarton was the centre of the independent Kingdom of Strathclyde. St Patrick is said to have been born here. A royal castle stood on Dumbarton Rock, a majestic 240ft-high rock commanding the river, until the Middle Ages. Little survives of medieval Dumbarton Castle, but 17th- and 18th-century fortifications can be seen. A 12th-century gateway and a dungeon survive, plus a sundial which was given to the town by Mary Queen of Scots during her brief stay at the castle in 1548. The castle is now used as a barracks.

DUMFRIES, Dumf & Gall   157 NX97

Affectionately known as 'Queen of the South', this ancient Royal Burgh was combined with its sister community of Maxwelltown in 1919. The central point of the town is an 18th-century complex of buildings known as Mid-steeple, comprising the old municipal buildings, courthouse and prison. The 15th- and 16th-century remains of Lincluden College, including the fine collegiate church and provost's house, can be seen just outside the town. Relics from this and other periods of the burgh's history are preserved in Dumfries Museum. Robert the Bruce changed the course of Scottish history when he stabbed the Red Comyn in the former Greyfriars monastery, and some 500 years later, in 1791, the poet Robert Burns made his home in the town. His house is now a Burns Museum.

DUNBAR, Lothian   161 NT67

Dunbar is an old fishing port and Royal Burgh situated on the edge of rich farming country. The ruins of Dunbar Castle perch high on a rock above the harbour, forming a prominent local landmark. In 1339 the castle was besieged, and its final destruction came after the downfall of Mary Queen of Scots in 1568.

DUNDEE, Tayside   *164 NO33*

One of the largest cities in Scotland, Dundee covers some 20 square miles of hillside above the north bank of the Firth of Tay. The only surviving gate of the strong walls that protected the town in medieval times is the Cowgate Port. One of the oldest buildings is 15th-century St Mary's Tower, which was built to house a bell and is now a museum. Also of interest are the Mills Observatory, the Spalding Golf Museum in Camperdown House, and the comprehensive local collections shown in the City Museum and Art Gallery. Exhibits relating to local shipping and industry can be seen in the Barrack Street Museum. Victoria Dock contains 19th-century HMS *Unicorn*, the only floating wooden warship in the country.

DUNFERMLINE, Fife   *160 NT08*

Scotland's capital for six centuries, Dunfermline was the burial place of Robert the Bruce and the birthplace of James I and Charles I.

Andrew Carnegie, a Scottish ironmaster who emigrated to America and became an industrial millionaire and a great philanthropist, was born in the town in 1835. His cottage is now a small museum containing personal mementoes. The first of nearly 3,000 Carnegie libraries was established here in 1881, and Carnegie presented Pittencrieff Glen – with its beautiful park – to the town in 1903. A fine 17th-century mansion in the park houses galleries of costumes and works of art.

The great Benedictine abbey was founded by Queen Margaret, wife of Malcolm Canmore, in the 11th century. The foundations of her modest church lie beneath the present nave, a splendid piece of late Norman work. Of the monastic buildings, only ruins remain.

Dunfermline Museum in Viewfield Terrace has displays of local history, domestic utensils and linen – a traditional product of the town.

Dunfermline's abbey church preserves fine Norman work and is noted for its stained glass

DUNKELD, Tayside   *164 NO04*

Telford spanned the Tay with a fine bridge here in 1809, but this delightful small town is best known for the lovely ruins of its ancient cathedral. It was founded in the 9th century, was desecrated in 1560, and considerably damaged in the 17th-century Battle of Dunkeld. The 14th-century choir has been restored and is now in use as the parish church.

DUNS, Borders   *161 NT75*

Although little more than a village, Duns became the county town of old Berwickshire after Berwick was declared a neutral town in 1551. The summit of Duns Law, on which the town stood before being destroyed by English invaders in 1545, is crowned by the Covenanters' Stone, commemorating a camp made there in 1639 by General Leslie and his Covenanters before they marched to Newcastle.

The Burgh Chambers in Newtown Street house the Jim Clark museum, which exhibits trophies won by this world-championship racing driver. Clark lived in Duns before he was killed in Germany in 1968.

EAST LINTON, Lothian   *160 NT57*

The River Tyne flows through a tiny gorge here and is spanned by a 16th-century bridge. The famous engineer John Rennie was born east of the village in 1761, and his memorial can be seen beside the by-pass. On the river bank near East Linton is 17th-century Preston Mill, the oldest water-mill in Scotland still in working condition. To the north is the Church of Prestonkirk, which was built in 1770 and is now a mortuary chapel. It retains an interesting 13th-century square chancel from an earlier structure.

EDINBURGH, Lothian   *160 NT27*

Scotland's finest city and its capital since 1437, Edinburgh stands on seven hills between the waters of the Firth of Forth and the 2,000ft summits of the Pentlands. Until 200 years ago this great centre of culture and learning was little more than a cluster of houses along the Royal Mile, a cobbled slope between Castle Hill and the Palace of Holyroodhouse. The foremost building here is the castle, which overlooks the picturesque streets of the Old Town and has a history that stretches back at least 1,000 years. Canongate Tolbooth dates from 1591, 15th-century John Knox's house was built by goldsmiths to Mary Queen of Scots, and 17th-century Gladstone's Land features rooms decorated with fine tempera paintings. Lady Stair's House is a restored 17th-century building housing a museum, and off Canongate is 16th- and 17th-century Holyroodhouse – Scotland's finest royal palace. Ruins of the 12th-century Chapel Royal foundation adjoin the palace. The 14th-century stronghold of Craigmillar Castle is associated with Mary Queen of Scots, and 17th- to 19th-century Parliament House is where the Scottish parliaments met before the Union of 1707. Near the Castle Mound are the Royal Scottish Academy and the National Gallery of Scotland, where many fine paint-

Edinburgh's elegant streets are dominated by the stern outline of the castle buildings

ings by artists from various schools can be seen, and in Chambers Street the Royal Scottish Museum exhibits one of the most comprehensive general displays in Britain. There are many other fascinating museums, galleries, workshops, and studios in the city. Every year since 1947 Edinburgh has hosted the International Festival, a cultural extravaganza that is held in late summer.

ELGIN, Grampian   *164 NJ26*

A Royal Burgh and market town, Elgin is perhaps best known for its ruined cathedral of 1224, one of the finest ecclesiastical buildings in Scotland. The cathedral and part of the town were burnt in 1390 by the notorious Wolf of Badenoch, the outlawed son of Robert II, who terrorized the district. In spite of this, a great deal of 13th-century work is still preserved. A notable example is the choir, in which lies the founder's grave and an ancient cross-slab – perhaps of 6th-century date – carved with strange Pictish symbols. The Panns Port – or East Gate – is the only surviving gate from the cathedral precincts, and a wing of the Bishop's Palace dating from 1406 still stands. Near one of the park entrances is the Elgin Museum, which exhibits collections of fossils and prehistoric weapons and depicts the heritage of Elgin and Moray.

FORFAR, Tayside   *164 NO45*

Before the county reorganizations Forfar was the chief town of Angus, but it has now been absorbed into the new Tayside. In the 11th century there was a royal residence here, and an ancient octagonal turret marks the site of the castle which was destroyed many years later by Robert the Bruce. His son was buried near Loch Fithie in Restenneth Priory, a 12th-century foundation in beautiful surroundings. Forfar's Town House preserves a gruesome pronged bridle that was used to silence victims before and during execution.

FORT WILLIAM, Highland   *163 NN17*
The first fort built here was a wattle-and-daub structure erected by General Monk in 1655, but the town takes its name from a stone stronghold that replaced it by order of William III. The fort was garrisoned until the mid 19th century, by which time its redundancy was obvious and it was demolished. Relics from these and earlier days can be seen in the West Highland Museum, and include a curious picture of Prince Charles Edward that can only be seen in its reflection on a curved and polished surface. The town itself is a major resort and touring centre for the West Highlands and is dominated by the massive bulk of Ben Nevis.

GALASHIELS, Borders   *161 NT43*
The bustling Border town of Galashiels is noted for its tweeds and woollens. Every June there is a pageant, the Braw Lads' Gathering, when the history of the town since its charter was granted in 1599 is re-enacted. Galashiels motto 'Sour Plums' can be seen on the municipal buildings, and refers to a Border foray of 1337 when a party of English soldiers was slain while picking wild plums. Old Gala House dates from the 15th and 17th century, with modern alterations, and is now an art centre. The Bernat Klein Exhibition in Waukrigg Mill illustrates the process of design from concept to finished product, and the relationship between the designer and his environment.

GLAMIS, Tayside   *164 NO34*
This picturesque village boasts famous Glamis Castle, which stands in fine grounds bordered by Dean Water. A fortification has been here from very early times, and Malcolm II is said to have died here in 1034. The present 14th-

The exotic Templeton Carpet Factory lends a Moorish touch to Glasgow's architecture

century structure is the ancestral home of the Earl of Strathmore, father of the Queen Mother, and was rebuilt in the 17th century. Portions of the high square tower's 15ft-thick walls are original, and Duncan's Hall, the oldest complete portion of the castle, is traditionally associated with Shakespeare's Macbeth, who was Thane of Glamis. Housed within the building are fine collections of china, tapestry, furniture, paintings and armour. Restored cottages in the village contain the fascinating Angus Folk Museum, illustrating 200 years of domestic and farm life.

GLASGOW, Strath   *159 NS56*
Glasgow is the largest city in Scotland, and grew very quickly after the Industrial Revolution to become one of the major shipbuilding

and heavy engineering centres in the world.
Traditionally Glasgow was founded by St Kentigern – also called St Mungo – who built his church here in AD543. The first cathedral was erected on the site of this church in 1136, over the remains of the saint's body. Glasgow Cathedral is the only complete medieval cathedral on the Scottish mainland. Part of the original crypt of 1197 remains, and wonderful 13th-century work survives in the choir and tower. A little to the west of the cathedral is Provand's Lordship, which was built in 1471 for the priest in charge of the old St Nicholas Hospital, and may be Glasgow's oldest house.

The art gallery and museum in Kelvingrove Park was opened in 1901, and the galleries contain the finest municipal collection in Britain. On Glasgow Green is the People's Palace, containing a museum which illustrates Glasgow's domestic history. The fascinating Museum of Transport stands in Albert Drive and houses tramcars, motor-cars, horse-drawn vehicles, bicycles and historic Scottish locomotives. In 1451 Bishop Turnball obtained Papal authority to start a university in Glasgow, and the first lectures were held either in the cathedral or in the Black Friars' monastery in the High Street. The university stood in the High Street for 400 years before it was moved to its present commanding site on Gilmorehill in 1870. It includes the Hunterian Museum, where collections of early printed books, manuscripts, coins, paintings, and archaeological specimens are on display.

The Zoological Park lies south-east of the city near Calderpark. The Botanic Gardens cover 42 acres to the north-west of the city. Kibble Palace has a unique collection of trees and plants from temperate areas of the world.

The civic centre of Glasgow is George Square, where the stately City Chambers overlook the Cenotaph, designed by Sir John Burnet

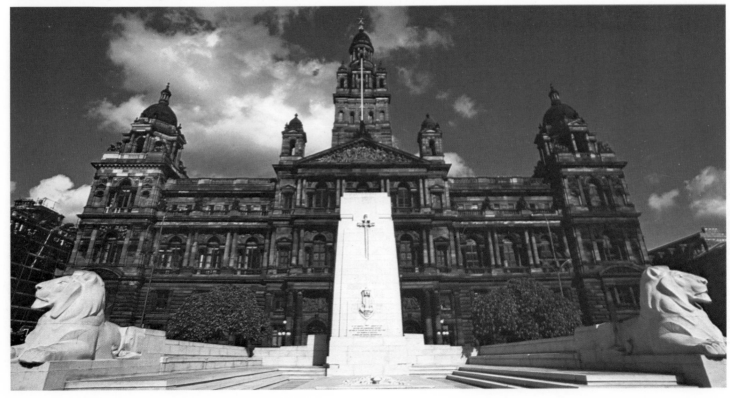

The hill on which Inverness Castle stands commands panoramic views along the River Ness (above). Beside the castle stands a statue of the famous Scottish heroine Flora Macdonald (right)

GLENCOE, Highland   *163 NN15*

The village of Glencoe lies in what is probably the finest and most famous glen in Scotland, Glen Coe, scene of the notorious massacre. In the early hours of a February morning in 1692, a troop of soldiers led by Robert Campbell of Glen Lyon slaughtered some 38 of the Macdonalds of Glencoe after 12 days' hospitality. The Macdonalds had failed to give up the Jacobite cause and swear allegiance to William III by the date set by the government. All the hamlets in the glen were burnt down, and many of those Macdonalds who fled into the mountains died of exposure. There are mementoes of the Macdonald family in the Glencoe and North Lorn Folk Museum.

GLENLUCE, Dumf & Gall   *156 NX15*

Old Wigtown's largest village, Glenluce lies a little to the west of the Water of Luce near its estuary in Luce Bay. Glenluce Abbey lies in ruins north of the village. This Cistercian house was founded around 1192 by the Lord of Galloway, and has an intact 15th-century vaulted chapter house.

GLENLIVET, Grampian   *164 NJ13*

Fine malt whisky has been distilled in this small village for many years, and although there is a modern distillery here, the method has changed little since the days of clandestine stills.

GORDON, Borders   *161 NT64*

Associated with the 'Gay Gordons' who moved to old Aberdeenshire in the 14th century, Gordon lies 1 mile west of the Eden Water. A circular clock-tower stands in the main street, and north of the village lie the ruins of a fine turreted tower house known as Greenknowe Tower, which was built in 1581.

Mellerstain House, 3 miles south, was designed by William and Robert Adam and is one of the most attractive houses open to the public in Scotland. It is noted for its beautiful interior decoration and fine walled Italian gardens.

HADDINGTON, Lothian   *161 NT57*

Once a county town, Haddington is a gracious Royal Burgh situated on the River Tyne. The town was laid out in a long, narrow triangle in the 12th century, and these original boundaries can still be traced by following the line of High Street, Market Street and Hardgate. Alexander II was born here in 1198, and the town is also thought to have been John Knox's birthplace in 1505. William Adam – father of Robert Adam – designed the splendidly proportioned Town House in 1748. The local library houses the 17th-century book collection of John Gray, who was born in the town in 1646, and St Mary's Church is a cruciform building dating from the 15th century. It has been somewhat restored, and is known as the Lamp of Lothian because of a lantern which once hung in the tower. Both Haddington House and Moat House (Eastgate) date from the 17th century, and Kinloch House is the gabled 18th-century town mansion of the Kinlochs of Gilmerton. Two fine old bridges span the Tyne; Nungate Bridge was once a place of public hanging.

HAMILTON, Strath   *159 NS75*

A rare example of an attractive industrial town set in relatively unspoilt surroundings, Hamilton is also a Royal Burgh. William Adam designed the octagonal parish church in 1732, and opposite stands the Celtic Netherton Cross. The District Museum in Muir Street includes local crafts, farming equipment and early modes of horse and motor transport.

INVERARAY, Strath   *159 NN00*

Picturesque woodland surrounds this smart Royal Burgh, where white-walled buildings make an attractive cluster on the banks of lovely Loch Fyne. At one time the village site was near the ancient castle that can be seen nearby, but after burning down it was replaced by the existing town and castle in the 18th century.

INVERNESS, Highland   *163 NH64*

Often referred to as the Capital of the Highlands, Inverness has a magnificent setting between the Beauly Firth and the Moray Firth. It also commands the northern entrance to Glen More, the great geological fault-line that divides the Highlands.

The oldest surviving building in the town is 16th-century Queen Mary's House. Just a little later is Abertarff House, which was built in 1593 for Lord Lovat and has a turnpike staircase. Nowadays it contains an exhibition detailing the origins and history of the Gaelic peoples, and is the headquarters of the Highland Association, *An Comunn Gaidhealach* – an association dedicated to the preservation of Gaelic language and culture. Inverness Castle dates from the 19th century, and stands on the site of two earlier fortresses. It overlooks a statue of Flora Macdonald, who helped Bonnie Prince Charlie to escape after the Battle of Culloden. The fortunes of the Jacobites are also recalled in the museum and art gallery.

Jedburgh's magnificent ruined abbey was founded by King David I in 1118

KILMARNOCK, Strath   *159 NS43*

Johnnie Walker was a grocer in Kilmarnock's King Street; he started to blend whisky in 1820 and today the whisky bottling concern that he began is one of the largest in the world. The first edition of Burns' poems was printed in the town in 1786 and a copy of this is exhibited in a museum housed in the red-sandstone Burns Monument in Kay Park. The Dick Institute contains a fascinating museum of rural life.

Two old towers are preserved at Dean Castle, a 15th-century fortification lying 1 mile north of Kilmarnock near Fenwick Water. European armour and early musical instruments are on display here and there are 42 acres of grounds.

KINGUSSIE, Highland   *163 NH70*

A popular pony-trekking centre surrounded by the wooded countryside of Strath Spey, Kingussie was chosen as the site for the superb Highland Folk Museum when it was moved from its place of foundation on Iona. Exhibits relate to the everyday life of the Scottish people and include farming implements, domestic tools, dress, tartans, relics of old crafts, and several much larger items such as a complete cottage furnished in traditional style, a mill from the Isle of Lewis, a traditional islander's black house, and a curious clack mill.

JEDBURGH, Borders   *161 NT62*

A popular walking, climbing and riding centre, Jedburgh's finest attraction is the abbey, which is roofless and in ruins but nevertheless magnificent. It was one of David I's Border abbeys and was burned in 1523. Mary Queen of Scots is associated with the town, and the 16th-century Mary Queen of Scots' House incorporates a museum devoted to her life. The castle at the top of Castlegate is a 19th-century construction on the site of the 12th-century stronghold built by Scottish kings. It houses a grisly gaol museum, where displays show the 'reformed' system of the early 19th century. The medieval custom of Candlemas Ba' takes place in Jedburgh every Shrove Tuesday, when a game of handball is played through the streets between Uppies, born above the mercat cross, and Downies, born below it.

JOHN O' GROATS, Highland   *167 ND37*

The shortest distance by road between this village, the most northerly on the British mainland, and Land's End in Cornwall is 877 miles. Its name is derived from that of a Dutchman who came to Scotland in the 15th century, and its beach is famous for the attractive little seashells known as Groatie Buckies.

KELSO, Borders   *161 NT73*

This bustling Border town was described by Sir Walter Scott, who lived and went to school here, as 'the most beautiful, if not the most romantic, village in Scotland'. Its abbey was the largest and probably the most splendid of the Border abbeys. Fine Norman workmanship can be seen in the surviving fragments of the abbey church. The cobbled town square features the elegant Town House of 1816, and John Rennie built the town's splendid Tweed Bridge in 1803.

Floors Castle, the largest inhabited house in Britain, stands about 1 mile to the north-west of the town. Built by Vanbrugh in 1718, this vast mansion boasts 365 windows.

KILLIN, Central   *163 NN53*

An old five-arched bridge over the River Dochart here offers fine views of the spectacular Falls of Dochart. Below the bridge is Inch Buie, a wooded island that is the ancient burial ground of the chiefs of the Clan MacNab. Just to the north of the village is Finlarig Castle, the former seat of the Campbell clan. Now in ruins, the castle is described in Scott's *Fair Maid of Perth*.

KIRKCALDY, Fife   *160 NT29*

Often known as Lang Toun, Kirkcaldy has a four-mile-long main street and has been a Royal Burgh since 1450. Several fine 17th-century and earlier houses which have all been restored by the National Trust for Scotland can be seen in an area near the harbour known as the Sailor's Walk. There are three museums in the town; the Industrial Museum, the town museum and art gallery and the John McDonall Stuart Museum in Dysart.

Gaunt, impressive ruins of Ravenscraig Castle, built by James II in 1460, lie on a rocky promontory between Kirkcaldy and Dysart.

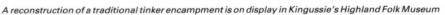

A reconstruction of a traditional tinker encampment is on display in Kingussie's Highland Folk Museum

KIRKCUDBRIGHT, Dumf & Gall   *156 NX65*

This ancient burgh stands in the heart of an area known as the Stewartry and was once a bustling port. Much of the local history is displayed in the Stewartry Museum, and the town is dominated by the handsome ruins of 16th-century Maclellan's Castle. Close to the 17th-century mercat cross is the old Tolbooth, once a prison for John Paul Jones, who became famous for his daring exploits as an officer in the early days of the American Navy. He was born in Kirkcudbrightshire in 1747. A fine collection of pictures by E. A. Hornel can be seen in 18th-century Broughton House.

KIRKOSWALD, Strath   *159 NS20*

Kirkoswald churchyard contains the graves of two of Robert Burns' best loved characters, Tam O' Shanter and Souter Johnnie. In real life Tam was Douglas Graham of Shanter, who supplied grain to an Ayr brewery, and his crony 'Souter' was a village cobbler named John Davidson. Davidson's thatched 18th-century cottage now houses a Burns' museum belonging to the National Trust for Scotland.

KIRRIEMUIR, Tayside   *164 NO35*

Sir James Barrie, creator of *Peter Pan*, was born in Kirriemuir in 1860. His birthplace in Brechin Road, and the wash-house which he used as a theatre, now form a Barrie Museum containing sections of original manuscripts, personal possessions, and mementoes of actors and producers associated with his plays. The author was buried in the new church cemetery in 1937. The Auld Licht Manse stands opposite his birthplace, and a gable of the Auld Licht Kirk is preserved in the new church, designed by Sir Ninian Comper. A camera obscura can be seen near the cemetery.

LANARK, Strath   *159 NS84*

Nothing remains of the 12th-century castle built here by David I, though there are still ruins of the 12th-century Church of St Kentigern. The Whuppity Scoorie ceremony takes place in the town every March, and is believed to be a relic of a pagan festival intended to chase away winter. On the Thursday following 6 June, pageants are held to celebrate Lanimer Day, or Beating the Bounds. New Lanark lies 1 mile south and was founded as a socialist experiment in 1784 by Richard Arkwright and David Dale. The textile mills and complete planned community layout became a European showpiece by the early 19th century.

LINLITHGOW, Lothian   *160 NS97*

Linlithgow is famous for the fine ruins of its Royal Palace, which stand on a knoll above the loch. Successor to an older building which was burned in 1424, the palace was itself destroyed by a fire – probably accidental – started by General Hawley's troops in 1746. The palace's chapel and magnificent great hall show late 15th-century work, and the handsome quadrangle has a richly carved fountain. A fine gateway in the town leads into the palace precincts, which also contain St Michael's Church, one of the finest parish churches in Scotland. Also rebuilt after the disastrous fire of 1424, the church carried a crown steeple which was removed in the 1820s. A recent appeal fund provided a modern, and controversial, golden spire in the shape of a crown. Beautiful window tracery includes particularly fine work in Katherine's Aisle.

There are some interesting late 16th-century houses in the High Street, where, facing the County Buildings, is a plaque which records the shooting in the street of the Earl of Moray – Regent of Scotland – in 1570.

MAUCHLINE, Strath   *159 NS42*

Visitors come to Mauchline for its rich associations with Robert Burns, who was married here and began his married life with Jean Armour in a house, now called Burns House, in Castle Street in 1788. Gavin Hamilton, friend and one-time landlord of Burns, is buried in a churchyard which also contains the graves of some of Burns' children. A Burns exhibition has been set up at Auld Nanse Tinnock's as part of the Burns Heritage Trail. The Burns Memorial Tower, a mile north of the town, houses a museum of his personal relics.

Mauchline was once well-known for its fine snuff boxes, and curling stones are still produced in the town. Five Covenanters were hanged on Loan Green in 1685, and a memorial has been set up to them.

MAYBOLE, Strath   *159 NS30*

Maybole was once the seat of the very powerful Kennedy family, who were the earls of Cassillis. An ancient tower that was once a Kennedy stronghold forms the centrepiece of nearby Culzean Castle, which was designed by the talented Robert Adam in 1777. Everything about the building prompts superlatives, but the Round Drawing Room and magnificent staircase are probably its finest features. Scotland's first countryside park was created in the 565-acre grounds of Culzean Castle this century, but the lovely walled garden was established in 1783 and the buildings of the Home Farm were designed by Robert Adam while he was extending the castle. The farm has been adapted as a reception and interpretation centre for the park.

MELROSE, Borders   *161 NT53*

Border raids in the 14th and 16th centuries destroyed most of David I's beautiful Cistercian abbey at Melrose. Parts of the nave and choir remain, but the most spectacular survivals are the red sandstone windows with their rich tracery. The heart of Robert Bruce was buried in front of the altar. A museum of carved stones and treasures from the abbey occupies the 15th-century Commendator's House.

Two miles west is Abbotsford House, internationally famous as the home of Sir Walter Scott. It was designed by the writer himself, who died here in 1832. It has been preserved in his memory, and the library contains a staggering collection of some 20,000 rare books.

MEY, Highland   *167 ND27*

Grey seals are a common sight in the little coastal bays of the Pentland Firth, and views across the water from this village take in the distant Orkneys. One of the best vantage points in the area is in the gardens of the 17th-century Castle of Mey.

MUSSELBURGH, Lothian   *160 NT37*

This manufacturing town on the sandy Esk estuary has a 16th-century Tolbooth which preserves an ancient clock given by the Dutch in 1496. Jacobean Pinkie House, now part of a school, incorporates a 14th-century tower but mainly dates from about 1590.

The house in Kirriemuir where J.M. Barrie was born in 1860 is now a museum to his memory

The fine ironwork of Nairn's Victorian bandstand epitomizes the resort's dignified character

NAIRN, Highland   *163 NH85*

Fine sands, bathing, golf and fishing are offered by this well-known resort on the Moray Firth. Once known as Invernairn, it has been a market town and fishing port for many centuries, though it was only after the railway arrived in 1850 that it became popular with holidaymakers. Lovely wooded countryside and the spectacular reaches of the River Findhorn near Dulsie Bridge and Ferness can be reached from the town, which stands on the border between the Highlands and the Lowlands. Near the harbour is Fishertown, built by Telford in 1820 and badly damaged by floods in 1829.

NEW ABBEY, Dumf & Gall   *157 NX96*

New Abbey is beautifully situated amid woodland on the Pow Burn. The village is best known for its lovely red-sandstone ruins of the Cistercian New or Sweetheart Abbey. Devorgilla, mother of the vassal king John Balliol, founded the abbey in 1273. When her husband John Balliol the Elder died she became one of the richest women in Europe. She built the 13th-century bridge over the Nith at Dumfries, and founded Oxford's Balliol College in her husband's memory.

NEWTONMORE, Highland   *163 NN79*

Highland ponies can be hired for rides into the bleak Monadhliath Mountains from this town, which was the first place in Britain to offer pony-trekking as a recreation. Overlooking the site of a clan battle fought nearby in 1386 is 2,350ft Craig Dhu, the ancient gathering place of the Clan Macpherson. Macpherson House features clan history and relics of the 1745 Jacobite Rising. They include the green banner under which the clan never saw defeat.

NORTH BERWICK, Lothian   *161 NT58*

One of Scotland's most popular east coast resorts, the Royal Burgh and fishing village of North Berwick has a sandy beach and facilities for golf, sailing, and swimming. Out to sea 3 miles north-east of the town is the famous 350ft-high Bass Rock, with its powerful lighthouse. Traces of old fortifications and a chapel can be seen here, and the rock with its satellite islands forms a nature reserve.

OBAN, Strath   *162 NM83*

In the 200 years of its existence, Oban has become a major centre in the West Highlands. Its busy port offers steamer services to many of the islands, making the town a thriving tourist resort. One of its most remarkable buildings is McCaig's Folly, which was begun in 1897 to relieve local unemployment but never finished. It was intended to be a replica of Rome's Colosseum and to house a museum and art gallery. St Columba's Cathedral was built by Sir Gilbert Scott. Macdonald's Mill, ½ mile south of the town centre, has a fascinating display of the story of spinning and weaving.

PAISLEY, Strath   *159 NS46*

Said to be the largest thread-manufacturing centre in the world, the industrial town of Paisley grew up around the fine Cluniac Abbey Church. This was founded in 1163 by Walter Fitz Alan and monks from Wenlock Abbey in Shropshire. Paisley's museum and art gallery houses a priceless collection of famous Paisley shawls, the 'pine' motif of which was introduced from Kashmir in 1770. The English destroyed the Abbey Church in 1307, and most of the present building dates from the mid 15th century. Parts of the abbey buildings were incorporated into the 17th-century Place of Paisley.

PEEBLES, Borders   *160 NT24*

Anglers come here to fish for the great Tweed salmon, but this attractive old Royal Burgh also offers facilities for golf, tennis, and pony-trekking. It has been the home of such famous people as the author Robert Louis Stevenson and Mungo Park, whose exploration helped to open up Africa. William Chambers and his brother Robert, publishers of the first Chambers' encyclopaedias and dictionaries, were born here and donated the Chambers Institute, a library, and a museum to the town. Relics of the town's history include the ruins of 13th-century Cross Kirk and the old shaft of a former parish cross.

PERTH, Tayside   *160 NO12*

Once known as St Johnstoun, the fair city of Perth is an old Royal Burgh set at the head of the Tay estuary between the meadows of the North and South Inch. In early times the area attracted the attention of English forces, and the town was taken and fortified by Edward I in 1298. Its single year as the capital of Scotland ended with the murder of James I at the former Blackfriars Monastery in 1437. One of the most important buildings to have survived is St John's Kirk, a fine medieval and later church that has been attended by many members of English and Scottish royalty. Also of interest are the Museum and Art Gallery, and the Black Watch Regimental Museum, which occupies Balhousie Castle. In North Port is the house of Catherine Glover, Scott's 'Fair Maid of Perth'. The 14th-century building has been restored and is now a craft centre.

On the western outskirts of the city is Huntingtower Castle, a 15th-century mansion noted for its painted wooden ceilings. Another fortified mansion is ruined Elcho Castle, which stands on the River Tay to the east.

Fishing boats and island steamers are usually to be seen in Oban's busy harbour

Queen Victoria slept in this bedroom at Scone Palace, whose royal connections date back to the 9th century

PETERHEAD, Grampian   *165 NK14*
Peterhead is a busy Buchan herring port and boat-building town at the mouth of the River Ugie. The old parish church, or Muckle Kirk, dates from 1806. The links to the south of the town include the remains of 12th-century St Peter's Kirk; the bell-tower of 1592 contains a bell which was cast in Holland in 1647. Arbuthnot Museum and Art Gallery has an exhibition on the fishing industry.

POOLEWE, Highland   *166 NG88*
The salmon-rich River Ewe flows into the head of Loch Ewe at Poolewe after its short course from Loch Maree. Poolewe lies near the 58th parallel, a latitude farther north than Moscow, yet features a remarkable collection of sub-tropical plants which thrive 1 mile north in the gardens of Inverewe House.

PORTREE, Highland   *162 NG44*
Skye's pleasant little capital town of whitewashed houses stands on Portree Bay, which is sheltered by high cliffs on three sides. Well situated as a touring centre for the island, the town has a charming harbour and receives all kinds of light boat traffic at its pier.

ROSLIN, Lothian   *160 NT26*
Scott mentioned this former mining village's famous chapel in the *Lay of the Last Minstrel.* It was founded in 1446 by William Sinclair and contains many fine stone carvings, including the exquisite Prentice Pillar. Nearby Roslin Castle overlooks the North Esk River and picturesque Roslin Glen.

ROTHESAY, Isle of Bute,
Strath   *159 NS06*
The popular resort and Royal Burgh of Rothesay is the principal town of Bute. Clyde steamers call at the pier, near which lie the remains of Rothesay Castle, one of the most important of the surviving Scottish medieval castles. Today the building's strong walls, heightened and provided with four round towers in the late 13th century, still enclose a circular courtyard. A deep moat surrounds the castle, and nearby is the Chapel of St Michael, which probably dates from the 14th century. Behind the town, on the west shore of narrow Loch Fad, stands Kean's Cottage, built by the great 19th-century actor Edmund Kean.

ST ANDREWS, Fife   *161 NO51*
Historically this ancient Royal Burgh is one of the most significant places in Scotland. The cathedral, founded in 1160, had grown to become Scotland's largest church by the time the finishing touches were made in 1318. Sparse remains include parts of the east and west gables, a section of the south nave wall, and the Precinct Wall. Close by is small St Rule's Church, which was built in about 1130 and is one of the best of its type in Scotland. The Sessions House preserves reminders of harsher times in the form of two repentance stools and a barbaric scold's bridle. St Andrews University was founded in 1412 and is the oldest in Scotland. Its Chapel of St Salvator carries an octagonal broach spire and contains the tomb of its founder, Bishop Kennedy. St Andrews Castle dates from the 13th century.

SCONE, Tayside   *160 NO12*
Scone Palace, the home of the Earl of Mansfield, is a 19th-century mansion that stands on the site of the old Abbey of Scone. This was founded in about 1114 by Alexander I, and before it was destroyed by a mob of John Knox's reformers in 1559 it was the coronation place of all the Scottish kings up to James I. By tradition the kings were crowned on a stone that was brought to the ancient mote-hill of Scone by Kenneth Macalpine in the 9th century. This was removed from the site and placed under the Coronation Chair of Westminster Abbey by Edward I in 1297. The present mansion contains various relics and works of art.

As the abbey developed it attracted a little satellite community that grew into the village of Scone. In 1805 this was moved by the Earl of Mansfield to improve the landscape, and only the village cross and graveyard remain to mark its old site.

SELKIRK, Borders   *161 NT42*
A fine centre for exploring the lovely Yarrow and Ettrick valleys, Selkirk lies on Ettrick Water at the edge of Ettrick Forest. The picturesque old Border Riding ceremony is held here every year, and a nightly curfew is still sounded from the town hall, which is surmounted by a 110ft-high spire. Statues in the High Street commemorate Sir Walter Scott, Sheriff of Selkirk from 1799 to 1832; and Mungo Park, the famous explorer, who was born near the town. The town museum contains relics of the explorer's expeditions to Sumatra and the Niger.

STIRLING, Central   *159 NS79*
This Royal Burgh makes an ideal base for touring the Highlands, but is also worth visiting for its own sake. All round the foot of the rocky crag which carries its imposing castle are hilly streets of stone buildings, and the castle itself seems to grow from the stone on which it is built. Its 250ft site has been fortified for many centuries, but the oldest parts of the present building date back about 500 years to the reign of James III. Below the castle ramparts is the King's Knot, one of the earliest ornamental gardens in Scotland. Down the hill in the Old Town are many good examples of 16th- to 18th-century domestic architecture, interspersed with such fine public buildings as the Guildhall, the Tolbooth of 1701, and the church where Mary Queen of Scots and James VI were crowned. The Argyll Lodging is a 17th-century mansion that became a military hospital in the 18th century. Its exterior is considered the most impressive of its style and period in Scotland. The town's 15th-century Old Bridge was rebuilt in 1749 after having been blown up during the '45 Rising. Stirling became a university town in the mid 20th century. The campus occupies the lovely Airthrey estate, and features a 23-acre loch.

About 1 mile east of Stirling are the beautiful ruins of Cambuskenneth Abbey, which was founded in 1147 by David I and was the scene of Robert the Bruce's parliament in 1326. King James III was buried in the abbey in 1488.

STONEHAVEN, Grampian   *164 NO88*
Lovely cliff scenery lies to the north and south of this fishing port and holiday resort, which has a stone and shingle beach. The river divides the old and new parts of the town, and just before entering the sea is joined by the Cowie Water which flows through a lovely glen from lonely hills to the west. The 16th-century Tolbooth stands on the quay and is a former storehouse of the Earls Marischal. From 1748 to 1749 it held episcopal ministers, who baptised children through the windows. The Tolbooth now houses a museum of fishing and local history.

TARBOLTON, Strath   *159 NS42*
From 1777 to 1784 the Burns family lived near Tarbolton at Lochlea Farm, and it was here that the poet's father died. The town was enlivened at this time by the Bachelors' Club, a debating society founded in 1780 by Burns and his friends at a house which still stands. A year earlier Burns attended dancing classes at the same house, and he was initiated as a freeman here in 1781. The thatched house now contains a Burns museum exhibiting relics mostly from the Lochlea period. Tarbolton's church includes stone stairs leading to a loft, and carries a 90ft spire.

THORNHILL, Dumf & Gall   *159 NX89*
Known also as the Ducal Village because of its long association with the dukes of Queensberry and Buccleuch, Thornhill lies in the Nith valley and is backed by Lowland hills. North Drumlanrig Street is lined with lime trees planted by the Sixth Duke of Buccleuch during the last century. A museum in the Town House exhibits relics of Burns and the Covenanters, and a tall column set up in 1714 at the town centre supports a winged horse – the emblem of the Queensberrys. A few miles up Nithsdale from Thornhill is Drumlanrig Castle, built between 1676 and 1689. It was originally the seat of the dukes of Queensberry, and is now the home of the dukes of Buccleuch. Inside is a notable collection of paintings.

THURSO, Highland   *167 ND16*
An expanding resort and residential town on the sandy shores of Thurso Bay, this charming place is the most northerly town on the British mainland. Close to the harbour are well-restored houses dating from the 17th and 18th centuries, and ruined St Peter's Church stands on a site occupied since the Vikings. The remains that stand here today are of a 17th-century building. Thurso's interesting museum maintains good collections of plants and fossils, and boasts a lovely little Runic cross.

TRAQUAIR, Borders   *160 NT33*
Lying on a tributary of the Tweed known as Quair Water, this lovely hamlet is usually visited for Traquair House – probably the oldest inhabited house in Scotland. A thousand years of history lie behind the grey walls of this picturesque, turreted mansion, and it may be the original of Scott's Tully-Veolan in the novel *Waverley*. William the Lion held court here in 1209, and since that time the mansion has been visited by 26 other English and Scottish monarchs. Most of the mansion was rebuilt in 1642, but the tower is earlier and the wings were added on at a later date. Ale is still brewed at the 18th-century brewhouse, and the house contains silver, glass, tapestries and embroideries of the 13th century.

TURRIFF, Grampian   *164 NJ74*
In 1639 this thriving little market town was the scene of the Trot of Turriff, when Covenanters met Royalists in battle. A church of the Knights Templar stood here and the old Market Cross was re-erected in 1865. Pleasant woodland to the east of the town surrounds the great tower house of Delgatie Castle, a seat of the Clan Hay that has been in the family's possession for nearly 700 years. It was founded by the Hays of Delgatie in the 13th century and shows alterations up to the 16th century. Inside are various relics and pictures, and fine painted ceilings of about 1590.

WHITHORN, Dumf & Gall   *156 NX44*
St Ninian, the son of a local chieftain, founded a monastery at Whithorn in AD397 and may have built his *Candida Casa*, or White House, here. It was one of the first Christian churches in Scotland. Fergus Lord of Galloway built the priory in the 12th century, and a good late 12th-century carved doorway has survived. The ruins show some 15th-century work and are entered through the Pend, a 17th-century arch on which the Royal Arms of Scotland before the Union are displayed. Attached to the priory is a museum which preserves some ancient carved stones.

WICK, Highland   *167 ND35*
Situated at the junction of Wick Water and Wick Bay, this ancient Royal Burgh is a thriving market town and herring port with two good harbours. One of these was initially designed by Thomas Telford and later improved by Stephenson. The ruined Castle of Old Wick, also known as Castle Oliphant, stands 1½ miles to the south-east.

Now surrounded by lovely gardens, Stirling Castle was built by King James V, father of Mary Queen of Scots. The infant queen was crowned here in 1542

Acknowledgements

Most of the photographs in this book are AA copyright. The publishers gratefully acknowledge the following for the use of other photographs.

British Tourist Authority Photographic Library for Widecombe (p.16), Mullion Cove (p.30), Tintagel Castle (p.34), Buckler's Hard (p.43), Salisbury Cathedral (p.59), Conwy (p.111), York Minster (p.137), Dove Cottage (p.147) and Buckie (p.178).

J. Allan Cash Ltd for Perranporth (p.15) and Criccieth (p.112).

Jarrold & Sons Ltd for Buckland-in-the-Moor (p.25), Brighton (p.46), West Somerton (p.85), Castle Howard (p.149), Kenmore (p.173), Culloden and Glen Moriston (p.175) and Balmoral Castle (p.178).

Philip Llewellin for Melton Mowbray (p.95) and Old Oswestry (p.96).

S. & O. Mathews for fossil ammonite (p.28), Guildford (p.44), Stratfield Saye (p.60) and Spalding (p.97).

The Scottish Tourist Board for Aviemore (p.176).

Madame Tussaud's for wax figures (p.67).

FULL-PAGE PHOTOGRAPHS

Half-title: South Harting, W. Sussex. Photograph by S. & O. Mathews.

Title page: Stourhead, Wilts. Photograph by Jasper Spencer-Smith.

Contents: Bradford-on-Avon, Wilts. Photograph by S. & O. Mathews.

Introduction: Cromer, Norfolk. Photograph by S. & O. Mathews.

Pages 10–11: Corfe Castle, Dorset. Photograph by Robin Fletcher.

Pages 36–7: The Needles, Isle of Wight. Photograph by Robin Fletcher.

Pages 62–3: The City of London. Photograph by Martyn J. Adelman.

Pages 74–5: Anne Hathaway's Cottage, Shottery, Warwicks. Photograph by Trevor Wood.

Pages 100–1: Craig Goch Reservoir, Powys. Photograph by Colin Molyneux.

Pages 124–5: Hadrian's Wall near Housesteads, Northumberland. Photograph by Richard Surman.

Pages 154–5: Loch Nevis, Highland. Photograph by Martyn J. Adelman.

Endpapers: The Eildon Hills from Scott's View, Borders. Photograph by Eric Rowell, reproduced by courtesy of the British Tourist Authority.